AMERICAN TURQUOIS AND TURQUOIS MATRIX.

(Plate prepared in cooperation with the U. S. Geological Survey.)

FIG. 1. Pale-blue turquois; Gove Turquois mine, near Cottonwood, San Bernardino County, Cal.

FIG. 2. Turquois matrix; Royal Blue Turquois mine, in Nye County, near Millers, Nev.

FIG. 3. Turquois matrix; Weber mine, Belmont, Nye County, Nev.

FIG. 4. Dark-blue turquois; Azure mine, Burro Mountains, N. Mex.

FIG. 5. Cobweb turquois matrix; Southwest Turquois Co. mine, Mineral Park, Ariz.

FIG. 6. Nugget of turquois, polished on one side; Myers and Bona Turquois mine, 13 miles north of west of Millers, Esmeralda County, Nev.

FIG. 7. Split veinlet of turquois showing a "Y" pattern; presented to a student at Yale University; Los Angeles Gem Co. mine, Mineral Park, Ariz.

FIG. 8. Pendant of turquois matrix; Southwest Turquois Co. mine, Mineral Park, Ariz.

FIG. 9. Turquois in dark brown matrix; Royal Blue Turquois mine, near Millers, Nev.

FIG. 10. Intersecting veinlets of turquois in matrix; New Azure mine, Burro Mountains, N. Mex.

FIG. 11. Veinlet of turquois in matrix; Cameo Claim, Little Hachita Mountains, N. Mex.

FIG. 12. Nodular turquois; Southwest Turquois Co. mine, Mineral Park, Ariz.

FIG. 13. Turquois matrix; Los Cerrillos, N. Mex.   U. S. National Museum.

MEMOIRS

OF THE

NATIONAL ACADEMY OF SCIENCES

PISCHEL YEARBOOKS, INC.

P.O. Box 36, Marceline, Missouri 64658

MEMOIRS

OF THE

NATIONAL ACADEMY OF SCIENCES

Volume XII

Part II

SECOND MEMOIR
THIRD MEMOIR

GLORIETA, NEW MEXICO · 87535

© The Rio Grande Press, Inc.,
Glorieta, N.M. 87535

First edition from which this edition was
reproduced was supplied by
MacRAE'S INDIAN BOOK DISTRIBUTORS
P.O. Box 2632
Santa Rosa, California 95405
Which, with certain exceptions, is the
exclusive supplier of this title to
the book and museum shop trade.

A RIO GRANDE CLASSIC
First published in 1915

LIBRARY OF CONGRESS CARD CATALOG 70-175059
I.S.B.N. 87380-056-7

Sixth Printing 1974

The Rio Grande Press, Inc.
GLORIETA, NEW MEXICO · 87535

Publisher's Preface

If ever there was a book with an all-inclusive title and sub-title, this is it; the work contains everything you might want to know about Turquoise, but were always afraid to ask. If there is anything incomplete about it--especially in view of the emendations of the erudite Rex Arrowsmith of Santa Fe--we can't imagine what it would be.

As it stood, the first edition published in 1915 was a monument to thorough scholarship but of interest mainly to the Turquoise *especialista.* The first edition lacked but one thing--enough color plates to be of help to the *aficionado,* or the average collector. Turquoise exists only in color; black and white plates of this lovely gemstone are for all practical purposes virtually worthless.

We have always had a lot of encouragement from our customers to publish something on this subject, but until we encountered this volume, there was nothing we could locate worth re-printing. When we saw this marvelous study, we felt like Archimedes discovering the principle of specific gravity! *Eureka!* But alas, this otherwise excellent work displayed only two--*just two*--color plates. We of course wondered what to do about the lack.

We're members of the Santa Fe Corral of The Westerners, an informal international organization of Western history buffs, so we noised it about that we had Turquoise problems needing some authoritative solutions. Thus we came to know our own Westerner colleague Rex Arrowsmith of Santa Fe, a professional geologist specializing in Turquoise. What more could we ask?

Well, first we asked him if he would write an Introduction. "Easy," he said, with his slow, engaging grin. "What about a bibliography?"

"Fine," we said, hardly waiting a decent interval.

"Also," he said, "how about an update on currently-operated Turquoise mines?"

Who could say no?

"I can also provide some good color photos," he offered. Which is an account of how we hit the jackpot herein pictured. This Arrowsmith could not only provide everything we needed for the book, but he has a shop that most museums would envy. We could spend hours there, just looking! If we were rich, we would spend hours there just buying. It's a place for the connoisseur collector of Western relics and Indian arts and crafts. But let us quote from our Santa Fe Corral periodical publication *La Gaceta* (Vol. V, No. 2, July 1970) a bit of biography prepared by our own Al Schroeder; Al can get by with such flattery--we get a klunk in the head.

HOMBRE ESPECIAL—Rex Arrowsmith

Rex Arrowsmith has such a wide interest in various things that it is difficult to pin down any main interest. His wife, Bonnie, said, "I wouldn't mind if Rex just collected one thing . . . but, he is interested in everything!"

Rex was born in Belleville, Kansas, and as a very small boy became interested in collecting Indian artifacts from the many sites that he could hike to from his home. Having a father and a grandfather who had been ardent collectors too, whetted an interest in the West and particularly in the Southwest. Rex still has several items that were collected by his grandfather who drove cattle in Texas and New Mexico and was a Wells Fargo agent in the 19th Century.

After graduating from high school in Belleville, Rex enrolled at The University of Kansas. While there, he received an appointment to the Merchant Marine Academy. In World War II, he served in the Naval Reserve aboard a tanker carrying 6,000,000 gallons of aviation gasoline in the Atlantic and Pacific War theaters. Luckily, he did not get blown up and after WWII came back to the university to complete his studies for a degree in mining engineering and geology.

After graduation, he did exploration work for a mining company looking for mineral deposits in Arizona and Nevada. Later he formed his own geology and engineering business in Houston, Texas, and also got into the manufacturing business, making lenses and optical grinding machinery.

While in Houston, Rex continued collecting Indian items, firearms, edged weapons, primitive art from all over the world, paintings, and all sorts of other unusual items. The house began to look like a museum and the Arrowsmiths began to run out of room. They had talked many times about moving to Santa Fe and had thought some day that they would retire there. But, business was good in Houston, and they did not know for sure how they would make a living in New Mexico.

Ray Smith, an El Corral de Santa Fe Westerner, kept urging the Arrowsmiths to move to Santa Fe.

One evening, Bob Platt, our former *ladron* who was living in Santa Fe, called and said, "Rex, there is a building available across from the Oldest Church . . . why don't you get it and move to Santa Fe?" Rex turned to his wife and asked, "Do you want to move to Santa Fe?" She said, "Sure." So, Rex told Bob to get the building tied up, and they'd be out.

The Arrowsmiths sold everything in Houston, came to Santa Fe, and started Arrowsmith's Relics of The Old West, using Rex's collection as the inventory. Arrowsmith's over the years has grown into one of the most interesting stores and galleries in the country. You'll nearly always find a few Indians trading with Rex when you stop by. And you will find the finest in contemporary Indian arts and crafts as well as museum-quality pieces from prehistoric times.

The last time I stopped by to see Rex, he had just obtained three fine bronzes by Charles M. Russell. There was a Remington hanging in the gallery and a great collection of pre-Columbian artifacts that any museum would like to have. The old West will never die as long as there is a place like Arrowsmith's! If only those old guns, spurs, saddles, swords, and Indian costumes could talk . . . what stories they could tell!

Rex is a charter member and former Alguacil of El Corral de Santa Fe Westerners, President of the Southwestern Association of Indian Affairs, Chairman of The Old Santa Fe Association, a member of the American Institute of Mining, Metallurgical, and Petroleum Engineers, former President of the Houston Chapter of the Society of American Military Engineers, a member of Sigma Gamma Epsilon (honorary geology), Delta Tau Delta, and The Screen Actors Guild, and active in other organizations. He has lectured and written many articles on geology and mining engineering, Indian arts and crafts, and other subjects.

Therefore, to Rex Arrowsmith, of Santa Fe, our thanks for invaluable help in returning this splendid book to contemporary usefulness.

We should mention, meanwhile, the superb color photography of cameraman Len Bouche. It is not an easy job to photograph small items in small format with sufficient definition to allow for extra-large enlargement. Mr. Bouche took the pictures with a Hasselblad camera; with such a fine operator using such a splendid instrument, we obtained transparencies of exquisite color and detail.

But no color photographs can be printed without the TLC (tender loving care) of a dedicated and experienced printer. Hence, for the lovely, glowing color plates in this book, we must finally thank Richard Dell and his crew on the production staff at Pischel Yearbooks, Inc., Marceline, Mo. We're so very pleased. What we have here is the product of the coordinated teamwork of many men and women, all of special skill and training and each of them doing the best he can possibly do. We know a nice sense of satisfaction as we survey our finished product.

Now to the book itself.

This paper by Joseph Ezekiel Pogue, A.B., M.S., Ph.D., was first published in 1915 by the National Academy of Science. It was the second paper in Volume XII, Second Memoir. The folio (pagination) sequence ran consecutively from page one through page 162 for the text, with the black and white full page plates carrying the folios on through page 208. These plates are identified in the original as "Third Memoir". We have not changed or altered the original pagination except in two particulars.

The unnumbered frontispiece, one of the two original color plates, has been repositioned to the front endpaper. Plate 18, the second of the two original color plates, has been moved to the back endpaper. The color plates we have added are positioned, for technical reasons, back to back every 16 pages beginning opposite page 18. In the first edition, all of the plates were printed on a paper stock different from the text stock. This made it easier, in a way, for our printer to make facsimile negatives since the black and white contrast was sharper. We are writing these words before the books goes to press; we pass this information along to account for any possible difference in coloration that may be visible between the pages ending with folio 162 and those beginning with folio 163. There should be no difference at all, but if there is, it was unavoidable.

Author Pogue was born in Raleigh, N.C., On June 6, 1887. He took his A.B. in 1906, and his M.S. in 1907, at the University of North Carolina. He took his doctorate at Yale in 1909. To 1911, he was a special student at the University of Heidelberg, in Germany. He was an assistant curator of minerology and petrology at the Smithsonian Institution from 1909 to 1913. He joined the U.S. Geological Survey in 1913, leaving to become an associate professor of geology and minerology at Northwestern University in 1914. It was during this period Dr. Pogue wrote this paper for the National Academy of Sciences. He rejoined the Smithsonian staff in 1917, going on from there to an incredible number of distinguished and honored positions in the fields of petroleum and geological technology. His output of scientific papers has been prolific, far too extensive to enumerate here. He is undoubtedly one of the country's greatest authorities in these fields. At the age of 85, Dr. Pogue in 1971 is living in retirement in Florida.

For information, there is hardly anything to beat the dictionary. Because Dr. Pogue wrote his paper spelling the word "turquoise" without a final "e", we checked the American Heritage Dictionary of the English Language and found that as of today, he spelled it incorrectly – although in 1915 he may have been absolutely correct to omit the "e". We also found that turquoise is a mineral of aluminum and copper, mainly $CuAl_6(PO_4)_4(OH)_8 \cdot 4H_2O$. We thought you would like to know.

For the particular benefit of our friends in the book reviewing fraternity, we believe it worthwhile to mention the specific differences between the original edition and this edition. We have mentioned these differences in our acknowledgment earlier to the scholarly Rex Arrowsmith, professional photographer Len Bouche and printer Dick Dell with his fine staff of graphic arts craftsmen at Pischel Yearbooks, Inc., but for emphasis–and to be explicit–the differences between the editions are these:

    1. A new Publisher's Preface.

    2. A new scholarly introduction.

    3. A new alphabetical listing of currently-operating turquoise mines.

    4. A new and extensive list of references and bibliography.

    5. Sixteen (16) new full color plates, with captions and table.

This is the 83rd title in our continuing line of beautiful Rio Grande Classics. In view of the ever-mounting public interest in the arts, crafts and culture of the American Indian, we believe republication of this work is both warranted and timely. It is the Indians of the American Southwest who today are using in their handsome handmade jewelry the lovely turquoise gemstone. A true turquoise in some ornament of personal jewelry is usually always an indication that someone of perfect taste is from or has been to this lonely and lovely land. We are delighted to republish this exceptionally fine book.

Robert B. McCoy

La Casa Escuela
Glorieta, New Mexico
February 1972

Addendum

In our first printing of this title, early in 1972, we inadvertently duplicated color plates, Numbers 7 and 8. The photographer photographed the same object from a different angle, reversing the Indian rug background so that at a casual glance, we had two different photographs. To our chagrin, this went unnoticed until the book was placed in distribution. We have corrected this fault in this edition. Plate No. 7 is from a color transparency taken by John F. Bennett, an attorney in Colorado Springs who apparently can make a camera sit up and talk. The turquoise jewelry pictured in the plate is contemporary Zuni and Navajo work better identified in the caption. Mr. Bennett took the photograph through the courtesy of the Broadmoor Drug Store, the Broadmoor Hotel, Colorado Springs, Colo. Mrs. Edna Mae Bennett is the author of *Turquoise and The Indian* (Swallow Press, $5.00), a current book available throughout the Southwest, as well as the wife of John F. Bennett. We greatly appreciate the cooperation of all concerned.

Robert B. McCoy

Introduction

Being a fellow Westerner of the Corral de Santa Fe, El Diputado Robert (Bob) McCoy came along one day and said he was going to reprint *Turquois,* by Dr. Joseph E. Pogue; it was, he said, to be republished as one of the beautiful Rio Grande Classics. He asked me if I would consider bringing the material up to date. Hardly without thinking, I said "yes."

Having been educated as a geologist and being currently in the Indian trading business, I had read *Turquois* and knew it would have great popular interest today if it was available again. It it still the leading book on this subject, even after all of these years--it was first published in 1915. A first edition is extremely hard to come by.

Most of the material in the book needed no updating, and the main task that I could see was to name and locate the various turquoise mines, claims and prospects in the Southwestern United States and in Mexico. Those of us in the Indian trading business who buy and sell rough and cut turquoise and finished jewelry know that we are asked nearly every day (at least once) to identify a piece of turquoise and guess which mine it came from.

I have found from my own personal experience and from talking with turquoise cutters, miners, traders and Indians that in some cases it is impossible to identify which mine a stone comes from. The turquoise from some mines does indeed have distinguishing characteristics that can narrow the field down, such as the iron pyrite in the matrix of Morenci turquoise (not usually found in other turquoises), the black spider-web matrix from the Number 8 Mine, the unusual black matrix from Smith's Black Matrix Mine, the unusual color and form of some of the Fox turquoise, the color of some of the Lone Mountain turquoise, and other features such as matrix color and composition. Each mine produces different grades of turquoise and the top grade is usually more easily identified than the lower grades that all tend to look more alike.

Since 1915, when *Turquois* was published, the excavation of various archaeological sites in the United States, Mexico and Central America have continued to yield artifacts made of turquoise. Some of the more important items excavated since then are:

(a) A turquoise necklace of 2,500 hand-drilled beads was found buried with four ear pendants under 15 feet of sand during the National Geographic Society's Pueblo Bonito Expedition of 1921-1927 in New Mexico. This necklace and the four ear pendants are pictured in color as a frontispiece in *Indians of the Americas* (see bibliography: Sterling, Matthew W.).

(b) In 1943, J.C. McGregor excavated a burial at Ridge Ruin, near Flagstaff, Arizona, dating Pueblo III. This burial of "an early magician" contained over 600 artifacts which included elaborate turquoise mosaics, lignite mirrors, carved, painted and inlaid sticks, awls, small bows and arrows and various other ceremonial objects including wood wands with wing-shaped turquoise inlaid sections. In the room above were the skeletons of two parrots. (McGregor, J.C., *"Burial of an Early American Magician"*, Proc. Amer. Phil. Soc., 86, 270-298, 1943.)

(c) Excavated in the Guatemalan Highlands was ". . .a painted copper bird head originally mounted, with a bell inside, on a turquoise-decorated stone disc." *(Archaeology of Southern Mesoamerica*, Vol. 2, Page 176.)

(d) During the 1930-31 excavations of Tomb 7 at Monte Alban, a beautiful necklace of 20 strands of turquoise, coral, red shell, gold and pearls, and with gold rattle pendants, was found. It is pictured in *Archaeology of Southern Mesoamerica*, Vol. 3, Page 952.

The case for believing that a brisk trade between the Pueblo Indians of the Southwest with the turquoise which they mined, and the Indians of distant other areas for products that they produced or were native to their areas, has been considerably strengthened. No large deposits of turquoise have been found in Mexico or Central America that would supply the quantity needed for the many items that have been found, or which must still lie buried. Thus, several reliable writers have concluded that turquoise was an important item of trade in prehistoric times.

One writer (Vall, 1941, Pages 117-125) says: ". . .New Mexico turquoise reached Mexico City and the Mayan cities. . .", and that the early trade in Southwestern turquoise extended ". . .from the West Indies and Yucatan on the south to Ontario on the north. . .and from California on the west to Mississippi and Arkansas on the east. . ." He notes that writer Earl Morris found a mosaic plaque set with 3,000 pieces of turquoise at Chichen Itza, Yucatan. Vall concludes that this turquoise ". . .doubtless was largely of New Mexican origin."

It is apparent that to the Pueblo Indians of the Southwest, turquoise had not only value as personal adornment and for ceremonial purposes, but was probably their most valuable trade item.

As used by the Indians of New Mexico and Arizona, turquoise in their jewelry is a study of its own. The art of setting turquoise in silver probably was first practiced by the Navajo about 1878. Of course, prior to this date the Indians had worked in turquoise making beads, pendants, mosaics, ceremonial objects and carvings since prehistoric times.

At the present time, there is a great interest not only in Indian jewelry containing turquoise, but in lapidary and hand-crafted hobby jewelry by craftsmen all over the world. Fine quality turquoise has always been in demand, but it is even more so today. Many of the old deposits are now either worked out or are no longer in existence due to the activities of miners or mining companies in their search for other ores or minerals. Since turquoise is very often associated with copper deposits, many of the fine turquoise areas are now or have been made into copper ore mines.

Because of the public demand for turquoise, and the age of plastics, resins and epoxies, many new methods of treating turquoise to change the color, make the color permanent, change the appearance of the matrix, or to fabricate complete imitations of turquoise have been developed since author Pogue wrote this book.

The buyer of turquoise jewelry should always deal with a known and reputable dealer in order to be sure he is getting a good stone. Although treated turquoise is not as desirable as fine quality untreated, today's technology in the treatment of the gemstone is able to produce a stone that will hold its color and will be harder than the original soft turquoise that is used for treatment. In the past, particularly in less expensive jewelry, soft and porous stones were used that would absorb greases, body oils, hand creams or soaps, and might change the color from blue to a disagreeable dull green. Hard turquoise is less likely to change color for these reasons.

Unlike other precious stones, it is very difficult to say which is the "best" type of turquoise. Some people prefer the green stones and some the various shades of blue. Some like the turquoise without matrix and others prefer the stones showing spiderweb markings and various shades of brown, red, gray, yellow, black or white matrix with the turquoise.

It is my feeling that turquoise is underpriced at this time in comparison with other gemstones according to the demand, the rarity, the cost of production and future reserves estimates. Fine turquoise stones and jewelry set with fine stones are items that can be enjoyed by the owner as something of real beauty. But they are undoubtedly also a fine investment that will do nothing but increase in value with the passing of years.

I might mention here, or perhaps should have even mentioned it at the outset of these words, that the two spellings of the word–turquois and turquoise–do not indicate inconsistency. When Dr. Pogue wrote his work, the dictionary spelling omitted the final "e". Today, the final "e" is proper. And for those who might want to refer to some additional reading on turquoise, the following references are offered.

Rex Arrowsmith
Geologist

Sante Fe, New Mexico
February 1972

Books and publications referring to Indian jewelry and turquoise:
1.   Adair, John. *The Navajo and Pueblo Silversmiths.* Univ. of Okla. Press, Norman, 1944.

2.   Hegemann, Elizabeth Compton. *Navajo Silver.* Southwest Museum leaflet 29, Los Angeles, 1962.

3.   Mera, Harry P. *Indian Silverwork of the Southwest.* Dale S. King, Globe, Arizona, 1959.

4.   Neumann, David L. "Navajo Silversmithing", *El Palacio,* Vol. 77, No. 2, Pages 13-32, Museum of New Mexico, Santa Fe, 1971.

5.   Tanner, Clara Lee. *Southwest Indian Craft Arts,* Univ. of Ariz. Press, Tucson, 1958.

6.   Woodward, Arthur. *A Brief History of Navajo Silversmithing.* Bulletin 14, Museum of Northern Arizona, Flagstaff, 1938.

Maps availabe for reference to particular turquoise producing areas:
1.   Map of Known Nonferrous Base and Precious Metal Mineral Occurrences in Arizona. Arizona Bureau of Mines, Univ. of Ariz., Tucson, 1969.

2.   Map of Known Nonmetallic Mineral Occurrences in Arizona. Arizona Bureau of Mines, Univ. of Ariz., Tucson, 1965.

3.   Map of Mineral and Water Resources of Arizona. *"Copper in Arizona",* P. 120, Fig. 18.

Arizona Bureau of Mines., Univ. of Ariz., Tucson, 1969.

4. Map of Mineral and Water Resources of Arizona. *"Gem Materials in Arizona"*, P. 358, Fig. 54. Arizona Bureau of Mines, Univ. of Ariz., Tucson, 1969.

5. Map of Mineral and Water Resources of Arizona. *"Sedimentary and Volcanic Rocks"*, P. 39, Arizona Bureau of Mines, Univ. of Ariz., Tucson, 1969.

Alphabetically:

6. Disbrow, Alan E. and Stoll, Walter Co. *"Geology of the Cerrillos Area, Santa Fe County, New Mexico."* Bulletin 48, State Bureau of Mines and Mineral Resources, New Mexico Institute of Mining and Technology, Socorro, N.M., 1957. Good maps are included with this bulletin.

7. Gillerman, Elliot. *"Mineral Deposits of Western Grant County, New Mexico."* Bulletin 83, State Bureau of Mines and Mineral Resources, New Mexico Institute of Mining and Technology, Socorro, N.M., 1964. Good maps also included with this bulletin.

8. Hewitt, Charles H. *"Geology and Mineral Deposits of the Northern Big Burro Mountains-Redrock Area, Grant County, New Mexico."* Bulletin 60, State Bureau of Mines and Mineral Resources, New Mexico Institute of Mining and Technology, Socorro, N.M., 1959. Good maps with this bulletin, too.

9. Horton, Robert C., Bonham, H.F., and Longwill, W.D. *"Copper Occurrences in Nevada by District, Map 13."* Nevada Bureau of Mines, Mackay School of Mines, Univ. of Nevada, Reno, 1962.

10. Johnson, Cy. *"Western Gem Hunters Atlas"*. Cy Johnson and Son, Susanville, Calif., 1970. Maps of many areas in this booklet.

11. Morrissey, Frank R. *"Turquoise Deposits in Nevada"*. Nevada Bureau of Mines, Mackay School of Mines, Univ. of Nevada, Reno, 1964. Very good map included with this book.

12. Murphy, J.B. *"Turquoise and Variscite Occurrences in Nevada, Map 23"*. Nevada Bureau of Mines, Mackay School of Mines, Univ. of Nevada, Reno, 1964.

13. Pearl, Richard M. *"Colorado Gem Trails and Mineral Guide"*. Sage Books, The Swallow Press, Inc., Chicago, 1965. Contains sketch maps and mileage logs to various mines and prospects.

14. Schmidt, Paul G. and Craddock, Campbell. *"The Geology of the Jarilla Mountains, Otero County, New Mexico."* Bulletin 82, State Bureau of Mines and Mineral Resources, New Mexico Institute of Mining and Technology, Socorro, N.M., 1964. Good maps included with this bulletin.

15. Terrell, John Upton. *"Traders of the Western Morning"*. Map showing main prehistoric trade trails of the Southwest, P. 97, Southwest Museum, Los Angeles, 1967.

16. U.S. Geological Survey. *"Geologic Map of New Mexico"*, P. 22; *"Generalized Tectonic*

Map of New Mexico", P. 32; *"Map of Copper in New Mexico"*, P. 165, Plate 41; *"Map of Gem Materials in New Mexico"*, P. 269, Plate 54. Mineral and Water Resources of New Mexico, Bulletin 87, State Bureau of Mines and Mineral Resources, New Mexico Institute of Mining and Technology, Socorro, N.M., 1965.

17. Zeller, Robert A. Jr. *"Geology of the Little Hatchet Mountains, Hidalgo and Grant Counties, New Mexico."* Bulletin 96, State Bureau of Mines and Mineral Resources, New Mexico Institute of Mining and Technology, Socorro, N.M., 1970. Good maps with this bulletin.

Various topographic and geological maps of the turquoise-producing states are available from the following places:

1. **Arizona**: The Arizona Bureau of Mines, The Univ. of Ariz., Tucson, Ariz. 85721.

2. **California**: The California Division of Mines and Geology, Division Hq., Resources Bldg., Rm. 1341, 1416 Ninth St., Sacramento, Calif. 95814.

3. **Colorado**: The Colorado Geological Survey, 254 Columbine Bldg., 1845 Sherman St., Denver, Colo. 80203.

4. **Nevada**: The Nevada Bureau of Mines, Mackay School of Mines, Univ. of Nevada, Reno, Nev., 89507.

5. **New Mexico**: The New Mexico State Bureau of Mines and Mineral Resources, New Mexico Institute of Mining and Technology, Campus Sta., Socorro, N.M. 87801.

6. **United States Geological Survey**, Geologic Inquiries Group, Washington, D.C. 20242.

Rex Arrowsmith standing at the entrance to the Tiffany Mine, Santa Fe County, N.M.

An interior view of one of the rooms in Arrowsmith's shop in Santa Fe.

Bibliographic Note

The note "The Turquois, Pogue, p.___" refers the reader to the present volume.
Amerial in parentheses refers to other works cited. Full bibliographic information is given in the text with the following three exceptions:

Mineral and Water Resources of Arizona. The Arizona Bureau of Mines. Bulletin 180. Tucson, The University of Arizona, 1969.

Mineral Deposits of Western Grant County, New Mexico. Elliot Gillerman. Socorro, N.M. Bureau of Mines and Mineral Resources, 1964.

Turquoise Deposits of Nevada. Frank R. Morrissey. Nevada Bureau of Mines, Mackay School of Mines, Report 17. Reno, University of Nevada, 1968.

Bibliography

Aberle, Sophia. "The Pueblo Indians of New Mexico, Their Land, Economy and Organization", *American Anthropological Association Memoirs,* 70: 93, January, 1948.

Adair, John. *The Navajo and Pueblo Silversmiths.* Norman, Okla: University of Oklahoma Press, 1946.

Adams, William Y. *Shonto, A Study of the Role of the Trader in a Modern Navajo Community.* Bureau of American Ethnology Bulletin No. 188. Washington: U.S. Government Printing Office 1963.

Aitkens, I. "Turquoise", *U.S. Bur. Mines Inf. Circ. 6941:* 17pp, 1931.

Amsden, Charles Avery. *Prehistoric Indians of the Southwest from Basketmaker to Pueblo.* Los Angeles: Southwest Museum, 1949.

Anonymous. "Note on Good Specimens from the Old Castilian Turquois mine, Cerrillos", *Eng. and Min. Jour.,* 29: 307, 1879.

--------. "News Dispatch from Turquesa, Santa Fe County", *Min. World* (Las Vegas), 1 (5): 7, January 1881.

--------. "Los Cerrillos", *Min. World* (Las Vegas), 2 (19): 260-261, July, 1882.

--------. "Turquoise", *Min. World* (Las Vegas), 5 (2): 23, October, 1885.

--------. "Production of Rare Minerals", *Min. and Sci. Press,* 84: 281, 1902.

--------. "Burro Mountain Turquoise", *South-Western Mines,* 1 (1): 5, October, 1908.

--------. "Tiffany Turquoise Mines Robbed by Santa Domingo Indians", *South-Western Mines,* 2 (8, should be 9): 9, November 1910.

Arrowsmith, Rex (ed). *Mines of the Old Southwest.* Santa Fe: Stagecoach Press, 1963.

Ayer, E.E. *The Memorial of Fray Alonso de Benavides, 1630* (Translation by Mrs. E.E. Ayer), Chicago, 1960. 309 pp.

Bahti, Tom. *Southwestern Indian Arts and Crafts.* Flagstaff, Arizona: KC Publications, 1966.

Baldwin, Brewster and Kottlowski, Frank E. *Scenic Trips to the Geologic Past, No. 1, Santa Fe.* Socorro, New Mexico: State Bureau of Mines and Mineral Resources, New Mexico Institute of Mining and Technology, 1968.

Ball, Sydney H. "Sandstone Copper Deposits at Bent, New Mexico", *Min. and Sci.* Press, 107: 132-135 (2 figs., map), 1913.

--------. *Mining of Gems and Ornamental Stones by American Indians.* Bureau of American

Ethnology, Anthropological Paper, Bulletin No. 128. Washington: U.S. Government Printing Office, 1941.

Bartlett, Katherine. "Prehistoric Mining in the Southwest", *Museum of Northern Arizona Museum Notes,* 12: 41-44, October 1935.

Beals, Ralph. *Comparative Ethnology of North America before 1750.* Berkley: University of California Press, 1932.

Benedict, Ruth. *Zuni Fetishes.* Bureau of American Ethnology, Bulletin No. 96. Washington: U.S. Government Printing Office, 1929.

--------. *Tales of the Cochiti Indians.* Bureau of American Ethnology Bulletin No. 98 (pp. 191-197). Washington: U.S. Government Printing Office, 1931.

Bennett, Edna Mae. *Turquoise and the Indian.* Chicago, Illinois: Swallow Press, 1970.

Berry, Rose V.S. "American Inter'Tribal Indian Art", *Art and Archeology,* 32: 147-158, November 1931.

Beaglehole, Ernest and Pearl. "Lost City of Nevada", *Scientific American,* 135: 14, July 1925.

--------. "Hopi of Second Mesa", *American Anthropological Association Memoirs,* 44: 5-65, 1935.

Blackman, Frank W. *Spanish Institutions of the Southwest.* Baltimore: Johns Hopkins Press, 1891.

Blake, W.P. "Observations on the Mineral Resources of the Rocky Mountain Chain, Near Santa Fe, and the Probable Extent Southwards of the Rocky Mountain Gold Field", *Boston Soc. Nat. Hist. Proc.,* 7: 64-70; Min. Mag., 1: 22-27, 1859.

--------. "Observations on the Geology of the Rocky Mountain Chain in the Vicinity of Santa Fe, New Mexico", *Edinburgh New Phil. Jour.,* 10: 301-304, 1859; *Am. Assoc. Adv. Sci. Proc.,* 13: 314-319, 1860.

--------. "New Locality of the Green Turquois Known as Chalchuite, and on the Identity of Turquois with the Callais or Callaina of Pliny", *Am. Jour. Sci.,* 25 (3): 197-200, 1883.

Bryan, Bruce. "Excavation of Galez Ruin, Mimbres Valley, New Mexico", *Art and Archeology,* 32: 35-42, November-December 1931.

Bullock, Alice. *Living Legends of the Santa Fe Country.* Denver, Colorado: Green Mountain Press, 1970.

Bunzell, Ruth L. *Zuni Katcinas.* Forty-seventh Annual Report of Bureau of American Ethnology, p. 1032. Washington: U.S. Government Printing Office, 1929-1932.

Clarke, F.W. *A Report of Work Done in the Washington Laboratory during the Fiscal Year 1883-84.* U.S. Geol. Survey Bull. 9, 1884.

--------. *Mineral Analyses from the Laboratories of the United States Geological Survey, 1880 to 1903.* U.S. Geol. Survey Bull. 220, 1903.

--------. *Analyses of Rocks and Minerals from the Laboratory of the United States Geological Survey, 1880 to 1914.* U.S. Geol. Survey Bull. 591, 1915.

--------, and J.S. Diller. "Turquoise from New Mexico", *American Journal of Science,* 3rd Ser., 32: 511-523, September 1888.

--------. *Crystallized Turquoise from Virginia.* U.S. Geol. Survey Bull. 509, pp. 42-47, 1912.

--------. *The Turquoise Copper-Mining District, Arizona.* U.S. Geol. Survey Bull. 530, pp. 124-134, 1913.

Clews, Elsie Worthington. *Isleta, New Mexico.* Forty-seventh Annual Report of the Bureau of American Ethnology, pp. 201-459. Washington: U.S. Government Printing Office, 1930.

--------. "War God Stories of the Laguna and Zuni Indians", *American Anthropologist,* n.s., 20 : 381-405, October-December 1918.

Cosgrove, Harriett Silliman and C.B. "The Swarts Ruin, a Typical Mimbres Site of Southwest New Mexico", *Papers of the Peabody Museum of Archeology and Ethnology,* 15 (1): 62-68, 1932.

Coolidge, Dave and Mary Roberts Coolidge. *Navajo Indians.* Boston: Houghton-Mifflin, 1930.

Cowan, John L. "Turquoise Mining of New Mexico", *Great Southwest Magazine,* May 1907.

--------. "Turquoise Mines of New Mexico", *Mineral Collector,* 15: 110-112, 1908.

Crawford, Wm. P. and Frank Johnson. "Turquoise Deposits of Courtland, Arizona", *Economic Geology,* 32: 511-523, 1937.

Cummings, Byron. *First Inhabitants of Arizona and the Southwest.* Tucson: Cummings Publishing Council, 1953.

Curtis, Natalie. *The Indian's Book.* New York: Harper and Bros., 1907.

Cushing, Frank Hamilton *et al.* "Contributions to Hopi History", *American Anthropologist,* n.s., 24: 253-298, March 1922.

Dana, E.S. *The System of Mineralogy of James Dwight Dana, 1837-1868.* New York: John Wiley & Sons, 1892.

Disbrow, Alan E. and Walter C. Stoll. *Geology of the Cerrillos Area, Santa Fe, New Mexico.* Socorro, New Mexico: State Bureau of Mines and Mineral Resources, New Mexico Institute of Mining and Technology, 1957.

Dodge, Natt N. and Herbert S. Zim. *The Southwest.* New York: Golden Press, 1955.

Douglas, Andrew Elliott. "The Secrets of the Southwest Solved by Talkative Tree Rings", *National Geographic Magazine,* 56: 737-770, December 1929.

Douglas, Frederick H. *Navajo Silversmithing,* 4th ed; Denver Art Museum Leaflet, No. 15. Denver: Denver Art Museum, 1951.

Duffield, M.S. "Aboriginal Remains in Nevada and Utah", *American Anthropologist,* 6: 148-

150, January 1904.

Ekholm, Gordon F. and Gordon R. Willey (eds.). *Archaeological Frontiers and External Connections*, Vol. 4, Handbook of Middle American Indians. Austin, Texas: University of Texas Press, 1966.

Farrington, O.C. *Gems and Gem Minerals*. Chicago: A.W. Mumford, 1903.

Fewkes, Jesse Walter. "Pueblo Ruins near Flagstaff, Arizona", *American Anthropologist*, n.s. II: 422-450, March 1900.

--------. *Casa Grande, Arizona*. Twenty-eighth Annual Report of the Bureau of American Ethnology. Washington: U.S. Government Printing Office, 1912.

--------. *Prehistoric Ruins in New Mexico, Colorado and Utah*. Smithsonian Miscellaneous Collections 67 (9). Washington: U.S. Government Printing Office, 1917.

Frost, Max (ed.). *New Mexico: Its Resources, Climate, Geography, Geology, History Statistics, Present Conditions and Future Prospects*. Santa Fe: New Mexico Bureau of Immigration, 1894.

--------, and Paul A.F. Walter. *To the Land of Sunshine*. Santa Fe: New Mexico Bureau of Immigration, 1906.

--------. *Santa Fe County: The Heart of New Mexico, Rich in History and Resources*. Santa Fe: New Mexico Bureau of Immigration, 1906.

Galbraith, Frederic W. and Daniel J. Brennan. *Minerals of Arizona*. Tucson, Arizona: University of Arizona Press, 1959.

Gifford, Edward Winslow. "The Southeastern Yavapai," *American Archeology and Ethnology*, 27: 176-252, April 1931.

--------. "Northeastern and Western Yavapai," *American Archeology and Ethnology*, 34: 247-354, April 1936.

Gillerman, Elliot. *Mineral Deposits of Western Grant County, New Mexico*. State Bureau of Mines and Mineral Resources Bulletin 83. Socorro, New Mexico: New Mexico Institute of Mining and Technology, 1964.

Gregg, Andrew K. *New Mexico in the Nineteenth Century*. Albuquerque, New Mexico: University of New Mexico Press, 1968.

Haile, Berard. *An Ethnologic Dictionary of the Navajo Language*. Germany: The Franciscan Fathers, Saint Michaels, Arizona, 1929.

Halloran, J.H. (ed.) "Turquoise Mining in Arizona and New Mexico," *Mining and Scientific Press*, 85: 102-103, August 1932.

Hammond, George P. and Agapito Rey. *Narratives of the Coronado Expedition, 1540-1542*. Coronado Historical Series, II. Albuquerque, New Mexico: University of New Mexico Press, 1940.

Harrington, E.R. "Digging for Turquoise in America's First Mines," *New Mexico Magazine*, 17, July 1939.

--------. "Chalchihuitl, A Story of Early Turquoise Mining in the Southwest," Eng. and Min.

Jour., 141 (6): 57-58, 1940.

Harrington, Mark R. "Primitive Pueblo of Nevada," *American Anthropologist,* n.s; 29: 268-269, July 1927.

Haury, Emil. *Bear Ruin.* Museum of Northern Arizona Bulletin No. 12. Tucson: University of Arizona, 1940.

Hawley, Florence M. "Bear Mountain Pueblo of Southwest Arizona," *Art and Archeology,* 33: 227-236, May 1932.

Helps, Arthur. *The Spanish Conquest in America, I.* London: John W. Parker and Sons, 1855.

Hewett, Charles H. *Geology and Mineral Deposits of the Northern Big Burro Mountains, Red Rock Area, Grant County, New Mexico.* State Bureau of Mines and Mineral Resources Bulletiin 60. Socorro, New Mexico: New Mexico Institute of Mining and Technology, 1959.

Hewett, Edgar Lee. *The Chaco Canon and its Monuments.* Albuquerque: University of New Mexico, 1936.

————. *Ancient Life in the American Southwest.* Indianapolis: Bobbs-Merrill

————. "Chaco Canon in 1932," *Art and Archeology,* 33: 147-157, 1932.

————, and A.F. Bandelier. *Indians of the Rio Grande.* Albuquerque: University of New Mexico Press, 1937.

Hill, Gertrude Frances. *Turquoise, Its History and Significance in the Southwest.* Unpublished Masters Thesis, University of Arizona, 1938, Library of University of Arizona.

————. *"Zuni Turquoise," Kiva,* 13: March 1947.

————. "Turquoise and the Zuni," *Kiva,* 13: May 1948.

Hilton, John W. "About Indian Jewelry," *Desert Magazine,* 6: July 1938.

Hodge, Frederick Webb. *History of Hawikuh, New Mexico.* Los Angeles: Southwest Museum, 1937.

————. *Turquoise Work of Hawikuh, New Mexico.* Leaflets of the Museum of the American Indians, No. 2. New York: Heye Foundation, 1922.

————. *Fray Alonso de Benavide's Revised Memorial of 1634.* Coronado Historical Series, IV. Albuquerque: University of New Mexico Press, 1944.

————, *et al,* (editorial board). *Introduction to American Indian Art.* New York: The Exposition of Indian Tribal Arts, inc., 1931.

Holmes, W.H. *Handbook of Aboriginal American Antiquities.* Bureau of American Ethnology Bulletin No. 60, Part 1. Washington: U.S. Government Printing Office, 1923.

Howard, E. Viet. *Metalliferous Occurrences in New Mexico.* Santa Fe: New Mexico State Planning Office, 1967.

Hyde, D.C. *Mount Chalchuitl; Description of Property and Mines of the Turquoise Gold & Silver Mining Company, Los Cerrillos, Santa Fe County, New Mexico.* (Promotional brochure published apparently between 1880 and 1890, 15 pp., 1 fig.)

Jeancon, J.A. *Excavations in Chama Valley, New Mexico.* Bureau of American Ethnology Bulletin No. 81. Washington: U.S. Government Printing Office, 1923.

Johnson, Cy and Son. *Western Gem Hunters Atlas.* Susanville, California: Cy Johnson and Son, 1966.

Johnson, Paul Willard. *A Field Guide to the Gems and Minerals of Mexico.* Mentone, California: Gembooks, 1965.

Jones, Fayette Alexander. *Epitome of the Economic Geology of New Mexico.* Albuquerque: New Mexico Bureau of Immigration, 1908.

--------. "Notes on Turquoise in the Southwest; Concerning its Original Workings, its Geology and its Modern Method of Mining," *South-Western Mines,* 1 (12): 1-2, September 1909.

--------. *The Mineral Resources of New Mexico.* Min. Res. Survey Bull. 1, New Mexico School of Mines, 1915.

------. *Selections from the Writings of Old Mining Camps of New Mexico, 1854-1904.* Santa Fe: Stagecoach Press, 1964.

Judd, Neil Merton. *Archeological Investigations at Pueblo Bonito, New Mexico.* Smithsonian Miscellaneous Collections 77, Part II. Washington: U.S. Government Printing Office, 1954.

Jung, H. "Uber Turkis," *Chemie der Erde,* 7: 77-94, 1932.

Kelley, Lillian. "Southwest Indian Silverwork," *Desert Magazine,* 27: November 1960.

Kidder, Alfred Vincent. "The Artifacts of Pecos," *Papers of the Phillips Academy Southwest Expedition, No. 6.* New Haven: Yale University Press, 1932.

------ (Rev. ed.). *An Introduction to the Study of Southwest Archeology.* New Haven: Yale University Press, 1962.

Kirk, Ruth Falkenburg. *Introduction to Zuni Fetishism.* Santa Fe: Papers of the School of American Research, Archaeological Institute of America, 1943.

--------. "Southwestern Indian Jewelry," *El Palacio,* 52 (2 and 3): 1945.

Kluckhohn, Clyde and Dorothea Leighton. *The Navajo.* Rev. ed. Garden City, New York: Natural History Library Anchor Book, Doubleday and Company, Inc., 1962.

Knaus, Charles L. "Sky Stones," *New Mexico Magazine,* 26: 40, March 1948.

Kneale, Albert. *Indian Agent.* Caldwell, Idaho: Caxton Printers, 1950.

Kroeber, A.L. *Anthropology.* New York: Harcourt, Brace and Company, 1932.

Kunz, George Frederick. "Precious Stones," *Mineral Resources of the United States.* U.S. Geological Survey Twelfth Annual Report, Part II, p. 910. Washington: U.S. Government

Printing Office, 1890.

———. "Precious Stone," *Mineral Resources of the United States.* U.S. Geological Survey, pp. 539-551, 1891; pp. 756-781, 1892.

———. "Turquoise; New Mexico," *Mineral Resources of the United States, 1903,* pp. 951 - 955, 1904. (This is a review of D.W. Johnson, 1903.)

———. "Gem Stones of Mexico," *Mining World,* 31: 16, July 1909.

Lange, Charles H. *Cochiti, A New Mexico Pueblo Past and Present.* Austin, Texas: University of Texas Press, 1960.

Lasky, S.G. "Geology and Ore Deposits of the Little Hatchet Mountains, Hidalgo and Grant Counties, New Mexico," U.S. Geological Survey Prof. Paper 208, 101 pp. 27 pls. (incl. maps), 18 figs. (incl. maps), 1947.

LeConte, J.L. *Notes on the Geology of the Survey for the Extension of the Union Pacific Railway, E.D., from the Smokey Hill River, Kansas, to the Rio Grande,* 76 pp., map, Philadelphia, 1868.

Libhart, Myles. "The American Indian," *Craft Horizons,* 24: May-June 1944.

Lincoln, Francis Church. "Mining Districts and Minerals," *Resources of Nevada.* Reno: Nevada Newsletter Publishing Company, 1923.

Manly, R.L., Jr. "The Differential Thermal Analysis of Certain Phosphates," Am. Mineralogist, 35: 108-115 (4 figs.), 1950.

Matthews, George Washington. "The Mountain Chant, A Navajo Ceremony," *Fifth Annual Report of the Bureau of American Ethnology.* Washington: U.S. Government Printing Office, pp. 421-455, 1884.

McCluney, Eugene B. "A Mimbres Shrine at the West Baker Site," *Archaeology,* 21 (3): 196-205, June 1968.

McGibbeny, J.H. "Hopi Jewelry," *Arizona Highways,* 26: July 1950.

McGregor, John C. *Southwestern Archaeology.* New York: John Wiley & Sons, Inc., 1941.

McIlhargey, A.L. "Indian Jewelry," *Great Southwest Magazine,* II: 53, May 1907.

———. "Notes." *Great Southwest Magazine,* II: 129, August 1907.

McNitt, Frank. *The Indian Traders.* Norman: University of Oklahoma Press, 1962.

Mera, Harry P. *Indian Silverwork of the Southwest, I.* Globe, Arizona: Dale Stuart King, Publisher, 1960.

Morris, Earl. "Aztec Ruins, New Mexico," *Anthropological Papers of the Museum of Natural History,* 26 (Part II): 109-138, 1919.

Morrissey, Frank. *Turquoise Deposits of Nevada, Report 17.* Reno, Nevada: Mackay School of Mines, University of Nevada, 1968.

Murburger, Nell. "Turquoise Mine in Nevada," *Desert Magazine,* 21: 15, January 1963.

Murphy, J. Bartlett. *Gems & Gem Material* (mimeo). Reno: Nevada Bureau of Mines.

--------. *Turquoise and Variscite Occurrences in Nevada.* Reno, Nevada: Mackay School of Mines, University of Nevada, 1964.

Murphy, Merrell O. "Turquoise in the Cerrillos Hills," *Lapidary Journal,* 14: 720-741, 1962 .

Neumann, David L. "Modern Development in Indian Jewelry," *El Palacio,* 42: 173-181, 1950 .

--------. "Navajo Silversmithing," *El Palacio,* 77 (2): 13-32, 1971.

Newberry, J.S. *Geological Report,* in Ives, J.C., Report upon the Colorado River of the West, explored in 1857 and 1858 by Lieutenant Joseph C. Ives, Corps of Topographical Engineers, under the direction of the Office of Explorations and Surveys, U.S. War Dept., U.S. 36th Cong., 1st Sess., House Exec. Doc. 90, pt. 3, 154 pp., illus. (incl. maps), 1861.

Northrup, Stuart A. "Minerals of New Mexico" (Geo. Series), *University of New Mexico Bulletin,* 6 (1): 1942.

--------. *Minerals of New Mexico.* Albuquerque: University of New Mexico Press, 1959.

O'Bryan, Aileen O. *Origin Myths of the Navajo,* Bureau of American Ethnology Bulletin No. 163. Washington: U.S. Government Printing Office, 1941.

Opler, Morris Edward. "Myths and Legends of the Lipan Apache Indians," *Memoirs of the American Folk Lore Society.* New York, J.J. Augustin, Publisher, 1940.

Otero, M.A. *Report of the Governor of New Mexico* (to the Secretary of the Interior) *for the Year Ending June 30, 1899,* 376 pp., illus., Washington, D.C., 1899.

--------. *Report of the Governor of New Mexico* (to the Secretary of the Interior) *for the Year Ending June 30, 1900,* 445 pp., Washington, D.C., 1900.

--------. *Report of the Governor of New Mexico* (to the Secretary of the Interior) *for the Year Ending June 30, 1901,* 546 pp., Washington, D.C., 1901.

--------. *Report of the Governor of New Mexico to the Secretary of the Interior, 1902,* 632 pp., Washington, D.C., 1902.

--------. *Report of the Governor of New Mexico to the Secretary of the Interior, 1903,* 661 pp., Washington, D.C., 1903.

Parsons, E.C. "Social Organization of the Tewa of New Mexico," *American Anthropological Association Memoirs,* 36: 1929.

Pearl, Richard M. "Turquoise Deposits of Colorado," *Economic Geology,* 36: 336-342, 1941.

--------. *Colorado Gem Trails,* 3rd ed., American Gem Trail Series. Colorado Springs: Mineral Book Company, pp. 36-39; 40-44; 66-67, 1953.

--------. *Colorado Gem Trails and Mineral Guide,* 2nd ed. Denver: Sage Books, Alan Swallow, Publisher, 1965.

Petersen, (Carl) Theodor. *Zur Kenntniss der natürlichen Phosphate; I. Türkis aus* Neu-Mexiko. Jarhresbericht des Physikalischen Vereins zu Frankfort am Main (1896-1897), pp. 77-80, 1898; Neues Jahrbuch für Min., Geol., und Pal., Band 2, Ref. p. 31, 1900.

Pogue, Joseph Ezekial. "The Turquoise," *National Academy of Science Memoirs.* 3rd Memoir, 12 (Part 2): 3-136, 1915.

Pough, Frederick H. *A Field Guide to Rocks and Minerals,* 2nd ed. Boston: Houghton-Mifflin, 1955.

Powell, John Wesley. *Report of Explorations in 1873 of the Colorado of the West and Its Tributaries.* Washington: U.S. Government Printing Office, 1874.

Reiter, Winifred S. *Personal Adornment of the Ancient Pueblo Indians.* University of New Mexico Unpublished Master's Thesis, 98 pp., illus., 1933.

Roberts, Frank Harold Hannah, Jr. *Shabik' eschee Village.* Bureau of American Ethnology Bulletin No. 92. Washington: U.S. Government Printing Office, 1929.

——. *Early Ruins of the Piedra District of Southwest Colorado.* Bureau of American Ethnology Bulletin 96. Washington: U.S. Government Printing Office, 1930.

——. *The Ruins of Kiatuthlanna, Eastern Arizona.* Bureau of American Ethnology Bulletin No. 100. Washington: U.S. Government Printing Office, 1931.

——. *Village of the Great Kivas on the Zuni Reservation.* Bureau of American Ethnology Bulletin III. Washington: U.S. Government Printing Office, 1932.

——. *Archeological Remains in the Whitewater District of Eastern Arizona.*

Rösler, H. (Title not known; Pogue, 1915, cites reference to origin of turquoise at Cerrillos) , Neues Jahrbuch fur Min., Geol., and Pal., Beilage Band 15, p. 286, 1902. (Not seen)

Sahagun, Bernardino de. *A History of Ancient Mexico,* I. Trans. Fanny R. Bandelier from Spanish version of Carlos Marie de Bustamente; I. Nashville: Fisk University Press, 1932.

——. Florentine Codex: *General History of the Things of New Spain, I.* Trans. C.E. Dibble; rev. ed. Santa Fe: New Mexico, School of American Research and the University of Utah, 1963.

Saville, Marshall H. *Turquoise Mosaic Art in Ancient Mexico,* Vi. Greenwich, Connecticut : Museum of the American Indian, Heye Foundation, 1922.

Schmidt, Paul G. and Campbell Craddock. *The Geology of the Jarilla Mountains, Otero County, New Mexico.* Socorro, New Mexico: State Bureau of Mines and Mineral Resources, New Mexico Institute of Mining and Technology.

Schole, F.V. "Civil Government and Society in New Mexico in the Seventeenth Century," *New Mexico Hist. Rev.,* 10: 71-111, 1935.

Schrader, F.C., R.W. Stone and Samuel Sanford. *Useful Minerals of the United States.* U.S. Geol. Survey Bull. 624,412 pp., 1917.

Scott's *Manual of Common Rocks and Minerals,* revised. Ft. Collins, Colorado: Rocky Mountain Minerals, 1949.

Silliman, Benjamin. "W.P. Blak's Visit to Cerrillos," *American Journal of Science,* Ser. 1, 25: 227, July 1858.

Sinkankas, John. *Gem Stones of North America.* Princeton, New Jersey: D. Van Nostrand Co., Inc. Pp. 213-228 and a 12 page bibliography on gems. 1959.

Smith, Helen M. "Turquoise," *Arizona Highways,* 15: 23, March 1939.

Spicer, Edward H. and L.R. Caywood. *Two Pueblo Ruins in West Central Arizona.* University of Arizona Bulletin, No. 10. Tucson: University of Arizona Press, 1936.

Starr, Frederick. "Shrines Near Cochiti, New Mexico," *American Antiquarian,* 22: 219-223, March 1900.

Sterling, Matthew. *Origin Myth of Acoma.* Bureau of American Ethnology Bulletin No. 135. Washington: U.S. Government Printing Office, 1942.

Sterrett, D.B. "Gems and Precious Stones," *Mineral Resources of the United States, 1909.* U.S. Geological Survey Part 2, pp. 789-795, 1911.

------. "Gems and Precious Stones," *Mineral Resources of the United States, 1912.* U.S. Geological Survey Bull. 530, pp 383-388, 1913.

------. "Gems and Precious Stones," *Mineral Resources of the United States, 1914.* U.S. Geological Survey Part 2, p. 334, 1916.

Stevenson, J.J. *Report upon geological Examinations in Southern Colorado and Northern New Mexico during the Years 1878 and 1879.* U.S. Geog. and Geol. Surveys West of the 100th Meridian (Wheeler), Vol. 3-Supplement, 420 pp., illus. (incl. maps), 1881.

Stevenson, James. *Illustrated Catalogue of Collections Obtained from the Pueblos of Zuni, New Mexico and Walpi, Arizona in 1879.* Third Annual Report of the Bureau of American Ethnology. Washington: U.S. Government Printing Office, 1894.

Stevenson, Mrs. Matilda Coxe. *The Sia.* Eleventh Annual Report of the Bureau of American Ethnology. Washington: U.S. Government Printing Office, 1874.

------. *The Zuni.* Twenty-third Annual Report of the Bureau of American Ethnology. Washington: U.S. Government Printing Office, 1904.

Stewart, T. Dale (Volume Editor). *Physical Anthropology.* (Volume 9, *Handbook of Middle American Indians)* Austin, Texas: University of Texas Press, 1970.

Stirling, Matthew W. *Indians of the Americas.* Washington D.C.: The National Geographic Society, 1955.

Sun, Ming-Shan. *The Nature of Chrysocolla from Inspiration Mine, Arizona, Reprint* Series No. 16. Socorro, New Mexico: State Bureau of Mines and Mineral Resources, New Mexico Institute of Mining and Technology, 1963.

Talmage, S.B. and T.P. Wootton. "The Non-Metallic Mineral Resources of New Mexico and Their Economic Features (Exclusive of Fuels)," *New Mexico Bur. Mines and* Min. Res.

Bull. 12: 159 (2 pls., incl. map, 4 figs., incl. maps), 1937.

Tanner, Clara Lee. *Southwest Indian Craft Arts.* Tucson: University of Arizona Press, 1958.

------. "Contemporary Southwest Indian Silver," *The Kiva* (Arizona State Museum, University of Arizona), 25 (3): February 1960.

Terrell, John Upton. *Traders of the Western Morning.* Los Angeles: Southwest Museum, 1967.

Thornton, W.L. (should be "T.") *Report of the Governor of New Mexico to the Secretary of the Interior, 1893,* 33 pp. Washington, D.C., 1893.

Underhill, Ruth. *Pueblo Crafts.* Indian Handcraft Series No. 6, Bureau of Indian Affairs, U.S. Department of the Interior, Brach of Education. Washington: Phoenix Press, 1944.

United States Geological Survey. *Mineral and Water Resources of New Mexico Bulletin 87.* Socorro, New Mexico: State Bureau of Mines and Technology, 1965.

------. *Mineral and Water Resources of Arizona Bulletin 180.* Tucson: The University of Arizona, 1969.

Van Valkenburgh, Richard. "Trail to Turquoise," *Desert Magazine,* 15:22, February 1947.

Webster, Robert. "Turquoise: Natural, Treated, Synthetic and Simulated," *Lapidary Journal,* 16: 758-777, November 1962.

Weight, Harold A. "Ghost Town Miners." *Desert Magazine,* 11: 20, May 1948.

Wheat, John Ben. *Crooked Ridge Village.* University of Arizona Bulletin, No. 24. Phoenix: University of Arizona Press, 1954.

Willey, Gordon R. (Volume Editor). *Archaeology of Southern MesoAmerica,* Parts 1 and 2. Handbook of Middle American Indians. Austin, Texas: University of Texas Press, 1965.

White, Leslie. "Pueblo of San Felipe," *American Anthropological Association Memoirs,* 38: 7-67, 1932.

------. Pueblo of Santa Domingo," *American Anthropological Association Memoirs,* 43: 7-199, 1935.

------. *Pueblo of Sia.* Bureau of American Ethnology Bulletin No. 184. Washington: U.S. Government Printing Office, 1962.

Woodbury, Richard E. *Primitive Stone Instruments of Northeast Arizona.* Peabody Museum Papers: Reports of Awatowi Expedition, 34, (6), p. 152, 1954.

Woodward, Arthur. *Brief History of Navajo Silversmithing,* 2nd. ed.; Bulletin No. 14. Flagstaff: Museum of Northern Arizona, 1946.

Wormington, Hanna Marie. *Prehistoric Indians of the Southwest.* Popular Series No. 7. Denver: Colorado Museum of Natural History, 1947.

Wuestner, Herman. "A Check List of Minerals from Kelly, New Mexico," *Rocks and Minerals,* 5: 127-131 (illus.), 1930.

--------. The Minerals of Silver City, New Mexico, District," *Rocks and Minerals,* 7: 121-125, 1932.

Wyman, Leland C. *The Windways of the Navajo.* Colorado Springs: The Taylor Museum, Colorado Springs Fine Arts Center, 1962.

Zeller, Robert A., Jr. *Geology of the Little Hatchet Mountains Hidalgo and Grant Counties, New Mexico.* Socorro, New Mexico: State Bureau of Mines and Mineral Resources, New Mexico Institute of Mining and Technology.

Mines and Prospects

American Gem and Turquoise Co. New Mexico, Grant County. See Parker Mine. Property acquired by Phelps Dodge Co. See The Turquois, Pogue, p. 56.

American Turquoise Co., The, New Mexico. See Hachita District. See The Turquois, Pogue, p. 57.

American Turquois Co., The, New Mexico, Santa Fe County. See Cerrillos Area.

Antler Prospect. Nevada, Lander County. Located in the Toiyabe range 6.5 miles south of Hall Creek Ranch, in Sec. 9, T.22N., R.45E. Hard, deep-blue turquoise occurs in the shale and quartzite, and some greenish turquoise is associated with a single metamorphosed tuff (?) bed. The enclosing rocks are little altered. (Turquoise Deposits of Nevada, p. 21)

Aranzazu Mining District. Zacatecas (state), Mexico. Turquoise mined here. Located southwest of Saltillo.

Arizona Turquoise Co., The. Arizona, Mohave County, Mineral Park Area. See Mineral Park Mines.

Arkansas Claim, The. Colorado, Conejos County. See The King Mine.

Arrowhead Mine. Nevada, Lander County. Also called "The Super-X." Located about 2.5 milesnorth-northwest of Tenabo in the NE ¼ Sec. 32, T.29N., R.47E. The host rock is a strongly faulted chert. The turquoise occurs in a breccia and gouge zone, where it forms nodules in the gouge together with veinlets in the gouge and breccia. Contains high grade spider web turquoise with golden-colored lines. (Turquoise Deposits of Nevada, p.2, 15)

August Berning Mine. Nevada, Eureka County. Located 1,000 feet southwest of the Number 8 Mine and 700 feet below it on the east side of a north-south ridge. Turquoise occurs within black shale and along the contact between the shale and intrusive quartz monzonite (?) The turquoise forms seams along bedding planes in the shale and nuggets along brecciated shear zones. High grade turquoise, slightly greenish blue in color, has been found both as clear pieces and as the black-matrix, spider-web variety. (Turquoise Deposits of Nevada, p. 10)

Aztec Claim. Nevada, Clark County. See Simmons Mine.

Aztec Claim. New Mexico, Grant County, Hachita District. See Robinson and Porterfield Mines. See The Turquois, Pogue, p. 57.

Aztec Turquoise Co. Arizona, Mohave County, Mineral Park Area. See Mineral Park Mines.

Azure Claim, The. New Mexico, Grant County, Hachita District. See The Robinson and Porterfield Mines. See The Turquois, Pogue, p. 57.

Azure Mine. New Mexico, Grant County. Located in the NE ¼ sec. 15, T.19S., R.15W, 3300 feet N 30°W of the Burro Chief Shaft. Was the largest producer of turquoise in the area and according to Zalinski (1907) produced several million dollars worth of fine stones. The turquoise is found within a wide fractured zone in granite, which at the mine is a medium grained, slightly porphyritic rock, typical of much of the granite in the Burro Mountains. The vein is 40 to 60 feet wide with distinct hanging and footwalls. Between the walls the material is mostly sheared and altered granite with streaks and blebs of kaolinite and secondary silica. The turquoise occurs within, and is confined to the vein. The following description of the Azure Mine is from Sterrett (1908, p.829): "Turquoise occurs as veins and veinlets filling the joints and fissures in the rock and as nuggets. In places these veinlets are mere films, and in others they are as much as three fourths of an inch thick. Part of the turquoise is found in groups of small rounded masses resembling nuggets, fitted roughly together though separated from one another by kaolin or clay and enveloped in it. These groups of nuggets generally fill a flattened lenticular-shaped pocket in one of the veinlets. The Elizabeth pocket was discovered in this mine in 1893. It is thought to be the richest single pocket of turquoise ever discovered. It was 100 feet long, 40 feet wide, and 40 to 50 feet high. The turquoise was very pure with little matrix except that some of the nodules had small quartz crystals in them. The vein rock near this pocket is cut by an unusually large number of quartz seams and veinlets up to half an inch wide. These contain crystal lined cavities in places, and veins of turquoise sometimes contain quartz crystals penetrating them. The quartz veinlets sometimes give place to turquoise veinlets or include patches of turquoise. Where portions of the rock are less altered and pink feldspars occur, turquoise of a bright blue color is found. Turquoise veinlets of different shades of color are found crossing each other indicating different periods of deposition and different sources of material.

"Good turquoise was found at places in the vein other than in the Elizabeth pocket. To the northeast of this pocket, much of the turquoise had a greenish cast, while still farther along a good blue variety was more plentiful. To the northeast of the open cut in a drift several hundred feet long, the Azure Mine did not yield much turquoise of good color. To the southwest of the open cut, the vein is readily traced for several hundred yards up Morrill's Canyon. It contains very little turquoise, however, but has proved to contain rich copper ores.

"Mr. William R. Wade, who has directed the openings of this vein for copper, reports that a little turquoise was found in The Copper King Mine at a depth of 410 feet. In the workings at the Azure Mine, the best turquoise was found at depths of less than 100 feet. Pyrite or sulphides were not observed associated with the turquoise, though the walls are covered red with hematite in places. Where the feldspars of the rock have been most extensively kaolinized, turquoise is found mostly in nugget form. In less altered rock, hard vein turquoise is found, and both varieties are found in moderately altered rock."

In 1959, Phelps Dodge Co. acquired the property of the Azure Mine. See Burro Mountains, Grant County, The Turquois, Pogue, p.55-56.

Badger Mine. Nevada, Lander County. Located 3 miles northwest of Tenabo in the SE¼ Sec. 29, T.29N., R.47E. The turquoise is found in thinly bedded, silicified, and ironstained shale. Turquoise cements some of the quartzite breccia along a fault exposing shale below the quartzite. Turquoise in the northern and southern areas forms veinlets cutting the shale. Very good blue turquoise, some in slabs but mostly in nodules, evenly matched in color. (Turquoise deposits of Nevada, p. 16)

Barium Claim. Nevada, Lander County. See Blue Matrix Mine. (Turquoise Deposits of Nevada, p.18)

Basalt Mine. Nevada, Mineral County. Also called the Blue Gem Number 1. Located on the west side of state highway 10, about 1.5 southwest from the Blue Jay Gem Mine, in the NW¼ Sec.3, T.2N., R.33E. Turquoise forms nodules and veinlets along bedding planes and fractures in a sequence of shale and limestone. (Turquoise Deposits of Nevada, p.24)

Battle Mountain. Nevada, Lander County, Copper Basin District. The host rock is an altered quartz monzonite. Turquoise is contained in limonitic shear zones that cut the quartz monzonite as veinlets and as nodules. "Battle Mountain Turquoise" has become a general name for turquoise from this area.

Big Blue Claim. Nevada, Lander County. See Blue Gem Mine. (Turquoise Deposits of Nevada, p.17)

Bisbee Mine. Arizona, Cochise County. Turquoise is found herein the open pit copper mine. (The Lavender Pit). Some very fine quality turquoise is found here with good color, hard, and some with beautiful dar colored matrix. Found as stringers up to a few inches wide and small nuggetlike masses in granite and quartzite. Also as minute stringers in massive pyrite. Some turquoise found at the 1,200 ft. level of the Cole Shaft.

Black Rock Mine, The. Nevada, Lander County. Also called the Leighton Mine.

Blue Mine. Nevada, Esmeralda County. See Blue Boy Mine.

Blue Bell Claim, The. New Mexico, Santa Fe County. Beautiful turquoise has been produced from this claim. Located near the Castillian Mine.

Blue Bell Prospect. Nevada, Esmeralda County. The exact location of this prospect is unknown. It was reportedly covered by a flash flood. It was an undeveloped occurrence of turquoise on the variscite claims of Carl Riek and W.K. Botts, presumably about 4 miles north of Coaldale on the west side of the Monte Cristo Range. The turquoise occurs in veinlets, seams, and small nodules ranging up to an inch in thickness. It is very hard and has a deep, sky-blue color. Some specimens have a delicate brown spider-web marking. (Turquoise Deposits of Nevada, p.7)

Blue Boy Mine. Nevada, Esmeralda County. Known also as the Miss Moffet Mine, Blue Mine, Persian Blue Mine, and Los Angeles Gem Co. Mine. It is located in the southern part of Sec. 7, T.3N, R.36E. about 4.5 line miles southeast of Candelaria. The deposit is in a sheared, kaolinized shale. The turquoise is of good quality and occurs mainly within the narrow zones of strongest argillization. Variscite is found about a mile northeast of the property. On the Pirate Number 3 claim a seam of turquoise more than an inch thick was found in a dark-gray, cherty rock. Part of this turquoise was fairly dark blue and very hard. A little greenish, variscite-like material also was found here. Also, small seams of dark blue, very hard turquoise were found in a dark jasperoid. These seams were not abundant and none over half an inch in thickness was found. The very dark brown and black matrix in this turquoise yielded very beautiful gems. (Turquoise Deposits of Nevada, p.5-6) See The Turquois, Pogue, p.50.

Blue Eagle Mine. Nevada, Lander County, Bullion District. Also called the Campsite Mine and the Blue Sky Mine. Located in the extreme SW corner of Sec. 21, T.29N., R.47E. about 1,000 feet northeast from the Color Back and New Blue Mines. The mine is about 4,000 feet north-northeast of the Badger Mine. Turquoise occurs as veinlets along bedding planes and fractures in the chert adjacent to an argillized quartz monzonite dike. Some of the turquoise is spider-web and some is clear blue slab. (Turquoise Deposits of Nevada, p.17)

Blue Fern Mine. Nevada, Lander County, Bullion District. Located in Sec. 35, T.28N., R.46E. About 1.5 miles west-southwest from Gold Acres. The turquoise appears to be associated with a highly altered dike that cuts silicified shale. A great number of prospects are in this area. (Turquoise Deposits of Nevada, p.14)

Blue Friday Mine. Nevada, Esmeralda County. Located 1 mile southwest of Crow Spring in the SW¼ Sec. 33, T.5N., R.39E. Turquoise occurs within bleached, argillically altered zones. The turquoise occurs in seams cutting a fine-grained quartzite. Seams range from paper thin to nearly ½ inch thick. The turquoise ranges from pale blue to pure blue of a fairly dark color. Some matrix with brown and red markings has been obtained. Also called the Crow Spring Mine or William Petry Mine. (Turquoise Deposits of Nevada, p.7) See The Turquois, Pogue, p.49)

Blue Gem Lease Mine. Nevada, Lander County, Copper Basin Area. Formerly the Pedro Lode Claim belonging to the Copper Canyon Mining Co. Located in the SE ¼ Sec.29, T.32N., R.44E. about 4,000 feet north-northeast of Copper Basin. Also called the Turquoise Tunnel and the Contention. The turquoise occurs in argillized quartz monzonite cut by two limonite-stained shear zones. An enormous amount of turquoise came from this mine. It is still active but is in the center of a major copper deposit being developed by Duval Corp. (Turquoise Deposits of Nevada, p.13)

Blue Gem Mine. Nevada, Lander County, Bullion District. Located about 500 feet north of the Color Back Mine. Located near the SE corner of Sec. 20, T.29N., R.47E. Also called the New Blue Mine. The turquoise is associated with an argillized and opalized sill. The turquoise is almost exclusively in clear blue slabs, some of relatively large size. Also some fine greenish stones from this mine. The Big Blue Claim, The Missing Link Claim, the New Blue Claim, and the Wee Nugget Claim located here. (Turquoise Deposits of Nevada, p.17)

Blue Gem Mine. Nevada, Nye County. See The Easter Blue Mine.

Blue Gem Number 1 Mine. Nevada, Mineral County. See Basalt Mine.

Blue Goose Mine. Nevada, Lander County, Bullion District. Located on the southern tip of Hot Spring Point in Sec. 9, T.24N., R.47E. Thinly bedded, black and brown chert and shale constitute the host rock. The turquoise is closely associated with quartz veins in the chert and shale. The mine has been a small producer but of very fine quality turquoise. Also called The Jimmy Allen Mine. (Turquoise Deposits of Nevada, p.21)

Blue Jay Gem Mine. Nevada, Mineral County. Five miles north of Basalt in the NW ¼ Sec. 35, T.3N., R.33E. Turquoise is found in fractures and along bedding planes in shale and limestone. (Turquoise Deposits of Nevada, p.24)

Blue Jay Mine. Nevada, Esmeralda County. See The Lone Mountain Mine.

Blue Jay Mining Lode. Nevada, Esmeralda County. See The Lone Mountain Mine.

Blue Matrix Mine. Nevada, Lander County, Bullion District. Located in the SE corner of Sec. 19, T.29N., R.47E. about 1 mile west of the Old Campground Mine, and 4 miles NW of Tenabo. An argillized sill intrudes dark, cherty beds. Turquoise forms veinlets along bedding planes and filling fractures in the chert. The turquoise is clear-blue slab and spider-web. An interesting feature of this mine is that boulders laying on the surface with no indication of turquoise in them, when broken revealed high-grade turquoise in seams up to a quarter of an inch thick. The claims adjacent to the discovery were named Campground One, Campground Two, and Tungsten (later named Barium) In 1950 Marvin Symes and his father produced turquoise from this mine and called it "Indian Blue." (Turquoise Deposits of Nevada, p.2, 18-19)

Blue Mountain Mine. Nevada, Nye County. See The Easter Blue Mine.

Blue Nugget Prospect, The. Nevada, Lander County, Bullion District. Located on the north side of Indian Creek Canyon, 2 miles north-northwest of Tenabo, in the NW ¼ Sec. 33, T.29N., R.47E. Turquoise is contained in a limonite breccia zone about 2 ft. wide. (Turquoise Deposits of Nevada, p. 15)

Blue Silver Mine. Nevada, Esmeralda County. Located in the NW ¼ Sec. 7, T.1N., R.41E. Discontinuous nodules and veinlets of turquoise are contained within an altered diorite. Minor amounts of secondary copper minerals and galena are associated with the turquoise. (Turquoise Deposits of Nevada, p.8)

Blue Stone Claim. Nevada, Lander County, Bullion District. See Dry Creek Mine. (Turquoise Deposits of Nevada, p.21-22)

Blue Stone Claim, The. Nevada, Lander County, Copper Basin Area. See Myron Clark Mine (Turquoise Deposits of Nevada, p.13)

Bona Mine. Nevada, Esmeralda County. See Carrie Mine. (Turquoise Deposits of Nevada, p.6-7)

Bunker Hill Mine. Nevada. Located on the Nye-Esmeralda County Line about 24 miles northwest of Tonopah in the Royston District. This mine is located about ½ mile north of the Royal Blue Mine. Turquoise occurs in altered quartzite and ranges from royal blue to greenish blue with brown and white matrix. Turquoise is mainly in the form of slabs from 1/16 to 1 inch thick. (Turquoise Deposits of Nevada, p.27)

Burnham Mine. Nevada, Lander County, Bullion District. Also known as the Dry Creek Mine or the Godber Mine. See Dry Creek Mine. (Turquoise Deposits of Nevada, p.21-22)

Burro Chief Mine. New Mexico, Grant County. Turquois is found here but not of commercial quantity. This mine is located SE of the Azure mine (approximately 3,300 feet South 30°East of the Azure) The turquoise occurs in granite and in quartz monzonite porphyry. The rock in the vicinity of the deposits is much altered. The turquoise occurs in veins and veinlets and as nodular masses in wide fractures zones in the altered rock. See The Turquois, Pogue, p.55-56.

Burro Mountains. New Mexico, Grant County. See The Turquois, Pogue, p.55-56.

Cactus Peak Mine. Nevada, Nye County.

Cameo Claim, The. New Mexico, Grant County, Hachita District. See The Robinson and Porterfield Mines. See The Turquois, Pogue, p.57.

Campground Claims. Nevada, Lander County. See Blue Matrix Mine.

Campsite Mine. Nevada, Lander County. See Blue Eagle Mine. (Turquoise Deposits of Nevada, p.17-18)

Candelaria Mine. Nevada, Mineral County, Candelaria Mining District. Primarily Variscite here.

Candelaria-Sigmund Group. Esmeralda County. Located on the Mineral County line. Turquoise and Variscite here.

Canyon Creek. Arizona, Gila County. Prehistoric turquoise mines are located on the east side of Canyon Creek just above where it intersects with the Salt River.

Carl Riek Mine. Nevada, Esmeralda County. Located just north of the Miss Moffet Mine. Turquoise reported here. (Turquoise Deposits of Nevada, p.5)

Carlin Black Matrix Mine. Nevada, Elko County. Reported to be in the Merrimac or Lone

Mountain Mining District. (Turquoise Deposits of Nevada, p.5)

Carr-Lovejoy Mine. Nevada, Esmeralda County. Located in Monte Cristo Range about 9 miles northeast of Blair Junction. According to the 1910 edition of *"Mineral Resources of the United States"* the country rock is a dull gray, slaty rock cropping out in the rough rocky ledges." The turquoise has a botryoidal surface and some is of a very fine blue color and is especially hard. (Turquoise Deposits of Nevada, p.7-8) See The Turquois, Pogue, p.50.

Carrie Mine. Nevada, Esmeralda County. Also known as the Hidden Treasure Mine and the Myers and Bona Mine. It is in the Monte Cristo Range in an unsurveyed area about 2½ miles southeast of the old mining camp of Gilbert. The country rocks are principally volcanic material and black slate. Turquoise occurs as nodules, seams, and veinlets along the contact between the slate and volcanic rocks. The best quality of turquoise is found in the black slate. The turquoise found in the volcanic rocks is generally soft with a poor color. The best material is hard with a beautiful sky blue color. (Turquoise Deposits of Nevada, p.6-7) See The Turquois, Pogue, p.49.

Castillian Mine. New Mexico, Santa Fe County. Located ½ miles south of the Tiffany Mine. Fine quality blue turquoise similar in appearance to Persian turquoise was mined here. See The Turquois, Pogue, p.52-55

Castle Dome Mine. Arizona, Gila County. Turquoise mined in conjunction with copper mine. All qualities of turquoise found here.

Castle Dome Mountains. Arizona, Yuma County. Some turquoise is found in shallow deposits.

Cerrillos Area. New Mexico, Santa Fe County. The strata of the area have been intruded by a series of monzonitic stocks, plugs, laccoliths sills, and dikes. The erosion-exposed remnants of these bodies form the Cerrillos Hills. See The Turquois, Pogue, p.52-55.

The Chamberlain. New Mexico. Also called R.S. Chamberlain Mine. See Hachita District.

Chapman Turquoise Mine. New Mexico, Grant County. Located on the SE side of Saddle Mountain in Sec. 25, T.21S., R.15W. In the White Signal District. High grade turquoise has been mined here. Turquoise probably occurred in fractures in the shattered areas and in pockets along the veins.

Chino Valley. Arizona, Yavapai County. Located southwest of Prescott. Some shallow deposits of turquoise here.

Clara Mine. Nevada, Mineral County. Located on the Dunwoody-Pritchard group of claims 8 miles southwest of Sodaville on the east end of the Excelsior Mountains. Small amounts of turquoise have been recovered. Some material is probably variscite. Also called the Halley's Comet Mine. (Turquoise Deposits of Nevada, p.23)

C.O.D. Claim. Nevada, Nye County, Royston Mining District. Located on the Esmeralda County Line.

Cold Day Mine. Nevada, Lander County, Bullion District. Located in the NE ¼ Sec. 17, T.20N., R.45E. The turquoise is found in a brecciated quartz zone about 10 inches wide. The production has been low in this mine but good quality heavy nuggets have been found. Also called the Green Tree Mine. (Turquoise Deposits of Nevada, p.21)

Coleman Mine. New Mexico, Grant County. See Parker Mine.

Color Back Mine. Nevada, Lander County, Bullion District. Located near the SE corner of Sec. 20, T.29N., R.47E. Chert adjacent to an opalized sill is brecciated and contains most of the turquoise. Also called the Turquoise Boy Mine. (Turquoise Deposits of Nevada, p.17)

Colorado Turquoise Mining Co. Colorado, Conejos County. See The King Mine.

Columbus District. Nevada, Esmeralda County. See the variscite claims of the Los Angeles Gem Co. See The Turquois, Pogue, p.50.

Consul Mahoney Claim, The. New Mexico, Santa Fe County. Beautiful turquoise has been produced from this claim. Located near the Castillian Mine.

Contention Mine. Nevada, Lander County, Copper Basin Area. See Blue Gem Lease Mine. (Turquoise Deposits of Nevada, p.13)

Copper Basin Area. Nevada, Lander County. See Turquoise King, Myron Clark, Blue Gem Lease, Contention, Pedro Lode, Turquoise Tunnel, Battle Mountain.

Copper Blue Mine. Nevada, Nye County. Located about 5 miles south-southwest from Belmont and ½ mile west of the ruins of Monarch Ranch in unsurveyed T.8N., R.45E. Host rock for the deposit is a strongly silicified shale. The shale is cut by brecciated shear zones that are recemented by iron oxide minerals, but locally they are argillized and devoid of iron oxides. Soft turquoise occurs within the argillized zones. (Turquoise Deposits of Nevada, p.25)

Copper Canyon Mining Co. Nevada, Lander County. See Blue Gem Lease Mine.

Copper Cities Mine. Arizona, Gila County. See Sleeping Beauty Mine.

Copper King Claim. Nevada, Mineral County, Pilot Mt. Mining District.

Copper King Mine. New Mexico, Grant County. Located northwest of Tyrone. Turquoise was found here at a depth of 410 feet which is unusual for turquoise. The best grades of turquoise were found at a depth of less than 100 feet, though. Located southwest of the Azure Mine.

Copper Queen Mine. Nevada, Esmeralda County. Located 2 miles east of Crow Spring on the east side of Sec. 35, T.5N., R.39E. Turquoise occurs in quartz monzonite where it has been argillically altered along easterly trending shear zones. This mine produces gem-grade turquoise in nodules and slabs with an unfading, uniform blue color. Also called the Marguerite Mine and the Star Mine. (Turquoise Deposits of Nevada, p.7)

Cortez Mine. Nevada, Lander County, Bullion District. See Fox Mine. (Turquoise Deposits of Nevada, p.20)

Courtland Area. Arizona, Cochise County. See The Turquoise District, Arizona.

Cow Spring District. New Mexico, Grant County. Thin seams of turquoise of good color found here. See The Turquois, Pogue, p.56.

Cracker Jack Mine. Nevada, Lander County, Bullion District. This deposit is along the NE side of Sec. 7, T.28N., R.47E. Turquoise occurs both in a gray shale and a white tuff. The shale contains both greenish and blue turquoise. The tuff contains blue turquoise which coats particles and acts locally as a cementing agent. Also called the Little Gem Mine. (Turquoise Deposits of Nevada, p.15)

Creede District, The. Colorado, Mineral County. Turquoise is found in this district.

Crescent Peak Mine. Nevada, Clark County. See Simmons Mine. (Turquoise Deposits of Nevada, p.3-5)

Cripple Creek. Colorado, Teller County. Located adjacent to the city of Cripple Creek. Small production of nodules and vein material. Some greenish turquoise and some light to dark blue with brown matrix.

Crocker, The. New Mexico. See Hachita District. Also called M.M. Crocker Claims. See The Turquoise, Pogue, p.57.

Crow Spring Mine. Nevada, Esmeralda County. See Blue Friday Mine.

DeMeules Property, New Mexico, Otero County, Jarilla District. Some fine turquoise from this mine. The turquoise occurs in seams and crevices in trachyte. Some of the turquoise faded on contact with light. See The Turquois, Pogue, p.58.

Dragoon Mountains Area. Arizona, Cochise County. Located northeast of Tombstone. Turquoise found in this area is usually of poor quality and needs treating. Color from pea green to apple green. Some of the turquoise resembles Cerrillos turquoise. The turquoise occurs in joints and small irregular fractures in a bed of Cambrian quartzite near contact with decomposed granitic rock.

Dry Creek Mine. Nevada, Lander County, Bullion District. Located in the SW ¼ Sec. 13, T.19N., R.46E. This mine has also been known as the Godber Mine and as the Burnam Mine. Host rock for the deposit is a light brownish-gray to grayish-black shale, with maroon interbeds. Turquoise is mainly confined to argillized zones in the shale. The turquoise ranges from medium to dark blue, mostly of high quality spider-web variety. The three claims comprising this property are the Last Chance, the Blue Stone, and the Homesite. (Turquoise Deposits of Nevada, p.21-22)

Dunwoody Claims. Nevada, Esmeralda County. Located about 8 miles southwest of Sodaville. Variscite and poor quality turquoise occurs both in a decomposed porphyry and ryolite. Color is dark greenish-blue to bright green in color and resembles variscite. See The Turquois, Pogue, p.51.

East Camp. California, San Bernardino County. See Stone Hammer Mines.

Easter Blue Mine. Nevada, Nye County. Also called The Blue Gem Mine and the Blue Mountain Mine. Located in Sec. 27, T.7N., R.39E., about 8 miles northwest from the Royston District. Turquoise occurs as thin veinlets along altered shear zones in a fine-grained, white quartzite. (Turquoise Deposits of Nevada, p.25)

Eureka, The. New Mexico. See Hachita District.

Evans Turquoise. Mine located east of Ensenada in Baja California, Mexico. Also known as Mexico Turquoise

Fox Mine. Nevada, Lander County, Bullion District. Located in the NE ¼ Sec. 34, T.27N., R.47E. Also called the Cortez Mine. The mine is located in a faulted, argillized block of chert. Turquoise occurs in greenish and blue colors in silicified, limonitic veinlets that follow the bedding. This mine was mined by the Indians in prehistoric times. Many large nuggets have been found in this mine. The Fox Mine has been Nevada's largest producer of turquoise. Much of the turquoise has been quite hard but of poor color. These stones were suited for treating and many were sent to Germany for this purpose. Many fine hard stones from here. (Turquoise Deposits of Nevada, p.20)

Fresno County, California. Pseudomorphs of turquoise after apatite found in a prospect pit in granite on Taylor's ranch on the Chowchillas River. See The Turquois, Pogue, p.46.

Galilee Claim, The. New Mexico, Grant County, Hachita District. See The Robinson and Porterfield Mines. See The Turquois, Pogue, p.57.

Garnet Mine, The. New Mexico, Otero County. Located in the SE ¼ Sec. 34, T.21S., R.8E. See The Jarilla Mountain Area.

Gem Claim, The. New Mexico, Santa Fe County. See The Morning Star Claim.

Gem Mine. Nevada, Lander County, Bullion District. See McGinnes Mine. (Turquoise Deposits of Nevada, p.21)

Gem Turquoise and Copper Co. New Mexico, Grant County. See Parker Mine. This is the site of ancient Indians workings.

German-American Turquoise Co., The. Nevada, Mineral County. Opened prior to 1910. See The Montezuma Mine. See The Turquois, Pogue, p.49.

Godber Mine. Nevada, Lander County, Bullion District. See Dry Creek Mine. (Turquoise Deposits of Nevada, p.21-22)

Gold Acres. Nevada, Lander County. See Steinich Mine.

Gove Turquoise. California, San Bernardino County. Located about 2 miles west of Cottonwood Siding, on the Santa Fe Railroad. First operated in 1908 by the California Gem Co. The Turquoise is found along the contact of an intruded rhyolite and the country rock a fine-grained biotite gneiss. The turquoise forms seams and nuggets in both rocks. The turquoise is generally associated with limonite or quartz, or with both. The best stones from this mine have a light to fairly dark, pure-blue color. See The Turquois, Pogue, p.47)

Green Tree Mine. Nevada, Lander County, Bullion District. See Cold Day Mine. (Turquoise Deposits of Nevada, p.21)

Hachita District, The. New Mexico, Grant and Hidalgo Counties. This District lies in the Little Hatchet Mountains, Townships 27-29 South, R.16W. Turquoise occurs in this area in altered rocks around the borders of an altered monzonite stock just west of old Hachita. Turquoise has also been mined from an altered iron-stained monzonite stock which crops out on the north slope of Howells Ridge near Smuggler's Pass. Both of these stocks have hematite-bearing siliceous zones in the rocks immediately overlying the monzonite. The Hachita District is divided into two subdistricts. The Eureka Subdistrict is in Grant County, and the Sylvanite subdistrict is in Hidalgo County. The turquoise mines in this area date back to prehistoric times. Some of the turquoise mines and claims in this area are the Aztec, the Azure, the American Turquoise Co. Claims, the Galilee, the Eureka, the Cameo, the Crocker, the Chamberlain, the LeFeve, and several other claims on Turquoise Mountain. The Turquoise from this area is dark blue to greenish with some soft pale blue stones. Much matrix turquoise from this area. In the Eureka Subdistrict mineralization occurs as veins and as bedded and irregular bodies in Cretaceous Strata. In the Sylvanite Subdistrict the mineralization occurs in quartz veins in a large mass of quartz monzonite cut by lamprophyre and syenite dikes, and in limestone which adjoins the porphyry on the south. (Geology of the Little Hatchet Mountains, Hidalgo and

Grant Counties, New Mexico, Zeller) See The Turquois, Pogue, p.57-58.

Hall Mine. Colorado, Saguache County. See Villa Grove.

Halley's Comet Mine. Nevada, Mineral County. See Clara Mine. (Turquoise Deposits of Nevada, p.23)

Harcross Group. Nevada, Lyon County. See Taubert Number 1. (Turquoise Deposits of Nevada, p.22)

Hidalgo. New Mexico, Grant County. Located in the Red Hill District.

Hidden Treasure Mine. Nevada, Esmeralda County. See Carrie Mine. (Turquoise Deposits of Nevada, p.6-7)

Himalaya Mining Co. California, San Bernardino County. See Stone Hammer Mines. Located 12 miles N.60° E. of Silver Lake.

Himalaya Mining Co. Nevada, Nye County, Royston District. See The Royal Blue Mine.

Holland Claim. Nevada, Esmeralda County, Coaldale Mining District.

Holy Cross District, The. Colorado, Eagle County.

Homesite Claim. Nevada, Lander County. See Dry Creek Mine. (Turquoise Deposits of Nevada, p.21-22)

Homestead Claim, The. Nevada, Lander County, Copper Basin Area. See Myron Clark Mine. (Turquoise Deposits of Nevada, p.13)

I Mine, The. New Mexico, Otero County. Located next to the Nannie Baird Mine. See The Jarilla Mountain Area.

Independence area. California. Turquoise found 8 miles east of Independence.

Indian Blue Mine. Nevada, Nye County. Located in the SE ¼ Sec. 16, T.15N., R.46E. Turquoise occurs as nuggets along bedding planes in gray to brown fossiliferous shale. These deposits were worked by Indians in prehistoric times. Produced high quality brilliant blue and very hard turquoise. (Turquoise Deposits of Nevada, p.24-25)

Indian Blue Turquoise. Nevada, Lander County. See Blue Matrix Mine.

Iron Mask Mine. Located adjacent to the Turquoise Chief Mine about 7 miles northwest of Leadville, Colorado. (Colorado Gem Trails, p.81)

Ithaca Peak Copper Mine. Arizona, Mohave County. Site of Duval Corporation's Openpit Copper Mine. See Mineral Park Mines.

Jane Claim, The. Nevada, Lander County, Copper Basin Area. See Myron Clark Mine. (Turquoise Deposits of Nevada, p.13)

Jarilla Mountain Area, The. New Mexico, Otero County. In the Tularosa Basin. Many showings of turquoise are present in these mountains and specimens can be collected in many of the mine cuts.

Possible early producers in this area were the Garnet Mine, the Nannie Baird Mine, the Lucky Mine, the I Mine, and the Three Bears Mine.

Some fine blue turquoise found here within 40 ft. of the surface but faded on contact with air due to the evaporation of water in the stone. There were extensive prehistoric mines in this area. Also old mines near Grants, Organ, Dona Ana, Eureka, and Red Mountain. There is some good turquoise from this area but most of it fades on exposure to air. See The Turquois, Pogue, p.58.

Jimmy Allen Mine. Nevada, Lander County, Bullion District. See Blue Goose Mine. (Turquoise Deposits of Nevada, p.20-21)

John Boitano Mine. Nevada, Lander County, Bullion District. See Lone Pine Mine. (Turquoise Deposits of Nevada, p.20)

Josie May Prospect. Located about 2,000 feet southwest of the Turquois Chief mine and about 6½ miles northwest of Leadville, Colorado. There are two other turquoise prospects in the area, one about 750 feet and another about 2,300 feet northeast of the Josie May. The turquoise here is associated with chrysocolla, malachite, and radioactive torbernite. (Colorado Gem Trails, 81)

King Mine, The. Colorado, Conejos County. Located about 9 miles east of Manassa. Has been worked extensively by the Indians since prehistoric times. Was mined in the early 1900's by the Colorado Turquoise Mining Co. The names of the claims here are the Lickspittle, the La Jara, the Sunset, the Arkansas, the Mexico, the Nelly Bly, and the Last Chance. The country rock is an altered trachyte or porphyry. This porphyry is cut by a dike of phonolite and capped with a 20 foot ledge of chert. The turquoise forms veins occupying joints in the trachyte and also occurs as irregular masses and nodules scattered through the rock. The turquoise runs in color from a pale-blue to a deep sky-blue and is very hard with a conchoidal fracture. Some specimens contain a brown limonite matrix and there is some spider-web matrix. There is also some greenish turquoise. (Colorado Geological Survey Letter, Sept. 3, 1971) See The Turquois, Pogue, p.47-48.

La Barranca Copper District. Sonora (state) Mexico. Two deposits of turquoise here in a volcanic rock.

La Jara Claim. Colorado, Conejos County. See The King Mine.

Last Chance Claim, The. Colorado, Conejos County. See The King Mine.

Last Chance Claim. Nevada, Lander County, Bullion District. See Dry Creek Mine. (Turquoise Deposits of Nevada, p.21-22)

Last Chance Mine, The. Colorado, Mineral County. Located about 1 mile north of Creede. The turquoise here is thought to come from a point high up in the mountains. Turquoise found here in green and blue colors. Some of the turquoise is clear with no matrix and some has a brown matrix. Turquoise can also be picked up at several places between the Commodore and the Amethyst Mines along West Willow Creek. (Colorado Gem Trails, p.57-58)

Lavender Pit. Arizona, Cochise County. See Bisbee.

Leadville. Colorado, Lake County. Turquoise from this area sometimes called "Leadville." See the Turquois Chief Mine and the Iron Mask Mine.

Le Feve, The. New Mexico, Grant County. See Hachita District.

Leighton Mine, The. Nevada, Lander County. Also called the Black Rock Mine.

Lickspittle Claim, The. Colorado, Conejos County. See King Mine.

Lincoln County. Nevada. Turquoise reported at the foot of Sugar Loaf Peak. Reported to be light blue in color and occurring within a dike cutting mica schist. Prehistoric mining here. Also, turquoise found in 1909 at Searchlight where a nugget weighing 320 carats was claimed to have been found. See The Turquois, Pogue, p.51.

Little Cedars Mine. Nevada, Nye County, Royston District. Supposed to be located about 6 miles north of Tonopah. Turquoise occurs as nodules and veinlets in altered quartz monzonite porphyry. This area is now within the boundary of the Las Vegas Bombing and Gunnery Range and is withdrawn from prospecting and mining activity. (Turquoise Deposits of Nevada, p.28)

Little Chief Mine. Nevada, Lander County, Bullion District. Located in the extreme NE corner of Sec. 31, T.29N., R.47E. Turquoise occurs in argillized, brecciated shale and quartzite. (Turquoise Deposits of Nevada, p.15)

Little Gem Mine. Nevada, Lander County, Bullion District. See Cracker Jack Mine. (Turquoise Deposits of Nevada, p.15)

Little Gem Mine. Nevada, Near Beowawe, Eureka County.

Lively Mine. Nevada, Esmeralda County. Located in an unsurveyed strip in T.1S. between R.40 and 41E. About 2.7 miles N.30°W. from the SW corner of Sec. 31, T.1S., R.41E. A small quantity of high-grade turquoise was produced from seams and nodules in metamorphosed shale. The turquoise is mainly within clay gouge along shears. (Turquoise Deposits of Nevada, p.9)

Lone Mountain Mine. Nevada, Esmeralda County. Located about 1 mile east of Paymaster Canyon in the NW ¼ Sec. 18, T.1N., R.41E. Turquoise occurs here as nodules in a thinly bedded calcareous shale. The turquoise from this mine is noted for not fading and for holding its color. The color of the turquoise ranges from clear blue to spider-web. The clear blue is found in the hard shales and the spider-web in the softer argillaceous zones. Some nuggets found in moss agate. A find with these inclusions was made in 1956. Also known as the Blue Jay Mine. (Turquoise Deposits of Nevada, p.8-9)

Lone Pine Mine. Nevada, Lander County, Bullion District. Also called the John Boitano Mine. Located near the center of Sec. 35, T.27N., R.47E. Veinlets of turquoise cut altered quartzite and a four-foot thick breccia layer. The production of this mine has been small but the quality of the turquoise good. (Turquoise Deposits of Nevada, p.20)

Los Angeles Gem Co. Mine. Arizona, Mohave County. See Mineral Park Mines.

Los Angeles Gem Co. Mine. Nevada, Esmeralda County. See Blue Boy Mine. (Turquoise Deposits of New Mexico, p.5-6)

Lucky Mine, The. New Mexico, Otero County. Located in the NW ¼ NE ¼ Sec. 10. T.22S., R.8E. See Jarilla Mountains Area.

M.M. Crocker Claims, The. New Mexico, Grant County, Hachita District. These two claims are located on the southwest end of Turquois Mountain and on a small knob ½ mile SW of Turquois Mountain. See The Turquois, Pogue, p.57-58.

McGinness Mine. Nevada, Lander County, Bullion District. Located 10 miles northeast of Austin near the center of Sec. 17, T.20N., R.45E. Turquoise occurs in three parallel, brecciated zones, each about 2 feet wide, that cuts cherts and siliceous shales. Most of the turquoise mined here has been of fair quality. Also called the Gem Mine. (Turquoise Deposits of Nevada, p.21)

Manvel District. California, San Bernardino County. See Stone Hammer Mines.

Marguerite M., The. Colorado, Teller County. Located near Cripple Creek.

Marguerite Mine. Nevada, Esmeralda County. See Copper Queen Mine. (Turquoise Deposits of New Mexico, p.7)

Maricopa County, Arizona. Turquoise reported 12 miles east of Morristown.

Maroney's Prospect. New Mexico, Grant County. Located along the road leading to Silver City a few miles northeast of Leopold. Good quality stones but small quantity. Possibly the same as the Porterfield Mine. See The Turquois, Pogue, p.56.

Mazapil. Zacatecas (state) Mexico. See Santa Rosa District.

Mexico Claim, The. Colorado, Conejos County. See The King Mine.

Mexico Turquoise. Mine located east of Ensenada in Baja California, Mexico. Also known as Evans Turquoise. See Evans Turquoise.

Middle Camp. California, San Bernardino County. See Stone Hammer Mines.

Mimbres Mine. New Mexico, Grant County.

Mineral Park Mines. Arizona, Mohave County. Located 15 miles northwest of Kingman on the southwest side of the Cerbat Mountain Range, in the Wallapai Mining District. The turquoise is found in the area of Aztec Peak and Ithaca Peak. The most extensive prehistoric workings in Arizona are located here. Production is from several claims including the Monte Cristo, the Turquoise King, the Queen, the Peacock and the Ithaca Peak Copper Mine, the site of Duval Corporation's open-pit copper mine. Turquoise occurs as veins, seams, and masses in altered and mineralized granitic rock. Much of the turquoise is of a poor quality and requires treating but some is of fine gem quality. Turquoise from the Aztec Mountain area is found in seams of 1 to 4 inches thick. Good blue turquoise comes from these mines but some turns green on contact with the air. Some turquoise and matrix from this area was shipped east to be made into statuettes, mantels, and pedestals. Mined by the Southwest Turquoise Co., the Los Angeles Gem Co., the Aztec Turquoise Co., the Arizona Turquoise Co., and the Mineral Park Turquoise Co. (Mineral and Water Resources of Arizona. Bulletin 180) See The Turquois, Pogue, p.45-46.

Mineral Park Turquoise Co. Arizona, Mohave County, Mineral Park Area. See Mineral Park Mines.

Miss Moffet Mine. Nevada, Esmeralda County. See The Blue Boy Mine. (Turquoise Deposits of Nevada, p.5)

Missing Link Claim. Nevada, Lander County, Bullion District. See Blue Gem Mine. (Turquoise Deposits of Nevada, p.17)

Mohave Sink Area. California. Turquoise deposits here. See Stone Hammer Mines.

Monitor Valley Mine. Nevada, Nye County. Located between Belmont and Potts.

Monte Cris Mine. Nevada, Esmeralda County. See Monte Cristo Mine. (Turquoise Deposits of Nevada, p.6)

Monte Cristo, The. Arizona, Mohave County. See Mineral Park Mines.

Monte Cristo Mine. Nevada, Esmeralda County. Located about 8 miles northeast of Coaldale in Sec. 12, T.3N., R.37E. Also known as the Monte Cris Mine. Solid Blue and Spider-web turquoise occurs as nodules in calcareous shale. (Turquoise Deposits of Nevada, p.6)

Montezuma Mine. Nevada, Mineral County. Located at the southern end of the Pilot Mountains about 14 miles east-southeast from Mina and 4 miles southwest from the site of the old Dunham Mill. Small intrusive bodies of argillized quartz monzonite are the host rocks for the turquoise. The turquoise occurs in seams, veinlets, and nodules up to an inch or more in thickness. It is variable in color, ranging from a hard, very dark blue, to dark blue with a greenish cast, to a pale-blue, softer material. There is much dark brown to yellow limonite stain associated with and filling the fractures in the turquoise. The best colored and hardest stones generally were found in the hard, iron-stained portions of the intrusive, and the softer, pale-blue stones were in the light-colored, soft parts of the intrusive. Strong contrasts in brown and blue with mottled patterns were obtained and yielded beautiful gems. Also known as the Troy Springs Mine, the German-American Turquoise Co., and the Western Gem. Co. (Turquoise Deposits of Nevada, p.23-24) See The Turquois, Pogue, p.49.

Moqui-Aztec Mine. Nevada, Mineral County. Located at the southern end of the Pilot Mountains, about 1½ miles west of the Montezuma Mine. Turquoise is associated with irregular bodies of quartz monzonite. The quartz monzonite is altered to argillic products in the vicinity of the turquoise deposits. The turquoise forms veinlets and nodules marked with limonite stains. A large amount of pale-blue turquoise has been mined, although some of it is low in hardness. Some excellent light-blue stones with delicate brown markings have been cut. Also known as the S. Simmons Mine. (Turquoise Deposits of Nevada, p.23) See The Turquois, p.50)

Morenci. Arizona, Greenlee County. Turquoise is produced here by a lessee from the Morenci open-pit copper mine which is operated by the Phelps Dodge Corp. Some turquoise of fine quality is produced here and iron pyrite inclusions in the blue turquoise make it a beautiful gem stone. Indians mined here in prehistoric times.

Morgan Mine. Nevada, Clark County. Located in the SW ¼ Sec. 29, T.28S., R.61E. The Turquoise forms narrow veinlets in quartz monzonite that is cut by rhyolite dikes. (Turquoise Deposits of Nevada, p.5)

Morning Star Claim. New Mexico, Santa Fe County. Located in 1891. Bought by the American Turquoise Co. about 1892. Located at Turquesa near the Castillian Mine. Also adjacent to this claim are the Sky Blue and the Gem Claims.

Mt. Chalchuitl. New Mexico, Santa Fe County. The turquoise mineralization in this area runs in a north-south line about 3 miles long. Claims were scattered all along this area. The turquoise at the north end of the area was of a better quality than that in the Mt. Chalchuitl area. See Cerrillos Area. See The Turquois, Pogue, p.52-55.

Mud Springs Mine. Nevada, Lander County, Bullion Mining District.

Muñiz Claim, The. New Mexico, Santa Fe County. Dates to 1889. Supposed to have been one of the best claims in the Castillian Mine Area.

Myers Mine. Nevada, Esmeralda County. See Carrie Mine. Also known as the Myers and Bona Mine. (Turquoise Deposits of Nevada, p.6-7)

Myron Clark Mine. Nevada, Lander County, Copper Basin Area. Located in the north-central part of Sec. 32, T.32N., R.44E. The host rock is altered quartz monzonite. Limonitic shear zones cut the quartz monzonite and contain turquoise as thin veinlets and small nodules. This mine has reportedly yielded a large quantity of high-grade turquoise. The deposit was first discovered by Myron Clark who staked four claims, the Turquoise, the Blue Stone, the Jane, and the Homestead. (Turquoise Deposits of Nevada, p.13)

Nannie Baird Mine, The. New Mexico, Otero County. Located in the SW ¼ NW ¼ Sec. 11, T.22S., R.8E. See The Jarilla Mountain Area.

Nelly Bly Claim, The. Colorado, Conejos County. See The King Mine.

New Azure Mine, The. New Mexico, Grant County. Located 500 feet east and across the road from the main pit of the Azure Mine. Old Indian workings consisting of tunnels and openings filled with rubbish, were exposed in the upper part of this mine. The turquoise is within a wide, fractured zone in granite which at the mine is a medium grained, slightly porphyritic rock, typical of much of the granite in the Burro Mountains. (Mineral Deposits of Western Grant Co., N.M. Bulletin 83, p.49-50) See The Turquois, Pogue, p.56.

New Blue Mine. Nevada, Lander County. See Blue Gem Mine.

New Blue Mine. Nevada, Lander County, Bullion District. See Blue Gem Mine. (Turquoise Deposits of Nevada, p.17)

New Mexico Turquoise. New Mexico, Grant County. This is a general term for turquoise from the Burro Mountain area south of Silver City.

Nogal District. New Mexico, Lincoln County. Small amount of turquoise reported here.

No Name Number 1 Prospect. Nevada, Lander County, Bullion District. Located in the south-central part of Sec. 28, T.29N., R.47E. There appears to have been no important production of turquoise. (Turquoise Deposits of Nevada, p.16)

No Name Number 2 Mine. Nevada, Nye County. Located 2 miles south of Belmont in the NW ¼ Sec. 2, T.8N., R.45E. Greenish-blue turquoise has been recovered in somewhat silicified, black silty limestone. The turquoise forms veinlets along bedding planes. (Turquoise Deposits of Nevada, p.25)

Number 8 Mine. Nevada, Eureka County. Located on the west side of the Tuscarora Range in the NW ¼ Sec. 4, T.35N., R.50E. Host rocks for the Number 8 deposit consist of intensely altered quartz monzonite (?) shale, and thinly bedded black chert, which are complexly folded, faulted, and much altered. Turquoise is concentrated along quartz veins in the intrusive rock and along faults in the sedimentary rocks. The turquoise is mainly in a nodular form, but only about 10 percent has been rated as good quality gem material. In 1950, a deposit of some of the finest spider-web turquoise ever found was uncovered. This Number 8 spider-web was mostly in nodules and one of them weighed more than 9 pounds. A specimen weighing 150 pounds of excellent color and hardness was uncovered in 1954. Total production of the Number 8 Mine is estimated at more than $1,400,000 and in addition the property has produced copper and gold. (Turquoise Deposits of Nevada, p.10)

Occidental and Oriental Turquoise Mining Co. New Mexico, Grant County. See Parker Mine. This is the site of ancient Indian workings.

Old Campground Mine, The. Nevada, Lander County, Bullion District. Located in the south-central part of Sec. 20, T.29N., R.47E. Turquoise is found in limonitic lenses within a flat-lying zone of brecciated chert and shale. Minor amounts of turquoise occur also within silicified shale beds. (Turquoise Deposits of Nevada, p.18)

Orogrande District. New Mexico, Otero County. There are a number of mines and prospects in this area. Much prehistoric mining carried on here.

Oscar Wehrend Mine. Nevada, Nye County, Royston District. Located on the Nye-Esmeralda County line about 24 miles northwest of Tonopah, and about 1/3 mile from the mail workings of the Royal Blue Mine. The turquoise is in highly altered rocks where it forms seams, coatings, and nodules as much as 2 inches thick. It is mostly soft, pale, and not of very good quality, but some of it is used in making treated turquoise that turns out harder and bluer. (Turquoise Deposits of Nevada, p.27-28) See The Turquois, Pogue, p.49.

Owa Claim. Nevada, Esmeralda County. See Smith Black Matrix Mine. (Turquoise Deposits of Nevada, p.9)

Pam Group. Nevada, Lyon County. See Taubert Number 1 Mining Area. (Turquoise Deposits of Nevada, p.22)

Parker Mine. New Mexico, Grant County. Turquoise deposits originally found by "Turquoise John" Coleman. Called Occidental and Oriental Turquoise Mining Co. (1882). In 1901 became the Gem Turquoise and Copper Co.; a few years later the American Gem and Turquoise Co., since known as the Parker Mine. Located about 2,000 feet SE of the Azure Mine. About 500 feet NW of the Parker Mine are some old Indian Workings. The turquoise here occurs in films, seams, nuggets, and irregular masses in sheared and altered country rock. The turquoise is of high quality and similar to the turquoise found in other mines in the Burro Mountains. Some stones of robin-egg blue. See The Turquois, Pogue, p.56.

Peacock, The. Arizona, Mohave County. See Mineral Park Mines.

Peanut Group. Nevada, Lyon County. See Taubert Number 1 Mining Area. (Turquoise Deposits of Nevada, p.22)

Pearce Vicinity. Arizona, Cochise County. Turquoise reported near here.

Pedro Lode Claim. Nevada, Lander County, Copper Basin Area. See Blue Gem Lease Mine. (Turquoise Deposits of Nevada, p.13)

Persian Blue Mine. Nevada, Esmeralda County. See The Blue Boy Mine. (Turquoise Deposits of Nevada, p.5)

Pinal County. Arizona. Old claims 2 miles south of Kelvin.

Pinto Mine. Nevada, Lander County, Bullion District. Located near the SW corner of Sec. 16, T.26N., R.44E. Excellent quality turquoise is found in thinly bedded brown and black shale. Turquoise forms seams and nodules along bedding planes and in close association with limonitic and carbonaceous zones, but the host rocks are little altered. Also called the Watts Mine and the Valley of the Moon Mine. (Turquoise Deposits of Nevada, p.19)

Pirate Number 3 Claim. Nevada, Esmeralda County. See Blue Boy Mine. (Turquoise Deposits of Nevada, p.5-6)

Poor Boy Lode. Colorado, Lake County. Located adjacent to the Iron Mask Mine. Mostly poor quality turquoise.

Porterfield Mine, The. New Mexico, Grant County. Located about ½ mile south of the Azure Mine on the west side of St. Louis Canyon and the Tyrone-Leopold Road, SW of the Burro Chief Mine. Located near the mouth of a small gully. Choice turquoise of a deep robin's egg blue was mined. Yielded one color gems of up to 20 to 30 carats. Much mottled turquoise and turquoise with matrix was also found. The turquoise was found in veins, in veinlets, and in nuggets in lens-shaped masses. A major part of the filling of the seams in some places is white clay coated turquoise nuggets. Associated with the turquoise in this mine is quartz, hematite, limonite, nuggets of waxy green halloysite, opal, and chalcedony. Possibly the same mine as "Maroney's Prospect" as described by Zalinski (1907) (Mineral Deposits of Western Grant Co., N.M. Bulletin 83, p.48, 51-52).

Queen, The. Arizona, Mohave County. See Mineral Park Mines.

R.S. Chamberlain Mine, The. New Mexico, Grant County, Hachita District. Located on the east side of the northeast end of Turquois Mt. See The Turquois, Pogue, p.58.

Ralph King Prospect, The. Nevada, Lander County, Bullion District. Located on the east side of the Shoshone Range in Sec. 4, T.20N., R.42E. In the vicinity of this mine tightly folded shale beds form the host for veinlets and nodules that occur along bedding planes in the thinly bedded rock. (Turquoise Deposits of Nevada, p.21)

Red Hill Turquoise Mine. New Mexico, Grant County. In the White Signal District. Located about 2 miles NW of White Signal in the NE quarter Sec. 16, T.21S., R.15W. An altered zone of sericite and clay minerals is shattered and fractured with many narrow veinlets and seams of talc, clay, quartz, and turquoise filling the fractures. The turquoise is mostly soft and greenish but a few nodules of hard blue turquoise have been found. The shattered and fractured zone containing the turquoise veins is radioactive.

Riek and Botts Claims. Nevada, Esmeralda County. Located 4 miles northeast of Coaldale. The country rock is rhyolite and altered quartz porphyry. The turquoise occurs both as veinlets and in nodules. The best quality stones have a fine blue color and good hardness. Some of the turquoise has a brown spider-web matrix. See The Turquois, Pouge, p.50.

Right Blue Claim. Nevada, Clark County. See The Simmons Mine. (Turquoise Deposits of Nevada, p.3)

Robinson and Porterfield Mines. New Mexico, Grant County, Hachita District. These mines named for the owners in 1909 include the Azure, Cameo, Galilee and Aztec Claims. The turquoise occurs along the contact of an altered trachyte and monzonitic porphyry. The turquoise forms seams filling fractures and ranges in color from various blue to greenish-blue. The Aztec claim also has nuggets distributed through the rock. This name was evidently used to identify an area during this period and not. See The Turquois, Pogue, p.57.

Royal Blue Mine, The. Nevada, Nye County, Royston District. Located on the Nye-Esmeralda County Line about 24 miles northwest of Tonopah. The Royal Blue is the main mine in this district. The turquoise occurs in a fine-grained, altered porphyry which is soft in places but hardened by silicification in many areas. The turquoise is found principally in seams and veinlets, with minor amounts in nodules and lenses. The turquoise ranges in color from dark sky-blue to a pale light blue. Some of the dark blue has a slightly greenish cast. The lighter colored turquoise is generally softer and the dark blue and the greenish cast stones are very fine grained and hard. The best turquoise is generally found in limonite-stained rock and the pale-blue and softer turquoise is found in light colored softer porphyry. The quality of the best pure blue turquoise from the Royal Blue Mine is equal to that found in any American mine. The hard turquoise specimens are coated with a crust or stain of dark to light limonite, some having a yellow color. This limonite stain penetrates the turquoise along seams and cracks producing beautiful matrix designs. This mine has been one of Nevada's principal producers of fine turquoise. Sold in 1907 by the Himalaya Mining Co. (Turquoise Deposits of Nevada, p.26-27) See The Turquois, Pogue, p.48-49.

Rufan Mine. Nevada, Lander County, Bullion District. Located 4 miles north of Gold Acres near the SE corner of Sec. 1, T.28N., R.46E. Exceptionally hard turquoise occurs as veinlets in brown and gray shale. (Turquoise Deposits of Nevada, p.15)

S. Simmons Mine. Nevada, Mineral County. See Moqui-Aztec Mine. (Turquoise Deposits of Nevada, p.23)

San Pedro. Nevada, Lander County.

San Rita. New Mexico, Grant County. Turquoise found here in conjunction with copper mining operation.

Santa Rosa District. Zacatecas (state), Mexico. Located near the town of Bonanza. Turquoise is found here in a mine of argentiferous galena. Occurs in veins and as nodules here. The turquoise is of good color and hardness. Also an occurrence of turquoise nearby at Mazapil.

Second Chance Claim. Nevada, Lyon County. See Taubert Number 1. (Turquoise Deposits of Nevada, p.22)

Sigmund Claim. Nevada, Esmeralda County. Located about 3½ miles south of Redlich. Found as veinlets and nuggets some with a fine dark-blue color. See The Turquois, Pogue, p.51.

Silver Night. New Mexico, Grant County. Ancient turquoise mines reported here. Located about 20 miles southwest of Eureka District Mines. This would place this mine in the Animas Range across the Playas Valley. See Hidalgo. See The Turquois, Pogue, p.58.

Simmons Mine, The. Nevada, Clark County. The principal workings are located in the SW ¼ Sec. 26 and the NW ¼ Sec. 35, T.28S., R.61E. Host rock for the deposit is sheared, argillized granite and quartz monzonite that locally contains abundant vuggy quartz veins. Turquoise occurs as veinlets and nodules, some of which are intimately associated with quartz veinlets. This is also known as the Crescent Peak Mine and is mainly on two patented claims, the Aztec and the Right Blue. This mine was worked extensively in prehistoric times by the Indians. (Turquoise Deposits of Nevada, p.3-5)

Sky Blue Claim, The. New Mexico, Santa Fe County. See The Morning Star Claim.

Sleeping Beauty Mine. Arizona, Gila County. Turquoise of all qualities mined here in conjunction with copper mining operations. Also called Copper Cities Open-pit mine. Turquoise is produced from the oxidized part of the open-pit mine.

Smith Black Matrix Mine. Nevada, Esmeralda County. Located on the Owa Claim on the east side of a small dark hill, about ¾ mile east of Klondyke Peak and 1 mile south of Klondyke, in the SW ¼ Sec. 29, T.1N., R.43E. The turquoise forms veinlets, seams, and breccia fillings in limonite-stained cherty limestone and slate. Seams of turquoise range up to ¾ of an inch thick and turquoise-cemented breccia masses are more than an inch across. The thicker seams of turquoise generally contain breccia fragments. The limonite of the host rock is in places integrated with the turquoise. The turquoise from this mine is usually in small pieces. The blue turquoise and the black chert matrix present a pleasing contrast and there are some beautiful stones cut from these specimens. Some of the specimens also have a gray quartz or a brown stain in with the other colors. (Turquoise Deposits of Nevada, p.9) See The Turquois, Pogue, p.50.

Smithson-Phillips Mine. Nevada, Clark County. See Simmons mine for approximate location and description. (Nevada Bureau of Mines. Turquoise and Variscite Occurrences, Map 23)

Snow Storm Claim. Nevada, Nye County, Royston Mining District. Located on the Esmeralda County Line.

Southwest Turquoise Co. Mine. Arizona, Mohave County. See Mineral Park Mines.

Stampede Mine. Nevada, Elko County. Located about 9½ miles southeast of Tuscarora in the SE ¼ Sec. 9, T.38N., R.52E. Turquoise occurs as nodules and seams along bedding planes in brecciated black chert and gray quartzite. Solid blue, spider-web, and matrix turquoise has been found. The turquoise has good color and is very hard. (Turquoise Deposits of Nevada, p.5)

Star Mine. Nevada, Esmeralda County. See Copper Queen Mine. (Turquoise Deposits of Nevada, p.7)

Steinich Mine. Nevada, Lander County, Bullion District. Located near the south side, center, of Sec. 19, T.28N., R.47E. Beds of gray shale and chert contain nodules of turquoise concentrated in the darker shale layers. The turquoise grades from blue to greenish-blue and is mostly in the form of small nuggets. Also called Gold Acres, and Stone Cabin Mine. (Turquoise Deposits of Nevada, p.14)

Stone Cabin Mine. Nevada, Lander County, Bullion District. See Steinich Mine.

Stone Hammer Mines. California, San Bernardino County. Just west of Nevada-Arizona Border. In 1904 three groups of claims were being worked at East Camp, Middle Camp and West Camp by the Toltec Gem Co. and others nearby by the Himalaya Mining Co. abandoned now. These mines were worked by Indians in prehistoric times. Located in the Manvel District. The turquoise occurs at the Himalaya Mine in a decomposed porphyry in association with limonite, Kaolin, sericite, jarosite, and quartz. The turquoise occurs as nodules and in veinlets filling joint planes and fracture zones. The best quality stones range in color from light blue to fairly dark blue and are of good quality. See The Turquoise, Pogue, p.46-47.

Sullivan Mine. Nevada, Clark County. See Yellow Diamond Mine. (Turquoise Deposits of Nevada, p.3)

Sunset Claim, The. Colorado, Conejos County. See the King Mine.

Super-X Mine. Nevada, Lander County, Bullion District. See Arrowhead Mine. (Turquoise Deposits of Nevada, p.15)

Taubert Number 1. Nevada, Lyon County. Located near the center of the boundary between Sec. 9 and Sec. 10, T.13N., R.24E. Turquoise occurs in highly fractured zones that end to show strong to moderate argillic alteration. Turquoise usually forms veinlets but sometimes nodules along the joints. Some of the veinlets are up to ½ inch in thickness. Color ranges from dark blue to bluish green to green. Much of the turquoise is very hard and the pure-blue variety is slightly translucent. Some of the turquoise, especially the greenish colored has patches and dendritic markings of limonite through it. Some of the claims here are the Harcross group, the Peanut group, the Pam group, and the Second Chance claim. (Turquoise Deposits of Nevada, p.22). See The Turquois, Pogue, p.51)

Taubert Number 2. Nevada, Lyon County. This prospect is located about 1½ miles north-northwest of Yerington. There are shallow pits here in altered quartz monzonite where turquoise forms seams and nodules. Most of the turquoise is pale-blue but there is also some darker pure-blue turquoise. (Turquoise Deposits of Nevada, p.22)

Tenabo Group. Nevada, Lander County, Bullion District.

Texas. El Paso County. Reported north of El Paso. Turquoise is greenish with matrix. See The Turquois, Pogue, p.58.

Three Bears Mine, The. New Mexico, Otero County. See The Jarilla Mountain Area.

Tiffany Mine. New Mexico, Santa Fe County. Located at the north end of the turquoise bearing area about 3 miles north of Mt. Chalchuitl. Hard gem quality turquoise mostly of greenish color was mined here. American Turquoise Co. owned these mines when last worked. Location is 5½ to 6 miles east of north of Cerrillos in Sec. 21, T.15N., R.8E. The turquoise occurs here in fracture zones or veinlets cutting altered intrusive rocks. See The Turquoise, Pogue, p.52-55.

Toltec. Nevada, Clark County. See The Simmons Mine for approximate location and description. (Nevada Bureau of Mines. Turquoise and Variscite Occurrences, Map 23)

Toltec Gem Co. California, San Bernardino County. See Stone Hammer Mines.

Tom Cat Mine. Nevada, Lander County, Bullion District. Located about 1,000 feet east of the Rufan Mine in the extreme NW corner of Sec. 7, T.28N., R.47E. Host rock for this deposit is a granular thinly bedded black quartzite. Turquoise occurs in a kaolinized layer that marks a bedding-plane fault. The greenish-blue color of the turquoise distinguishes it from the bluer material found elsewhere in this district, and the turquoise is relatively hard. (Turquoise Deposits of Nevada, p.15)

Tom Molly Mine. Nevada, Nye County. Previously called the Train Prospect. Located along the east side of Sec. 13, T.8N., R.43E. Turquoise, together with other phosphate minerals and some secondary copper minerals occur along shear zones in shale and slate. (Turquoise Deposits of Nevada, p.25)

Torpedo Mine. New Mexico, Dona Ana County. Located in the Organ District. Turquoise production here small. Replaces Kaolinite.

Train Prospect. Nevada, Nye County. See The Tom Molly Mine. (Turquoise Deposits of Nevada, p.25)

Troy Springs Mine. Nevada, Mineral County. See Montezuma Mine. (Turquoise Deposits of Nevada, p.23)

Tungsten Claim. Nevada, Lander County, Bullion District. See Blue Matrix Mine. (Turquoise Deposits of Nevada, p.18)

Turquoise Bonanza Mine. Nevada, Mineral County. Located on the east side of the Pilot Mountains, about 5 miles N. 65°E. from Pilot Peak, 2½ miles north of the Moqui-Aztec Mine, and just south from the Gunmetal tungsten Mine. The turquoise occurs as cementing material and veinlets in an altered, brecciated zone within quartzite. The turquoise from this mine was mainly of an excellent blue color with some showing a slight greenish tinge. (Turquoise Deposits of Nevada, p.23)

Turquois Chief Mine, The. Colorado, Lake County. Located 7 miles northwest of Leadville, Colorado. The turquoise occurs in veins and as nodules. The turquoise is found mainly along faults in the St. Kevin granite. Located adjacent to the Iron Mask Mine. Mostly poor quality turquoise. (Colorado Geological Survey Letter, Aug. 27, 1971; Colorado Gem Trails, p.81)

Turquoise Claim. Nevada, Lander County, Copper Basin Area. See The Myron Clark Mine. (Turquoise Deposits of Nevada, p.13)

Turquoise District, The. Arizona, Cochise County. Located on the west flank of turquoise ridge, ¾ mile west of Courtland. Turquoise occurs as stringers and nuggets in both Bolsa quartzite and in a granite that intrudes the quartzite. Some fine turquoise from this deposit.

Turquoise 50 Mine. Nevada, Lander County, Bullion District. Located near the center of Sec. 12, T.27N., R.46E. Turquoise occurs as seams and veinlets in shale and a thin, highly altered unit that may represent an intrusive sill. (Turquoise Deposits of Nevada, p.14)

Turquoise King, The. Arizona, Mohave County. See Mineral Park Mines.

Turquoise King Mine. Nevada, Lander County, Copper Basin Area. Located near the west side, center of Sec. 32, T.32N., R.44E. The deposit is in an altered quartz monzontie containing limonitic seams, quartz veinlets, and minor fractures oriented in several directions. Turquoise occurs in the veinlets and fractures. (Turquoise Deposits of Nevada, p.12-13.)

Turquoise Mine. Nevada, Clark County. See Simmons Mine. (Turquoise Deposits of Nevada, p.4)

Turquoise Mountain. Arizona, Cochise County. Prehistoric mines located here.

Turquoise Ridge. Arizona, Cochise County. Located east of Gleason. Turquoise found in this area.

Turquoise Tunnel Mine. Nevada, Lander County, Copper Basin Area. See Blue Gem Lease Mine. (Turquoise Deposits of Nevada, p.13)

Valley of the Moon Mine. Nevada, Lander County, Bullion District. Also known as Watts Mine and Pinto Mine. See Pinto Mine.

Villa Grove Mine. Colorado, Saguache County. Also known as the Hall Mine. Located northwest of the town of Villa Grove near Turquoise Creek on Turquoise Ridge. Many bright blue gems mostly in nodules have been mined. Also some poorer yellow-greenish and greenish-gray turquoise has been mined.

Wallapai Mining District. Arizona, Mohave County. See Mineral Park Mines.

Watts Mine. Nevada, Lander County, Bullion District. Also known as Valley of the Moon and Pinto Mine. See Pinto Mine. (Turquoise Deposits of Nevada, p.19)

Weber Mine. Nevada, Nye County, Belmont Mining District. Produces turquoise with peculiar matrix. Many bluish-green stones with white outline around blue portion, then surrounded by brown matrix. (Nevada Bureau of Mines. Turquoise and Variscite Occurrences in Nevada. Map 23)

Wee Nugget Claim. Nevada, Lander County, Bullion District. See Blue Gem Mine. (Turquoise Deposits of Nevada, p.17)

West Camp. California, San Bernardino, County. See Stone Hammer Mines.

Western Gem Co., The. Nevada, Mineral County. Acquired by Western Gem Co. in 1910. See The Montezuma Mine.

White Horse Mine. Nevada, Lander County, Bullion District. Located about ½ mile north of the Fox Mine. Veinlets of turquoise are associated with a highly altered dike where it intrudes chert. (Turquoise Deposits of Nevada, p.20)

White Signal District. New Mexico, Grant County. Located near White Signal. The turquoise here seems to lie along a porphry dike that cuts through granite. See The Turquois, Pogue, p.56.

William Petry Mine. Nevada, Esmeralda County. See Blue Friday Mine. (Turquoise Deposits of Nevada, p.7)

Wilson-Capps Claim. Nevada, Esmeralda County, Coaldale Mining District.

Woods Mine. Nevada, Clark County. See Simmons mine for location and description. (Nevada Bureau of Mines. Turquoise and Variscite Occurrences, Map 23)

X-15 Prospect. Nevada, Lander County, Bullion District. Located in the NW ¼ Sec. 11, T.25N., R.45E. toward the south end of the Red Mountains. Turquoise occurs as veinlets along fractures and bedding planes in brown to black shale. (Turquoise Deposits of Nevada, p.20)

Yavapai County. Arizona. Turquoise occurrence northeast of Wittmann. Located west of Carrizo Creek on the Fort Apache Indian Reservation about halfway between the Salt River and the north border of the reservation.

Yellow Diamond Mine. Nevada, Clark County. Also known as the Sullivan Mine. Located in the SW ¼ Sec. 25 and the NW ¼ Sec. 36, T.22S., R.64E. The Turquoise occurs in sheared and altered rocks. (Turquoise Deposits of Nevada, p.3)

Zabrisky Mine. Nevada, Nye County. Located about ½ mile east of the No Name Number 2 Mine. Turquoise was discovered here in old copper workings. The best grade of turquoise from this mine is dark-blue material with a small amount of white mineral in a dark-gray and chocolate-colored matrix. Along with this variety of turquoise was found a larger quantity of ordinary blue and greenish turquoise with brown matrix. (Turquoise Deposits of Nevada, p.25)

Zuni Mountain. Nevada, Lincoln County.

List of Color Plates

MEMOIRS

OF THE

NATIONAL ACADEMY OF SCIENCES

Volume XII

Part II

SECOND MEMOIR
THIRD MEMOIR

WASHINGTON
1915

NATIONAL ACADEMY OF SCIENCES.

Volume XII.
THIRD MEMOIR.

THE TURQUOIS.

A STUDY OF ITS HISTORY, MINERALOGY, GEOLOGY, ETHNOLOGY, ARCHÆOLOGY, MYTHOLOGY, FOLKLORE, AND TECHNOLOGY.

BY

JOSEPH E. POGUE, Ph. D.,

ASSOCIATE GEOLOGIST, UNITED STATES GEOLOGICAL SURVEY, FORMERLY ASSISTANT CURATOR
DIVISION OF MINERALOGY AND PETROLOGY, UNITED STATES NATIONAL MUSEUM,
FELLOW OF THE GEOLOGICAL SOCIETY OF AMERICA.

PREFACE.

Some years ago the writer undertook a study of turquois, with the purpose of presenting an account not only of its mineralogy and geology, but of its history, ethnology, and technology as well. He entered upon this task with no adequate conception of its magnitude or appreciation of its difficulty, and was enabled to bring it to conclusion only through a position that placed at his command excellent library facilities and the Government collections and gave him access to advice of many experts on subjects not his own. While he has aimed at reasonable completeness in its execution he realizes that much of importance has escaped him. He is aware also of many deficiencies in the treatment of subjects in which he has had little experience. In spite of these drawbacks it is hoped that the present treatise may arouse a greater interest in a fascinating field—that concerned with precious stones in their relation to mankind.

The investigation was carried on while the writer was in charge of the mineralogical collections of the United States National Museum, and he is indebted to the officials of that institution, particularly to Dr. George P. Merrill, Head Curator of Geology, not only for opportunity of doing this work, but also for encouragement and cooperation during its progress. He feels that he owes more than can be adequately acknowledged to ideas, suggestions, and help on the part of many who have been so kind as to take an interest in the undertaking. Special thanks are due Dr. Walter Hough, Curator of Ethnology in the National Museum, for information, references, and experience, a critical examination of a portion of the text, and constant encouragement and interest; Mr. Douglas B. Sterrett, of the United States Geological Survey, for use of unpublished notes on the turquois localities of this country, review of the portion of text covering these occurrences, and cooperation in the preparation of the colored plate shown in the frontispiece; and Dr. Berthold Laufer, Associate Curator of Asiatic Ethnology in the Field Museum of Chicago, for invaluable information, numerous references, and especially for a most thorough and scholarly treatment of the turquois in India, Tibet, and China—a contribution originally planned to appear as an appendix to this monograph, but which, because of unavoidable exigencies, has been published in advance.[1] Dr. Laufer's critical and searching study, which appears under the modest title, "Notes on Turquois in the East,"[2] is the fruit of high attainment in a field difficult of access to the westerner, and it offers a wealth of information that would have long remained buried but for the efforts of that accomplished scholar. The present writer has attempted to include in this treatise the main results set forth in Dr. Laufer's paper, but the critical reader must be referred to the original for the detail that could not be here admitted without reprinting the entire paper.

Other friends and workers have generously supplied information or aided the study in other ways, and to these the writer wishes to extend his grateful acknowledgment, as follows:

Prof. Max Bauer, University of Marburg.

Dr. R. S. Bassler, United States National Museum.

Dr. A. E. Wallace Budge, British Museum.

Dr. I. M. Casanowicz, United States National Museum.

Mr. A. Stanley Clarke, India Museum, London.

Prof. Ellsworth Huntington, Yale University.

Dr. J. Walter Fewkes, Bureau of American Ethnology.

Mr. C. G. Gilbert, United States National Museum.

---

[1] In July, 1913.   [2] Field Museum of Natural History, publication 169, Anthr. Ser., vol. 13, No. 1, 1913.

PREFACE.

Prof. Victor Goldschmidt, University of Heidelberg.

Mr. S. M. Gronberger, Smithsonian Institution.

Mr. F. W. Hodge, Bureau of American Ethnology.

Prof. W. H. Holmes, United States National Museum.

Dr. A. Hrdlička, United States National Museum.

Mr. T. A. Joyce, British Museum.

Mme. A. Kornacoff, Kiachta, Siberia.

Dr. George F. Kunz, New York.

Mrs. F. B. Laney, Denver.

Dr. Nicolas Leon, Museo Nacional, Mexico.

Mr. Sidney Paige, United States Geological Survey.

Prof. W. M. Flinders Petrie, University College, London.

Dr. W. T. Schaller, United States Geological Survey.

Dr. Eduard Seler, Museum for Ethnology, Berlin.

Miss I. D. Singleton, Washington.

Prof. E. A. Smith, State Geologist of Alabama.

Mrs. John Wetherill, Kayenta, Arizona.

During the course of the study the following libraries have been used: Library of Congress, library of the United States Geological Survey, library of the Surgeon General's Office, libraries of the Smithsonian Institution and of the United States National Museum, library of the Bureau of American Ethnology, British Museum Library, Bibliothèque nationale (Paris), library of Heidelberg University, and library of the University of Berlin.

In addition to the material in the United States National Museum, the collections in the following institutions have been consulted during the investigation: American Museum of Natural History, New York City; Metropolitan Museum of Art, New York City; The Field Museum, Chicago; British Museum, London; Victoria and Albert Museum, London; The India Museum, London; Museum of Natural History, South Kensington, London; Museum of Practical Geology, London; The Wallace Collection, London; The Louvre, Paris; The Trocadéro Museum, Paris; Musée Guimet, Paris; Museum for Natural History, Paris; Museum for Ethnology, Berlin; Museum of Industrial Art, Berlin; Museum of Natural History, Berlin.

CONTENTS.

LIST OF ILLUSTRATIONS.

*

THE TURQUOIS.

INTRODUCTION.

Turquois is a mineral prized for its perfection of color; for, being opaque, it lacks the brilliant luster that forms the chief attraction of the transparent gems. When of finest quality it possesses a blue tone, soft and pleasing, like the color of clear sky; but often its value is lessened by a greenish cast, and in many stones the green predominates. The mineral is but slightly harder than glass, and may be worked with ease, even by primitive people possessing the crudest tools. Chemically, it is a phosphate of aluminum carrying small quantities of copper and iron, to which its color is due, and with variscite, a green mineral of similar character but of less value and beauty, is the only phosphate to find a place among the precious stones.

At the present day, among civilized nations, the turquois is outranked in value by the diamond, ruby, emerald, sapphire, and some other gems, although over some minds the wonderful blue of that precious stone wields a fascination shared by no other. With many semi-civilized peoples, however, the turquois takes foremost rank, and its value depends not only upon its intrinsic worth but also upon the mystic properties and religious signification it is supposed to possess. It is at once the most highly prized possession of the Navaho Indian in the deserts of Arizona and of the Arab Bedawyn on the plains of Arabia; and the Tibetan and Mongolian natives esteem this gem no less than do the Hopi and Zuñi pueblo dwellers in our own Southwest. By virtue of its parallel use in parts of the Orient and America, and its curious introduction into legends and myths of diverse and widely separated peoples, the turquois carries considerable ethnologic interest.

In the past, even more than the present, has the turquois played an important rôle. From the dawn of civilization down to the present it has found a variety of uses, both ornamental and religious, and always held in high esteem it has frequently been invested with marvellous virtues. The tombs of the earliest Egyptian kings have yielded jewelry of considerable beauty wrought of gold and inlaid with turquoises from the Sinai Peninsula. The inhabitants of Central Asia have long valued the turquois and been lavish in its use, while the Persians and neighboring races of western Asia have from time immemorial drawn upon the famous Nishapur deposits near the Caspian Sea, which furnished stones of the choicest character. The Europeans, during the Middle Ages and thereafter, esteemed the Persian stone which came to them by way of Turkey, and the mineral was known in Europe even prior to the Christian Era. The Aztecs of old Mexico, at the time of the Spanish Conquest under Cortés, employed turquois and "chalchihuitl," an allied or similar stone of greenish hue, in many of their ceremonies, and a number of remarkable turquois mosaics carried by the Conquerors to Europe attest the skill and taste of these Indian artisans. The Spaniards, on first entering the region now occupied by New Mexico and Arizona, lured on by the tales of fabulous riches, found the turquois here too held in high regard, and recent excavations in the ancient pueblos and cliff dwellings of these two States have revealed a wealth of turquois ornaments that reflect considerable credit on the artistic ability of their makers.

Turquois occurs at comparatively few places on the globe, and strangely enough is confined almost exclusively to regions of barrenness and aridity. It is also a remarkable fact that, with

7

a few unimportant exceptions, no occurrence is now known near which traces of prehistoric mining have not been discovered. Productive deposits are found in Asia, notably at Nishapur in Persia, long the most important locality in the world, and at several places in Central Asia about which very little information is available. On the Sinai Peninsula are remains of extensive workings executed during the Egyptian Era, but these mines have been exhausted, or, at least, have not been successfully operated for a very long period. The southwestern portion of the United States has recently become an important source, and mines in New Mexico, Arizona, California, Nevada, and Colorado are now producing stones of good quality, rivals of the Persian gems.

CHAPTER I.

THE HISTORY OF TURQUOIS.

The temple I frequent is high,
A turkis-vaulted dome—the sky,
That spans the world with majesty.
Omar Khayyam: Translation by Louisa Stuart Costello.

Because the city gave him of her gold,
Because the caravans brought turquoises.
Kipling: Evarra and his Gods.

The turquois was known and used as an ornament in remote antiquity. Recent excavations in Egypt show that this precious stone found employment in that country prior to the first dynasty—a time to which history scarcely penetrates. The earliest direct reference to turquois occurs in ancient Egyptian hieroglyphics, in which the word *mafkat* finds repeated mention. This term was translated at first as malachite, an ore of copper, but is now believed by competent authorities to refer to turquois. Rock carvings including this word are abundant on the cliffs and monuments surrounding turquois mines in the Sinai Peninsula, and the translation of these ancient documents shows that mining operations in search of turquois were intermittently prosecuted there under Egyptian direction from the first to the twentieth dynasties. The word also holds a place in Egyptian literature and a legend in which turquois figures has been translated from an early papyrus.[1]

In the earliest writings turquois fails to be identified. The Bible, which refers to the use of a number of minerals for purposes of adornment, has not been found to contain mention of turquois, although the modern equivalents of the precious stones of the Bible have been the subject of research on the part of several able investigators.[2]

Aristotle (384–322 B. C.) is accredited by the Arabian authority, Ahmed Teifascite (thirteenth century), with the statement that turquois prevents death by accident and is beneficial for scorpion and reptile stings; but this characterization appeared under the caption Σάπφειρος, a term generally regarded as the equivalent of lapis-lazuli, and consequently it can not be accepted that Aristotle had any knowledge of turquois.[3]

Theophrastus, scholar of Aristotle, has left a treatise on precious stones entitled Περὶ τῶν Λίθων written about 315 B. C., a very good English translation[4] of which was published in London in 1774. This work contains no reference to turquois, but gives a brief account of copper-stained fossil ivory, "which," affirms the translator, "although generally esteemed a stone, is in reality no other than the bones and teeth of animals." The citation is mentioned because it includes the first notice of a substance known as *odontolite*, or *bone turquois*, which, resembling somewhat inferior turquois, has been constantly confounded with the real mineral, as will be noted later.

Dioscorides, who lived during the first century and wrote (about A. D. 50) a five-volume treatise on Materia Medica, a portion of which deals with the medicinal properties of minerals,

---

[1] See pp. 28–34, 69–71, 111 for a detailed discussion of turquois in Egypt.

[2] Lommer in 1776 (Abhandl. einer Privatgesellsch., Böhmen, vol. 2, 1776, pp. 112–118) stated that turquois was known to the Patriarchs, and found a place in the breastplate of the High Priest Aaron. This ornament of the Jewish High Priest is described in Exodus, XXVIII, 17–20, and while the modern equivalents of the ancient gems used in its adornment are not in every case certain, the accepted identifications, as given by Adler and Casanowicz (U. S. Nat. Museum, Ann. Rept., 1895–96, pp. 979–982) and in several Biblical encyclopedias, do not include turquois. Kunz (The curious lore of precious stones, 1913, pp. 275–306) in a detailed discussion of the high-priest's breastplate says in regard to the *shoham*, a stone usually rendered beryl or onyx, that the high priest in addition wore on his shoulders two *shoham* stones, and ventures the suggestion that the latter were turquoises.

[3] See p. 12 for statement regarding a *lapidarium* wrongly attributed to Aristotle.

[4] Theophrastus, History of stones. Trans. by John Hill, London, 1774. See p. 159.

9

either fails to mention turquois or else he treats it under a name which now can not be definitely recognized. In book V of De Medica Materia [1] Dioscorides writes:

It is believed that by swallowing a lapis-lazuli (Σάπφειρος) one is rendered immune to scorpion's stings. It is also taken in drink for internal ulcerations. Besides this, it represses growths in the eyes, such as warts and pustules, and even glues together their broken membranes.

These properties ascribed by Dioscorides and his predecessors (Aristotle and Theophrastus) to lapis-lazuli were later by Arabian authors of the 13th century (Ibn-el-Beithar, 1197–1248 A. D.; and Teifascite, 1253 A. D.) attributed to turquois; [2] and, while probably a mistake on the part of the latter,[3] this circumstance may suggest, as King [4] has noted, that the Ancients looked upon turquois as a variety of lapis-lazuli.

Pliny,[5] in book 37 of his Natural History, first published in A. D. 77, treats with great wealth of detail and in very interesting fashion, all the precious stones known to the Ancients. Under several different names he describes minerals that a number of authorities have correlated with turquois.

The *Callaina*, to which Pliny devotes an entire chapter, has some characteristics in common with turquois, although the correspondence is far from satisfactory. He says of it: [6]

CALLAINA.

With this stone [chrysolite and possibly green agate] we must also couple another, which resembles it more closely in appearance than in value, the stone known as "callaina," and of a pale green color. It is found in the countries that lie at the back of India, among the Phycari, namely, who inhabit Mount Caucasus, the Sacae, and the Dahae. It is remarkable for its size, but is covered with holes and is full of extraneous matter; that, however, which is found in Carmania is of a finer quality, and far superior. In both cases, however, it is only amid frozen and inaccessible rocks that it is found, protruding from the surface, like an eye in appearance, and slightly adhering to the rock; not as though it formed an integral part of it, but with all the appearance of having been attached to it. People so habituated as they are to riding on horseback can not find the energy and dexterity requisite for climbing the rocks to obtain the stones, while, at the same time, they are quite terrified at the danger of doing so. Hence it is that they attack the stones with slings from a distance, and so bring them down, moss and all. It is with this stone that the people pay their tribute, and this the rich look upon as their most graceful ornament for the neck. This constitutes the whole of their wealth, with some, and it is their chief glory to recount how many of these stones they have brought down from the mountain heights since the days of their childhood. Their success, however, is extremely variable, for while some, at the very first throw, have brought down remarkably fine specimens, many have arrived at an old age without obtaining any.

Such is the method of procuring these stones, their form being given them by cutting, a thing that is easily effected. The best of them have just the color of smaragdus, a thing that proves that the most pleasing property in them is one that belongs of right to another stone. Their beauty is heightened by setting them in gold, and there is no stone to which the contrast of the gold is more becoming. The finest of them lose their color by coming in contact with oil, ungents, or undiluted wine even; whereas those of a poorer quality preserve their color better. There is no stone, too, that is more easily counterfeited in glass. Some writers say that this stone is to be found in Arabia also, in the nest of the bird known as the "melancoryphus."

The *callais* of Pliny, although treated in scant detail, bears likewise some analogy to turquois. All that is said of it is, "The *callais* is like *sapphiros* [lapis-lazuli] in color, only that it is paler and more closely resembles the tint of the water near the seashore in appearance." [7]

Many authorities hold that both *callaina* and *callais* represent turquois, but the evidence adduced is not conclusive. This question, however, has elicited many opinions, not all of them in accord. King [8] was one of the earliest students of the subject to oppose the identification of *callaina* as turquois. While admitting *callais* to be turquois, he has argued that *callaina* is peridot (olivine), maintaining that Pliny's description fits a pale-green, transparent stone such

[1] Coloniae, 1529, p. 693.

[2] See pp. 13, 14.

[3] See Fühner, Lithotherapie. Strasburg, 1902, p. 107.

[4] Antique gems and rings. London, 1872, vol. 2, p. 13. King merely states that the Ancients considered the turquois to be a light-blue variety of "sapphire," without giving his reasons for so believing.

[5] Pliny drew much of his information on precious stones from numerous mineralogists, chiefly Greeks, whom he mentions by name at the end of book 37. Of his sources only the treatise of Theophrastus and a poem on gems by the Pseudo-Orpheus are now extant. (King, The natural history, ancient and modern, of precious stones and gems. London, 1865, p. 2.) The latter, a good translation of which is given by King (ibid, pp. 375–396), occupies itself with ornate descriptions of many of the gems, but makes no mention of turquois. Pliny is said to have taken the liberty to quote considerably from Dioscorides without acknowledging the author.

[6] The translation is that of Bostock and Riley, Pliny's Natural History. London, 1857, book 37, chapter 33.

[7] Pliny, Natural History, Bostock and Riley's transl. London, 1857, book 37, chap. 56, vol. 6, pp. 444–445.

[8] Op. cit., 1865, p. 167.

Plate No. 1.

Rex Arrowsmith, left, and photographer Len Bouche with the camera set-up used to photograph the remaining color plates.

Turquoise figurines and fetishes.

as the peridot.　Blake,[1] however, has taken exception to King's statements, believing that Pliny's description of *callaina* does agree with inferior greenish turquois.　Middleton[2] considers the *callaina* to be *green* turquois; the *callais, blue* turquois.　Dana[3] states that both *callaina* and *callais* are probably turquois.　Laufer[4] takes a decided stand on the question and goes so far as to say, "The supposed identification of Pliny's *callaina* or *callais* with the turquois is no more than a weak guess, and one that is highly improbable; and a mere guess, even though it may be repeated by a dozen or more authors, will never become a fact."

In another place Pliny[5] speaks of the stone *callaica* (turquois matrix ??) thus: "Callaica is the name given to a stone like a clouded callaina; a number of them are always united, it is said."[6]　In chapter 54 of book 37,[6] he states that "*Augetis* is thought by many to be identical with *callaina*."　Several other statements by Pliny have been interpreted as referring to turquois. In chapter 18, book 37, Pliny[7] writes:

Next　*　*　*　the smaragdus of Ethiopia is held in high esteem.　*　*　*　Democritus includes in this class the stones that are known as "herminei," and as "Persian" stones; the former of which are of a convex, massive shape, while the latter are destitute of transparency, but have an agreeable uniform color, and satisfy the vision without allowing it to penetrate them; strongly resembling, in this respect, the eyes of cats and of panthers, which are radiant without being diaphanous.

King[8] has voiced the belief that both the "herminei" and "Persian" smaragdus are turquois.　Of the "Persian" smaragdus Dana[9] explains that "it may have been turquois; yet, as with most of Pliny's descriptions (owing to his mixing different things of similar aspect), when all the other characters given are weighed, they leave doubt."

Farther on Pliny gives a description of 14 varieties of *iaspis*, or jasper, in which he says:[10]

*　*　*　that of Persia is sky-blue, whence its name, "aerizusa."　Similar to this is the Caspian iaspis　*　*　*. A fourth kind, which is called by the Greeks "boria" [northern], resembles in color the sky of a morning in autumn; this, too, will be the same that is known as "aerizusa."

Commenting upon this statement in 1644 de Boot[11] pointed out that "many believe that turquois was formerly placed among the jaspers and was identical with Pliny's boria.　The Greeks call it azure-blue jasper."　King,[12] however, as well as Beckman,[13] questioned whether the turquois was meant by *iaspis aerizusa;*[13] on the other hand, Salmasius accepted this correlation and Berthold Laufer,[14] considering Pliny's statement in connection with that of Trallainos,[15] was led to believe that this jasper is not jasper in fact, but turquois and probably identical with the Persian turquois from Nishapur.

It has been asserted that Pliny[16] signified the turquois by his *cyanos*, but King[17] rightly maintained that this is ultramarine.

If it could be accepted without question that Pliny's *callaina* and *callais* referred to turquois, we would be safe in assuming that this mineral was described by other writers of that early period.　The *Periplus Maris Erythraei*, a Greek work of an unknown author, written

[1] Amer. Journ. Sci., vol. 25, 1883, p. 199.

[2] The engraved gems of classical times.　Cambridge, 1891, p. 149.

[3] System of Mineralogy, 1892, p. 845.

Damour in 1864 (Compt. rend., vol. 59, 1864, pp. 936–940) referred a green hydrous phosphate of alumina, found in the form of ornaments in a Celtic grave in Lockmariaquer, Morbihan, France, to the *callais* of Pliny.　It bears more resemblance, however, to Pliny's *callaina*, and Dana (ibid, p. 825), recognizing this, proposed *callainite*, a modification of *callaina*, as a name preferable to *callais*.　Blake (op. cit., p. 199), considered it an altered greenish turquois; although Dana lists it as an independent species.　Bauer (Edelsteinkunde, Leipzig, 1896, p. 457) has suggested it to be a variety of variscite.

[4] Field Mus. Nat. Hist., publ. 169, Anthr. Ser., vol. 13, No. 1, 1913, p. 2, note 2.

[5] Ibid., book 37, chap. 56, vol. 6, p. 445.

[6] Ibid., p. 442.

[7] Ibid., pp. 411–412.

[8] Op. cit., 1865, p. 138.

[9] Loc. cit.

[10] Ibid., p. 430, book 37, chap. 37.

[11] Le parfaict ioaillier ou histoire des pierreries.　Ed. by André Toll.　Lyon, 1644, p. 338.

[12] Op. cit., 1865, p. 137.

[13] A history of inventions, discoveries, and origins.　Trans. by Wm. Johnston.　London, 1846, p. 471, note.

[14] Private communication to the writer.

[15] See p. 12.

[16] Ibid., vol. 6, p. 432.　Book 37, chap. 40.

[17] Antique gems and rings.　London, 1872, vol. 2, p. 13.

between 80 and 89 A. D., states that the *cullean* stone was exported from the Indian port Barbaricon.[1] The *Cyranides*,[2] an old Greek work on natural history, of uncertain date, which was first published as an anonymous Latin translation, and later appeared in a second Latin edition printed at Frankfort in 1681, describes a stone called *xifios*, which is compared to the *kalainos*, as shown in the following citation:

Xifios is a stone known to every one. It is abundant all over the earth like pebbles, and in color is like the kalainos. It is mined in the country of the Assyrians, and quadrupeds about to be sacrificed are stained and fumigated with this color.

After the first century there followed a long period of intellectual darkness, during which the literary output of the entire world was small. Mineralogy during that time was but a subordinate branch of medicine, and the few writers who touched upon minerals at all did so only indirectly in works of a medical nature. All learning, in Christendom at least, was confined to the cloister, and any advance in knowledge was blocked by the spirit of the times, which was one not of inquiry but of acceptance. While this was the state of affairs in Europe the torch of knowledge was kept more brightly burning by the Arabians, who, from the seventh to the fourteenth century in particular, cultivated the arts and sciences and toward the end of that period produced scientific treatises of some merit. As will appear, the few allusions to the turquois made during the ten centuries following the time of Pliny are of little importance.

Galenus, the most celebrated of the ancient medical writers, born in the year 130 A. D., is accredited[3] with the statement that the best turquois is obtained from Neisabur (Nishapur, Persia), whence it is exported to all parts of the world.

The Greek physician, Alexander Trallianos (sixth century A. D.), mentions in his treatise on epilepsy, Περὶ ἐπιληψίας,[4] a remedy which is quoted from a lost work of Archigenes (first century A. D.; lived in Rome):

Wear on your finger a jasper shining blue-green like the turquois and you will be cured from the disease (*i. e.*, epilepsy); it is of great value. * * * Wholesome, if worn on the finger, are also the chrysolite and the jasper, which shine blue like the atmosphere or green-blue like turquois.[5]

The jasper here referred to is the same as Pliny's *iaspis aerizusa*, and hence itself may be turquois.

Hispalensis Isadorus, Bishop of Seville, in book 16 of his "De Natura Rerum," written in the seventh century, alludes to the frequent use of turquois in the ears of Orientals.

In the eighth century the turquois finds its earliest notice in Tibetan literature, although the mineral was previously known to the people of that country. In the biography of a famous physician of that period, it is related how immense quantities of turquoises and other precious stones were miraculously heaped upon the roof of his house by gods and demons.[6] In "The Four Tantra," an ancient Tibetan work based on a standard Sanskrit treatise translated into Tibetan in the middle of the eighth century, two varieties of turquois are described, but the work contains so much material subsequently interpolated that the historical value of specific statements is questionable.[7]

An old work, De Lapidus,[8] wrongly imputed to Aristotle,[9] but which according to Ruska was composed before the middle of the ninth century, includes a brief section[10] descriptive of turquois, as follows:

This stone is green, and the green color is like that of the sea. It changes its color according to the changes in the air, as is also said to be the case with the emerald. And it is to be noted that all precious stones, the colors of which change with the air, are not well adapted to be worn in rings. In this stone gold is found intermixed with copper. It is not a stone of great value, and kings and magnates do not wear it. Oil dulls its color.

---

[1] Through Laufer, op. cit., p. 2, note 2. Laufer thinks that the reference has no connection with turquois, although W. H. Schoff (The Periplus of the Erythraean Sea, London, 1912, pp. 38, 170) takes the opposite view.

[2] The Greek text is quoted by Mely (Les lapidaires de l'Antiquité et du moyen age. Vol. 2: Les lapidaires Grecs. Paris, 1898. See page 32), and consists of a series of letters, of which paragraph 3 of letter 10 pertains to *xifios*.

[3] See Ibn-el-Beithar, p. 13, of this work; also p. 35.

[4] See Puschmann, Alexander von Tralles, Wien, 1878, vol. 1, pp. 566, 570.

[5] The reference and translation were kindly furnished the writer by Berthold Laufer.

[6] See p. 113.

[7] Laufer, op. cit., p. 6.

[8] Quoted in Latin by Rose in Zeitschr. deutsch. Alterthum, vol. 18, 1875, pp. 321–455.

[9] J. Ruska, Das Steinbuch des Aristoteles. Heidelberg, 1912, p. 151.

[10] Rose, ibid., p. 391.

A poem on temperance by the Byzantine Meliteniote was published in 1858 by Emmanuel Miller from the sole manuscript in the Bibliothèque nationale, Paris. It contains a lengthy enumeration of precious stones, and certain extracts are quoted by Mely,[1] including a reference to the *callaida* and *callaina*, which are mentioned in connection with Cappadocia.

The earliest Arabic author to refer to the Persian turquois was Ibn Haukal (978 A. D.), who, following Iṣṭakhri (951), reported:

> The villages and towns in the plain around Nishapur are numerous and well populated. In the mountains of Nishapur and Tus are mines, in which are found brass, iron, turquoises * * *[2]

He was succeeded by the traveler al-Beruni (973–1048) and al-Ta'alibi (961–1038), both of whom mentioned the turquois mines at Nishapur.[3]

A Persian manuscript entitled "Nozhat Namah Ellaiy," written in the eleventh century by Sehem Ad'din, transcribed in 1304, and in the possession of Ouseley[4] in 1811, is accredited with the statement that the Piruzeh (Persian for turquois) is a stone without brilliance, but one regarded as auspicious and lucky on account of its name, which signifies victorious or fortunate.

Arnoldus Saxo,[5] in "De virtutibus lapidum" (Properties of stones), a Latin work written near the beginning of the thirteenth century, remarks:

> The turquois (turcois) is a stone of a yellow color, verging on white. It is so called from the regions of Turkey, whence it originates; it has the quality of preserving the eyesight from external injuries when superimposed on the eyes, and it induces hilarity.

This passage serves to explain the origin of the word *turcois*, the French form of which is *turquoise*, and forms the earliest instance known to the writer of its use.

Albertus Magnus, who lived between 1193 and 1280 and wrote a treatise on minerals, "De Mineralibus," referred to the turquois in these terms:

> This stone is of a golden yellow color, glistening and glowing as if milk had entered the golden yellow color and leaped back to the upper surface. It is neither clear nor of a loose texture. Moreover, they say it preserves sight and protects those wearing it from harmful accidents."[6]

The famous Arabic botanist Ibn-el-Beithar, born about 1197 in Malaga, Spain, and who died at Damas in 1248, has left a treatise on Remedies, in which 2324 articles, dealing with medicaments, are arranged in alphabetical order. This extensive work which has secured for him a well-deserved reputation in the Orient and in the West is based on original research carried on during many years of travels in Egypt, Arabia, Syria, and Mesopotamia, but carefully embodies also the notes of his predecessors, Greeks and Arabs; quotations from Dioscorides and Galenus occupy almost half of his book. The entire work has been admirably translated into French by L. Leclerc.[7] Under No. 1713, Ibn-el-Beithar gives the following notes on turquois:

FIROUZEDY, TURQUOIS.

The Book of Stones.—It is a green stone mixed with blue, very pleasant to look at. It shines when the air is pure, and gets pale when the air is dim. It is soft and a bit fragile; it does not enter the adornment of sovereigns. Its substance is little dense.

Ibn Massa.—It is cold and dry. It comes from Neisabur, where it is found in the mines in the state of fragments from a drachme to five stateves. It is employed in alchemy. It enters into the remedies of the eye. Triturated and administered as a potion, it is useful against the sting of scorpions.

Dioscorides, Book V.—It is a species of stone the employment of which is considered advantageous against the stings of scorpions. It is given also for intestinal ulcerations.[8]

Galenos, IX.—It comes from a mine situated in a mountain of Neisabur, whence it is exported into all countries. There is one species found elsewhere; but that of Neisabur is preferable. Two species are distinguished, the one called *sakhamy*, and the other *fidjidjy*.[9] The most precious is that which is ancient and of the variety called *sakhamy*;

---

[1] Les lapidaires de l'antiquité et du moyen age. Vol. 2: Les lapidaires grecs. Paris, 1898. See p. 207 (lines 1155–1165).

[2] A. V. W. Jackson, From Constantinople to the home of Omar Khayyam. New York, 1911, p. 254.

[3] See Laufer, op. cit., pp. 40–41.

[4] Travels in various countries of the East; more particularly Persia. London, 1819, vol. 1, pp. 210–212.

[5] See Rose, Zeitschr. für deutsch. Alterthum, Berlin, vol. 18, 1875, p. 446.

[6] Translated by Mrs. F. B. Laney from an anonymous Latin work, published at Vienna (no date), entitled "Lapidarium Omni Voluptate Refertum" (a famous work about stones and filled with every delight).

[7] Traité des simples par Ibn-el-Beïthar *in* Notices et Extraits des Manuscrits de la Bibliothèque nationale, Paris, vol. 23, 25, 26, 1877–1883.

[8] See p. 10. This description was given by Dioscorides of Σάπφειρος.

[9] Another Arabic author, Tememy, speaks also of two kinds from Neisabur which he designated as male and female.

but the best is that which is of an entire purity of color, of a perfect polish, and of a wholly uniform hue. It is especially employed as a set stone (in French: *chaton*).

El-Kindy reports that he has seen a specimen of the weight of one ocque and a half. It takes a finer polish than the lapis-lazuli, and has more splendor. In contact with an oily substance it alters and changes color. Perspiration, too, alters it and completely deprives it of its color. The contact of musk acts similarly, and deprives it of its whole price. Aristotle is of opinion that a stone thus changing color is worth nothing for its wearer.[1]

Marco Polo,[2] in his remarkable journey across Asia in the latter half of the thirteenth century noted the production of turquoises in the Province of Kerman in Persia and Caindu (present Sze-ch'uan) in China.

Ahmed Teifascite, a well-known Arabian authority on precious stones, born about 1253, treats at length the turquois, as follows:[3]

THE TURQUOIS.

The turquois is a stone of the same nature and quality as copper and is produced from the vapors of that metal, which are exhaled from copper mines, as we say—may it please God—in speaking of the formation of other stones of the same kind.

Regarding its good and bad qualities and its mining—I refer to the places in which the mines of the turquois are found—it may be stated that this stone is extracted from the mountains of Nissabur, whence they are transported to all countries of the world. There is, however, a kind of stone to be found in Nescinar, but the one from Nissabur is better.

As to its good and bad qualities, there are two species of the turquois, of which one is called *buscechica*, and the other *lahahica*. But the perfect and marvelous stone in every respect is the *buscechica*, and its most beautiful specimens have a resplendent and clear sky-blue color and are, in addition, very limpid, smooth and endowed with a very even color. Although this gem is not found otherwise than in small pieces adapted for wearing on rings, nevertheless El-Kendite relates that he has seen a stone that weighed an ounce and a half.

REGARDING ITS PROPERTIES AND USES.

In the first place, the turquois possesses the quality of becoming clarified or bright in time of serene and clear weather, and vice versa, becomes dull and obscure when the weather is dark and cloudy. Referring to this we take pleasure in relating that Aristotle has said that all stones which naturally change their colors and aspect are a base ornament to those who wear them. The turquois, moreover, possesses the quality of becoming affected by fatty substances, which obscure it and make it change its color. The same effect is produced by perspiration, which disfigures it entirely, according to an experiment made by myself. Likewise musk also, when it comes into contact with the stone, spoils it and takes away all its beauty. Coming now to the particulars of its usefulness, the stone brightens and refreshes the vision when it is looked at fixedly, and it is similarly beneficial to the eyes when it is used together with eye salves. As to its special qualities I deem it well to quote here a verbatim translation from the end of Alexander's letter regarding the proper government of a kingdom. "The turquois," says Aristotle.[4] "is a stone with which the Kings of Damascus never omitted to adorn their necks and hands and to employ for many other purposes because, among the great, the stone possesses the property of removing from its wearer the danger of being killed, and is therefore never to be seen on the hands of or worn by a person killed. Furthermore, when reduced to powder it is of assistance in case of stings of scorpions and dangerous and venomous reptiles."

REGARDING ITS PRICE OR VALUE.

The turquois, as we have indicated above, is generally found in small pieces, worn or set in rings, and as such stones vary not a little as to their beauty or lack of it, one may perhaps be worth only a farthing (*denarium*), and then another a whole *drachm*, although both may be of the same weight. This difference in price is owing to what we have already stated regarding the good and bad qualities of the stone. The turquois is very much desired and sought after by the Mograbinian princes, and the latter heightened its price to such an extent that they sometimes paid 10 *denarii* of their own country for a small stone adapted for wearing in a ring. The use which they make of it was to place it and wear it on the hilt (handle) of their arms, as well as on the rings with which they adorn their fingers. Vulgar persons believe and maintain that turquois is still used in alchemistic processes, but this is entirely without foundation in fact.

Muhammed Ibn Mansur, in an Arabian work on mineralogy, written about 1300, gives an extensive and detailed account of the turquois,[5] which must rank as the first really scientific description accorded it. Considering the time this was written and the nature of contemporary writings in Europe, it forms a striking example of the superiority of the science of the

---

[1] The reference and translation were furnished the writer by Berthold Laufer.

[2] The travels of Marco Polo. Trans. by Henry Yule. London, 1903, vol. 1, p. 90; vol. 2, p. 53.

[3] Translated for the writer by S. M. Gronberger from an Italian version entitled: "Fior di Pensieri sulle Pietre Preziose di Ahmed Teifascite." Bologna, 1906, pp. 70–73.

[4] See pp. 9 and 10 of this treatise.

[5] Quoted by Schindler, Jahrb. k. k. geol. Reichs., vol. 36, 1886, pp. 303–314.

near-by Orient to that of Europe, asleep in the night of the Dark Ages.[1] Europe must wait several hundred years before producing a description so complete. Ibn Mansur enumerates the sources of the turquois, its different grades, and its imitations, and gives an account of the Nishapur deposits and of famous stones, ending with a description of the value and supposed virtues of this mineral.[2]

An interesting Chinese work, "Cho keng lu,"[3] first published in 1366, contains a brief account of the Mohammedan precious stones that were traded into China. These include three kinds of *tien-tse*, obtained respectively from Nishapur, Kerman, and Siang-yang (a city and prefecture of Hu-pei Province, China). This statement probably represents "the oldest Chinese reference to a turquois-producing locality in China proper * * * and the first authentic use of a word for turquois in the Chinese language."[4]

An Arabian manuscript entitled *Nozhat al Colub*, by Hamdallah Cazwini, written between 1300 and 1400, deals in part 1, in a chapter on minerals and jewels, with the firuzdje (turquois). It is here stated[5] that this precious stone was chiefly worn by women, and considered inferior to the *zumrud* (emerald). Toward the middle of the fourteenth century Sir John Mandeville[6] wrote of the turquois, referring to two kinds, the one consisting of bone and the other coming from the Orient and possessing wonderful properties.

In the fifteenth century the turquois finds its earliest description of moment in Hindu literature, its supposed properties being briefly noted in a small treaties written at one of the native courts by Narahari,[7] a physician from Kashmir.

In 1502 in Italy, Camillus Leonardus wrote a work, later translated into English under the title "The mirror of stones," in which (pp. 235–6) the turquois is briefly characterized as follows:

Turchion, or *Turchesia*, the *Turcois*, is a yellow Stone bordering upon white, and if passed thro' Milk, is of a yellow Colour, is very agreeable to the Sight, and took its Name from the Country. There is a vulgar Opinion, that it is useful to Horsemen, and that so long as the Rider has it with him, his Horse will never tire him, and will preserve him unhurt from any Accident. It strengthens the Sight with its Aspect. It is said to defend him that carries it from outward and evil Casualties.

Georgius Agricola, an early German mineralogist, in "De natura fossilium,"[8] written during the first half of the sixteenth century, described the *callais* of Pliny, giving all the latter said of it.[9] Farther on[10] appears the following, which is of interest in this connection:

Thus far about transparent stones. Now I shall speak of the stones which have such a great variety of color that different kinds of gems seem grouped under one name. Among these is the jasper, which is green and copies the color of smaragdus. The Norican variety, of a rich blue, occurs in Thrace and a like stone of rich gray in India. There is a variety, green and suffused with milk, which the country of the Lygians produces in great abundance near the town of Striga. The Cyprian variety is a pale green like Callais—which Dioscorides writes terebinthizusa, and Pliny called by an inappropriate name. A variety as blue as a calm sky or like an early autumn sky is found in Cappadocia, near the river Thermodos. It is a deep blue suffused with milk. Some of the ancients call it for this reason ἀείζασαν and others boreas, but moderns call it Turcica. Such are the Caspian and Persian stones. The former are found around the Caspian Sea and especially near Lake Neusin and also near the Iberians and Hircanians. The latter are mined from the mountains surrounding the city of Crerma. They are found also in Scythia, beyond the Imans in the region which they call Cuniclum. However, that from Striga is very seldom like this. There is a purple variety as if dyed with flowers which comes from the very deepest mines of Mount Ida, and a purple-blue kind found in Cappadocia.[11]

---

[1] "Muhammed Ibn Mansur," says King (The natural history of precious stones. London, 1865, p. 8), "may justly claim the honour of being the first to compose a really scientific and systematic treatise on the subject. * * * The knowledge of the character of minerals displayed throughout this treatise is absolutely miraculous, considering the age that produced it. He actually anticipates by many centuries the founders of the modern science in Europe, Haüy, Mohs, etc., in several points, such as in defining the different species of the Corundum, and in basing the distinctions upon the specific gravity and the hardness of the several kinds. * * * What gives the treatise a special interest is the evident fact that the author drew from the fountain head of that science, whence the early Greek mineralogists had obtained, though imperfectly, their information."

[2] A translation of Ibn Mansur's description is given on pp. 71–72. Muhammed Ibn Mansur was followed by al-Akfani (died 1347–48), who likewise deals with the turquois in his treatise on precious stones (Ed. by Cheikho, Al-Machriq, vol. 11, 1908, pp. 751–765. Through Laufer, op. cit., p. 41.)

[3] See Laufer, op. cit., p. 56.

[4] Ibid. p. 57.

[5] According to Ouseley, Travels in various countries of the East. London, 1819, vol. 1, pp. 210–212.

[6] Le Grand Lapidaire. Edited by Is. del Sotto, Vienne, 1862, p. 109.

[7] Trans. from the Sanskrit into German by Garbe, Die indischen Mineralien. Leipzig, 1882, p. 91.

[8] Printed at Basil, 1657.

[9] Book 6, p. 623.

[10] Ibid. pp. 626–627.

[11] Translated for the writer by Mrs. F. B. Laney.

This passage hardly calls for comment, in the light of what has been given in connection with Pliny. However, it should be noted that while Agricola is evidently describing colored varieties of quartz, he expressly states that the "boreas" or "sky-blue jasper" of the Ancients is turquois.

Following the discovery of America in 1492, and particularly the conquest of Mexico in 1519, the turquois found frequent mention in the writings of the Spanish chroniclers, Sahagun, Diaz, Gomara, Torquemada, Coronado, and Niza. Their works also contain numerous references to a green stone, highly prized by the Aztecs and called by them *chalchihuitl*, which is so imperfectly and conflictingly described that its true nature can not be affirmed with certainty, but which appears to include both jade and turquois.[1] During the Spanish occupation of Mexico a number of very fine turquois-incrusted masks and other ornaments were brought to Europe. As early as 1553 a mask, now preserved in Rome, was noted in the *Inventorio della Guardaroba Medicea* and other similar objects, some of which are still extant, were listed in catalogues of 1596, 1643, 1647, and 1677.[2] Twenty-three examples of this interesting art, to be described later (pp. 93–96), are now displayed in several of the leading European museums and are ranked with the choicest treasures of their collections.

According to a communication of Prof. Georg Jacob to Dr. Berthold Laufer,[3] the turquois is described in a Turkish work on mineralogy written in 1511–12 by Jahja Ibn Muhammad al-Gaffari (manuscript in Leipzig, Catalogue of Fleischer, No. 265, p. 508). Five principal kinds are enumerated and described—Nishapuri, Gaznewi, Ilaqi, Kermani, and Kharezmi—and an account is given of the celebrated turquoises in the history of Islam.[4]

In 1547 there appeared in Paris a Latin work on gems by Franciscus Ruëus[5] from which the following citation anent the turquois has been translated:

> The turquois is regarded so highly by almost all people that many think they are not at all in a position suited to their rank until they have acquired a very fine one. There are two varieties, each named from the place of its origin. The less desirable is called Spanish, the other Indian or Eastern. Yet both are alike dense and not at all transparent. The Spanish is of a greenish color, pale and indeed unattractive, and on this account is regarded as least desirable. But the Indian, of grass-green to dark-blue color, with somewhat milky luster, inspires no common delight. It exhibits a color from green to dark-blue slightly tinged with milky shadows. It is rarely found without crack or vein. Yet the most desirable is the one which, freest from flaws, and evenest in composition, most faultness and without imperfection in color, renders its own beauty acceptable.[6]

Garcia ab Horto, in his "Aromatum et simplicium aliquot," published at Antwerp in 1567, points out (p. 199) that Mesue, in "Electuario de Gemmis" confuses turquois with the emerald, because of an error in translation whereby the Arabic word *Peruzegi* (a corruption of *Peruzaa*, turquois) becomes changed to *Feruzegi*, due to a similarity between the letters P and F.

In the year 1608 Boetius de Boot, a native of Antwerp and physician to Emperor Rudolph II, published a very famous work entitled "De Gemmis et Lapidus." The Latin edition in 1644 was translated into French by Andre Toll, with the addition of many notes, and was published at Lyon under the caption of "Le parfaict ioaillier ou histoire des pierreries." In many respects this is a very remarkable treatise. As King[7] remarks: "Whoever desires to peruse a work breathing in every line the spirit of those times, an extraordinary mixture of credulity with the most extensive and various learning and great practical experience, will be amply repaid for his trouble in going through this book, written * * * by the confidant and helper of the imperial alchemist and virtuoso." Each precious stone is treated in great detail, with much space devoted to its supposed mystic and therapeutic properties, which in most instances are combated in a manner far in advance of the period of writing. The section on the turquois will serve to illustrate the temper of the entire work:

---

[1] For consideration of this perplexing question see Chap. VI.
[2] See pp. 93–96.
[3] See Laufer, op. cit., p. 1.
[4] This work is evidently based on that of Muhammed Ibn Mansur, see p. 71.
[5] De Gemmis. Paris, 1547. Caput XVIII, pp. 139–140.
[6] Translated from the Latin for the writer by Mrs. F. B. Laney.
[7] The natural history of precious stones. London, 1865, p. 12.

Chapter 114.

On the turquoise.—Among the opaque precious stones, the finest of all is the turquois, called by the Germans *einturkes*. It is known among all nations by this name, because it is brought from Turkey hither. Many believe that it was formerly placed among the jaspers and it is Pliny's *borea*. The Greeks called it *ἰασσης ἀεριζῶσα*; others, *calaiden*. Mesuë calls it *ferruzegi*, a corruption of the Arabic word *peruzaa*, which means turquois. This precious stone has a color composed of green, of white, and of blue; and, if it is fine, a gray-green color, commonly called air green.

Chapter 115.

Its nature; its natal place; and its fineness.—There are two kinds of turquois; Oriental and Occidental. The Oriental is that whose color is composed more of blue than of green. The Occidental is that which is more green or which whitens uncommonly. The first kind occurs in Persia and the eastern part of India; the second, in Spain, Germany, Bohemia, and Silesia near the town of Strigonum in the vicinity of Isere. In Persia it grows among black rocks, as if it might be their excrement or transudation; and there it occurs in great quantity. Specimens that I have seen rarely surpass the size of a walnut.

It is said that there is in the cabinet of the Duke of Etruria a stone of great size, upon which is engraved the likeness of Julius Cæsar. As for myself, I have never seen a stone larger than a hazelnut. The Oriental stones, moreover, are divided into two kinds. One kind retain perpetually their color, and these are called *of the old rock*. The other kind slowly lose their color and become green; and these are called *of the new rock*.

Chapter 116.

The nature, properties, and virtues of the turquois.—(This chapter embodies a very curious and interesting account of the supernatural properties with which the turquois at that period in particular was so richly endowed. Its translation will be deferred to Chapter VII, for which it is more suitable.)

Chapter 117.

The dignity, value, and use of the turquois.—The turquois possesses such authority that no one thinks his hand well adorned, nor has satisfaction in his luxury, unless he wears a fine one. Yet the women are not accustomed to carry this precious stone, because it is not sold at a great price, inasmuch as it is brought in great abundance from the Orient. Its pleasing color gives its value; yet jewelers consider whether its color is going to fade. Those the size of filberts, of a fine sky-blue shade and not discolored by black veins, bring 200 thalers, or even more. The smaller ones are lower in value, and their breadth establishes their price. Those the size of a large pea bring 6 thalers. Preferable to all others are those which perfectly express the greenish cast of clear gray and show an agreeable greenish-blue color diluted by the color of milk. Those with black veins, or which are too green or too milky, are of no value. The people of Mauritania use the turquois medicinally, calling it *peruzegi* or *perusaa*.

Chapter 118.

Imitations of turquois and means of restoring its color.—The glass makers of Venice perfectly imitate the turquois. I know a certain Frenchman who copied it so perfectly by introducing small veins that it could not be distinguished from the true. He sold it for counterfeit, and with great pride, because it was fine. I think he made it of natural chrysocolla and a petrifactive water, with some other ingredients. In order to renew its lost color, some melt the color of ultramarine in the water of chrysocolla; this being drawn off by distillation, the residue is dried, and in this the turquois is rubbed. Some others place it first in water of chrysocolla, and after it is taken out and wiped, allow it to stand a short time in vinegar, and then plunge it into very cold water, whereupon it becomes more deeply colored. But by these artifices the color is only changed on the surface, and soon the stone becomes more disagreeable and less valuable than formerly. A good test is to wash the stone in oil of vitriol, so that the color which lies beneath shows through.

The people in our country wash and clean the turquois by rubbing it with emery and polishing it with tripoli. If its color within is sky-blue its natural color can be restored, otherwise it can not.

Mylius,[1] in an alchemical treatise published in 1618, says of the turquois:

The turquois is a gem originating in Turkey. There are two species of it: the Spanish and the Indian, but the Indian is the best; while the other, being inferior, is not considered as valuable. Its color is a light or venetian blue, of a greenish luster or as if suffused with a lacteal fluid; both are of a solid composition, but the Spanish is the more obscure and thicker. It has the virtue of soothing the sense of vision and the mind (or *heart*), and of guarding against all external dangers and accidents; it brings happiness and prosperity to its wearer. Suspended in a glass it sounds the hour. When worn by the immodest, it loses all its power and color. [2]

---

[1] Opus medico-chymicum. Tractatus II, Basilicae chymicae, lib. 4, cap. 13 (pp. 360–361). Francofurti, 1618.
[2] Translated for the writer from the Latin by S. M. Gronberger.

25200°—15——2

In 1628 Gui de la Brosse [1] in Paris described odontolite or bone turquois, calling it a "licorne minerale." "The Licorne," says he, "is a stone having the shape of a horn, and the consistence of a stone, which, being exposed to a graduated heat, gives the true turquois." This confusion between copper-stained bone and the mineral turquois, and the belief in the transformation of the one into the other by the aid of heat, were very persistent and striking features in the writings of many ensuing investigators, as noted below.

John Swan, in a very curious work entitled "Speculum Mundi, or a glass representing the face of the world; shewing both that it did begin, and must also end: the manner how, and time when, being largely examined," published at Cambridge in 1635, says of the turquois (p. 296):

Turcois is dark, of a skie colour, and greenish. It helpeth weak eyes and spirits; refresheth the heart; and, if the wearer of it be not well, it changeth colour and looketh pale and dim, but increaseth to his perfectness as the wearer recovereth to his health.

> The sympathizing Turcois true doth tell
> By looking pale, the wearer is not well.

The following year, 1636, there appeared at Lyons the "Mineralogia" of Caesius. In this (p. 601) the turquois is described as follows:

You ask in the fifth place, what is there to be observed about the turquois?

In the first place it is to be noted that this gem is called Turchois by Mylius and Albertus Magnus; Turchois by Rueius; and Turca by Caussinus.

In the second place it should be observed that it is called Torquoise or Turca from the place of its origin, because it originates in Turkey.

In the third place it is to be observed that this gem is so highly prized by nearly everybody that many consider their own luxury somewhat complete only when they have obtained a particularly brilliant stone of this kind.

It should be noted in the fourth place that there are two kinds of turquoises, namely the Spanish, and the Indian or Oriental; of these the Indian is the best, while the other, being more common, is held in less esteem.

In the fifth place it is to be observed that the turquois is of a cerulean blue color or venetian blue, shifting into green as if suffused with milk or some such less transparent substance. Rueius describes the color of this gem in the following words: "The Spanish turquois," he says, "is of so little value that it is looked upon as worthless. The Indian stone, on the other hand, finds uncommon favor, being of a grassy-green or milk-white colour or brightness; it shows a colour verging into blue or green, and one would imagine it to be suffused with something like milk. It is rarely found without a crack or vein, but the most excellent stone is the one which sets off its brilliancy to advantage by exhibiting a most plain, clear, and homogeneous color substance without any blemish." Albertus Magnus makes the following statement about the color of this gem: "The turquois is a stone of a yellow color of a dazzling whitish hue as if milk had penetrated into the yellow color and is reflected from it to the surface." [2]

Thomas Nicols, in his "Arcula Gemmea," printed in London in 1653, gives the following entertaining account of the turquois.[3] Its dependence upon de Boot's previous description is evident.

OF THE TURKY STONE.

The *Turky stone* is a very hard gemm of no transparency, yet full of beauty, as giving the grace of its colour in a skie colour out of a green, in the which may be imagined a little milkish perfusion; Indico will give the perfect colour of it, and the Verdigrease hath a perfect resemblance of it: and a clear skie colour free from all clouds will most excellently discover the beauty of a *Turky stone*. Non-transparent stones, and wholly shadowed gemms admit of no foyls, therefore nothing concerning them must be here expected. The *Turky stone* is throughout of the same beauty, as well internally as externally; it wants no help of tincture to set it off in grace, the constancy of its own beauty without any extraneall help is the support of it, and beareth it up against all defects. It is an excellent gemm of a most simple substance, in every part like itself, most pure in colour, and without spot, and the constancy of its beauty is a sufficient commendation for itself.

OF THE IMITATION OF THE TURKY, AND THE CORRECTION OF ITS COLOUR IF IT VANISH.

The Venetians have a very pretty way by which they will neatly imitate this gemm, and that is with Venice glasse, prepared with a convenient skie-coloured tincture.

If at any time there do appear any kind of vanishing of colour of the *Turky stone*, it may be recovered by rubbing it with oyl of Vitrioll.

---

[1] Sur la nature et l'utilitate des plantes. Paris, 1628, p. 421.

[2] Translated for the writer from the original Latin by S. M. Gronberger. The remainder of this citation, dealing with the mystic properties of the turquois, is given in Chap. VII, p. 120.

[3] Pp. 146–151, ch. 33.

OF ITS NAME.

In Greek βόρεα. It is in Latine called *Turchus, Turchicus, Turchina, Turchesia, Turchoys;* Pliny calleth it *Boreas,* which Martinus Rulandus maketh the sixth kind of *Jasper,* which he saith is ceruleous like unto a serene heaven, and is called *Turcica* in Latine and in Dutch *ein Orientischer Turckise.* It is of the Greeks called *Jaspis Aerizusa;* Mesuë calleth it *Feruzegi.* It hath its name *Turcicus,* either because of its excellent beauty, or because it is brought from the Turks, saith Baccius.

THE KINDS OF IT.

There are saith Baccius two kinds of it, an Orientall one, which is of tendency to a skie colour rather than to a green; and a Spanish one, of an obscure green colour, with an ingratefull aspect and seldome without a chink or vein.

Rulandus maketh this stone, the sixth kind of *Jasper* of a skie colour, which Pliny reckoneth as the third kind of Jasper and calleth it *aerizusa;* but in Greek it is called βόρεα, because it hath a clear representation of the serene morning of an Autumnall heaven. Dioscorides even as Pliny, reckoneth *aerizusa,* as a third kind of *Jasper.*

THE PLACE.

The Orientall ones are brought from Persia and from the Indies into Turky, and into these parts; these are seldome bigger than a filberd and very rarely seen so big as a walnut. It is reported of the Duke of Hetruria that he had one of this bignesse, on which was engraven the image of C. Julius Ceasar, which he kept in his repository as a gemm of very high esteem.

Boetius saith that he never saw one of these gemms bigger than a filberd.

I was once master of one of the best Orientall ones of a very pleasing delightfull beauty, about the bignesse for breadth of the nail of a mans little finger, and for thicknesse of the small kernell of a filberd, in which was engraven a Lion Rampant with the year of its engraving, and so excellently as that no whit of the beauty of the gemm was in the least kind empaired by it.

Some of the Orientall ones are said to keep their colour perpetually, and those are called *Turkies* of the old rock, and some of these gemms are said by degrees to loose their colour and to grow greenish, and these are called *Turkies* of the new rock.

There are also Occidentall ones, or Western *Turchoys* which are more greenish than ordinary, or else whitish more than is meet, and these are found in Spain, Germany, Bohemia, and Siberia.[1]

OF ITS DIGNITY AND VALUE.

The excellency of the colour of this stone doth set its price, and the breadth of it doth much enlarge the price.

It is of great esteem with Princes and much pleasure they take in its beauty; and it being set in gold they wear it on their fingers.

The Mauritanians use this stone in physick and call it *Peruzegi,* or *Perozaa.* Mesues useth it *in electuario de gemmis,* as Garcias *ab horto* hath observed.

Those *Turchoys* that are of the bignesse of a filberd, and have an excellent colour like unto a serene skie, and not at all obscured with any black veins, are sold for two hundred crowns apiece and more. The breadth of the body of this stone doth appoint the price. That which is of the exact colour of verdegrease, or like unto a serene skie, without any black veins, is excellent.

Adam Olearius, who traveled in Persia in 1637, reported in his "Voyages and Travels of the Ambassadors,"[2] that while at Cazvin he purchased turquoises the size of peas for half-a-crown each. He further mentioned Nichapur and Firuzkuh as yielding these stones in abundance. "In the country around Mesched," he says, "there is a mountain, where are found such excellent turquezes, that the king permits them not to be sold to any but himself."

Robert Boyle, in an old Latin work, "Exercitatio de Origine et Viribus Gemmarum," published at London in 1673, very briefly alluded to the turquois.

Jean Baptiste Tavernier, the celebrated traveling jeweler, made several trips into the East during the seventeenth century. In the account of his journeys[3] he gives a brief description of the Nishapur mines, noting as did his predecessors that the best stones (of the *old rock*) were guarded for the sole use of the King, whereas all the world was permitted to buy the product of the *new rock,* which was of inferior and less permanent color.[4]

In 1697 Boccone[5] observed that the turquoises of the new rock are artificial stones chemically prepared.

During the seventeenth century there appeared, probably at one of the native courts in India, a compilation on precious stones entitled the "Juaher Namah," or "Book of jewels," in

---

[1] The section following on the supposed properties of the turquois is given in Chap. VII, p. 121.
[2] Trans. by John Davies. London, 1669, p. 148.
[3] Travels in India. Trans. by V. Ball, London, 1889, vol. 2, pp. 103-104.
[4] See also Tavernier, Voyages en Turquie, en Perse, et aux Indes. Amsterdam, 1678, pt. 1, p. 421: pt. 2, p. 374.
[5] Intorno le Turchine o Turquoises della nova rocca. Museo di Fisica, 1697, p. 278.

which were recounted the principal localities for turquois in eastern Asia and the prevailing notions regarding its virtues.[1] The best kind of turquois produced at Nishapur, it was pointed out, was worthy of imperial ownership, because of the wonderful results it could accomplish.

In 1715 Reaumur[2] demonstrated that the "turquois" found in France is nothing more than the copper-stained bones and teeth of certain animals and stated that the osseous portion of teeth could be converted into turquois by the action of fire. His views appear to have attracted considerable attention. In 1719 the members of the Academy of Science of Bordeaux experimented with numerous bones recently found in the Parish of Haux, with a view to determining under what conditions a bone could be changed into turquois.[3] According to Buffon,[4] who reported the proceedings, "a number of these were heated without taking on a blue color. The investigators went further and experimented with a number of recent bones, which only blackened, with the possible exception of a few small fragments that assumed a blue color. From this they concluded that a bone, to become turquois, must remain for a very long period in the earth, and that the same matter that causes the black in recent bones, produces the blue in those which have been buried for a long time, whereby they have gradually acquired a certain maturity."

At the beginning of the eighteenth century, to recapitulate, the turquois was considered to be of two kinds, oriental and occidental; although the true difference, namely, that the one kind was a mineral while the other was a copper-colored fossil bone, was not yet clearly recognized by all. When Reaumur showed that the "turquois" familiar to him was not a mineral, others were led to believe that all turquois was of organic origin; and it was a hundred years before this erroneous idea was fully banished from the then dawning science of mineralogy. Moreover, there arose confusion in the use and meaning of the terms *oriental* and *occidental*, and *old rock* and *new rock*. De Boot, as has been noted, first used all four terms, but with clear distinctions: *Oriental* turquois referred to the real mineral; *Occidental* turquois was the blue fossil bone found in Europe (although its nature was not then known); *turquois of the old rock* included the best quality oriental stones, of permanent color; *turquois of the new rock* embraced the inferior grades, which soon lost their color. These distinctions held for a considerable period, but subsequently the terms *old rock* and *new rock* came to be practically synonymous with *oriental* and *occidental*. Finally the terms were used only as designations of quality, irrespective of the nature or origin of the stones.

Carreri, in an account of a trip around the world, published at Paris in 1719,[5] told of the valuable turquoises extracted from the mountains of Pyruskou near Meshed. He specified that two grades were distinguished, those of the old rock being retained for the king, since they have a finer color and are less liable to fade than the stones of the new rock.

In 1730 the Capuchin friar, Francesco Orazio della Penna di Billi in his "Breve Notizia del Regno del Thibet"[6] noted the occurrence of turquois in Tibet.

Chardin,[7] in his Travels in Persia, printed in 1735, mentioned the Persian turquoises. He observed that these gems were mined in Nishapur and in a mountain between Hyrcanie and Parthide, four days' journey from the Caspian Sea, called Phirous-Cou or Mont de Phirous, after an ancient king of Persia during whose reign the deposit was discovered. Chardin noted, moreover, the division of the Persian stones into the old and the new rock, and stated that the trappings of royalty were richly adorned with turquoises.

In the year 1747 Mortimer[8] took up the question of the real nature of turquois. He admitted that some stones sold for turquois are "fossil ivory tinged with copper," but maintained that the turquoises of the old rock of permanent color are "real mineral stones." "This sample now before us," he says, "seems to show this, from both the form and size. Its shape

[1] See Ouseley, Travels in various countries in the East. London, 1819, vol. 1, pp. 210–212.
[2] Mem. de l'Acad. Royale des Sci., 1715, pp. 174–202.
[3] Histoire de l'Academie des Sciences, 1719, pp. 24–25.
[4] Histoire naturelle. Ed. by Sonnini, Paris, 1802, vol. 13, pp. 318–319.
[5] Voyage autour du monde. Paris, 1719, vol. 2, p. 212.
[6] C. R. Markam, Narrative of the mission of George Bogle to Tibet, etc., London, 1876, p. 317. Through Laufer, op. cit., p. 17.
[7] Voyages en Perse et autres lieux de l'Orient. Amsterdam, 1735, vol. 2, p. 70; vol. 3, pp. 30–31.
[8] Philos. Trans., vol. 44, pt. 2, 1747, pp. 429–432.

shows it not to be part of any animal bone; but its botryoid form is to me a demonstration that it is the product of fire, which had once melted this substance; and that when it cool'd, its surface was formed into bubbles and blisters, in the same manner as the *Haematitis botryoides* or bloodstone, whose surface consists of knobs, resembling a bunch of grapes." Furthermore, he found from examination in the chemical way that the mineral turquois was a "very rich ore of copper," and proposed that all stones of the ivory origin should be called *Pseudo-Turchesiae* or bastard turquois.

In 1774 Hill, in a letter appended to his translation of Theophrastus,[1] affirmed that the color of the turquois as well as that of the sapphire is due to particles of copper, and not to the presence of what was supposed to be *native zaffer.*

In 1776 Lommer[2] related that a tooth found near Lissa in Bohemia had been converted into turquois by being exposed to violent fire in the muffle of an assay furnace. He added that, while the turquois is ordinarily considered a precious stone, it is really an artificial product formed by the action of fire upon fossil teeth.

In 1793 Agaphi[3] described briefly the Nishapur turquois mines which he had visited the previous year, and concluded that the Persian stone is really a mineral substance and not organic, as many had supposed. Yet in 1797 Bruckmann[4] held that the turquois described by Agaphi was merely a kind of green copper or malachite, and since all the "turquois" seen by him possessed the structure of bone, was led to believe that there is no such thing as mineral turquois. On the other hand, Meder,[5] in 1799, maintained that the oriental turquois, on account of its occurrence, must be a mineral substance and distinct from bone turquois.

In 1801 Cuvier,[6] the great French naturalist, expressed the opinion that the occidental turquoises, particularly those occurring in France, are the copper-stained teeth of the English and American mammoth, or carnivorous elephant.

In 1802 Buffon,[7] in his Natural History, gave an extended discussion of turquois and bone turquois, drawing a clear distinction between the two. Of the latter he says that they "take on a fine color only by the action of fire * * *. They are, so to speak, artificial stones, while natural turquoises, which have obtained their color within the earth, preserve it always, or at least a very long time, and deserve to be placed in the rank of fine opaque stones." He quotes from many authorities, and gives considerable information on the occurrence and nature of bone turquois, and on the cause of its blue color, which he considers due to a "metallic tincture." In one place[8] he states his belief that iron is the coloring matter in real turquois, although this constituent "is not its base, as of hematite."

John,[9] in 1806, very clearly distinguished between bone turquois and true turquois by making an analysis of the latter, which was thus shown to be clay (alumina) colored by copper oxide. The same year Bouillon Lagrange[10] analyzed a bone turquois, thinking it a real or oriental stone, and concluded that iron was the coloring agent instead of copper, inasmuch as he found none of the latter present. Likewise in 1806 Fischer[11] characterized at some length the two sorts of turquois, and for the mineral proposed three varietal names, based upon differences in color, fracture, weight, and occurrence, as follows: (1) *Johnite;* vitreous or scaly, occurring in siliceous schists; named after J. F. John, who had thus far furnished the best analysis of the turquois; (2) *Agaphite;* conchoidal variety occurring in a porphyry or lava; named in honor of Demetreus Agaphi, who examined the Persian deposits at the risk of his life; (3) *Calaite;* a mammilary or botryoidal variety, whose occurrence had not yet been examined,

---

[1] History of Stones. Trans. by John Hill, London, 1774.
[2] Abhandl. einer Privatgesellsch. Böhmen, vol. 2, 1776, pp. 112–118.
[3] Neue Nordische Beyträge, vol. 5, 1793, pp. 261–265.
[4] Chem. Ann. (Crell), 1797, pp. 300–301.
[5] Ibid., 1799, pp. 185–199.
[6] Journ. de physique, vol. 52, 1801, p. 263.
[7] Histoire naturelle. Ed. by Sonnini, Paris, 1802, vol. 13, pp. 311–325.
[8] P. 321.
[9] Mem. soc. imp. nat., Moscou, vol. 1, 1806, pp. 131–139; also Journ. Chem. und Phys., Berlin, vol. 3, 1809, pp. 93–97.
[10] Ann. de chimie, vol. 59, 1806, pp. 180–195.
[11] Mem. soc. imp. nat., Moscou, vol. 1, 1806, pp. 140–149.

supposed to be the *callais* of the ancients. Fischer [1] later summarized his ideas regarding mineral and bone turquois in a rather comprehensive treatise published in Moscow in 1816.

To illustrate how slowly the mineral nature of turquois was accepted we have only to refer to Mawe's "Treatise on diamonds and precious stones," published in London in 1815, where it is stated that there are two kinds of turquois; the one bone or ivory colored by phosphate of iron, the other "probably a peculiar mineral substance." A further quotation from the same writer will serve to show how the terms oriental and occidental finally came to have the quality significance originally given by de Boot to *old rock* and *new rock*. Thus (p. 153):

> In commerce, however, the two varieties of turquois are, for the most part, confounded together, the distinction of oriental and occidental, in this, as in many other analogous cases, serving only to discriminate the finest from the inferior specimens, without any reference to the real or supposed place of their origin, or the difference in their chemical composition.

From this time on the identity of turquois as a mineral species was fairly well established, although Ouseley,[2] a Persian traveler, stated in 1819 that recent experiments had cast some doubt upon the propriety of ranking the turquois among stones. Succeeding workers, however, soon proved beyond question the true nature of turquois, and while this mineral never commanded equal scientific interest with many well-crystallized species, yet its variable composition and the difficulties attendant upon assigning it a definite formula, have rendered considerable work necessary to fully elucidate its properties.

The foremost workers upon its chemical composition have been Carnot, Church, Clarke, Penfield, and Schaller. Its microscopic character, first studied by Fischer in 1869, has been further examined by Büching, Jannetaz, Diller, and Schaller. Its occurrence and other characters have commanded the services of numerous investigators, and the work of Blake, Bauer, Fraser, Frenzel, Hidden, Johnson, Koksharow, Kunz, Lindgren, Moore and Zepharovich, Peterson, Pohl, Schindler, Silliman, Snow, Sterrett, Zalinski, and Paige has added much to our knowledge of this mineral.

---

[1] Essai sur la turquoise et sur la calaite. Moscou, 1816.
[2] Travels in various countries of the East. London, 1819, vol. 1, pp. 210–222.

CHAPTER II.

THE MINERALOGY OF TURQUOIS.

Out upon her! it was my turquoise:
I had it when I was a bachelor.

Shakespeare: Merchant of Venice.

PHYSICAL PROPERTIES.

Turquois ranges in color from a beautiful sky-blue to an unsightly pale green and presents a wide diversity of intermediate shades. The most approved tint, from our viewpoint, is a pure blue, called in the trade *sky-blue* or *robin's-egg blue*. So unique is the finest color of this material that it becomes difficult to find anything in nature with which to compare it, and hence *turquois-blue* has come to be a standard of comparison itself. Comparatively few stones, however, are entirely free from a green element, and with increasing greenness the value in general lessens. Yet this is not exclusively the case, for certain semicivilized and savage peoples of the past as well as the present have not so keenly discriminated against the green as we ourselves have done.

The large proportion of all turquois mined is utterly worthless, so inferior and unattractive is its color. Upon the rarity of the finest-colored specimens is dependent to large degree the value of this mineral as a gem.

The frontispiece shows a selection of characteristic American specimens. The plate is reproduced from photographs colored by hand [1] from actual specimens. Allowing for loss in reproduction and subsequent fading, the figures produce a fair conception of the range of shades displayed by commercial material. In most stones the color is evenly distributed, but in some the coloring matter is dustlike or forms patches of indefinite outline. In others, like the example from Millers, Nevada (frontispiece, Fig. 2), two shades are present, with distinct though irregular boundaries. In rare cases, as illustrated by some of the Sinai stones, a fine net-work of lighter streaks upon a darker background is visible. The polishing that the turquois undergoes before being worn strengthens the color and color contrasts, a fact to be borne in mind in selecting rough material for cutting and polishing.

The most valuable stones are those of the approved tint that contain no inclusions of foreign matter. Many cut stones, however, both by chance and design, show more or less of the accompanying material, which is usually yellow to reddish limonite, quartz (colorless or iron stained), or vein matter (mainly colored by iron and perhaps other metallic oxides). A specimen containing an appreciable amount of such associated material is called *turquois matrix*.

The turquois owes its color to the presence of copper in its molecule, and it is probable that iron, a variable quantity of which (in unknown state of combination) always enters into its constitution as an impurity, exerts a modifying influence upon its shade. The state of combination of the copper has not been established by experiment, although the ready change of color of the mineral upon heating and even, in frequent instances, upon exposure to weather suggests the presence of an unstable hydrated compound of this metal. The explanation often advanced that the blue tones of turquois are caused by a copper compound and the green shades by an iron compound, the color of a given specimen resulting from the relative preponderance of the copper or iron,[2] can not be regarded as thoroughly established, although it is more plausible than a hypothesis attributing variation in color to variation in state of

---

[1] This work was skilfully executed by Miss Frances Wieser upon photographs made by D. B. Sterrett, both of the U. S. Geological Survey.

[2] On this basis the change from blue to green upon gentle heating (the proportion of copper and iron being thereby not altered) would be explained by the assumption that the copper compound was more readily decomposed than the iron.

23

combination of the copper. The few views that have been put forward on the cause of color in turquois are discordant. Büching [1] in 1878 attributed the color of this mineral to a phosphate of copper, decomposable by heat into brown cupric oxide. Moore [2] concluded, from microscopic examination and chemical analysis, that the color resulted from the presence of a copper salt, either intermixed or in isomorphous replacement, which he thought to be a copper aluminate analogous to the mineral namaqualite. Clarke [3] considered the blue color due to a copper salt, supposed to be a hydrous copper phosphate and present as an impurity, and ascribed the degradations of this color toward green to the admixture of salts of iron. Penfield,[4] however, expressed the opinion that iron phosphate would have little effect upon the color of the stone, since the hydrated ferric-phosphate, strengite, and the hydrated ferric-arsenate, scorodite, are both light-colored minerals.

Much turquois fades to an unsightly grayish color or takes on a greenish cast soon after it is mined. This tendency varies greatly with different localities; the Nishapur stones, for instance, are noted for their permanency of color, while those from Sinai have a bad reputation for fading. In general, however, each locality has furnished stones of permanent color as well as those that soon altered. A stone that holds its color for a reasonable period is very likely to retain it permanently if carefully treated. Sir Richard Burton [5] noted in the stock of a Bedawyn matchlock a bright-blue turquois that had been exposed to the weather for 50 years without loss of color. Some of the Sinai turquoises mined thousands of years ago still retain a good color, and many stones used by the American aborigines show beautiful shades.

The cause of the alteration in color is not clearly understood. The change is probably a chemical one, and has been attributed to the gradual drying out of the water contained (spontaneous dehydration).[6] Various devices are resorted to for improving the color of turquois (see p. 133), and various precautions must be observed to preserve the delicate hue of a fine stone (see p. 133).

Turquois is opaque in the mass, but a very thin slice is translucent to semitranslucent. Its luster is waxlike and dull upon fresh break; a polished surface, however, has a slightly vitreous cast. Its fracture is slightly conchoidal to uneven, and massive varieties show no cleavage.

The mineral occurs in veins and seams, as crusts and concretionary masses partly filling cavities, and in disseminated grains and nodules. It weathers easily when exposed, losing its color, whitening, and finally crumbling to a white powder. Many pieces with a white shell are found to be of good quality and color within.

Turquois is about 6 in the scale of hardness.[7] It is the same as feldspar and is readily scratched by quartz. It scratches window glass and is itself scratched, though with difficulty, by a knife blade of good quality. In comparison with other gem stones it is soft and is readily marred by rough usage. It is rather brittle and somewhat resembles ivory in consistency. Its streak (i. e., powder) is white to pale-green. The specific gravity varies from 2.60 to 2.88, although values below the limit assigned have been noted.[8]

CRYSTALLOGRAPHY.

Turquois is almost exclusively massive, and until 1911 no crystallized examples of this mineral were known. Recently, however, W. T. Schaller [9] of the United States Geological Survey has identified as turquois a bright-blue crystallized mineral from Campbell County, Va.

---

[1] Zeitschr. Kryst., vol. 2, 1878, pp. 163–168.

[2] Zeitschr. Kryst., vol. 10, 1885, p. 250.

[3] Amer. Journ. Sci., vol. 32, 1886, p. 214. U. S. Geol. Surv. Bull. 42, 1887, p. 41.

[4] Amer. Journ. Sci., vol. 10, 1900, p. 347.

[5] The gold mines of Midian and the ruined Midianite cities. London, 1878, p. 302.

[6] Heating and usually exposure to weather causes blue turquois to turn green. Schaller (Amer. Journ. Sci., vol. 33, 1912, p. 38) found that the Virginia crystallized turquois retained its blue color up to 200°; between this temperature and 650° all the water was given off and the mineral became greenish in color. Büching (Zeitschr. Kryst., vol. 2, 1878, p. 167) noted that the heat of molten Canada Balsam is sufficient to develop a green color in some thin sections of turquois.

[7] The hardness of turquois is not absolutely uniform and depends upon its texture, chemical condition (whether silicified, unaltered, or altered), etc. Some vein turquois is slightly above 6 in hardness, but the average cut-stone is perhaps a trifle under 6. Hardness is, of course, a very desirable quality.

[8] 2.39 by Frenzel. 2.426 by Blake.

[9] Amer. Journ. Sci., vol. 33, 1912, pp. 35–40.

The turquois from this locality occurs as minute crystals, rarely exceeding a third of a millimeter in length, either forming small spherical masses of a botryoidal surface or cementing fragments of glassy quartz. The mineral is triclinic and its angles closely approximate those of chalcosiderite (isomorphous with turquois, see p. 27). It shows the following forms: b {010}, a {100}, m {110}, M {1$\bar{1}$0}, k {0$\bar{1}$1}.

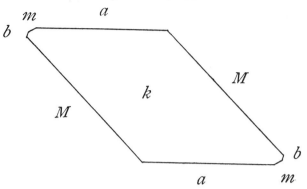

On account of the close agreement in angular values with chalcosiderite, and because the turquois crystals were poorly adapted for very accurate measurements, the crystallographic elements and orientation of chalcosiderite are adopted for turquois. The values [1] for turquois are then:

$$a : b : c = 0.7910 : 1 : 0.6051$$
$$\alpha = 92° 58'; \ \beta = 93° 30'; \ \gamma = 107° 41'$$
$$aM = 44° 50'; \ am = 31° 10'; \ bm = 40° 54'$$
$$mM' = 104° 00'; \ kM' = 105° 36'; \ ka = 95° 45'$$
$$km = 109° 36'; \ kb = 119° 19'.$$

The habit and appearance of the crystals are shown in the accompanying figure.

MICROSCOPIC CHARACTER.

The first to study the microscopic character of turquois was Fischer.[2] Others who have turned the microscope upon this mineral are Büching,[3] Silliman,[4] Moore and Zepharovich,[5] Clarke and Diller,[6] Penfield,[7] Johnson,[8] and Schaller.[9] The turquois is so dense that only a limited amount of information has been obtained in this way, and the various observations are not entirely in accord.

In general a thin slice of turquois when viewed under the microscope appears a dense, confused mass of minute irregular grains, semitransparent, of pale color, and with rather high index of refraction.[10] Upon revolution of the stage between crossed nicols the polarized light is admitted through the thinnest edges, indicating that the material is doubly refracting. In some

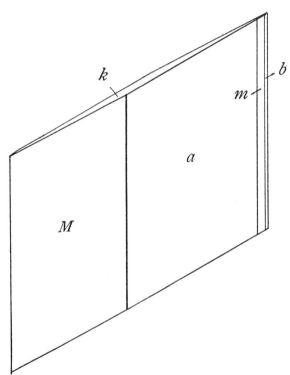

Fig. 1.—Top and side view of crystal of turquois from Campbell County, Va. (After Schaller, 1912.)

instances the turquois has a fibrous texture, and the fibers show slightly inclined extinction.

The crystallized turquois from Virginia, studied by Schaller,[11] is transparent and distinctly pleochroic (colorless to pale-bluish). Extinction is inclined and values of 5°, 12°,

[1] Schaller, ibid.

[2] Kritische microskopisch-mineralogische Studien. Frieburg, 1869, p. 69. Also Archiv. Anthr., vol. 10, 1878, pp. 177–214.

[3] Zeitschr. Kryst., vol. 2, 1878, pp. 163–168. Ibid., vol. 3, 1879, pp. 81–82.

[4] Amer. Journ. Sci., vol. 22, 1881, p. 70.

[5] Zeitschr. Kryst., vol. 10, 1885, pp. 240–251.

[6] Amer. Journ. Sci., vol. 32, 1886, pp. 214–217.

[7] Amer. Journ. Sci., vol. 10, 1900, pp. 346–350.

[8] School of Mines Quart., vol. 25, 1903, pp. 91–97.

[9] Amer. Journ. Sci., vol. 33, 1912, pp. 35–40.

[10] Lacroix (Minéralogie de la France et de ses colonies, 1910, p. 530) gives 1.63 for the mean refractive index of turquois.

[11] Loc. cit.

and 35° were measured upon pieces of uncertain orientation. The refractive indices are: $\alpha = 1.61$; $\gamma = 1.65$. The double refraction is about 0.04.

CHEMICAL COMPOSITION.

The earliest analyses of turquois, made by John [1] and Bouillon Lagrange [2] have only historical interest and have been adverted to under the historical chapter. Excepting these, 21 analyses of turquois have been published, and are shown in the table following:

List of analyses of turquois.

	1	2	3	4	5	6	7	8	9 a	10	11
P_2O_5	30.90	38.9	28.90	13.930	32.86	29.57	34.42	28.14	28.40	33.21	31.96
Al_2O_3	44.50	54.5	47.45	50.755	40.19	29.17	[35.79]	41.09	38.61	35.98	b 39.53
H_2O	19.00	1.0	18.18	18.125	19.34	18.85	18.60	20.96	20.69	19.98	19.80
CuO	3.75	1.5	2.02	1.420	5.27	4.04	7.67	4.54	3.32	7.80	6.30
Fe_2O_3	7.80	2.8	1.10	1.100	....	....	3.52	1.08	....	2.99	....
FeO					2.21	4.35					
CaO			1.85	9.810		1.61			3.95		.13
MgO									.15		
MnO			.50	.600	.36						
SiO_2				4.260		12.57			4.37		1.15
									c .68	c .66	
									d 4.49		
Sum	99.95	98.7	100.00	100.00	100.23	100.16	100.00	....	100.15	99.96	98.87
Sp. gr.	....	....	2.621	....	2.75	....	2.887	....	2.70	2.806	....

	12	13	14	15	16	17	18	19	20	21 e
P_2O_5	32.86	28.63	29.43	30.38	28.29	31.90	27.09	34.18	34.89	34.13
Al_2O_3	36.88	37.88	42.17	44.82	34.32	36.236	32.14	35.03	31.60	36.50
H_2O	19.60	18.49	18.59	11.86	18.24	21.0	15.58	19.38	f 19.33	20.12
CuO	7.51	6.56	5.10	7.40	7.41	7.45	4.92	8.57	8.84	9.00
Fe_2O_3	2.40	4.07	....	....	....	1.264	1.33	1.44	....	.21
FeO			4.50	5.32	.91					
CaO	.38	....	....	Trace.	7.93	1.70	5.23	....		
MgO					Trace.		g .89			
MnO				.22	Trace.					
SiO_2	.16	4.20				.50	8.71	....	1.70	
			h .21		i Trace.			j .93		
					k 2.73					
Sum	99.79	99.83	100.00	100.00	99.85	100.05	95.89	99.53	96.36	99.96
Sp. gr.	2.805					2.67		2.791		2.84

a Average of 2 analyses.
b Includes Fe_2O_3.
c H_2SO_4.
d Organic matter (bitumen).
e Recalculated composition, after deducting 12.57 per cent insoluble matter (quartz).
f 1 per cent at 100°; remainder, over 100°.

g Includes Na_2O and K_2O.
h Clay.
i Fl.
j Insoluble.
k Quartz or clay.

1. Jordansmühl, Silesia. John, Bull. scient. nat., 1827, p. 440, through Rammelsberg, Mineralchemie, 1860, p. 337.
2. Jordansmühl, Silesia. Zellner, Isis, 1834, p. 637, through Rammelsberg, Mineralchemie, 1860, p. 337.
3. Persia, fine blue. Hermann, Journ. für prakt. Chem., vol. 33, 1844, pp. 282–285.
4. Persia, green. Ibid.
5. Nishapur, Persia. Church, Chem. News, vol. 10, 1864, p. 290.
6. Los Cerrillos, N. Mex. Loew, Report Chief of Engineers, 1875, pt. 2, p. 1027.
7. Karkaralinsk District, Kirghise Steppes, Russia, greenish-blue. Nicolajew, published in Koksharow, Materialen zur Mineralogie Russlands, vol. 9, 1881, p. 87.
8. Alexandria, Egypt (probably brought from Sinai), dark-green. Frenzel, Tschermak's Min. u. Petr. Mitth., vol. 5, 1883, p. 184.
9. Wadi Maghara, Sinai, blue-green. Ibid., p. 185.
10. Fresno County, Cal. Pseudomorphous after apatite. Moore and Zepharovich, Zeitschr. für Kryst., vol. 10, 1885, p. 247.
11. Los Cerrillos, N. Mex., bright-blue. Clarke and Diller, Amer. Journ. Sci., vol. 32, 1886, p. 212.
12. Los Cerrillos, N. Mex., pale-blue. Ibid.
13. Los Cerrillos, N. Mex., dark-green. Ibid.
14. Persia, blue-green. Carnot, Comp. rend., vol. 118, 1894, pp. 995–998.
15. Nevada. Ibid.
16. Burro Mountains, N. Mex., blue. Carnot, Bull. soc. franç. min., vol. 18, 1895, p. 120.
17. Bodalla, New South Wales, sky-blue. Curran, Journ. & Proc. Roy. Soc. N. S. W., vol. 30, 1896, pp. 214–285.
18. Burro Mountains, N. Mex. Peterson, Jahresber. physik. Ver., 1898, through Neues Jahrb. für Min., etc., vol. 2, 1900, Ref. 31.
19. Lincoln County, Nev., sky-blue. Penfield, Amer. Journ. Sci., vol. 10, 1900, p. 346.
20. Santa Rosa, Mazapil, Zacatecas, Mexico. Bergeat, Neues Jahrb. für Min., etc., Beilage Band, vol. 28, 1909, p. 499.
21. Near Lynch Station, Campbell County, Va., deep-blue; crystallized. Schaller, Amer. Journ. Sci., vol. 33, 1912, p. 38.

The list of analyses shows a rather wide variation in the percentages of the components. This is due in part, as illustrated by the earlier analyses, to faulty analytical methods, and in

[1] Mem. Soc. Imp. Nat., Moscou, vol. 1, 1806, pp. 131–139.   [2] Ann. de chimie, vol. 59, 1806, pp. 180–186.

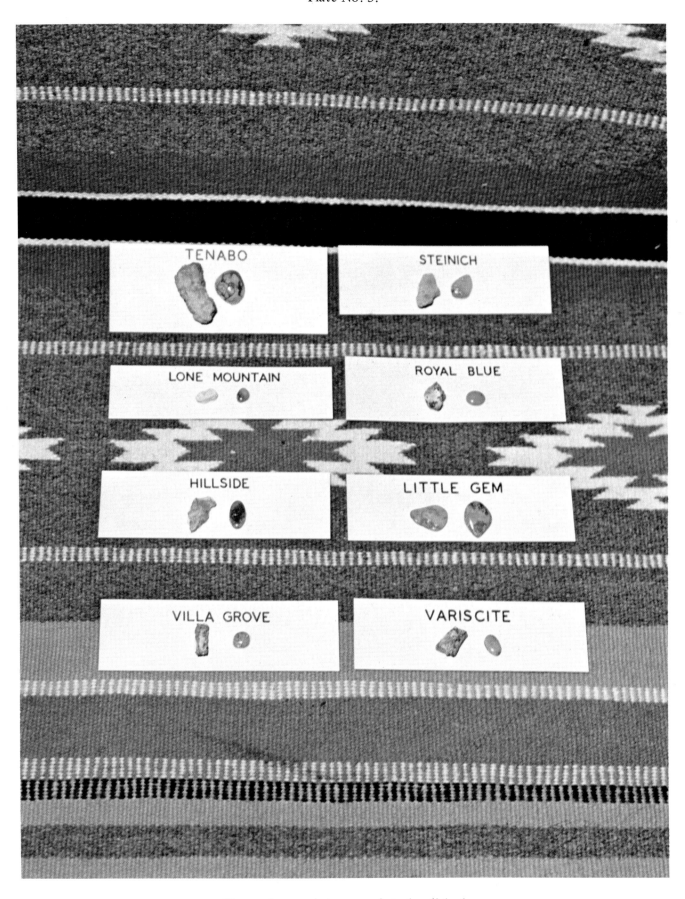

Turquoise specimens rough and polished.

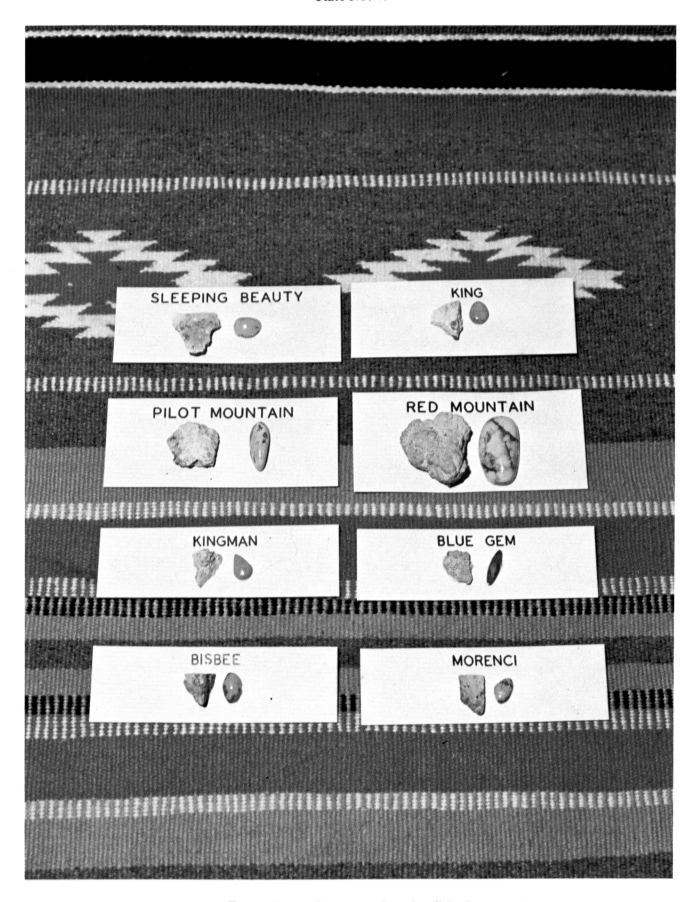

Turquoise specimens rough and polished.

part to the fact that turquois is ordinarily uncrystallized (semicolloidal) and lacks the purity possessed by well-crystallized species. Analyses 11–13 by Clarke, 19 by Penfield, and 21 by Schaller have proved of chief importance in disclosing the constitution of turquois, and the conclusions of these investigators only need be considered.

Clarke concluded from analyses of three specimens from Los Cerrillos, N. Mex. (columns 11, 12, 13), that turquois is a variable mixture of the two salts

$$2Al_2O_3.P_2O_5.5H_2O$$
$$2CuO.P_2O_5.4H_2O$$

of which the first may be regarded as turquois proper (written in rational form, halved, as $Al_2HPO_4(OH)_4$), and the second as an impurity, giving to the mineral its color.

Penfield, on the basis of an analysis of a fragment of exceptional purity and fine blue color from Lincoln County, Nevada (column 19), held that copper and iron were essential constituents and not impurities. Since water was not expelled at low temperatures he considered the hydrogen present as hydroxyl and not as water of crystallization. He interpreted turquois therefore to be a derivative of ortho-phosphoric acid, H_3PO_4, in which the hydrogen atoms are to a large extent replaced by the equivalent radicals $[Al(OH)_2]$, $[Fe(OH)_2]$, and $[Cu(OH)]$, between which there seems to be no fixed ratios, although the $[Al(OH)_2]$ radical always predominates. In accordance with this conception the constitution of turquois is formulated thus:

$$[Al(OH)_2, Fe(OH)_2, Cu(OH), H]_3 PO_4$$

Schaller analyzed crystallized turquois from Campbell County, Va. (column 21), and found that the molecular ratios derived from the percentage composition led to the formula:[1]

$$CuO.3Al_2O_3.2P_2O_5.9H_2O$$

turquois, therefore, being a hydrous phosphate of copper and alumina. On the basis of Penfield's suggestion that the hydrogen is present as hydroxyl instead of water of crystallization this formula may be written $CuOH.6[Al(OH)_2].H_5.(PO)_4$, in which the $Al(OH)_2$, CuOH, and H are present in fixed amounts, namely in the ratio 6:1:5, which is close to the ratio 7:1:6 derived by Penfield from his own analysis.

Additional light was thrown by Schaller upon the composition of turquois and his conclusion strengthened by comparison with the mineral chalcosiderite whose crystals are similar to those of turquois. The formula assigned chalcosiderite is $CuO.3Fe_2O_3.2P_2O_5.8H_2O$. If the amount of water present be taken as 9 molecules, as is probable from the inclusion of certain impurities in the material analyzed tending to lower its water content, the isomorphous character of this mineral with turquois becomes apparent:

Turquois: $CuO.3Al_2O_3.2P_2O_5.9H_2O$ Triclinic.
Chalcosiderite: $CuO.3Fe_2O_3.2P_2O_5.9H_2O$ Triclinic.

The important relation therefore is brought out that chalcosiderite differs from turquois in having ferric iron in the place of alumina.

BLOWPIPE REACTIONS.

The following simple reactions will be found useful in identifying turquois: It is attacked in powdered form by hydrochloric and nitric acids, with resultant destruction of color, but is only partly soluble in these acids. Held in the forceps and heated before the blowpipe it decrepitates, turns brown, and without fusing assumes a somewhat glassy appearance. Heated in a closed tube it decrepitates, gives off water, and leaves a brown or black mass. Heated in a covered crucible it crackles and yields a dark earthy mass, easily crumbling to a powder. In powdered form on a platinum wire it colors the flame green and, if moistened with hydrochloric acid, a distinct blue. Treated as follows it reacts for phosphoric acid: Fuse with sodium carbonate, dissolve in nitric acid and add a few drops of solution to an excess of cold or slightly warm ammonium molybdate solution, when a bright yellow precipitate of ammonium phospho-molybdate will be slowly thrown down.

---

[1] Special emphasis must be laid upon the results obtained by Schaller, because of the crystallized condition of the material analyzed.

CHAPTER III.

THE OCCURRENCE OF TURQUOIS.

Through caves, and palaces of mottled ore,
Gold dome, and crystal wall, and turquoise floor.

Keats: Endymion.

Important productive deposits of turquois are found only in Persia, central Asia (Tibet and China), and the southwestern portion of the United States. The mineral occurs also in Abyssinia, Nubia, Sinai, Turkestan, Bokhara, Afghanistan, Arabia, Australia, France, Germany, Siberia, Peru, Mexico, Alabama, Texas, and Virginia.

AFRICA.

Upon the African continent turquois has been found in limited quantity in Abyssinia and Nubia, and at two points on the Sinai Peninsula [1] are localities of great historical interest, though not now productive except in a small way.

ABYSSINIA.

The Nubian sandstone of Tertiary age, of wide distribution in Egypt and intervening Nubia, outcrops in Abyssinia also and in certain localities carries turquois.[2] At Got, near Angolola, in the southern portion of that country, a reddish, ferruginous phase forms the matrix for stones of good hardness and color;[3] the turquois-bearing bed has considerable horizontal extent and is capped by barren strata and basalt and flanked by porphyry. So far as known to the writer no deposits are or have been regularly worked in Abyssinia, although prior to 1851 Rochet d'Hericourt, a French geologist and explorer, is stated [4] to have brought back from that country a collection of stones closely resembling those found in Sinai and consisting of small globular concretions embedded in sandstone. The occurrence in Abyssinia seems to be similar to that in Sinai.

NUBIA, EGYPTIAN SUDAN.

According to Budge,[5] turquois occurs in Nubia and is sought at the present time to some extent. It is probably found in the Nubian sandstone as in Abyssinia. That this source was known to the ancient Egyptians is revealed from an ancient inscription found at Abydos, which reads, "I worked a mine with young men; I forced the old ones to wash out gold; I brought turquois," and refers to operations in the country of Heh (Nubia).[6]

SINAI PENINSULA.

The oldest mines of turquois in the world are situated on the Sinai Peninsula. These were extensively and systematically worked at various periods by the ancient Egyptians, but for the past 3,000 years have not been an important source of the mineral. They are of special interest in forming the earliest mining operations recorded by history.

Location.—The Sinai Peninsula is a triangular body of barren and almost uninhabited country that connects Africa with Asia and binds Arabia and Egypt closely together. It is of historical interest as the "Wilderness" through which the Children of Israel passed and of geological moment from a position at the intersection of the two greatest linear fractures known

---

[1] The Sinai Peninsula is strictly a part of Asia, but because of its close connection with Egypt it is considered under Africa.
[2] Suess, The face of the earth. Sollas translation, 1904, vol. 1, p. 370.
[3] Rochet d'Hericourt, Bull. soc. géol. France, vol. 3, 1846, pp. 544–545.
[4] Bristow, A glossary of mineralogy, 1861, p. 391.
[5] Personal communication to the writer.
[6] Budge, The Egyptian Sûdân; its history and monuments. London, 1907, vol. 1, p. 538.

on the face of the earth.[1]   Toward the south it is flanked by two chains of hills uniting at right angles and together forming the so-called Gebel et-Tîh.   In a region of sandstone, between the western branch of these hills and the Gulf of Suez, are situated the ancient turquois mines.   The remains of extensive mining operations may still be seen in the Wady [2] Maghareh and at Serabit el Khadem, 10 miles to the northeast.   The deposits are distant six days' journey on camel-back from Suez.[3]

Remains at Wady Maghareh.[4]—The red sandstone walls of the Wady Maghareh rise steeply to a considerable height.   The turquois mines are located on the western slope [5] near the mouth of the Wady Qenaiyeh, and a line of workings 170 feet above the valley bottom extends for 300 yards along the rock face.   Broad low openings, faced by heaps of débris, indicate the entrances to the ancient operations.   Wide tunnels, narrowing inward, penetrate nearly horizontally to a considerable distance, opening here and there into chambers of various sizes.   Sandstone pillars have been left at intervals to support the roof.   At many places the wall-rock contains small discolored turquoises, which may be detached with a knife blade.

Opposite the mines, upon the top of a small tableland at an elevation of 200 feet, may still be seen the ruins of some 125 huts, built to accommodate the ancient miners.   Other more pretentious huts, used doubtless by the overseers and officers of the mining colony, are grouped at the foot of the hill.   A wall, partly remaining, once extended from the plateau across the valley bottom and up the opposite slope almost to the mines.

Monuments and tablets near the mines, and carvings and writings on adjacent smooth sandstone walls bear ample witness of Egyptian occupancy.   They have been fully described by Petrie in his Researches in Sinai, and photographs of most of these early historic records may there be found.[6]

Remains at Serabit el Khadem.—On the elevated plateau at Serabit el Khadem, 10 miles northeast of the Wady Maghareh, are also extensive prehistoric turquois mines.   The region is similar and the occurrence identical with that just described.   The most important group of mines is located in a ridge between the heads of two valleys that open on the east into the Wady Serabit; many other workings, however, are to be found on the sides of adjacent ravines or canyons, but the chief operations were confined within a radius of one-half mile.[7]   The turquois stratum was attacked at eight separate places and much labor was expended in making the extensive system of tunneling now remaining.   One tunnel extends through 220 feet of rock and is connected with a shaft from above.   At one place a chamber 35 feet square, with caved roof, forms a deep pit; at another place the workings extend entirely through a ridge and connect with the plateau top by several shafts.

Many inscriptions are found within the mines and about their entrances, and upright sandstone slabs are located upon the plateau above some of the mines.   Elaborately carved steles, standing in the midst of stone enclosures, are abundant and commemorate the various kings under whom the district was exploited.   The most striking indication of Egyptian activity is an extensive temple, now in ruins, constructed of the local sandstone quarried nearby.   This reached the total length of 230 feet and by its size indicates the importance in which the district was held.[8]   In it may still be seen numerous inscriptions and carvings, many of them commemorating Hathor, the divinity of the Turquois Land.   In addition to numerous memorials inscribed with records of expeditions, a great quantity of tools, fragments of pottery, objects of worship, and so on, have been found.

---

[1] These are marked by the long, narrow basin of the Red Sea and the line of depressions occupied by the Dead Sea, the Jordan Valley, the Gulf of Akobah, and the narrow lakes of eastern Africa. (See Suess, The face of the earth.   Sollas translation, 1904, vol. 1, p. 369.)

[2] Wady means *valley*, but its significance is more nearly conveyed by our adopted word *canyon*.

[3] A map showing the location of the turquois mines and directions for reaching them may be found in Baedeker, Lower Egypt and the Peninsula of Sinai.   London, 1878, pp. 480–483.

[4] Petrie, Researches in Sinai, 1906.

[5] A detailed topographic map, showing the location of the mines, is given by Petrie, loc. cit., page 38.   A good map may also be found in Weill Recueil des inscriptions Egyptiennes du Sinai, vol. 1, 1904, p. 27.

[6] For many photographs, maps, and an earlier discussion of the inscriptions, consult the Ordnance Survey of the Peninsula of Sinai, 1868.   An entertaining account of an exploration of one of the Maghareh tunnels has been published by Lord in Leisure Hour, vol. 19, 1870, pp. 423–426.

[7] Petrie in Researches in Sinai, 1906, p. 54, gives a detailed topographic map showing the location of the mines and the chief historic remains.

[8] Petrie gives a detailed description of the temple, with many photographs.

Ancient history of the Sinai deposits.[1]—Preceding the first Egyptian dynasty, whose date is placed approximately at 5500 B. C.[2] there extended into the unknown past a period of vast duration concerning the extent and events of which very little is known; this is termed the prehistoric period of Egyptian history. There is little question that during this period, and probably well back into it, the Sinai deposits of turquois became known to the Egyptians. This seems amply demonstrated not only by the finding of turquois beads in prehistoric Egyptian graves,[3] but also by the advanced use to which this precious stone was put at the beginning of the first dynasty.[4]

The Monitu, who frequented the Sinai Peninsula from the dawn of history until comparatively recent time, when the Arabs became its inhabitants, at a very early period discovered deposits from which they extracted copper and turquois that later found their way to the Delta of the Nile.[5] The interest of the Pharaohs was aroused by the fame of these riches and expeditions were established in the midst of the mining district. The Monitu struggled against the Egyptians, who had either to pay tribute or to repulse the natives by force of arms. That the latter was the more usual procedure is amply evidenced by inscriptions, which the lapse of 70 centuries has not succeeded in effacing. The country as a whole was called Mafkat, or Country of Turquois; and the Egyptian goddess Hathor, the patroness of the turquois seekers, was termed the Lady of Mafkat, or Mistress of Turquois.

The first deposit exploited was that in the Wady Maghareh. The Egyptians had dispatched an expedition hither as early as the first dynasty, as indicated by a carving on a smooth sandstone face high above the bottom of the valley, in which Semerkhet (5300 B. C.), the seventh king of this dynasty, is represented as smiting a prostrate Bedawyn.[6] Pharaoh's laborers called this region the district of Bebit (country of grottoes), from the numerous tunnels their predecessors had left here; the present name, Wady Maghareh (Valley of Caverns) is merely an Arabic translation of the old Egyptian word.[7] Again during the third dynasty, the Egyptians were present, and Sneferu (4887–4757 B. C.) in particular, the last king of the third dynasty, furnished many records of his mining activity. The most striking is a bas-relief, still to be discerned upon the northwest slope of the Wady Maghareh, representing a Bedawyn sheikh cowering beneath the threatening hand of Pharaoh.[8] This indefatigable ruler opened also the mines at Serabit el Khadem, or, at least, was the first to record his presence there.[9]

During the fourth dynasty (4700–4500 B. C.), Khufu is the only Pharaoh whose presence in the Wady Maghareh is at all assured; but even the sculptures in which he figures have been badly smashed by modern turquois seekers and only one small fragment is sufficiently clear to admit of identification.[10] In the fifth and sixth dynasties (from about 4400–4000 B. C.), however, no less than seven kings dispatched expeditions to the Land of Mafkat, and the work of winning the precious turquoises was prosecuted with vigor and skill.

---

[1] The abundance of inscriptions, carvings, and monuments, as well as the mines and other remains of the ancient workers, have enabled Egyptologists not only to construct the past history of these deposits, but actually in some instances to throw light upon mooted points of Egyptian history. Those who have reaped a rich harvest from this field of inquiry have been Maspero, the well-known Egyptian historian, and W. M. Flinders Petrie, the noted Egyptian archaeologist. The first in his four-volume History of Egypt devotes many pages to the ancient mining operations; while the second in 1906, under the auspices of the Egyptian Exploration Fund, spent four months in the Wady Maghareh and at Serabit el Khadem and made a complete study of both localities, resulting in the publication of his readable and admirably illustrated Researches in Sinai and later of more formal scientific reports. The historical sketch presented here is based chiefly upon these authorities, particularly Petrie.

[2] This date, and those to follow in this section, are those assigned by Petrie. Authorities on Egyptian history differ rather widely in their chronology, particularly that of the ancient dynasties, and Petrie's views have not gone unchallenged by Egyptologists. While, for the convenience of the reader, therefore, the exact dates of Petrie have been freely used, it should be distinctly borne in mind that more conservative estimates place the events about 1,000 years nearer the present era and some authorities believe that in many instances it is quite impossible to allot any precise dates whatsoever. A good discussion of this question may be found in The Book of Kings by A. E. Wallis Budge (London, 1908.)

[3] Petrie, Researches in Sinai, p. 41. See also his Diospolis Parva, Publ. Egypt. Expl. Fund, London, 1901, where he gives an account of finding turquois beads in the cemeteries of Abadiyeh and Hu, indicating that they were in use from S. D. 55-63. The "S. D." refers to a system of "sequence dating," introduced by Petrie to cover the prehistoric age, where absolute dating is impossible, according to which the earliest prehistoric graves are S. D. 30 and shortly before S. D. 80, the first historic dynasty is entered. The possibility must be recognized, however, that the turquois of these early beads was obtained from Persia, along with the lapis-lazuli more abundantly found.

[4] See p. 69 for a description of elaborate golden bracelets inset with turquois found in the tomb of King Zer.

[5] See Maspero, History of Egypt, vol. 2, p. 161.

[6] Petrie, op. cit., p. 41.

[7] Maspero, op. cit., vol. 2, p. 162.

[8] Petrie, op. cit., p. 44, figs. 50, 51.

[9] Ibid., p. 97.

[10] Ibid, pp. 46, 259.

Following the reign of Pepy II (4107–4012 B. C.), the ruler of the sixth dynasty last to leave his impress upon the valley walls of Maghareh, there is no record of what became of the mining colony in Sinai for the next 500 years. Unless entirely abandoned the mines must have remained in comparative idleness, for the seventh, eighth, ninth, and tenth dynasties appear to have entirely neglected them; nor was their active exploitation resumed until the accession of the twelfth dynasty. The deposits in the Wady Maghareh were then much exhausted, but a series of fortunate explorations revealed the presence of untouched deposits at Serabit el Khadem,[1] only 10 miles from the mines that had so richly yielded in the past. Although these new deposits were known as early as Sneferu (about 4800 B. C.) and a carving of Mentuhotep III of the eleventh dynasty, found by Petrie,[2] indicates Egyptian presence about 3500 B. C., they do not appear to have been actively exploited until Amenemhat I (3559–3429 B. C.) ascended the throne of Egypt. This first ruler of the twelfth dynasty again directed attention to this region, and sent new settlers to its lonely valleys. From his time these new veins were worked and absorbed attention for several generations. No less than seven kings of this dynasty left abundant record of their interest in these deposits. Expeditions were dispatched from Egypt every few years, under the command of high functionaries, who were compelled, as the older mines became exhausted, to find new veins to meet the industrial demands. This task was often arduous, and the commissioners took good care to record their successes upon the rocks for the information of posterity. From time to time convoys of cattle and provisions were received from Egypt to augment the meager fare the peninsula afforded. The population increased rapidly and the great temple, dedicated to Hathor, was constructed, to which additions were made during the seventeenth, nineteenth, and twentieth dynasties.[3]

With the accession of Amenemhat III (3341–3303 B. C.) the demand for turquois became so great that the mines of Serabit el Khadem could no longer meet it, and attention was turned anew to those in the Wady Maghareh. In one inscription 734 soldiers are named as present at Maghareh in the beginning of his reign,[4] so that it is seen that these deposits were again actively exploited. Both sets of mines were worked with unabated vigor during the reign of Amenemhat IV (3259–3250 B. C.), and were still producing when the thirteenth dynasty succeeded the twelfth to the Egyptian throne in the year 3200 B. C.[5]

During the thirteenth, fourteenth, fifteenth, sixteenth, and seventeenth dynasties there ensued a long period of neglect, during which no expeditions were sent to Sinai. For 1,600 years no monuments were left at either Serabit or Maghareh to record the presence of Egyptian miners. With the advent of the eighteenth dynasty, however, we again find remains of an offering made at Serabit under Aahmes I (1570 B. C.),[6] and from the accession of Amenhotep I (1562 B. C.) through the entire eighteenth, nineteenth, and twentieth dynasties there are records in great abundance of Egyptian activity at Serabit el Khadem. The temple was considerably enlarged during the reign of Queen Hatshepsut, who was associated with her nephew Tahutmes III (1481–1449 B. C.); and several following rulers made further changes and improvements. Sety I of the nineteenth dynasty ended the growth of the temple, although later kings continued to make alterations. Ramessu VI (1161–1156 B. C.) of the twentieth dynasty was the last to record his presence at Serabit el Khadem; after him, there is no trace of any later constructing, offering, or mining.[7] Only a piece of Roman pottery found in a cave supplies a single point of history until the accounts of modern travelers.[8]

---

[1] Maspero, History of Egypt, vol. 2, p. 333.

[2] Op. cit., p. 96.

[3] Petrie, loc. cit., pp. 72–95.

[4] Ibid, p. 117.

[5] Maspero (op. cit., vol. 2, p. 336) says of this period:

"Tranquillity prevailed in the recesses of the mountains of Sinai as well as in the valley of the Nile, and a small garrison sufficed to keep watch over the Bedouin of the neighborhood. Sometimes the latter ventured to attack the miners, and then fled in haste, carrying off their meager booty; but they were vigorously pursued under the command of one of the officers on the spot, and generally caught and compelled to disgorge their plunder before they had reached the shelter of their *douars*. The old Memphite kings prided themselves on these armed pursuits as though they were real victories, and had them recorded in triumphal bas-reliefs; but under the twelfth dynasty they were treated as unimportant frontier accidents, almost beneath the notice of the Pharaoh, and the glory of them—such as it was—he left to his captains then in command of these districts."

[6] Petrie, op. cit., p. 102.

[7] Ibid, p. 108.

[8] Ibid, p. 108.

At Maghareh are not found so many traces of activity during these later dynasties; but that the mines were reworked at least during the eighteenth dynasty is evidenced by a tunnel inscribed with the name of Tahutmes III [1] (1481–1449 B. C.), who reigned toward the close of that dynasty. This was the latest inscription found by Petrie in the Wady Maghareh; but it is not unlikely that these deposits were exploited in a small way during the next dynasty and possibly also into the twentieth. They were fast becoming exhausted, however, and were doubtless abandoned before the mining colony was withdrawn from Serabit el Khadem.[2]

Ancient organization and methods of working.[3]—The Egyptians were great organizers and the carefully planned mining operations in the Sinai Peninsula give striking insight into their methods of administration. The expeditions were involved, with extreme subdivision of labor; to each member was assigned a definite task.[4] The head was always a high official skilled in organizing. Following the Nile inundation in November and December, the expedition, consisting usually of 400 to 500 men, would set forth for the peninsula, and there remain for several months actively prosecuting the mining. Before the hot weather arrived they would be back again in Egypt, having recorded in the rocks the events and success of their operations. The Egyptians never maintained a permanent garrison. At the most the expeditions were in alternate years, occasionally they were less frequent, and at several periods the mines were entirely abandoned.

The members of the party dwelt in stone huts near the workings, and their supplies were obtained from Egypt. Natives were occasionally employed to aid in the rougher work. The actual mining was done mostly with copper chisels, struck by heavy stone hammers with handles of wood. By this means blocks of matrix were detached, which were crushed in basalt pounders, and the turquois picked out by hand. The oxides of copper and manganese, obtained in limited quantity as by-products, were utilized for making enamel.

Modern history of the Sinai mines.—The ruins at Serabit el Khadem were discovered in 1762 by Niehbur,[5] sent to this region by the King of Denmark to search for inscriptions, and were thought to be the remains of an Egyptian colony. Niehbur did not ascertain the reason for this settlement, and it was a long time before subsequent explorers discovered the adjacent mines. Ruppell visited the ruins in 1817, and rightly attributed their origin to a mining colony. Laborde,[6] however, was the first to discover turquois there. In 1828 his guide found five stones, but set

---

[1] Petrie, op. cit., p. 49.

[2] *Meaning of "mafkat."*—The Egyptian word *mafkat* occurs repeatedly in the inscriptions about the Sinai mines. It refers to the material there mined, and is translated by most authorities as *turquois*. Some investigators, however, have rendered it *malachite;* and, since this meaning would affect the validity of the historical details given, which are partly based upon petroglyphs containing this word, a brief review of the question is necessary.

The earliest travelers (see for example Lepsius, Reise nach der Halbinsel des Sinai, 1846) to explore the mines of the Wady Maghareh and Serabit el Khadem supposed copper ore to be the substance mined. Indeed, the black outcropping of iron ore at Serabit was long considered a mass of copper slag. The fact, too, that copper was actually mined in Sinai and that at Wady Nasb are large slag heaps (estimated by Petrie at 100,000 tons) from ancient copper smelters has led some observers to believe that the ancient mines of Maghareh and Serabit were copper mines. Petrie's researches, however, have clearly shown that these mines primarily produced turquois, with copper as a secondary product; and recent geological descriptions verify this conclusion.

De Morgan (Recherches sur les origines de l'Egypte, Paris, 1896, p. 217) states that the Egyptians embraced under *mafkat* all stones of a green color, including the emerald, malachite, and turquois, but that the turquois is meant in the Sinai inscriptions. Weill (La Presqu'ile du Sinai, Paris, 1908, pp. 145–146) defines *mafkat* as a "mineral substance, used as green coloring matter and consisting of a mixture of pulverized turquois and different salts of iron and copper" and correlates (Recueil des inscriptions Egyptiennes du Sinai, vol. 1, 1904, pp. 21–25) the *mafkat* mined at Maghareh with turquois. Breasted (Ancient Records of Egypt, Chicago, 1906, vol. 1, pp. 314–323), a well-known American authority, published in 1906 a 5-volume work filled with translations of the principal records upon which Egyptian history is based. On pp. 314–323 of vol. 1 the author gives the Wady Maghareh inscriptions. The turquois is not mentioned, but malachite is repeatedly referred to and Hathor is characterized as "mistress of the malachite country." Breasted evidently considers *mafkat* to mean *malachite.* Maspero (op. cit.), Brugsch (Wanderung nach den Türkis-Minen und der Sinai-Halbinsel, Leipzig, 1866, p. 80. Geschichte Aegyptens unter den Pharaonen, 1875. A History of Egypt under the Pharaohs, London, 1881), and Petrie (loc. cit.) have rendered *mafkat* by *turquois.* Petrie (Researches in Sinai, 1906, p. 41) states "we know that *mafkat* means turquois," and again (private communication to the writer), "the *mafkat* of Egyptians is commonly rendered turquois, and it seems to be usually such, but it may include malachite. At least no independent word for the very common malachite is known. I rendered *mafkat* as *malachite* in the "Tale of the Magicians," issued in my Egyptian Tales, first series, p. 18, because at that time we did not know how common turquois was in early times. Since then I have found much of it, and it is probably the *mafkat.*" A. E. Wallis Budge (private communication to the writer) holds that the *mafkat* of the Sinai inscriptions refers to turquois.

[3] Petrie, Researches in Sinai, 1906, chs. 4 and 8, pp. 46–54, 109–121.

[4] Of the organization of the average party, Petrie (op. cit., p. 110) says: "Of the general officials, brought from regular official work in Egypt we find no less than 25 different grades in Sinai. Of the local officials who were concerned with the management of the special work of mining there are 11 varied titles; of the technical artisans who were employed, there are 8 classes; and of the laborers, who formed the bulk of the party, there are 9 varieties."

[5] Ritter, The Comparative Geography of Palestine and the Sinaitic Peninsula. Gage's translation, N. Y., 1866, vol. 1, pp. 352–354.

[6] Voyage de l'Arabie Petree. Paris, 1830, p. 44. Journey through Arabia Petræa to Mount Sinai. London, 1836, p. 84.

little value upon them. "They are washed out of the rocks so abundantly," said Laborde, "that a person spending a few days here might easily make a large collection."

During modern times nothing is known of the Wady Maghareh mines until 1845,[1] when they were visited by Maj. MacDonald. This singular man, a native of Scotland and a British cavalry officer, conceived the idea that wealth awaited the reopening of these deposits. He returned to England with a collection of turquoises, which were exhibited and obtained a medal at the great exhibition of 1851 in London.[2] In 1854, having perfected plans for a long stay in Sinai, he returned to the Wady Maghareh, where he engaged in systematic search for turquoises. He enlisted the aid of the native Bedawyn, who were furnished with powder and tools and paid a small daily wage for their services, with a bonus for extra-fine specimens. A stone house was built on the plateau opposite the mines, and in this MacDonald dwelt[3] and from its commanding position directed the operations that he fondly hoped would heap riches upon him. The first stones obtained were picked out of the rain-washed gravel, but soon a number of the ancient tunnels were reopened. The earliest consignments of turquoises found a ready sale at a good profit on the English market, and the venture promised well. Many of the stones, however, were soon found to fade and whiten; and then as larger shipments arrived the trade became suspicious of the Sinai stones, and the later packets could only be sold at auction at whatever they would bring.[4] The natives, too, soon discovered that the turquois found a ready sale in Suez and Cairo, and many of the choicest specimens found their way to those marts.

These and other difficulties conspired against MacDonald, who was forced to abandon his venture in 1866, after having spent 12 years in vain expectations of justifying his early hopes. He repaired to Serabit el Khadem for a year, and then retreated to Cairo, and died there in 1870, "a ruined and disappointed man." His life forms a melancholy example of the hope, so characteristic of the prospector, that continues in the face of every obstacle. Yet his interest was not a single one, nor were his efforts without value. In the words of Petrie[5] "He at least set the best example of a mining explorer, for he was always diligent to take paper squeezes of the inscriptions, to search out fresh ones, and to carefully preserve all that he could find. The great collection of squeezes at the British Museum is mainly due to his care."[6]

In 1866 a Frenchman, failing to profit by MacDonald's example, undertook to exploit the Maghareh deposits, but met with no success.[7] Lord, who visited this district in 1870 stated[8] that the Bedawyn worked the turquois in a sporadic fashion, obtaining a good price for the stones in Cairo. Shortly before 1900, J. de Morgan and a party of French engineers explored the ancient deposits at Maghareh[9] and collected material subsequently investigated by Berthelot.[10] Barron[11] visited the region in 1899 and found the deposits at Serabit el Khadem entirely abandoned, but those at Maghareh were being worked in a rude fashion by the natives and nearly every man of the district had spent a certain time there at some period of his life. In 1902 an English company[12] was engaged in mining the turquois and wantonly destroyed an untold

[1] Weill, La Presqu'ile du Sinai. Paris, 1908, p. 315.

[2] Bristow, A glossary of mineralogy. London, 1861, pp. 390–391. It is here stated that these were collected from five or six localities in the "country of Sonalby," 16 days' journey south of Suez. Either this is an error, or, if correct, the collection undoubtedly included stones from Maghareh. The Museum of Practical Geology, London, contains several specimens presented by MacDonald. *

[3] Its remains may still be seen. Petrie gives a photograph of it in his Researches in Sinai, p. 54.

[4] Lord, The Peninsula of Sinai, Leisure Hour, London, vol. 19, 1870, pp. 398–399.

[5] Researches in Sinai, p. 53.

[6] The data concerning MacDonald are derived principally from Petrie's Researches in Sinai, Weill's La Presqu'ile du Sinai and Recueil des Inscriptions Egyptiennes du Sinai, and Lord's Peninsula of Sinai in Leisure Hour, 1870. Tyrwhit (Vacation Tourists, 1862–3, pp. 337, 350), Palmer (The desert of the Exodus, 1871, p. 201), and Brugsch (Wanderung nach den Türkis-Minen und der Sinai-Halbinsel, 1866, p. 68), were entertained on different occasions in MacDonald's desert dwelling and formed interesting impressions of his unusual personality.

[7] Bauerman, Quart. Journ. Geol. Soc., vol. 25, 1869, p. 33.

[8] Op. cit., pp. 358, 360.

[9] Anon., Sci. Amer., vol. 82, 1900, p. 134. This brief article erroneously locates the turquois deposits upon the slopes of Mount Sinai. De Morgan himself published an account of his visit and a description of the district in his Recherches sur les origines de l'Egypte, Paris, 1896, pp. 217–225.

[10] Compt. rend., vol. 123, 1896, pp. 365–374. This French mineralogist identified three minerals in the samples collected; turquois, chrysocolla, and malachite.

[11] The topography and geology of the Peninsula of Sinai (western portion). Survey Dept. Egypt, 1907.

[12] The Egyptian Development Syndicate. See Mineral Industry for 1902, vol. 2, p. 251

wealth of inscriptions, but the enterprise proved unsuccessful and was soon abandoned. Since then the local tribes have resumed undisturbed possession of the deposits.[1]

Geological description of the Wady Maghareh deposits.[2]—The Wady Maghareh lies in reddish sandstone, from which nearby rise mountains of granite. On the valley slopes at the turquois deposits, a thin, ferruginous stratum separates a lower 170-foot bed of purplish Carboniferous sandstone from an overlying 430-foot layer of lighter-colored sandstone, probably to be correlated with the Nubian sandstone. The adjacent hills are capped by a basalt flow of Tertiary age. The turquois occurs near the top of the lower sandstone member just below the ferruginous stratum, and the purplish-brown or more highly ferruginous bands are the most productive. Numerous streaks of an ochreous friable sand thread the turquois bed and form pockets in the rocks, and from this sand and particularly the pockets the best gems are obtained. Thin veins and patches of inferior quality also line the joints, which are numerous. The mineral is very unevenly distributed, and the productive area is confined within narrow limits, owing to a fault on the north and the steep dip of the beds to the west.

The principal workings today are in the Wady Qenaia, but a few are in the Wadys Qena and Sidri. The stones of the best color come from a mine called Yahudia, which has a wide entrance chamber with two branching galleries. The other openings now exploited are called by distinctive names by the Bedawyn. The natives work the beds in a slovenly fashion. The small nodules of turquois are picked out by hand, after the rock is crushed, and the selected pieces rubbed on a coarse grit to ascertain the quality of their interior. From time to time small consignments of stones reach Suez and are there disposed of. Part of the output, however, is bartered with Arab merchants for gunpowder and other necessaries. Barron[3] believes that the deposits might prove fairly profitable under systematic exploitation.[4]

Geological description of the Serabit el Khadem deposits.[5]—The geology of Serabit is similar to that at Maghareh, the beds only being at a higher level. The turquois occupies joints traversing a bed of ferruginous sandstone—probably the Nubian sandstone—and is principally confined to a productive stratum 15 feet below a thin limestone layer capping the formation.

Other localities in Sinai.—Turquoises of good, permanent color are reported to occur outside the Maghareh Valley in the Serbal porphyry, and especially at a locality known as Nusaiph Springs, or Wells of Moses, between Suez and Mount Sinai.[6] The position of the deposits is not precisely known, since the natives carefully conceal traces of their activity;[7] one writer,[8] however, locates the Moses Well locality 5 miles north of Serbal.[9] The absence of turquois in the southeastern portion of the Sinai Peninsula is attested by a member[10] of the Egyptian Geological Survey, who writes: "In crossing the Nubian sandstone country turquois was sought for without success, the only record in Sinai being therefore its occurrence at Gebel Maghareh and Serabit el Khadem, both on the western side."

ASIA.

NISHAPUR, PERSIA.

Location.—The most important turquois deposits in the world are near the small village of Maden (i. e., mine), 36 miles in a northwesterly direction from Nishapur,[11] in the Province

[1] Thomas, Min. and Eng. World, vol. 37, 1912, p. 53.

[2] Barron, op. cit., pp. 209–212, is the chief authority. See also Fraas, Aus dem Orient. Stuttgart, 1867, pp. 9–10. Bauerman. op. cit. Petrie, op. cit. Lord, op. cit. De Launey, Les richesses minerales de l'Afrique. Paris, 1903, pp. 284, 285. Thomas, op. cit., p. 53.

[3] Loc. cit., p. 212.

[4] The South Kensington Museum, London, contains several specimens from Maghareh, one of which shows very good color.

[5] Bauerman, Quart. Journ. Geol. Soc., vol. 25, 1869, pp. 17–38.

[6] Bauer, Edelsteinkunde. Leipzig, 1896, p. 450. Büching (Zeitschr für Kryst., vol. 2, 1878, pp. 163–168), made microscopic examination of specimens from Moses Well.

[7] One traveller (Haughton, Nat. Hist. Rev., London, vol. 6, 1859, p. 33), searched in vain for the turquois locality, finding only a single pale stone in the sandstone 1½ miles from Nasaiph Springs.

[8] Fischer, Archiv. Anthr., vol. 10, 1878, p. 192.

[9] Serbal lies 25 miles southeast of Maghareh.

[10] Hume, The topography and geology of the Peninsula of Sinai (S. E. portion). Survey Dept. Egypt, Cairo, 1906, p. 123.

[11] Nishapur (nish-â-poor) is said to have been destroyed by Alexander the Great. It was founded by Shahpur II (309–379), from whom it derived its name; but was subsequently destroyed by the Arabs and the hordes of Tartary. Formerly a city of importance, it is now but a town of a few thousand inhabitants. The place is of literary importance, for here was born in the latter half of the eleventh century Omar Khayyam, the best known (in the west) of the Persian poets, and nearby is a small tomb in which his remains were interred (Fraser, Journey into Khorassan in the years 1821 and 1822, London, 1825, p. 401). Khorassan is distinguished in having furnished "nearly all that is best in the history and literature of Persia" (Pickering, National Review, vol. 16, 1890, pp. 506–521).

of Khorassan, Persia. The mines, of which there are an immense number actually worked, fallen in, or abandoned, occupy the southern slopes of a range of hills that rise from the broad open valley in which Maden is located. The mining and cutting give occupation to some 1,500 persons, who inhabit the Maden village and several small hamlets in the neighborhood.

The locality is about 225 miles east of the southern end of the Caspian Sea, and its position, close to important caravan routes, which for long were the chief arteries of commerce between the Orient and the Occident, has been of great importance in conditioning the distribution of the product.

History.—It can not be ascertained when the Nishapur deposits first became known. Berthold Laufer [1] goes into the question with care and is skeptical that there exists any substantial evidence for assuming any considerable antiquity for Persian acquaintance with the turquois. There is certainly thus far no conclusive proof that this occurrence was exploited earlier than the tenth century; nevertheless, there are certain considerations that lead one to suspect that the deposits were discovered long before that period. Their location near the center of ancient culture and the conspicuous surface appearance that the material presented must have been important factors in drawing early attention to the locality. Moreover, the ruins of Anau in Turkestan belonging to a culture period of great antiquity have yielded turquois beads, and explorations in tombs of the first to third centuries in the Caucasus have brought to light turquois ornaments in some abundance; and while the source of material in either instance is not definitely known, the comparative nearness of these finds to Nishapur may not be without significance. That the deposits were worked about 2,100 years B. C., is suggested by the name of one of its openings, called Isaac's Mine on account of a tradition that it was discovered by Isaac, the father of Israel.[2]

The Arabic botanist Ibn-el-Beithar [3] (1197–1248) quotes Galenus (second century) as stating that the turquois "comes from a mine situated in a mountain of Neisabur, whence it is exported into all countries." This allusion has not been verified in the extant writings of Galenus, and it may consequently represent a later interpolation; otherwise it would stand as the earliest reference to the Nishapur stones. This locality may have been known to Pliny as a source of *callaina*, but his geographical statements are too vague to warrant a definite conclusion in this regard.

We must come to the tenth century before we are on safe ground, so far as historical evidence is concerned. Arabian writers of this and the eleventh, twelfth, and thirteenth centuries [4] speak of active exploitation at Nishapur, and extensive cave-ins of the workings resulted from earthquakes in the years 1271 and 1273.[5] Muhammed Ibn Mansur,[6] writing about 1300, enumerates seven productive mines at this locality.

De Boot [7] in the sixteenth century noted that turquoises were comparatively cheap in Europe, because of the quantities imported from the East, and the Nishapur deposits therefore must have been actively producing at that period.

Olearius [8] visited Persia in 1637 and mentioned Nishapur as yielding turquoises in abundance. Kemp [9] in 1671 referred to the custom of the Persian Shah, established a few years previously, of reserving the deposits of the *old rock* (those of the best quality [10]) for his own enrichment, whereas anyone was permitted to exploit the inferior or *new rock* diggings at will. This scheme, however, did not always work to its full perfection, for the officers of the Shah frequently deceived His Majesty, selling the finest stones in Europe for their own profit.[11] Taver-

[1] Op. cit. 1913, pp. 38–40.
[2] Upon the authority of Mohammed Ibn Mansur. See Schindler, Jahrb. k. k. geol. Reichs., vol. 36, 1886, pp. 303–314. This tradition assumes greater weight because of a statement made by Schindler (Rec. Geol. Surv., India, vol. 17, 1884, p. 140) to the effect that some of the Maden villages claim that their ancestors were Jews.
[3] See p. 13.
[4] See p. 71.
[5] Khanikoff, Mémoire sur la partie méridionale de l'Asie centrale. Paris, 1862, pp. 326–329.
[6] See Schindler, Jahrb. k. k. geol. Reichs., vol. 36, 1886, pp. 303–314.
[7] See p. 17.
[8] Voyages and travels of the ambassadors, Davies' translation. London, 1669.
[9] The history of jewels. London, 1671, pp. 62–64.
[10] For explanation of the terms *old rock* and *new rock* see p. 20.
[11] Pinkerton, A general collection of the best and most interesting voyages and travels in all parts of the world. London, 1811, vol. 9, pp. 186–187.

nier,[1] the traveling jeweler, in 1676 gave a brief account of the Nishapur deposits, and in 1735 Chardin,[2] the traveler, visited them. In 1791 Agaphi[3], on a long journey from the East Indies to Russia, stopped off at the Nishapur locality and at imminent risk to his life inspected the occurrence and published a description of it in 1793. By means of first-hand information so obtained he was able to affirm, contrary to the views then held by many, that turquois was not of organic origin.

It is believed that in former times and during the prosperous period of the Sefawi dynasty, the mines were worked directly by the State.[4] In the anarchy and turbulence of the eighteenth century they were either neglected or left to the haphazard exploitation of the villagers. With the return of order, control was resumed by the Government, which throughout the nineteenth century farmed out the mines to the highest bidder. This policy resulted in the most careless and reckless working of the mines, each lessee trying only to obtain a maximum production, caring nothing for the condition in which his administration left the workings. Up until 1882 the Government was accustomed to receive about $16,000 annually for the turquois concession.[5] In that year the Shah leased out all the mines for a period of 15 years at a rental of $30,000 per year,[6] and A. Houtum Schindler was sent to direct the mining operations and act as governor of the district. Under his guidance the project neither gained nor lost, but so many difficulties were encountered in the way of interference and ill-advised directions on the part of the company that Schindler left in 1883; and in 1885, the venture having met with ill success, the mines were againd farmed out after the old fashion. Relieved of his duties Schindler turned his attention to describing these deposits and were it not for his labors in this direction very little would now be known concerning them.[7] The London firm of Streeter later thought of working the mines, but estimated that it would require nearly $300,000 to put them in good order, and nothing was done.[8] In 1896 the Reish mine, it is stated, was the only one operated on a large scale.[9] In 1899 the deposits were worked by the head of the merchants of Khorassan, at a yearly rental of $24,000. In 1906 the concession brought $30,170.[10]

Geology.—The geology of the Nishapur occurrence has not been investigated in detail. Schindler,[11] Tietze,[12] Toque,[13] and Bogdanowitsch[14] have furnished the best accounts of it.

The region surrounding the mines consists of nummulitic limestones and sandstones of Tertiary age, resting upon clay slates and inclosing immense beds of gypsum and rock salt. The strata are intruded by porphyritic trachyte and a diabasic rock, and are locally metamorphosed by them. Both the trachyte and the basic intrusive have a brecciated phase, and the trachyte contains needles of apatite, in places visible to the unaided eye. The turquois occurs both in a decomposed phase of the trachyte and in its corresponding breccia. In the trachyte, it forms an extensive system of small veins, from 2 to 6 mm. in thickness; fills small clefts and crevices irregularly distributed through the rock; and here and there replaces a feldspar crystal. In the breccia, it is confined to the spaces between the fragments. In nearly all places it is accompanied by limonite or yellow ocher, which partly or entirely incloses the turquois. The

[1] Travels in India. Trans. by V. Ball, London, 1889 vol. 2, pp. 103–104.

[2] Voyages en Perse et autres lieux d'Orient. Amsterdam, 1735, vol. 3, pp. 30–31.

[3] Neue Nordische Beyträge, vol. 5, 1793, pp. 261–265.

[4] Curzon, Persia and the Persian question. London, 1892, vol. 1, p. 265. The Sefawi dynasty lasted from 1499–1736, ending with the accession of Nadir Shah.

[5] Toque, Ann. des mines, vol. 13, 1888, p. 575. De Launey (La géologie et les richesses minerales de l'Asie, 1911, p. 107) states that in 1878, 14 mines were rented for 77,000 francs.

[6] Schindler, Rec. Geol. Surv. India, vol. 17, 1884, p. 137.

[7] Schindler's chief contributions on the Nishapur deposits are to be found in:
Jahrb. k. k. geol. Reichs., Wien, vol. 31, 1881, pp. 169–190.
Rec. Geol. Surv. India, vol. 17, 1884, pp. 132–142.
Diplomatic and Consular Reports, 1884, pt. II.
Jahrb. k. k. geol. Reichs., Wien, vol. 36, 1886, pp. 303–314.

[8] Bauer, Edelsteinkunde. Leipzig, 1896, p. 448.

[9] Anon., Eng. Min. Journ., vol. 62, 1896, p. 417; from report of British vice-consul at Meshed.

[10] Kennion, Min. Journ., London, 1906, p. 522.

[11] Loc. cit.

[12] Verh. k. k. geol. Reichs., No. 6, 1884, p. 93.

[13] Ann. des mines, vol. 13, 1888, pp. 563–577.

[14] Verh. Russ. Kais. Min. Gesellsch., vol. 23, Protoc. d. Sitz, 364–365. Abstract: Neues Jahrb., vol. 2, 1889, Ref. 18.

neighboring alluvium near the foot of the hills carries roughly-rounded pieces of turquois derived through the processes of weathering from the original veins. Many such pieces have a weathered crust which it is necessary to remove in order to judge the quality of the stone.[1] The highest spot at which turquoises have been found lies 5,800 feet above sea level; the lowest spot, 4,800.

Mines.[2]— The turquois mines are of two kinds: (*a*) The, mines proper, shafts and galleries in the solid rock, and (*b*) the Khaki mines, diggings in the detritus of disintegrated rock washed down toward the plain.

(*a*) The mines proper: The most easterly, and according to all accounts, the oldest mine is the Abdurrezzagi, formerly called the Abu Ishagi and so designated in the old books.[3] It is very extensive and has a vertical depth of 160 feet. Since 1880 very few stones have been obtained therefrom, but its turquoises are more esteemed than those of the other mines. Near by, in the same valley, are the Surkh, Shaperdar, and Aghali mines, now neglected. A little to the west of the Abdurrezzagi Valley, is the "Derreh-i-Safid" or white valley, containing the old Maleki, upper and lower Zaki, and Mirza Ahmedi mines. The first three are immense workings, but now almost entirely filled from cave-ins. The lower Zaki consists of a vertical depression 60 feet deep and about 250 feet in circumference; a recent shaft goes down 60 feet from the bottom of this depression without penetrating the old galleries. Several attempts have been made to clear this mine, but thus far without success. The mouth of the Mirza Ahmedi mine, which was probably once a part of the Zaki mines, lies 8 feet lower than that of the latter, and the opening is 80 feet deep. It still contains stones of good quality, but working in it is very dangerous. The stones of the "white valley" are very good, though of less value than those of the Abdurrezzagi. Many turquoises, usually small but of good color, are found in the rubbish of the old mines.

The next valley to the west is the Derreh-i-Dar-i-Kuh, containing several important mines, including the Kerbelai Kerimi and the Dar-i-Kuh. The opening to the Dar-i-Kuh mine extends to a depth of 150 feet. Its workings are very old and extensive, and some of its galleries extend as far as the Zaki mine. It is largely filled with débris from numerous cave-ins and is dangerous to exploit. Many shafts, now filled, formerly lighted and ventilated the mine. All the mines in the Dar-i-Kuh Valley were worked under Schindler (1882–3) and produced good turquoises.

Farther west is the "Derreh-i-Siyah," or black valley, with the old Ali Mirzai and Reish mines. The Ali Mirzai, especially the lower one of that name, is very dangerous, owing to the softness of its wall rock, which often falls into the mine. The turquoises here obtained are neither of good quality nor of permanent color. A little to the south of the Ali Mirzai mine lies the Khuruj mine, very extensive, but partly filled and abandoned. About 1820 it produced some very good stones. Near the top of the Reish mine a vein of turquois was discovered about 1880 and a new mine opened into it, with the name of Sar-i-Reish (the head of the Reish). Turquoises were obtained of fine color and large size, which preserved their color while damp, but upon drying assumed a dirty-green shade with white and gray spots. A stone of fine color as large as a walnut was found in this mine in 1881 and presented to the Shah of Persia; it had scarcely been in His Majesty's possession two days when it faded and became valueless.

The next valley to the west, called the Derreh-i-Sabz, or green valley, contains the old Ardelani and Sabz mines and the new Anjiri mines. The Ardelani was once a very great mine; more than 12 shafts, now filled, may still be seen; its present entrance is by a large cave; it is 85 feet deep and several parts of it are insufficiently ventilated. The turquoises produced are inferior. The Juaher Namah (book of jewels), written in the seventeenth century, states

---

[1] The weathered turquois after long exposure decomposes to a cream-colored, chalk-like mass, which the natives are said to eat with apparent zest. It is claimed to have medicinal properties. See Journ. Soc. Arts, vol. 45, 1896, p. 38.

[2] The most complete description of the mines is given by Schindler (Rec. Geol. Surv. India, vol. 17, 1884, pp. 134–136) and the following account is taken almost verbatim from his memoir.

[3] Muhammed Ibn Mansur, writing in 1300, states that the choicest turquois is obtained from this mine, which tradition says was discovered by Isaac.

that turquoises of the most inferior quality were produced by the Ardelani.[1] The Sabz mine formerly produced green stones, but is now filled up. The Anjiri mines are recent. Around 1880 they furnished a great quantity of fine-colored turquoises, which found a ready sale, but subsequently faded. Many stones were sent to Europe and kept moist in earthenware pots till sold, but when exposed to the air they lost color and in a year or two became quite white. The output from these mines and from the Sar-i-Reish, occasioned a fall in the price of the turquois in Europe.

The next and westernmost valley contains the Kemeri mine. It is full of water, and several attempts to unwater it have failed. It has some thick veins of turquois, but the stones are not of ring quality.

There are perhaps a hundred more mines, and more than that number of nameless workings; but they are either parts of those enumerated or unimportant.

Work in the various mines is carried on by means of picks and crowbars and gunpowder. The last was not used prior to 1850. Formerly all work was done by picks, with better results; for, whereas the blasting accomplishes more, it also breaks the stones into small pieces. It is evident that the mines were at one time well directed and skilfully exploited. Tunnels were driven in on the slopes of the mountain, following the lead of the turquois, and vertical shafts were cut at intervals for lighting and ventilation. With the advent of the system of farming out the mines, however, the supporting pillars and walls between shafts were carelessly cut away, and the roofs of many of the workings fell in. At the Reish[2] mine the material is brought to the surface in a sheepskin bag, which is raised by means of a wooden wheel turned by the feet of two men lying upon their backs. The fragments are broken by hammers and the larger pieces of turquois selected; the finer material is then sifted and hand picked by boys. The procedure at this one mine serves to illustrate the lack of all appliances for facilitating economic work.

(b) The Khaki mines are diggings in the débris collected at the foot of the mines and in the alluvial soil extending from the base of the mountain a mile or two down to the plain. The finest turquoises are obtained from these mines—in fact, good ring stones are seldom produced by the rock mines. The work is carried on in haphazard fashion, without any system whatever. The earth is brought to the surface, sifted, and searched for turquoises; the last-named work being usually done by children.

Classification.[3]—The turquoises are divided at the mines into three classes: (1) Angushtari, (2) Barkhaneh, and (3) Arabi.

1. All stones of pleasing, permanent color and favorable shape are called *Angushtari*, meaning ring stones, and are sold by the piece. No two stones are alike, and each turquois requires individual consideration of its special properties before appraisal. A stone two-thirds by two-fifths by one-half inch in dimensions, cut "peikani" (conical), was valued at Meshed at $1,500; another of about the same size, shape, and cut was valued at only $400. Turquoises of the size of a pea bring as much as $40. The most valued color is deep sky-blue; the slightest imperfection, or an almost inappreciable tinge of green, decreases the value considerably. A deep indigo-blue, called "talkh," or bitter, also lessens the value. A good stone, in short, must possess an indefinable property called the "zat," which is something like the "water" of a diamond or the luster of a pearl; a fine-colored turquois without the "zat" is not of much worth. The best ring stones are found in the Khaki diggings and in the Abdurrezzagi mine.

2. Stones of intermediate quality are called *Barkhaneh*, and are divided into four grades. They are sold by weight; the first grade brings at the mines $450 per pound, the fourth grade only about $22 to $25 per pound. At Meshed one can buy small cut stones of the third grade for about 75 cents per thousand. Only the first grade and part of the second, are sent to Europe; the others are sold to Persian artisans, chiefly at Meshed, who use them for inlaying

[1] Ibn Mansur (loc. cit. about 1300) mentions that the Andelibi turquoises are the most inferior produced in Persia. The similarity between Ardelani and Andelibi suggests identity.

[2] Anon., Eng. Min. Jour. vol. 62, 1896, p. 417. Kunz, 18 Ann. Rept. U. S. Geol. Surv., 1896–97, pt. 5, pp. 1209–1211.

[3] Schindler, Rec. Geol. Surv. India., vol. 17, 1884, pp. 137–138.

and incrusting jewelry, arms, trappings, etc. European jewelers use many of the best Bark-haneh stones for rings, but the fact that they are not classed at the mines as ring stones shows that they are not of the finest quality.

3. All stones not belonging to the first two kinds are called *Arabi*. The name originated from the ready sale, on one occasion, of a great quantity of inferior stones to the Arabs. Since then any pale-colored, greenish, or spotted turquois is called Arabi. The whitish stones of this kind are termed *shirbumi*, or *shirfam;* the round pieces with white crust, *chaghaleh*. A few of the Arabi stones reach Europe. The large flat pieces and slabs used for amulets, brace-lets, etc., at the mines called *tufal*, are now classed with the Arabi stones, though some are very much esteemed; pieces two by one by one-eighth inches being sometimes valued at $16. Twelve pounds of pale, uncut tufal stones on one occasion brought $300. Stones of a greenish color, called *Gul-i-Kasni* (chicory) are bought principally by Afghans.

Disposition.[1]—About 200 men of the village work in the mines and in the Khaki diggings, and about 30 of the elders of the village buy the turquoises and sell them to merchants at Meshed or commission agents who visit the mines. Work in the mines is difficult, but always yields a sure return. In the diggings the labor is comparatively easy, but the finding of a turquois is a matter of chance. Consequently the good workmen confine their attention to the mines; while the old and infirm, the weak and lazy, and some of the women and children, exploit the Khaki diggings. During the summer months many strangers try their hand at the diggings. The original finder of a turquois does not gain much. The elders make about 20 per cent upon their purchases; and the final selling price, in Europe or in the East, is from two to three times the first purchase price. The miners themselves seldom cut their turquoises, and therefore they rarely can judge the value accurately. The elders, however, often half cut the stones and are enabled to sort them. The ring stones are then set aside for separate sale, and often large profits are realized on fine stones. The annual output of the mines around 1880 was $40,000, valued at the mines; in 1890 the production amounted to $115,000.

The Persian stones reach nearly all parts of the world. They come to Europe chiefly through dealers in Moscow; and in the same way ultimately reach America. Many stones are sold in Constantinople, Bagdad, Teheran, Shiraz, Tiflis, and some go to the Persian Gulf by way of Yezd. An extensive trade is also carried on with India, where the product finds ready disposition. Through the agency of caravans and pilgrims[2] other adjacent parts of the East are supplied. It is difficult for an individual to procure good stones at Meshed or Nisha-pur, or even at Maden. Many travellers have reported the ruthless attempts at cheating on the part of the natives at those places. All the best stones are purchased at once by com-mission agents on the spot and are either exported or sold to Persian grandees.

OTHER PERSIAN SOURCES.

Turquois occurs at several other localities in Persia, but none are important producers and little information is available concerning them.

Tabbas, Province of Khorassan.—Turquois of inferior color was discovered a few years prior to 1881 at Zeberkuh, in the Tabbas district,[3] near the Afghanistan border. The mineral is stated to occur in schists.

Turshiz, Province of Khorassan.—The small district of Turshiz, north of Tabbas, is reported to have turquois deposits, which were leased by the Government in 1889.[4]

Kaleh Zeri, Province of Khorassan.—At Kaleh Zeri, near Basiran, between Birjand and Neh, is an unimportant deposit of turquois.[5]

Taft, District of Yezd.—A locality exploited in times past, lies near Taft, a small town noted for its carpets, 13 miles from Yezd.[6]

[1] Schindler, op. cit., pp. 138–139.
[2] Nishapur is only about 50 miles west of Meshed, where is located the mausoleum of Imam Riza, scarcely equaled in magnificence in all Persia and visited annually by over 100,000 pilgrims, who carry away numbers of turquoises and turquois ornaments.
[3] Schindler, Jahrb. k. k. geol. Reichs., vol. 31, 1881, pp. 169–190. Ibid., vol. 36, 1886, pp. 303–314.
[4] Curzon, Persia and the Persian Question. London, 1892, vol. 1, pp. 203, 264.
[5] Curzon, op. cit., p. 264.
[6] Khanikoff, Mémoire sur la partie méridionale de l'Asie centrale, 1862, pp. 326–329.

Kerman Province.—Turquois occurs in the Kerman Province at several points between the cities of Kerman and Yezd, within a northwest-running chain of volcanic mountains.[1] The workings are very old and are now largely abandoned. The region (called Carmania) was mentioned by Pliny[2] as a source of *callaina* (turquois); Marco Polo,[3] and Muhammed Ibn Mansur[4] refer to its exploitation during the thirteenth century. More recently some of the localities have been worked on a small scale. The stones have a greenish color, are prone to fade, and consequently are little esteemed.[5] The deposits are several in number and are situated as follows: (1) Three miles from Schehr-i-Babek,[6] 7 abandoned shafts;[7] (2) at Karik, northeast of Schehr-i-Babek, 2 shafts unworked since 1860;[8] (3) at Tchemen-i-Mo-Aspan, near God-i-Ahmer, productive around 1870;[9] and (4) near Mashiz on the slopes of the Tscheheltan mountains.[10]

Other localities.—Bogdanowitsch[11] reported in 1889 that turquois had recently been discovered 18 days' journey south of Meshed. The locality is not precisely stated, but it may correspond to the turquois-bearing mountains near Kerman, just described, since these are about 500 miles west of south from Meshed. A mountain in Azerbayan, the northwesternmost Province of Persia, was included by Ahmed[12] in an enumeration of Persian sources.

RUSSIAN TURKESTAN.

Northeastward beyond the confines of Persia turquois occurs in a number of places in Russian Central Asia, but the information in the literature concerning such localities is meager and unreliable.

Old deposits of turquois are known in Ferghana, a western Province of Russian Turkestan; records of their production go back to the tenth century.[13] Ibn Haukal (978 A. D.) specifies the district of Upper Nasiya as a source of this mineral.[14] M. Krasnokutsky, a Russian traveler who has visited the region, states[15] that turquois occurs in the Gros-Alai Mountain, about 62 miles south of Margelan. Williams[16] notes that the Belour Mountains of Turkestan abound in rubies, lazulite, and turquois.

A turquois deposit of some importance is situated on Mount Karamazar, 24 miles northeast of Khojend in the valley of Biriouza-Sai, near the Samarkand-Ferghana boundary. The region is composed of altered feldspathic porphyry, carrying numerous veins of ferruginous quartz and cut by dikes of diabase. The turquois occurs both in the quartz and in a decomposed phase of the porphyry, forming coatings and veinlets up to one-eighth inch in thickness and isolated masses up to 1 inch in diameter. There are numerous signs of ancient exploitation[17] and the deposits merits attention, although it is difficult of access and work would suffer for lack of water and wood.[18]

The Armenian Lapidarium, translated into Russian by K. P. Patkanov (Precious Stones, their Names and Properties according to the Notions of the Armenians, St. Petersburg, 1873, p. 48), cites Khojend (in Samarkand) as a source for turquois.[19] Ritter[20] mentions an occurrence

---

[1] Schindler, op. cit., 1881, p. 177.

[2] See p. 10. This has been questioned by Laufer, op. cit., p. 41, note 6.

[3] Travels, Yule's translation, 1903, vol. 1, p. 90.

[4] Through Schindler, op. cit., 1886, pp. 303–314.

[5] Benjamin, Persia, 1877, p. 408.

[6] Also spelled Shebavek.

[7] Schindler, op. cit., 1881, pp. 169–190. This locality was mentioned also by Ouseley (Travels in various countries of the East, 1819, vol. 1, p. 211) and in Juaher Namah (seventeenth century).

[8] Schindler, ibid.

[9] Schindler, ibid. Sykes (Ten thousand miles in Persia. London, 1902, p. 74), states that near God-i-Ahmer are turquois pits, some of which are close to the Pariz Road and others 20 miles to the north of Shehr-i-Babek. At the time of writing (1902) these were filled with water.

[10] Schindler, op. cit., 1881.

[11] Neues Jahrb., vol. 2, 1889, Ref. 18.

[12] Through Ouseley, Travels in various countries of the East, London, 1819, vol. 1, pp. 210–212.

[13] Ritter, Erdkunde, 1837, vol. 7, p. 746. See also Heyd, Histoire du commerce de Levant au Moyen âge, 1886, vol. 2, p. 653; and Laufer, op. cit., 1913, p. 68.

[14] See Laufer, op. cit., p. 68.

[15] Personal communication.

[16] Chinese respository, vol. 1, p. 173.

[17] The locality is said to have been known to Pliny (see Ahmed, loc. cit.), but this is certainly open to question.

[18] Mouchketoff, Les richesses minerales du Turkestan Russe, 1878, pp. 11–12. Lansdell, Russian Central Asia, 1885, vol. 1, pp. 497–498. See also, Romanowsky, Verh. Russ-Kais. Min. Gesellsch., St. Petersburg, vol. 10, 1876, p. 221.

[19] Laufer, op. cit., p. 36.

[20] Erdkunde, 1837, vol. 7, p. 735.

in the Myoghil Mountain in the Khojend district. In the Memoirs of Baber [1] appears this passage: "To the north of both the town (Khojend) and the river lies a mountain range called Munughul; people say there are turquois and other mines in it." In 1887, according to Bauer,[2] deposits worked at some unknown time in the past were further exploited in the Kara-tube Mountains, 31 miles from Samarkand, where the mineral occurs with limonite in siliceous schists; and in 1880 turquois was discovered near the town of Ibrahim-Olga, 15 miles from Samarkand.

Inferior stones of greenish color have been obtained from a copper mine in the Karkaralinsk district in the Kirghiz Steppes.[3]

The following information, kindly communicated by Dr. Berthold Laufer, is of importance in clearing up the vagueness of our knowledge in regard to the occurrence of turquois in Russian Turkestan:

In "Notes on the Turquois in the East"(p. 26), reference has been made to turquois mines of Ferghana and Samarkand, but the available evidence was of such a nature that I felt obliged to look upon it with some diffidence. I am just in receipt of a "Catalogue of Useful Minerals of Russian Turkistan" (188 p., with a map), compiled in Russian, in the course of three years, by a mining engineer, A. Andreyev (Tashkend, 1912, published by the author), where (on p. 108) the first exact indications of turquois mines in that region are given and simultaneously show that the previous statements made by other authors were all inexact and that my attitude of reserve toward them was fully justified. Mr. Andreyev points out five sites where turquois is quarried: 1, in the mountain Altyn-tau in the volost Tandyn, district of Amu-Darya, Province of Syr-Darya; 2, on the road to Lake Bugadjili near the source of the Ak-sumbe, in the volost Karatav, district of Chimkent, Province of Syr-Darya; 3, in the locality Taz-kazgoi, in the mountains Ak-tau, in the volost Kurgan-tubin, district of Djizak, Province of Samarkand; 4, in the locality Bir'uza-Sai, 15–16 verst northwest from the former post station Murza-Rabat, in the volost Ural, district of Khodjend, Province of Samarkand; 5, south of the place Shur-ab, 5 verst from the ramification of the roads into the valley Shur-ab, almost southward and a bit westward, in the volost L'ail'ak, district of Kokand, Province of Ferghana.

Thus the question of the location of turquois mines in Russian Turkistan seems to me to be settled.

BOKHARA.

In the Russian work on Precious Stones, by M. I. Pyl'ayev (St. Petersburg, 1888, p. 200), the statement is made that turquois of an inferior quality is found in the mountain Nurata in Bokhara.[4] Ibn Haukal [5] refers to celebrated turquois mines in Transoxiana (ancient Bokhara) near the mountains called Jabal-Buttam.

AFGHANISTAN.

A number of early writers [6] refer to the occurrence of turquois at Firuskuh.[7] According to Clement-Mullet,[8] this locality is among the mountains of Ghur, between Herat and Ghuzni, east of the Persian-Afghanistan border. The mine was discovered under King Firous,[9] from whom both the place and the precious stone appear to have derived their name. No information is available concerning its importance.

Turquois is also reported to occur in Badakhshan [10], a territory of Afghan Turkestan on the northwest declivities of the Hindu-Kush, noted for its spinel (balas ruby) mines and extensive deposits of lapis-lazuli. The Persian jewelers formerly recognized a variety of turquois termed *Badakshani*, but it has been maintained by some writers that this was odontolite, while others have held that it represented lapis-lazuli,[11] so that this fact can not be accepted in entire corroboration. Turquois is said also to occur in the region between western Tibet and Badakhshan.[12]

[1] See Laufer, op. cit., p. 68.

[2] Edelsteinkunde. Leipzig, 1896, p. 449.

[3] Kokscharow, Materialen zur Mineralogie Russlands, vol. 9, 1881, p. 85.

[4] This reference was furnished by Berthold Laufer.

[5] De Goeje's Bibl. Geogr. Arab., p. 362, through Laufer, op. cit., 1913, p. 68.

[6] Olearius, Voyages and travels of the ambassadors, 1669. Ahmed, Juaher Namah, 17th century or earlier. Carreri, Voyage autour du monde 1719, vol. 2, p. 212. Chardin, Voyages en Perse et autres lieux de l'Orient, 1735, vol. 3, pp. 30–31. Ouseley, loc cit., 1819.

[7] Also spelled Firuska, Pyrouskou, Phyrous-Cou, Pharis-Koue, Birouzkoue, etc.

[8] Essai sur la minéralogie Arabe. Journ. Asiatique, Paris, vol. 11, 1868, p. 154.

[9] Chardin, ibid.

[10] Heyd, Histoire du commerce du Levant au Moyen-âge, 1886, vol. 2, p. 653.

[11] Clement-Mullet, Journ. Asiatique, Paris, vol. 2, 1868, pp. 150–157. Prinsep, Journ. Asiat. Soc. Bengal, vol. 1, 1832, pp. 361–362. See page 261 of this paper.

[12] Hausmann, Handbuch der Mineralogie, 1847, vol. 2, p. 1091.

ARABIA.

Turquois is reported to occur in Arabia, especially in its western portion, east of the Gulf of Suez, in a region anciently of some importance known as the Land of Midian.[1] According to Streeter [2] three deposits are known; the northernmost is situated at Aynuneh, the southernmost on the coast near Ziba, while the location of the central one (called Jebel Shekayk) is not precisely known except to the Bedawyn. Sir Richard Burton visited the Ziba locality in 1879 [3] and found four pits 65 feet deep, as well as a number of smaller workings, where considerable material had been obtained from a "quartzose rock." The natives pretended ignorance of the occurrence, though stones therefrom were then being sold at Cairo and Suez and the region had been previously visited by Europeans in search of its product.

TIBET.

No geologic information is available concerning the occurrence of turquois in Tibet. The extensive use of turquois in that region, however, points to a local supply,[4] and scattered through the native literature are references designating Tibetan localities where this mineral has been obtained. Berthold Laufer [5] has critically reviewed this subject and from information assembled by him it appears that the following localities are or have been productive: (1) The region between Lhasa and the China-Tibetan border; particularly in the vicinity of Lhasa and near Chamdo, a small town of eastern Tibet, about 400 miles ENE. of Lhasa; (2) Djaya (or Draya), to the west of Bathang; (3) a mine of the Gangs-chan mountains of Ngari-Khorsum in western Tibet; and (4) several mountains of the great State of Derge in eastern Tibet.[6]

As to further details regarding these occurrences, few can be given.[7] The first mentioned locality is probably the most important. The third, also, is stated to have yielded good material. Most of the Tibetan turquois seen by the writer has been matrix material, in which turquois of greenish to bluish color occurs in rounded areas within a dark, iron-colored rock, the whole presenting a mottled appearance when polished. Material of such appearance has recently come into the London and Paris markets in some abundance.

CHINA.

Little is known of the occurrence of turquois in China, as no geologist has visited its localities in that country. Rockhill,[8] who passed through Si-ngan in 1889, was informed that turquois is found in the Honan Province. Berthold Laufer,[9] who visited the region in 1909, failed to confirm this statement, and suggested that the mines of Honan had since been worked out. He was told by turquois dealers in Si-ngan that the turquoises traded in there came from the prefecture of Yün-yang, Hu-pei Province; and the district of Chu-shan in the same prefecture was designated by one dealer as the special place of production.

[1] Bauer, Edelsteinkunde. Leipzig, 1896, p. 450.

[2] Precious stones and gems. London, 1898, p. 222.

[3] The Land of Midian (revisited). London, 1879, vol. 1, p. 115; vol. 2, p. 47. Burton noted the occurrence of turquois in Midian in an earlier work, The Gold Mines of Midian and the Ruined Midianite cities, London, 1878, p. 302.

[4] The turquois from Tibet that the writer has seen is so different from the Nishapur material as to preclude such a source for it.

[5] Op. cit., 1913, pp. 16–18.

[6] "It seems also that in the mountains to the north of Ta-tsien-lu in western Sze-ch'uan a turquois of inferior quality and sickly green is obtained; it is, however, so poor and insignificant that the Chinese traders there accustomed to the brilliant blue of their home product look down upon it as spurious." Laufer, op. cit., p. 18. Regarding the occurrence of turquois in Tibet, Rawling (The Great Plateau, London, 1905, pp. 294–295) says: "The rough stones are bought at the fairs held in the country and conveyed by the Indian merchants to Amritsar and Delhi, where they are mounted in gold and silver, and afterwards reimported. Practically every matrix originally comes from Tibet, but though inquiries were made at all the more important places, no information could be obtained as to the situation of the mines. The Phari people obtain their supply from Calcutta, Shigatse from Lhasa, Lhasa from China and Leh, and Leh from Lhasa, whilst at many other places the people merely said that they did not know where the stones came from, that they had had them for years, and that none were to be found in their district or anywhere near. Despite these unsatisfactory answers, the consensus of opinion leads one to believe that they exist in the greatest numbers in the country situated between Lhasa and the western border of China."

[7] *Firozeh nakis*, an inferior turquois, is enumerated amongst the mineral products of Tibet by Abdul Kadir Khan in the History of Cashmir. See Prinsep, Journ. Asiat. Soc. Bengal, vol. 1, 1832, p. 361.

[8] The Land of the Lamas. New York, 1891, p. 24.

[9] Op. cit., 1913, pp. 64–65.

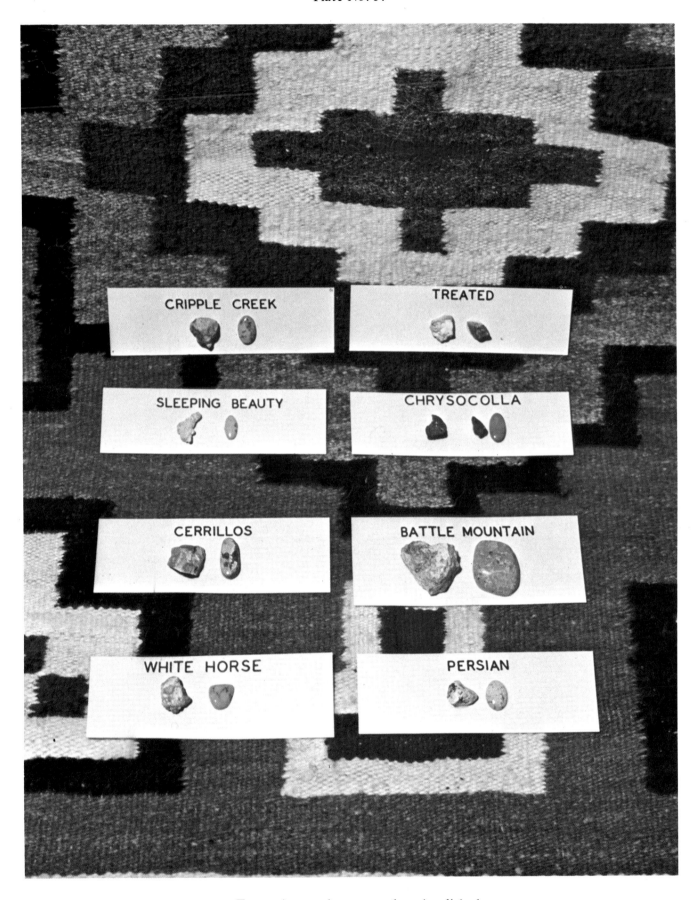

Turquoise specimens rough and polished.

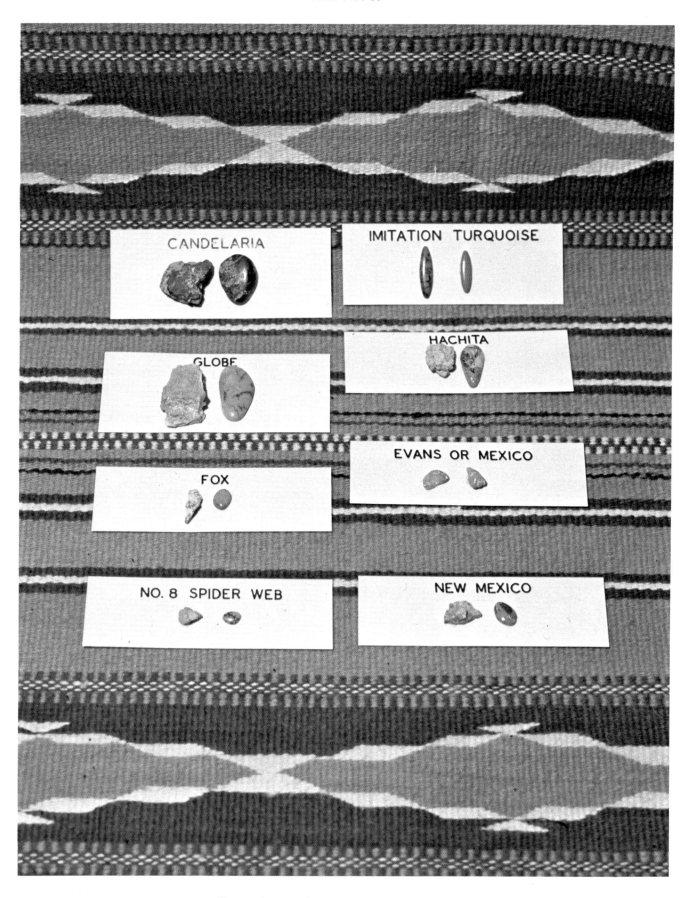

CANDELARIA

IMITATION TURQUOISE

GLOBE

HACHITA

FOX

EVANS OR MEXICO

NO. 8 SPIDER WEB

NEW MEXICO

Turquoise specimens rough and polished.

OTHER REGIONS.

In spite of occasional statements to the contrary,[1] turquois is not definitely known to occur in Burma, Ceylon, and India— countries rich in many other precious stones.[2] Prinsep[3] thought it possibly present among the copper ores of Rajauri in Ajmir, India, and Irvine[4] mentioned a report of its occurrence in the Ajmir hills and at Ramgarh in the Shakhwati country; but these occurrences may represent merely a blue copper ore.[5] The mineral is said to have been found near Multan in the Punjab province of India,[6] and is reported,[7] though with question, in Rajputana and the territory to the eastward of the Tenasserim River.

AUSTRALIA.

Turquois occurs in Australia in the states of Victoria, New South Wales, and Queensland; but thus far the Australian deposits have not proved of any commercial moment.

Lurg, near Benalla, Victoria.[8]—Turquois here occurs in thin veins and incrustations, of greenish-blue color, with quartz and slate.

Edi, King River district, Victoria.[9]—Here turquois forms thin veins, ranging from films to 1 inch in thickness, in a black, carbonaceous slate. Much of the material is green, but occasionally thin veins of good color are obtained. The regions consists of steeply dipping slates and sandstones of Ordovician (?) age. Decomposed pyrite (limonite) is invariably associated with the turquois. The future of the locality is doubtful.

Bodalla, County of Dampier, New South Wales.[10]—Turquois was discovered in 1894 on the north bank of Mummuga Creek, near Bodalla. In 1896 some mining was done, but little of the mineral proved marketable. The turquois is in thin crusts and concretionary masses in a dark, carbonaceous shale containing pyrite, and has a fairly good blue color, fading on exposure. A few of the stones, however, are of good quality, and appear promising.

Other localities.—Turquois also occurs on Mount Lougan, New South Wales,[11] where some work has been done in extracting it, but thus far without commercial success; at Wagonga, New South Wales,[12] in pale-blue veins, 3.5 mm. thick; and has been reported, though erroneously, in the Murcheson district, in western Australia.[13] In the Geological Museum of Sydney are specimens of turquois from Gippsland, Victoria, and Wanganilla, Queensland. The United States National Museum possesses a specimen (Mus. No. 61026) from Kepple Rock, near Rockhampton, Queensland. The South Kensington Museum, London, has a small green cut stone labeled Kepple Bay, Queensland.

EUROPE.

Turquois, greenish in color, occurs at a number of places in Europe, but none of the localities are commercially important.

In Silesia, Germany, the siliceous schists at Jordansmühl, near Domsdorf, carry small nodules of apple-green to grass-green turquois in the joints.[14] Near Steine, not far from Jordansmühl, turquois has also been found.[15] Between the Weckersdorf and Langenwolschendorf, in

1 Rochschild (Handbook of precious stones, 1890) cites Burma as a source of turquois.
   Fuchs & de Launey (Traite des Gites Mineraux et Metalliferes. Paris, 1893, vol. 1, p. 411) states that some turquois is obtained from India.
2 Bauer, op. cit., p. 451.
3 Journ. Asiat. Soc. Bengal, vol. 4, 1835, p. 584.
4 Topography of Ajmir, p. 162.
5 Note by W. K. appended to Schindler's article, Rec. Geol. Surv. India, vol. 17, 1884, p. 132.
6 Encyclopedia Britannica. Rev. Amer. Ed., 1881. In article on India, p. 766.
7 Mallet, A manual of the geology of India. Calcutta, 1887, pt. 4, p. 133.
8 Walcott, Proc. Roy. Soc. Victoria, vol. 13, 1900, pp. 253–272.
9 Atkinson, Proc. Roy. Soc. Victoria, vol. 9, 1896, pp. 68–119.
   Dunn, Rec. Geol. Surv. Victoria, vol. 2, 1908, pp. 170–174.
10 Curran, Journ. Proc. Roy. Soc. N. S. Wales, vol. 30, 1896, pp. 214–285.
   Pittman, The mineral resources of New South Wales. Sydney, 1901, p. 409.
11 Kunz, 18th Ann. Rept., U. S. Geol. Surv., 1896–97, p. 1217.
12 Card, Rec. Geol. Surv., N. S. W., vol. 4, 1894, p. 20.
13 Claremont, The gem-cutter's craft. London, 1906, pp. 248–252.
14 Glocker, Ann. Phys. und Chem. Pogg., vol. 64, 1845, pp. 633–636.
15 Glocker, Beiträgen zur mineralischen Kenntniss der Sudetenländer, vol. 1, 1827, p. 58. There is a specimen of green color from this locality in the South Kensington Museum.

southern Thuringia, central Germany, turquois has been identified in a quarry among siliceous slate of Middle Silurian age,[1] forming thin seams filling cavities in the rock. It has also been found near Oelsnitz, Zwickau, Saxony; a specimen in the South Kensington Museum shows a thin green coating on a dark rock.

In the tin deposits of Montebras, Department of Creuse, France, turquois of a fine blue color, but too porous to admit of a polish, accompanies wavellite and amblygonite.[2] In the kaolin deposits of the Colettes Forest, Department of Allier, turquois also has been identified.[3] It occurs likewise at Caceres, Estremadura, Spain,[4] associated with deposits of tin (cassiterite); and has been reported in Hungary.[5]

SOUTH AMERICA..

No important occurrence of turquois is known in South America. The mineral, however, has been found in Peru and reported in Chile. Its rather extensive use by the tribes formerly inhabiting what is now Peru and Argentina (see pp. 87–89) suggests other and more important sources than those now known.

According to Raimondi,[6] turquois occurs near Huari, between Huanta and Ayacucho, Peru, in the form of small green to grayish nodules, disseminated through a loose earth, which does not represent the parent ledges. The turquois is also stated to occur in Chile at San Lorenzo (Department of Ligua, Province of Aconcagua)[7] and near Copiapo (Province of Atacama).[8]

NORTH AMERICA.

Turquois deposits of commercial importance occur in Arizona, California, Colorado, Nevada, and New Mexico. The last mentioned is the oldest and largest producer; the others have more recently come into prominence. The mineral is found also in Alabama, Texas, Mexico, and Virginia and has been reported from New Jersey.[9] It is believed that certain Indian tribes of the Southwest still obtain stones from localities known only to themselves.[10]

ALABAMA.

Turquois was discovered in 1902 at several points near Idaho, Clay County, Ala., in the neighborhood of former copper mines.[11] According to Eugene A. Smith,[12] State Geologist, it also occurs in a railroad cut near Erin, a few miles to the northeast. It forms thin veins in graphitic schists of Carboniferous age. All the material thus far obtained has been taken from the surface and is light-green to yellowish-green in color. The deposit is undeveloped, but at depth might yield low-grade gem material. Unlike the western occurrences, there are no traces of aboriginal workings, nor have turquoises been found in Indian graves of this region.

ARIZONA.

Turquois occurs in Arizona near Tombstone, Cochise County, and at Mineral Park, Mohave County. It is also stated to have been found at Pierce,[13] and in Maricopa County, 12 miles east of Morristown and about 70 miles southeast of Wickenburg.[14]

---

[1] Anon., Zeitschr. naturw., vol. 72, pt. 6, 1900, p. 453; through Neues Jahrb., vol. 1, pt. 2, 1902, p. 187.
   Kunz, Min. Res. for 1902, U. S. Geol. Surv., p. 857.
[2] Fuchs & de Launey, Traite des Gites Mineraux et Metalliferes, Paris, 1893, vol. 1, pp. 411–414. Lacroix, Minéralogie de la France. Paris, 1910, p. 530.
[3] De Launey, Bull. soc. géol. France, vol. 16, 1888, p. 1067.
[4] Siret, L'Anthropologie, vol. 20, 1909, p. 138.
[5] Buffon, Histoire naturelle. Paris, 1802, vol. 13, pp. 311–325.
[6] Minerales del Peru. Lima, 1878, pp. 218, 222.
[7] Domeyko, Mineralogia, 3rd Ed., 1879, pp. 259–260.
[8] Molina (Histoire naturelle du Chile. Gruvel's translation, Paris, 1789, p. 56) says that the Province of Copiapo owes its name to the number of turquoises found in its mountains, explaining that most of these are bone turquoises, but some are quite hard and known as turquoises of the old rock (mineral turquoises).
[9] The rounded "turquois" pebbles reported in 1898 from the drift in Brown County, Nebr. (Kunz, 20th Ann. Rept. U. S. Geol. Surv., 1898–99, p. 580) turned out to be odontolite (Kunz, 21st Ann. Rept., ibid, 1899–1900, p. 455).
[10] See pp. 58 and 124.
[11] Kunz, Min. Resources for 1902, U. S. Geol. Surv., pp. 856–857.
[12] Personal communication. Prof. Smith also very kindly placed a small specimen of the turquois and country rock at the disposal of the writer.
[13] Johnson, School of Mines Quart., vol. 25, 1903, p. 95.
[14] Blake, Minerals of Arizona. Tucson, 1909, p. 58.

COCHISE COUNTY.

According to Blake,[1] light apple-green to pea-green turquois is found on an outlying spur of the Dragoon Mountains, 20 miles from Tombstone, where considerable ancient excavation had been undertaken. This locality has never been of importance, although the deposits under the head of the Gleason District are reported to have produced some fair-quality stones a few years prior to 1909.[2] In 1911 Ransome [3] published a brief note on this occurrence, stating that turquois occurs in joints and small irregular fractures in a bed of Cambrian quartzite near contact with decomposed granitic rock.

MINERAL PARK, MOHAVE COUNTY.[4]

The most important deposits of turquois in Arizona lie to the east and south of Mineral Park,[5] occupying certain of the hills and peaks along the western side of the Cerbat range. The precise localities are Ithaca Peak, 1 mile east of Mineral Park (see Fig. 1, Pl. 2); Aztec Mountain,[6] 1 mile south of Ithaca Peak; and the end of a range one-third of a mile west of south of Mineral Park. A mountain four-fifths of a mile east of south of Mineral Park is reported to carry turquois.

Turquois was discovered near Mineral Park prior to 1883, when some good stones were obtained.[7] In common with many other western deposits, however, the occurrence was known and worked by prehistoric Indians. In 1886 several claims were located, but the district remained undeveloped until fortunate prospecting in 1898 revealed promising deposits of gem material.[8] Since then considerable mining has been carried on by the Aztec Turquois Co., Arizona Turquois Co., Los Angeles Gem Co., Southwest Turquois Co., Mineral Park Turquois Co., and several individuals.

The region consists principally of pre-Cambrian gneisses and schists intruded by granites and by granite- and quartz-porphyry. The granite porphyry shows phenocrysts of quartz and orthoclase, with remnants of biotite crystals, in a medium-grained ground of the same minerals including as accessories sericite, microcline, zircon, and secondary epidote. The quartz porphyry is a phase of the granite porphyry, differing only in texture, having a finer ground and more prominent quartz phenocrysts. Both types of rock have suffered sericitization, kaolinization, and silicification, and in their more decomposed phases the turquois is found. The outcrops stand out prominently and near the deposits are seamed with quartz and stained by limonite, copper salts, discolored kaolin, and inferior turquois.

The turquois forms seams and veins (see Fig. 1, Pl. 1) in the porphyry and streaks and patches in the quartz veinlets, locally assuming a nodular form in the larger veins or within masses of kaolinized feldspar in the porphyry. Some specimens show a gradation from good turquois through soft "semiturquois" to copper-stained kaolin, and this is the case with certain patches probably representing altered feldspar phenocrysts. In one mine the "semiturquois" contains alum and a little copper sulphate. The best material obtained has a rich, deep-blue color and takes a good polish. The matrix stones afford pleasing contrasts of dark-blue turquois against the dark brown of limonite or the gray of quartz or porphyry. A great quantity of soft and off-color material, unfit even for low-grade matrix, is rejected. Prior to 1899 blocks of the blue-veined turquois-bearing rock were shipped to New York to be worked into pedestals, mantels, and other objects.[9]

---

[1] Amer. Journ. Sci., vol. 25, 1883, pp. 197–200.

[2] Sterrett, Min. Resources for 1909, pt. 2, p. 779.

[3] Bull. 530, U. S. Geol. Surv., p. 134.

[4] The best and most detailed description of this locality is given by Sterrett in Mineral Resources of the United States for 1908, pt. 2, pp. 847–852, published by the United States Geological Survey, and the following information is gathered mainly therefrom.

[5] Mineral Park is 4 miles southeast of Chloride, which is reached by a branch line leaving the Santa Fe Railroad near Kingman.

[6] The Turquois Mountain of this locality described by Kunz (20th Ann. Rept. U. S. Geol. Surv., pt. 6, 1898–99, p. 581) is identical with Aztec Mountain.

[7] Kunz, 20th Ann. Rept., U. S. Geol. Surv., pt. 6, 1898–99, p. 581. According to F. C. Schrader (cited by Sterrett, Min. Resources for 1906, p. 1234), turquois was discovered about 1885 by James Haas.

[8] Frenzel, Eng. Min. Journ., vol. 66, 1898, p. 697.

[9] Kunz, op. cit., p. 581.

A detailed description of the mining operations up to 1908 may be found in the report by Sterrett previously mentioned. It suffices here to state that the mining is chiefly done by means of open cuts and tunnels, the rock being blasted out and the turquois removed after careful breaking of the blocks. The most extensive operations have been confined to the upper slopes of Ithaca Peak and the northern and southern sides of Aztec Mountain.

Prehistoric excavations, consisting of small pits filled with rubbish, and several tunnels nearly 20 feet long, were found on the southern side of Aztec Mountain. A quantity of stone implements were discovered in the workings, and represent the means whereby the ancient Indians extracted their supply of the precious stone. The site has been modernly worked, but not so successfully as the nearby deposits. Small fragments of turquois found around the old pits are of better grade than the material latterly produced there.

CALIFORNIA.

Turquois occurs in Fresno County, Cal., and at several places in the northeastern part of San Bernardino County.

FRESNO COUNTY,

In 1864 several small,[1] hexagonal blue-green crystals were discovered by J. D. Whitney in a prospect pit in granite on Taylor's ranch on the Chowchillas River. These were later investigated by Moore and Zepharowich[2] and found to have the composition of turquois but the form of apatite, and hence were regarded as pseudomorphs of turquois after apatite. No further finds are reported from the locality.

SAN BERNARDINO COUNTY.

Turquois has been mined in the northeastern corner of this county in what may be termed the Manvel district and farther south in the Mohave Desert.

Manvel district.[3]—The principal deposits of turquois in California occupy a desolate and barren region near the Nevada line, about 100 miles northwest of Needles and 50 to 60 miles north of Manvel. The Toltec Gem Mining Co. owns three groups of claims known as East Camp, Middle Camp, and West Camp, within a few miles of each other. The Himalaya Mining Co. has operated a mine near West Camp and about 12 miles N. 60° E. of Silver Lake, a small station on the Tonopah & Tidewater Railroad.

In 1897 T. C. Bassett discovered a vein of turquois in this district and prospected it to a depth of 20 feet; two aboriginal stone hammers were found and the opening was called, in consequence, the Stone Hammer mine. In the meantime the State Mining Bureau had received several promising specimens, reported to have come from the same general region. In 1898 further discoveries were announced, and the press devoted much space to accounts, undoubtedly exaggerated, of the extensive excavations and other evidences of prehistoric activity in this inaccessible region. Finally interest was aroused to such a pitch that the San Francisco Call organized a party, headed by Gustav Eisen as archæologist, to explore the reported finds. A number of excavations, cave dwellings, and stone implements were discovered, and it became evident that the locality had been worked on a large scale by the prehistoric inhabitants of the region. Since 1898 the deposits have been operated to considerable extent,[4] but for the past few years no work has been done.

The region near West Camp is composed of schists and gneisses, intruded by granite and granite porphyry. At the Himalaya mine the turquois occurs in a decomposed phase of the granite porphyry in association with limonite, kaolin, sericite, jarosite, and quartz.[5] It forms veinlets and nodules, filling joint planes and fracture zones, and is found in disseminated patches in the country rock and the quartz veins traversing it. The best stones range from light-

---

[1] One measures 20 by 11 mm.

[2] Zeitschr. Kryst., vol. 10, 1885, pp. 240–251.

[3] Kunz, Gems, jewelers' materials, etc., of California, 1905, pp. 12–13, 107–110. Ibid, 20th Ann. Rept. U. S. Geol. Surv., 1898–99, pp. 582–583. Sterrett, Min. Resources for 1911, pt. 2, pp. 1071–1073.

[4] The yield in 1900 was estimated at $20,000.

[5] Sterrett, Min. Resources for 1911, pt. 2, pp. 1072–1073.

blue to fairly dark blue and are of good quality. Much matrix material, with a variety of markings and colors, has been obtained.

The remains of the ancient mining operations are very abundant. They appear as saucer-like pits from 15 to 30 feet across and of half that depth, many filled with débris, and scattered over an area 15 miles long by 4 miles wide. Many stone tools and turquois fragments are found around and in the old workings. In the words of Kunz: [1]

From an archaeological point of view this locality possesses remarkable interest. The canyon walls are full of caverns, now filled up to a depth of several feet with apparently wind-blown sand and dust, but whose blackened roofs and rudely sculptured walls indicate that they were occupied for a long time by the people who worked the mines. In the blown sand were found stone implements and pottery fragments of rude type, incised but not painted. The openings to these caves are partially closed by roughly built walls composed of trap blocks piled upon one another with no attempt at fitting and no cement, but evidently made as a mere rude protection against weather and wild beasts. The tools, found partly in the caves and largely in the mine pits, are carefully wrought and polished from hard basalt or trap, chiefly hammers and adzes or axes, generally grooved for a handle and often of large size. Some are beautifully perfect, others much worn and battered by use.

The most impressive feature, however, is the abundance of rock carvings in the whole region. These are very varied, conspicuous, and peculiar, while elsewhere they are very rare. Some are recognizable as "Aztec water signs," pointing the way to springs; but most of them are unlike any others known, and furnish a most interesting problem to American archaeologists. They are numbered by many thousands, carved in the hard basalt of the cliffs, or, more frequently, on large blocks of the same rock that have fallen and lie on the sides of the valleys. Some are combinations of lines, dots, and curves into various devices; others represent animals and men; a third and very peculiar type is that of the "shield figures" in which complex patterns of lines, circles, cross hatchings, etc., are inscribed within a shieldlike outline perhaps 3 or 4 feet high.

Mohave Desert.[2]—The principal deposit of this district, known as the Gove Turquois mine, is situated about 2 miles west of Cottonwood Siding, on the Santa Fe Railroad. It was first operated in 1908 by the California Gem Co.

The country rock is principally a fine-grained biotite gneiss, with nearly vertical dip, cut by a belt of rhyolite or porphyry. The latter has been severely mashed and in part converted into a sericite schist; it has also suffered considerable kaolinization. The turquois occurs along the contact of the rhyolite and the gneiss, forming seams and nuggets in both rocks. It is generally associated with limonite or quartz, or with both. The seams of turquois traverse the rocks in all directions, and many are too small to yield gem material. The nuggets range from a fraction of an inch to over an inch in thickness and are developed along limonite seams, in fracture zones, and within the hard rock. Most of them are elongated with the schistosity of the rock, and many are pale and too soft for cutting. The turquois from the gneiss is generally of better grade than that from the igneous rock. The best stones have a rather light to fairly dark, pure-blue color, those of the latter shade forming the principal yield. The production has not been great.

COLORADO.

The principal deposit of turquois in Colorado is near Lajara, Conejos County, in the south-central part of the State. The turquois is also reported to occur at Villagrove, Saguache County, about 25 miles south of Salida;[3] and in the Holy Cross mining district, 30 miles from Leadville.[4]

Lajara.[5]—Deposits of turquois are situated 13 miles S. 60° E. of Lajara,[6] in a small outlying hill or mesa 1½ miles west of the Rio Grande. The discovery of the mineral was announced in 1901,[7] and since then the locality has been considerably exploited with a series of pits, shafts, and tunnels by the Colorado Turquois Mining Co. In 1909 the mine was leased by several individuals, who established a lapidary shop in Colorado Springs to handle the output.[8] There

---

[1] Gems, etc., of California, 1905, pp. 108–109.
[2] From Sterrett, Min. Resources for 1909, pt. 2, pp. 780–781.
[3] Kunz, Min. Resources for 1893, p. 694.
[4] Kunz, Min. Resources for 1888, p. 582.
[5] Sterrett, Min. Resources for 1908, pt. 2, pp. 852–853.
[6] Near the New Mexican boundary; reached by the Denver & Rio Grande Railroad.
[7] Kunz, Min. Resources for 1901, p. 760.
[8] Sterrett, Min. Resources for 1909, p. 781.

are abundant evidences, in the form of stone hammers, pieces of deerhorn, etc., of prehistoric mining activity.[1]

The country rock is an altered trachyte or porphyry, composed principally of feldspar, but containing considerable sericite, kaolin, and limonite stains. It is cut by a dike of phonolite and capped with a 20-foot ledge of grayish to brownish chert. Diorite or andesite outcrops near-by and the neighboring hills are composed of basalt.

The turquois forms paper-thin to one-fourth inch veins occupying joints in the trachyte, and irregular masses and nodules scattered through the rock. The best material runs from pale-blue to a deep sky-blue, and is very hard, with a conchoidal fracture. Attractive matrix material is yielded by many specimens containing brown limonite.

MEXICO.

No important deposits of turquois are known in Mexico. The mineral, however, has been found in limited quantity at two points in the State of Zacatecas and at one locality in Sonora.[2]

Zacatecas.—Kunz[3] in 1903 announced the discovery of turquois in a mine of argentiferous galena, near the town of Bonanza in the Santa Rosa district, State of Zacatecas, Mexico. Mrs. V. M. Clement, a stockholder in the company operating the mine, is stated to have found on the dumps small pieces of blue mineral which aroused her curiosity and upon being sent to the City of Mexico were pronounced turquois. The mineral occurs in veins and nodules, of good color and quality; and when its nature was learned was worked to some extent.

Bergeat[4] later investigated the geology of the Santa Rosa district and found at Mazapil an occurrence of turquois which he called the most important of that region. An analysis was made (see No. 20 of table on p. 26) of a blue and fairly hard specimen, which was surrounded by a crust of whitish, weathered material, low in phosphoric acid (P_2O_5).[5]

Sonora.—According to an anonymous contributor to the Engineering and Mining Journal,[6] two deposits of turquois were found about 1901 by J. Owen in the La Barranea copper district, Sonora, Mexico. The mineral is said to occur in volcanic rock.

NEVADA.

The principal deposits of turquois in Nevada are confined to a region embracing portions of Esmeralda and Nye Counties. Less important occurrences are in Lincoln and Lyon Counties.

THE ESMERALDA-NYE COUNTY REGION.

Some very fine turquois has recently been produced from this region. The "mottled matrix" from some of the mines near Millers and the "black matrix" from near Klondike are particularly promising matrix stones. The deposits lie in eastern Esmeralda and western Nye Counties.

Royal Blue mine.[7]—The Royal Blue mine is in Nye County, southwestern Nevada, 12½ miles N. 12° W. from Millers. It was owned and operated for several years by William Petry, of Los Angeles, and sold in 1907 to the Himalaya Mining Co., under whose ownership it has been actively exploited. The deposits lie upon the eastern scarp of a plateau at an elevation of about 5,400 feet, and have been worked by a series of tunnels, shafts, and open cuts.

The country rock is a fine-grained light-colored porphyry, or altered trachyte. Under the microscope it is seen to be composed of feldspar crystals, largely changed to sericite and kaolin, inclosed within a fine feldspathic ground, also partly altered. Stains of limonite, from original pyrite crystals now weathered away, occur throughout the sections. The rocks of the region have been fractured and the resulting openings filled with quartz, limonite, and to some

---

[1] Kunz, Min. Resources for 1901, p. 760.

[2] Barrera (Gems and jewels, London, 1860, p. 150) states that turquois occurs in the "Provinces of Guanaxuato and Oaxaca."

[3] Min. Resources for 1903, p. 955.

[4] Bergeat, Neues Jahrb., Beilage-Band, vol. 28, 1909, p. 499. Ibid., Inst. Geol. Mex., Bull. 27, 1910, p. 58.

[5] In the gem collection of the American Museum of Natural History is a specimen of turquois matrix, of good color and cobweb pattern, labeled "Santa Rosa, Mexico."

[6] Vol. 71, 1901, p. 347.

[7] Sterrett, Min. Resources for 1909, pp. 781-783.

extent turquois. The last occurs principally in seams and veins, in places lenslike, up to 1 inch in thickness, and in nodules or irregular lumps with a maximum diameter of an inch or so. The best material is generally obtained from the harder limonite-stained rock, while the paler and softer turquois is found in the light-colored trachyte. The turquois varies from dark- to light-blue, and much of the best quality is free from greenish shades. The choicest stones are probably equal to any produced in America, and the matrix also is especially fine. Some of the veins and nuggets are stained with limonite along seams and cracks in such manner as to produce most pleasing patterns and contrasts of color when cut. Many of the matrix stones show a beautiful and striking combination of dark and light turquois with reddish matrix.

Oscar Wehrend prospect.[1]—A locality one-third mile north of the Royal Blue mine has been worked to some extent by Oscar Wehrend. The turquois here occurs as seams, splotches, and nodules in kaolinized trachyte. The material obtained is not high-grade, being quite pale and rather soft.

William Petry mine.[2]—This mine occupies the summit of a small knob, 10½ miles N. 40° W. of Millers, among the eastern foothills of the Monte Cristo Mountains. The work thus far (1909) is confined to several small pits. The hill is composed of fine-grained rhyolite, more or less altered and kaolinized, and showing under the microscope quartz and orthoclase, with epidote, zircon, and probably apatite. The turquois forms paper-thin to one-half-inch seams cutting this rock at all angles. It runs from pale-blue to pure-blue of fairly dark shade and the best stones are of good quality though not large. Some good matrix with brown and red markings is obtained and some of the seams upon a ferruginous base have been cut with good success into cameos.

Myers and Bona mine.[3]—This mine is 13 miles north of west of Millers in Esmeralda County, and occupies the northeast face of a small steep hill, upon the western slope of the Monte Cristo Mountains, at an elevation of about 6,400 feet. The workings are rather extensive, but have been principally developed for gold and silver, for which the mine was opened. The operations undertaken in 1908 were suspended in 1909.

The country rock is an altered quartz porphyry, inclosing bands of black slate with slightly calcareous and siliceous phases. The turquois occurs along the contact of the porphyry and slate, and forms nodules[4] and seams in both rocks. The former range from a fraction of an inch to over 2 inches in thickness, and occur either scattered through the rocks or in leads inclosed in softer gougelike matrix. The seams are a half inch or less in thickness; and are not regular nor continuous, but pinch and swell, in places containing nodular lumps. The best material occurs in the softer decomposed streaks in the slate; that in the porphyry is generally soft and of inferior color. Round balls of a hard white mineral, probably a hydrous aluminum phosphate, occur through the porphyry.

The best turquois from this mine is hard and has a fine sky-blue color, equaled in few localities in this country. Some specimens show a greenish color adjacent to the blue. Many of the larger nuggets are pale and deficient in hardness. Some of the matrix material with good iron stains yields pleasing patterns upon cutting.

Montezuma mine.[5]—The Montezuma mine is among the eastern foothills in Esmeralda County, on the north side of a small hill 12 miles N. 40° E. of Redlich and about 20 miles by road east of Sodaville. The German-American Turquois Co. opened up the deposit by a series of pits and tunnels prior to 1910, when the holdings were acquired by the Western Gem Co.[6] Other croppings of turquois occur on the same hill.

The turquois occurs in a decomposed trachyte as seams, veinlets, and nodules up to an inch or more in thickness. It varies in hardness and ranges in color from fine dark-blue through dark greenish-blue to pale-blue. The hardest and best-colored stones are generally obtained from the harder, iron-stained portions of the rock, while the softer, pale-blue stones come from its softer, light-colored portions.

---

[1] Sterrett, op. cit., p. 783.
[2] Sterrett, op. cit., pp. 783, 784.
[3] Sterrett, op. cit., pp. 784–785.

[4] Nodular specimen from this locality is shown in the frontispiece, Fig. 6.
[5] Sterrett, op. cit., pp. 785–786.
[6] Sterrett, Min. Resources for 1910, pt. 2, p. 887.

The choicest material resembles that from the Royal Blue mine, and fine contrasts of brown and blue with mottled patterns are obtained. The product, however, is chiefly low-grade, the cut stones retailing at about 50 cents per carat.

Moqui-Aztec mine.[1]—This mine, also known as the S. Simmons mine, lies about a mile southwest of the Montezuma mine on the south side of a ridge at an elevation of about 6,250 feet. It was worked by a series of tunnels, open cuts, and pits; but operations were suspended in 1908. In 1910 work was resumed and a small production was reported for that year.[2]

The turquois occurs as veinlets and nodules in a fine-grained, kaolinized quartz porphyry and in quartz masses included in the porphyry. The best grade is associated with limonite stains. Turquois of dark color is scarce, but considerable pale-blue material has been produced. A considerable quantity of the latter, with delicate brown markings, has been cut.

Smith Black Matrix mine.[3]—The deposit thus designated occupies one of a small group of hills about 3 miles northeast of Klondike, a station in Esmeralda County on the railroad between Tonopah and Goldfield. The workings at this mine are not extensive.

The region consists of limestone and shales of Cambrian age, with hard siliceous phases called jasperoid, to the south dipping beneath a rhyolite flow, which, before erosion, probably covered the turquois deposits and surrounding rock. The turquois fills joints and fractures in the black, slatelike jasperoid, forming paper-thin to three-fourths-inch veins distributed in all directions through it. It also, to less extent, cements the fragments of brecciated portions of the jasperoid, locally in this way forming masses an inch or two across. Many of the thicker turquois seams contain angular fragments of black jasperoid. Numerous limonite stains occur throughout the rock, many in intimate association with the turquois.

This unique mode of occurrence yields unusual and characteristic gems. Matrix material is alone produced, and obtains its beauty from the contrasts between black matrix and blue turquois and the many patterns afforded by their combination. Some cut stones show veins of turquois in black matrix; others, matrix fragments included in turquois; and still others, matrix breccia cemented with turquois. Some stones are cut to show brown iron stains or seams of gray quartz, which lend further contrast to the gems. The turquois itself runs in color from fairly pure blue to very light blue to greenish, the last resembling that of variscite.

Columbus district.[4]—Turquois has been found at two places on the variscite claims of the Los Angeles Gem Co., about 2 miles northwest of the abandoned Columbus mining camp in Esmeralda County. At the first locality it occurs in a dark-gray, cherty rhyolite; and at the second, in a dark jasperoid or silicified calcareous rock. The latter occurrence is similar to that of the Smith Black Matrix mine, and is capable of yielding beautiful matrix gems. Very little work has been done at either prospect.

J. E. Clayton is accredited with the discovery of the turquois near the Columbus district at a time when the Cerrillos deposits were the only ones known on this continent.[5] The date of the discovery can not now be ascertained, but it was probably during the seventies, since Hoffman[6] in 1878 reported the occurrence of turquois 5 miles north of Columbus, and in 1879 Büching,[7] in Germany, studied under the microscope pale blue-green specimens from the Columbus district.

Carr-Lovejoy claims.[8]—Turquois was discovered in 1910 on variscite claims 9 miles east of north of Blair Junction, Esmeralda County. The mineral forms veins and seams in rhyolite and in accompanying dikes of trachytic rock. The best material is of good hardness and fine blue color.

Rick and Botts claims.[9]—Turquois has been prospected on a turquois-variscite claim 4 miles northeast of Coaldale, Esmeralda County. The country rock consists of rhyolite and altered quartz porphyry; the turquois occurs in the former in veinlets and small nodules up to an inch in thickness. The best material is of superior hardness and has a fine blue color. Some of the matrix with delicate brown cobweb markings would yield attractive patterns.

---

[1] Sterrett, Min. Resources for 1909, pt. 2, p. 786.
[2] Sterrett, Min. Resources for 1910, pt. 2, p. 887.
[3] Sterrett, Min. Resources for 1909, pt. 2, pp. 786-787.
[4] Sterrett, Min. Resources for 1909, pt. 2, pp. 787-788.
[5] Silliman, Amer. Journ. Sci., vol. 22, 1881, p. 70.
[6] On the mineralogy of Nevada, U. S. Geol. and Geogr. Surv., vol. 4, Bull. No. 3, 1878, p. 740.
[7] Zeitschr. Kryst., vol. 3, 1879, pp. 81-82.
[8] Sterrett, Min. Resources for 1910, pt. 2, p. 886.
[9] Ibid.

Sigmund claim.[1]—Turquois has been recently discovered and worked to some extent at several points about $3\frac{1}{2}$ miles south of Redlich. It is found as nuggets and small seams, and some of the specimens have a fine dark-blue color.

Dunwoody claims.[2]—Turquois of poor quality is obtained from a group of variscite claims 8 miles southwest of Sodaville, Esmeralda County, where it occurs both in decomposed porphyry and rhyolite. It forms seams and veins up to three-fourths inch thick in a fracture zone and is dark greenish-blue to bright-green in color, resembling variscite.

Other localities.—Some turquois has been obtained from Belmont, Nye County.[3] The best of this shows dark-blue turquois fringed with white material, in a dark-gray or chocolate-colored matrix, and is very beautiful. In 1898[4] turquois was reported from Nevada, 18 miles east of Vanderbilt, Cal. The locality was discovered by George Simmons, and an ancient "village site" and stone tools were found. The turquois is stated to occur as veins and nodules associated with limonite in a trachytic rock. In 1901[5] a new deposit of turquois was announced on Cactus Mountain, 50 miles east of Butler, in Nye County. During 1910 turquois was found at several points in the neighborhood of Goldfield during the course of prospecting and mining for gold. Pale-green turquois, fading to white opaque masses, has been identified by Eakle[6] at Tonopah, where it occurs associated with black manganese oxides and kaolinite in crevices of the Mizpah vein at the 600-foot level.

LYON COUNTY.

Taubert mines.[7]—Turquois has been mined at two points near Yerington in Lyon County.

The first locality is about 8 miles N. 75° W. of Yerington, on the western slope of a ridge west of the Walker River, and has been worked by a shaft and open cut. The country rock is monzonitic in nature and has undergone kaolinization and sericitization, particularly around the deposits; in places it is indurated by silica. The turquois fills seams and joints and forms nodules in the weathered rock, and much of it is associated with limonite. In color the material ranges from dark sky-blue through bluish-green to green. The best grade is slightly translucent and of good quality. Some of the greenish varieties are marked by limonite dendrites and would yield attractive matrix stones.

The second locality lies about $1\frac{1}{2}$ miles N. 25° W. of Yerington, near a copper vein, in low hills in the Walker River Valley. The turquois has been found at a number of points within a hundred yards of one another. It forms seams and nodular segregations in a decomposed granitic porphyry and trachytic intrusive. Both pale-blue and darker pure-blue material has been obtained; the best grade is associated with limonite.

LINCOLN COUNTY.

In 1897[8] turquois was reported as recently discovered in Lincoln County at the foot of Sugar Loaf Peak. The mineral occurs within a dike cutting mica schist and is light-blue in color. The locality was worked to some extent and abundant signs of prehistoric mining were found.

In 1909[9] a discovery of turquois was reported at Searchlight in Lincoln County, where a stone weighing 320 carats and worth $2,600 was claimed to have been found.

NEW JERSEY.

Turquois was reported in 1904[10] to have been found at Somerville, N. J., occupying small veins 1,100 feet down an inclined shaft, in the workings of the American Copper Mining Co. on Watchung Mountain.

[1] Sterrett, Min. Resources for 1910, pt. 2, p. 886.

[2] Ibid, p. 887.

[3] Sterrett, Min. Resources for 1909, pt. 2, p. 788.

[4] Kunz, 20th Ann. Rept. U. S. Geol. Surv., pt. 6, 1898–99, p. 579.

[5] Kunz, Min. Resources for 1901, p. 761.

[6] Bull. Dept. Geol., Univ. Calif., vol. 7, No. 1, 1912, p. 17.

[7] Sterrett, Min. Resources for 1910, pt. 2, pp. 885–886.

[8] Kunz, 19th Ann. Rept. U. S. Geol. Surv., pt. 6, 1897–98, p. 504.   Anon., Eng. Min. Journ., vol. 64, 1897, p. 456.

[9] Jeweler's Circular Weekly, Mar. 5, 1909, through Sterrett, Min. Resources for 1908, pt. 2, p. 846.

[10] Kunz, Min. Resources for 1904, p. 957.

NEW MEXICO.

New Mexico has produced a greater quantity of turquois than any other State.[1] The mineral has been mined in four regions, namely, the Cerrillos Hills of Santa Fe County, the Burro Mountains and the Little Hachita Mountains of Grant County, and the Jarilla Hills of Otero County. The Cerrillos and Burro Mountains districts are the best known in this country, and the Hachita has recently come into prominence. The best grade New Mexican stones are noted for their excellence. At all four localities the deposits were worked by the aborigines and those near Cerrillos under Spanish rule also. The prehistoric excavations at the last named locality are of great extent.

CERRILLOS DISTRICT.[2]

The most important deposits of turquois in the United States, from the point of view of their history and past production, are within the Cerrillos mining district, Santa Fe County, in the north-central portion of New Mexico. They lie in a prominent group of hills, after which the district has been named, a few miles north of Cerrillos Station and about 20 miles south-southwest of the historic old city of Santa Fe. Turquois has been mined extensively at two localities 3 miles apart.[3] The first is situated on Turquois Hill, 6 miles east of north of Cerrillos, and includes the Tiffany and Castilian mines owned by the American Turquois Co. of New York. The second occupies the slopes of Mount Chalchihuitl (see Fig. 1, Pl. 3), a low knob near the center of the hills and about a mile east of Grand Central Mountain, and is now abandoned. Other localities in the neighborhood have been more or less exploited; some good material has been obtained from workings three-fourths mile southeast of Mount Chalchihuitl and from claims one-half mile west of north of Mount Chalchihuitl.

Ancient workings.—Mount Chalchihuitl (see Pl. 4) is the site of the most extensive prehistoric mining operations known on the American continent. The extent of the workings is "truly marvelous;" the whole north side of the hill has been quarried out, while less extensive excavations are found in other parts of the so-called mountain.[4] According to Johnson,[4] "It seems almost incredible that such a mass of rock could have been removed by a primitive people, without the aid of modern mining appliances." Blake[5] relates that he "was struck with astonishment at the extent of the excavations * * * it appears to be 200 feet in depth and 300 or more in width * * * at the bottom pine trees over a hundred years old are now growing. This great excavation is made in the solid rock, and tens of thousands of tons of rock have been broken out." In the words of Silliman,[6] "The observer is deeply impressed with the enormous amount of labor which in ancient times has been expended here. The waste or débris excavated in the former workings covers an area which the local surveyor assured me extends by his measurement over at least 20 acres. On the slopes and sides of the great piles of rubbish are growing large cedars and pines, the age of which * * * must be reckoned by centuries." According to measurements made by Sterrett[7] in 1911, the main pit is about 130 feet deep and 200 feet across, and the débris therefrom covers about 2½ acres. Many stone hammers (see Fig. 2, Pl. 3) and other primitive implements have been found in the débris of the ancient workings.

Ancient excavations have also been found at the other points modernly worked and at several places in Turquois Hill they exceed in extent the recent excavations.

History.—The immense excavations at Cerrillos are of great antiquity, and it seems beyond reasonable question that the greater portion was executed before the advent of the Spaniards. Indeed, this deposit must have supplied much of the turquois which was so widely used in pre-Spanish times, not only in the Southwest but in Mexico as well, for no other sources are now known at all adequate to account for the quantities employed.

---

[1] Its total production probably exceeds $5,000,000 in value.
[2] Pronounced *Sĕrēeōs.*
[3] Johnson, School of Mines Quart., vol. 24, 1903, p. 494.
[4] Johnson, op. cit., p. 495.

[5] Amer. Journ. Sci., vol. 25, 1858, p. 227.
[6] Amer. Journ. Sci., vol. 22, 1881, p. 68.
[7] Min. Resources for 1911, pt. 2, p. 1067.

During the sixteenth century the Tano guarded the Cerrillos workings jealously and the product proved quite a resource to them for purposes of commerce.[1]   Toward the close of that century the first successful Spanish colony was established in New Mexico under Juan de Oñate.   The Spaniards are said to have soon discovered deposits of the precious metals and of "charchihuites" (turquoises), which "were sought after principally by the Indians and used by them as ornaments, and by whom they were valued above all other earthly things."[2] The colonists shortly turned their attention to mining, and the natives were forced against their wills to labor in the mines.   Galled by this oppression and compelled to embrace Christianity, they finally rose against the Spaniards in 1680 and drove them out of New Mexico. There is a well-known tradition that in that year a large section of Mount Chalchihuitl fell in from the undermining of the mass by the Indians, killing a considerable number, and that this accident brought to head the discontent and was the immediate cause of the uprising.[3]

By the year 1700 the Spaniards had succeeded in reestablishing themselves in New Mexico, but only under the condition, it is said,[4] that mining should not be resumed.   To what extent this compact was kept can not be stated.   Jones[5] found in the archives at Santa Fe the record of a chalchihuitl (turquois) grant bearing the date 1763.   Evidently, then, at that time the excavation was again worked, and it is probable that the place was exploited by the Indians[6] in a desultory fashion and at intervals to the era of modern mining.

Little information is available concerning the modern development of the turquois deposits, as few observers have been permitted to examine the recent workings.   In 1858 the Indians, it was stated,[7] occasionally searched the surface about the excavations.   Shortly before 1881 considerable exploratory work was undertaken by J. B. Hyde on the slopes of Mount Chalchihuitl and shafts were sunk through the old workings on both sides of the hill.[8]   It was proposed to connect them by tunnels, and work the rock for both gold and turquois; but the project, after the expenditure of thousands of dollars, proved unsuccessful.[9]   Since then no systematic mining has been done at this point.

The deposits on Turquois Mountain were probably reopened in the seventies, for in 1879 some good specimens were reported[10] to have been taken from the old Castilian mine.   In 1885 this property was located and exploited by a man named Palmerly.[11]   In 1889 the Muniz claim, one of the most important in the district, was located by F. Muniz, a Mexican.   Other claims were located in 1891.   The following year the combined holdings were purchased by the American Turquois Co., which proved very successful in their operation.   The "Tiffany mine" in particular yielded good returns.   During the past few years work has not been actively prosecuted.

Between 1892 and 1904 several points near and adjoining the property of the American Turquois Co. on Turquois Mountain were exploited by J. P. McNulty.[12]   Recently Michael O'Neil and A. B. Renehan have opened deposits near Mount Chalchihuitl.

Description.—The Cerrillos deposits were first described by Blake[13] in 1858.   They have since been visited and studied by Loew,[14] Silliman,[15] Herrick,[16] Johnson,[17] Lindgren,[18] and Sterrett.[19]

---

[1] Bandelier, Final report of investigations among the Indians of the southwestern United States.   Cambridge, 1890, pt. 1, p. 163.

[2] Davis, Spanish Conquest of New Mexico, 1869, p. 271.

[3] Blake, op. cit., p. 229.   Sillman (op. cit., p. 69) describes the caved portion.   Bandelier (op. cit., p. 196) does not believe in the Spanish myths of the treasures taken from New Mexico, nor in the tale that the uprising of 1680 was produced chiefly by hard labor to which the Indians were forced in New Mexico.   He thinks that there was no mining undertaken by the Spaniards until after 1725 and that there was very little enforced labor.

[4] Anon., Eng. Min. Journ., vol. 31, 1881, p. 8.

[5] Jones, New Mexico Mines and Minerals, 1904, p. 268.

[6] For a long period the Queres of San Felipe were the chief traders in the Cerrillos product.

[7] Blake, Amer. Journ. Sci., vol. 25, 1858, p. 229.

[8] Silliman, Amer. Journ. Sci., vol. 22, 1881, p. 69.

[9] Kunz, Gems and precious stones of North America.   New York, 1890, p. 56.

[10] Anon., Eng. Min. Journ., vol. 29, 1879, p. 307.

[11] Jones, ibid., p. 274.

[12] Jones, ibid., p. 274.

[13] Amer. Journ. Sci., vol. 25, 1858, pp. 227–232.

[14] Geological and mineralogical report on portions of Colorado and New Mexico.   (In Rept. Chief of Engineers, 1875, pt. 2, p. 1027.)

[15] Amer. Journ. Sci., vol. 22, 1881, pp. 67–71.

[16] Rept. Gov. of N. M., 1990, pp. 257–260.

[17] School of Min. Quart., vol. 24, 1903, pp. 493–499; vol. 25, 1903, pp. 69–98.

[18] Prof. Pap. 68, U. S. Geol. Surv., 1910, pp. 163–167.

[19] Min. Resources for 1911, pt. 2, pp. 1066–1071.

The Cerrillos hills consist principally of intrusive monzonite porphyry exposed by the erosion and removal of overlying Cretaceous sediments. The matrix of the turquois is a decomposed and somewhat fractured phase of the monzonite porphyry. While the rock in many places answers to this description, only the areas on Mount Chalchihuitl and at either end of Turquois Hill have been found to carry any considerable quantity of turquois. This mineral forms seams, veins (see Fig. 2, Pl. 1), and kaolin-inclosed nodules, occupying fissures, joint planes, and fracture zones. Its color varies from green through greenish-blue to fine sky-blue. While many stones are marred by streaks of limonite (derived from accompanying pyrite) and inclusions of quartz or rock, and are suitable only for matrix material, considerable pure turquois is obtained and the best quality is equal to the Persian stones. Figure 13 of the frontispiece illustrates a fine piece of turquois matrix in the rough, in which patches of turquois of beautiful blue color are scattered through the whitish country rock.

The microscopic character of the turquois-bearing rock has been considerably discussed. According to Clarke and Diller,[1] it is a trachyte, consisting chiefly of orthoclase feldspar, considerably kaolinized, with biotite, epidote, pyrite, limonite, and an amorphous substance. Johnson[2] identified albite as the principal feldspar, with subordinate orthoclase; on this basis classifying the rock as andesitic in nature. He further believed the "amorphous substance" to be very probably fluorite. Lindgren[1] found the feldspar phenocrysts filled with microscopic sericite, the groundmass also carrying this mineral; and noted the presence of kaolin, small grains of tourmaline, very little epidote, and probably some fluorite. He concluded that the turquois area had evidently been greatly altered by mineralizing solutions before the formation of the turquois. Sterrett[3] noted the presence of apatite in thin section.

In the following table are given the available analyses of the fresh and altered country rock near the turquois deposits. On the basis of these analyses and the microscopic examination, Lindgren concluded that, in keeping with recent nomenclature, the igneous rocks of the Cerrillos Hills are monzonitic in character, and that the matrix of the turquois is a much altered phase of monzonite porphyry.

Analyses of rocks from Cerrillos district.

	1	2	3	4	5
SiO_2	48. 21	53. 99	56. 68	60. 82	52. 38
Al_2O_3	17. 96	....	16. 62	....	} 33. 49
Fe_2O_3	5. 18	....	6. 50	....	
FeO	4. 47	....	....	....	
MgO	4. 11	....	. 79	....	1. 17
CaO	9. 72	4. 89	. 59	. 25	Trace.
Na_2O	3. 68	4. 08	1. 03	5. 86	....
K_2O	2. 99	4. 90	11. 18	4. 94	....
H_2O+	1. 41	....	} 3. 28	....	12. 88
H_2O-	. 21	....		....	
TiO_2	. 84	....	....	....	
P_2O_5	. 58	....	. 73	....	
MnO	. 31	....	1. 02	....	
BaO	. 07	....	....	....	
FeS_2	....	....	2. 21	....	....
	99. 74	....	100. 63	....	99. 92

1. "Gabbro porphyry," Mount MacKenzie, Cerrillos Hills, George Steiger, Analyst. Johnson, op. cit., vol. 25, p. 90.
2. Monzonite porphyry, Cerrillos Hills, E. C. Sullivan, Analyst. Lindgren, op. cit., p. 165.
3. "Altered trachyte," Cerrillos Hills, F. W. Clarke, Analyst. Clarke & Diller, Bull. 42, U. S. Geol. Surv., p. 43.
4. Altered rock from turquois quarry, Cerrillos Hills, E. C. Sullivan, Analyst. Lindgren, op. cit., p. 165.
5. Kaolin, associated with turquois, Cerrillos Hills, George Steiger, Analyst. Johnson, op. cit., vol. 25, p. 90.

Considerable secrecy has been maintained as to the output of the productive portion of these deposits. However, with the possible exception of the mines in the Burro Mountains, the Cerrillos district has modernly been the most productive in this country. As the first important domestic occurrence to be developed, it was largely instrumental in replacing the Persian tur-

[1] Loc. cit.   [2] Op. cit., vol. 25, pp. 86–90.   [3] Min. Resources for 1911, pt. 2, p. 1070.

quois on the American market. The "Tiffany mine" is reputed to have produced a higher proportion of high-grade gem material than any other deposit in the United States; its choicest stones have been equalled in this country only by those from the Burro Mountains and some localities in Nevada. Good material has also been obtained from the Castilian mine, but much of its output had a greenish cast. The total yield from the holdings of the American Turquois Co., coming chiefly from the "Tiffany mine," is said to exceed $2,000,000 in value.

BURRO MOUNTAINS, GRANT COUNTY.[1]

Deposits of turquois, formerly of importance but now largely exhausted, are situated among the Burro Mountains, Grant County, near the southwest corner of New Mexico. The principal occurrence centers about the Azure mine, which lies 10 miles S. 35° W. of Silver City and 1½ miles north of Leopold, overlooking the Mangas Valley.

Turquois was mined in this region in prehistoric times; excavations and heaps of débris, containing stone implements and coiled pottery, mark the site of the ancient operations, and have determined the location of some of the modern workings. The deposits were probably exploited also under Spanish rule.[2] John E. Coleman, locally known as "Turquois John," is generally accredited with the first modern discovery of turquois.[3] He is supposed to have stumbled upon some old workings while on a hunting trip in 1875 and to have been instrumental in locating the first claim, the Calliate.

The Burro Mountains consist in the main of a core of pre-Cambrian rocks, chiefly granitic, intruded by quartz monzonite and quartz monzonite porphyry.[4] Much of the region has been severely fractured and mineralized, and to the south of the turquois deposits are copper veins formed through secondary enrichment. The turquois lies both in the granite and in the porphyry dikes traversing it, and is found in places along the contact. It has been deposited in fractures where the rock has undergone alteration.

Azure mine.—The Azure mine, located 10 miles S. 35° W. of Silver City, was opened in 1891 by the Azure Mining Co., of New York. It has been operated in modern times more extensively than any other turquois mine in this country, and its stones are the equal of the Persian gems. The total value of its output is stated to have been between $2,000,000 and $4,000,000.[5] The deposit has been worked by an open cut, measuring about 600 feet in length, 100 to 200 feet in width, and 60 feet in depth, with tunnels at several levels. In 1893 the famous "Elizabeth pocket" was entered, which produced more high-grade turquois than any single deposit on record.[6]

The country rock is granite,[7] and the turquois lies in a pronounced fracture zone, 40 to 60 feet wide, with northeast strike and dip of 45° to the southeast. This zone is a severely shattered phase of the granite that has undergone kaolinization, sericitization, and silicification. The joints produced during fracturing are principally of two kinds; those parallel to the walls of the fracture zone, and those with similar strike but northwest dip. The first set are the more prominent. The fractures are not confined to the "vein," although more pronounced therein. Dikes and masses of quartz monzonite porphyry[8] outcrop within a few hundred feet of the mine. A prominent fluorite vein is slightly over one-half mile distant.

---

[1] The best descriptions of the turquois deposits are by Zalinski, Econ. Geol., vol. 2, 1907, pp. 464–492; Eng. Min. Journ., vol. 86, 1908, pp. 843–846; Sterrett, Min. Resources for 1907, pp. 828–846; ibid., 1909, pp. 789–791; Graton, Prof. Paper 68, U. S. Geol. Surv., 1910, pp. 321, 324; and Paige Econ. Geol., vol. 7, 1912, pp. 382–392.

[2] A pick of crude workmanship with eye in one end was found in an old pit and thought to be of Spanish origin. (Jones, New Mexico mines and minerals. Santa Fe, 1904, p. 275.)

[3] Zalinski, Econ. Geol., vol. 2, 1902, p. 465. The names of W. J. Foley and Nicholas C. Ransome are also mentioned in this connection. Snow (Amer. Journ. Sci., vol. 41, 1891, p. 511) relates that in 1890 Foley, then of Silver City, was informed by a firm of Indian traders that the Navaho claimed that turquois occurred near Silver City and had been worked at a remote period in an extensive manner; search then instituted by Mr. Foley resulted in the finding of ancient excavations in the Burro Mountains.

[4] Paige, op. cit., p. 382.

[5] Sterrett, Min. Resources for 1909, pt. 2, p. 789. Zalinski, who was superintendent of the mine in 1905, estimates the value of its production at "several million dollars."

[6] Zalinski, op. cit., p. 475.

[7] Ibid. Sterrett (1909) called it granite porphyry.

[8] According to Zalinski, the granite is intruded by mica andesite porphyry, with dacitic affinity, and both are cut by dikes of mica andesite, evidently a later phase of the porphyry magma. The microscopic description of both the porphyry and dike rock suggests quartz monzonite porphyry, and following Graton (op. cit., p. 324) these rocks are accordingly so designated.

The turquois occurs as films to three-fourths inch veins filling joints, and as nuggets enveloped in kaolin-like material[1] and generally occupying lenticular pockets. The nuggets yield the finest gems and are generally found where the feldspars have undergone the most extensive alteration. Veins of different shades sometimes cross, indicating a period of minor fracturing between two successive depositions. Some of the turquois is penetrated by quartz crystals, or associated with olive-green and grayish masses and nuggets of halloysite. The best material came from the Elizabeth pocket, which extended 150 feet along the "vein" with a width of 40 feet and a depth of about 50 feet, where the country rock was cut by an unusually large number of quartz veinlets.

The turquois from the Azure mine has held an enviable position in the gem trade.[2] The cut gems of good quality are marked on the under side with a circle and guaranteed to retain their color. The stones show a variety of shades, but the most approved is a slightly translucent, deep-blue; and it is such that the "Elizabeth pocket" yielded so abundantly. The output includes both pure turquois and attractive matrix. Some "mottled matrix," showing two shades of blue, is also produced. The best grade material is over 6 in hardness and yields stones with good wearing qualities.

New Azure mine.[3]—In 1908 a new deposit of turquois was opened about 150 yards east of the old Azure mine, after the yield in the latter had considerably diminished. This deposit, anciently worked by the Indians, and recently developed by a series of shafts, drifts, and tunnels, was soon worked out. The turquois occurs in a fracture zone in granite, and the occurrence is similar to that of the old Azure mine.

American Gem & Turquois Co.'s mines.[4]—The American Gem & Turquois Co. have operated the Parker mine, one-half mile southeast of the Azure workings, and opened deposits near remains of prehistoric mining about 200 yards to the northwest. The total development consists of several tunnels and open cuts. The occurrence is similar to those already described; the turquois occurs along the contact of quartz monzonite porphyry and altered granite. In the prehistoric workings, numbers of stone hammers were found. They are made of the local altered granite, in some instances even containing turquois, and are of rounded form from 4 to 8 inches or more in diameter; evidently they were used without a handle.

Other localities.—Prospecting has been carried on at a locality one-half mile south of the Azure mine on the west side of St. Louis Canyon, which is stated to have produced some good-quality stones.[5] Turquois has also been found a few miles northeast of Leopold along the road leading to Silver City.[6] At Maroney's prospect, in this vicinity, the material is said to be of good quality, but limited in quantity and size.[7] The mineral also has been found at two places near the old Burro Chief copper mine,[7] about three-fourths mile east of south of the Azure mine. One of these was described in 1891 by Snow,[8] who stated that the locality was originally prospected for copper, the turquois having been mistaken for an ore of that metal. The turquois here is prevailingly greenish in color and forms a network of veinlets in a dike rock. The second point is nearby, where some green and blue earthy varieties of turquois were obtained from a shaft sunk for copper. The turquois at neither place is of gem quality. A few miles south of the Big Burros thin seams of turquois of good color have been noted in the Cow Spring district.[9] A little prospecting was done here as early as 1893.[10]

In the White Signal district, on the south side of the Burro Mountains, turquois has been found at several places.[11] At one of these it lies along the contact of a 2-foot porphyry dike with granite. In 1905 one turquois prospect was worked in this district. Turquois is reported also to have been found at a depth of 410 feet in the Copper King mine.[12]

[1] Probably a mixture of sericite and kaolin.
[2] Sterrett, Min. Resources for 1909, pt. 2, p. 791.
[3] Sterrett, ibid., pp. 789–790.
[4] Sterrett, Min. Resources for 1907, pt. 2, pp. 830–831.
[5] Sterrett, ibid., pp. 831–832.
[6] Graton, Prof. Paper 68, U. S. Geol. Surv., 1910, p. 324.
[7] Zalinski, Econ. Geol., vol. 2, 1907, p. 474.
[8] Amer. Journ. Sci., vol. 41, 1891, pp. 511–512.
[9] Zalinski, op. cit., p. 474.
[10] Hidden, Amer. Journ. Sci., vol. 46, 1893, p. 400.
[11] Graton, op. cit., p. 324.
[12] Sterrett, Min. Resources for 1907, pt. 2, p. 829.

HACHITA DISTRICT, GRANT COUNTY.[1]

The turquois deposits of the Little Hachita Mountains[2] lie about 6 miles west of Hachita, in Grant County, at elevations of 5,000 to 5,400 feet. They are situated in a semibasin country containing a small number of knobs and ridges, prominent among which is an elevation locally known as Turquois Mountain.

The region was considerably exploited for turquois by the prehistoric Indians. In modern times the deposits were worked between 1885 and 1888, at first for gold. The rediscovery of turquois during that period, however, led to their purchase by eastern capital. Hidden[3] in 1892 carried on a little work here, but abandoned the project because little good material was obtained. It was not until 1908 that the region was considerably developed, and in 1909 mining was actively prosecuted.

Geologically, the region consists of a series of sandstones, slates, and limestones, associated with rhyolitic, trachytic, and andesitic rocks, which occur as tuffs, flows, sills, and dikes. The turquois is present in altered phases of the trachyte and in places in what appears to be an altered andesite.

The various mines will be separately described folowing the information published by Sterrett,[4] who visited the region in 1909.

Robinson and Porterfield mines.—This group of mines, so designated from their owners (1909), include the Azure, Cameo, Galilee, and Aztec claims.

The Azure claim occupies the top of Turquois Mountain, (see Fig. 2, Pl. 2) and consists of two sets of workings, one at its northeast end and another a short distance to the southwest. The first has been developed by means of a lengthy tunnel and some open cuts; the second, only by open cuts. The former shows many signs of prehistoric mining and remains of later workings probably executed during the eighties. Here the turquois occurs along the contact of an altered trachyte (or monzonite) and monzonitic porphyry, principally in the first named, especially in its fractured and iron-stained phases. It forms thin to one-half inch, irregularly distributed seams filling fractures, and ranges in color from dark sky-blue through greenish-blue to pale-blue. The paler material is rather soft. The principal yield has been high-grade matrix including some good cameo material. The second locality has produced a little hard turquois, with a fine pure-blue color.

The Cameo claim is nearly one mile north of west of the northeast end of Turquois Mountain and has been developed by a shaft following an almost vertical veinlet of turquois in altered trachyte. The best turquois is pure-blue, locally greenish; some is cut into cameos with base of yellowish-gray to brownish wall rock. This deposit shows prehistoric excavations and stone implements, one of which was identified under the microscope as an andesitic breccia.

The Galilee claim is three-fifths mile southwest of Turquois Mountain and has been worked by a large pit. The turquois forms two main veinlets occupying iron-stained fracture zones.

The Aztec claim, so named from its prehistoric workings, lies 1½ miles west of south of Turquois Mountain, and has been modernly worked by means of a tunnel. The turquois occurs as seams filling pronounced joints in altered trachyte, and as nuggets irregularly distributed through the rock. The latter form of occurrence is said to yield the best material. Much of the product is rather soft and pale, and some fades on exposure.

American Turquois Co. mine.—This deposit is a few hundred yards west of the Cameo claim. It has been worked by shaft and open cut. The turquois forms veinlets in iron-stained, altered trachyte; and its best grade has a good blue color and is quite hard. The product has been mostly pure turquois.

M. M. Crocker claims.—These are two in number, located, respectively, on the southwest end of Turquois Mountain and on a small knob one-half mile south of west of Turquois Moun-

---

[1] Sterrett, Min. Resources for 1909, pt. 2, pp. 791–795.
[2] Also known as the Hachita Range.
[3] Amer. Journ. Sci., vol. 46, 1893, pp. 400–402.
[4] Min. Resources for 1909, pt. 2, pp. 791–795.

tain. The first has been exploited by means of a shaft and open cut; the second, by two pits. The occurrence presents no features different from those already described.

R. S. Chamberlain mine.—This deposit, marked by large prehistoric workings, lies on the east side of the northeast end of Turquois Mountain. A 40-foot shaft is reported to have followed ancient workings to that depth. The deposits appear to be along the contact of trachyte and monzonite (or andesite).

Other occurrences.—Turquois was reported one-third mile south of Turquois Mountain in a shaft sunk for silver. A little of the mineral was also found on the Le Feve claim, slightly over one-half mile S. 20° W. of Turquois Mountain. A deposit with ancient workings has been reported at Silver Night, about 20 miles southwest of the present district. A little turquois is said to have been found in some of the silver mines formerly worked in the present turquois region.

JARILLA DISTRICT, OTERO COUNTY.

The Jarillas are a low range of hills that rise out of a wilderness of sand in western Otero County, N. Mex., 50 miles north-northeast of El Paso, Tex., and about the same distance east of Las Cruces. Turquois was discovered here in 1892 by W. E. Hidden,[1] who rightly considered the old workings in the vicinity to have been developed in search of this mineral, and by the close of that year a permanent camp had been established and regular mining undertaken. About 1898 a series of fortunate explorations on the De Meules property resulted in the production of some fine stones.[2] Since then several other claims have been located and worked, but without particular success. The deposits are not now productive.

According to Hidden, the turquois occurs in seams and crevices in trachyte,[3] and was found all the way to the bottom of a 70-foot shaft. The associated minerals at the surface are limonite and kaolin; at the bottom, pyrite, chalcopyrite (rare), gypsum, jarosite, and kaolin. The material first obtained faded. A bright future was predicted for the occurrence, which has not yet been fulfilled.

Hidden considered that the old operations had been abandoned for several hundred years. A half score of ancient excavations were found, but they were very shallow and ended wherever hard rock was encountered.

OTHER LOCALITIES.

Turquois is reported to have been mined to some extent about 1891 in Sierra County, N. Mex., near Paschal.[4] Old trenches containing fragments of pottery and stone hammers indicate that prehistoric mining also had been undertaken here. According to Bandelier,[5] a turquois locality lies near San Marcos (a ruined pueblo 18 miles SSW. of Santa Fe), which the Tano Indians of Santo Domingo own and frequently visit to procure stones. Mrs. Stephenson[6] states that the Zuñi Indians know of deposits to the southwest of the Cerrillos mines, but seldom visit them for fear their situation will become known to the whites. (See page 124.)

TEXAS.

Turquois was reported in 1884 from a locality in Texas north of El Paso.[7] About 1910 a small quantity of greenish material, obtained from near Van Horn, in El Paso County, was cut into matrix stones.[8]

[1] Amer. Journ. Sci., vol. 46, 1893, pp. 400–402.

[2] Jones, New Mexico Mines and Minerals. Santa Fe, 1904, p. 277.

[3] More properly a monzonite porphyry. Graton (Prof. Paper 68, U. S. Geol. Surv., 1910, p. 185) states that the Jarilla Hills consist of carboniferous limestone strata domed up by an intrusion of fine-grained monzonite porphyry, and that the turquois is found in the latter.

[4] Anon., Eng. Min. Journ., vol. 51, 1891, p. 751.

[5] Final report of investigations among the Indians of southwestern United States. Cambridge, pt. 2, 1892. p. 93.

[6] Dress and adornment of the Pueblo Indians. Consulted in manuscript.

[7] Kunz, 16th Ann. Rept. U. S. Geol. Surv., 1894–5, pt. 4, p. 602.

[8] The Houston Post, through Jewelers' Circular Weekly, Nov., 1910, p. 89.

The wide bracelet at top is a Zuni "channel" bracelet. Bottom left: A Zuni wrought silver bracelet. Bottom right: A Navajo cast silver bracelet. All three items from collection of Broadmoor Drug Store, Broadmoor Hotel, Colorado Springs, Colo. Photo by: John F. Bennett. Selections were designed to show superb turquoise in contemporary handcrafted jewelry. Courtesy of the shop and Mr. Bennett is appreciated.

Various specimens from the collection of Joan Patania Wheeler.

VIRGINIA.

In 1911 a specimen of bright-blue *crystallized* turquois (see Fig. 3, Pl. 1) was collected by J. H. Watkins from a copper prospect near Lynch's Station, in Campbell County, Va., and described by W. T. Schaller.[1] This is the first recorded occurrence of this mineral in crystallized condition. The locality has not yet been examined geologically nor has the occurrence been exploited.

The mode of occurrence is quite different from that in the localities previously described. The turquois is found in quartz, filling small fractures and lining cavities therein. The specimen in the United States National Museum consists of fragments of glassy quartz cemented by thin seams of crystallized turquois and upon one side the turquois forms a drusy, botryoidal layer, cavernous in texture and inclosing many small fragments of quartz. The surface glistens as light is reflected from innumerable crystal facets. No mineral, except quartz, is in close association with the turquois, although a very subordinate quantity of kaolin and sericite occupies small seams and patches in the quartz. Evidently the turquois has been deposited from solutions containing little else than the constituents necessary for its formation.

The mineral is of good blue color, polishes well, and would make attractive matrix gems.

---

[1] Amer. Journ. Sci., vol. 33, 1912, pp. 35–40. Mr. Watkins presented the specimen to the U. S. National Museum (Cat. No. 86990).

CHAPTER IV.

THE ORIGIN OF TURQUOIS.

* * * he made
An image of his God in gold and pearl
With turquoise diadem and human eyes.

Kipling: Evarra and his Gods.

SUMMARY OF GEOLOGIC RELATIONS.

The significant data connected with the occurrence of turquois throughout the world are given in the following table. Occurrences are omitted the geological relations of which are doubtful:

Table giving summary of geologic features of important turquois deposits of the world.[1]

Locality.	Turquois occurs in—	Associated with—	Remarks.
Abyssinia	Ferruginous sandstone, intruded by porphyry and capped by basalt.		
Sinai Peninsula	Ferruginous sandstone capped by basalt	Limonite	
Nishapur, Persia	Altered trachyte and trachytic breccia	Limonite and kaolin	Trachyte contains apatite. Turquois replaces feldspar crystals.
Mt. Karamazar, Turkestan	Altered feldspathic porphyry, and in veins of ferruginous quartz.		
Bodalla, New South Wales	Carbonaceous shale	Pyrite	
King River, Victoria	Carbonaceous slate	Limonite	
Clay County, Ala	Graphitic schist		Geology not described.
Mineral Park, Ariz	Altered quartz porphyry and granite porphyry.	Limonite, kaolin, alum, copper sulphate.	Country rock has suffered kaolinization, sericitization, and silicification.
Fresno County, Cal	Granite		Pseudomorph after apatite.
Manvel District, Cal	Altered granite porphyry	Limonite, kaolin, sericite, jarosite, quartz.	
Mohave Desert, Cal	Altered rhyolite and biotite gneiss, along contact.	Limonite and quartz	Rhyolite in part a sericite schist; is considerably kaolinized.
Lajara, Colo	Altered trachyte	Limonite, kaolin, sericite	
Esmeralda-Nye County region, Nev. Royal Blue mine.	Altered trachyte	Limonite, kaolin, sericite, quartz.	
Same. William Petry mine	Altered rhyolite	Limonite and kaolin	Rhyolite contains casts of apatite crystals.
Same. Myers & Bona mine	Altered quartz porphyry and altered black slate, along contact.	Limonite	Porphyry contains much sericite.
Same. Montezuma mine	Altered trachyte	Limonite	
Same. Moqui-Aztec mine	Altered quartz porphyry and included quartz masses.	Kaolin, limonite, and quartz.	
Same. Smith Black Matrix mine.	Black siliceous jasperoid, near contact with rhyolite flow now eroded away.	Limonite	Turquois fills fractures and breccia spaces. Few copper stains in jasperoid.
Same, near Columbus	Rhyolite; also in silicified sedimentary rock (jasperoid).	Not stated	
Lyon County, Nev	Altered monzonite	Kaolin, limonite, sericite	
Cerrillos Hills, N. Mex	Altered monzonite porphyry (or augite andesite).	Fluorite (?), kaolin, limonite, quartz.	Porphyry contains both sericite and kaolin; also pyrite and apatite.
Burro Mountains, N. Mex. Azure mine.	Altered granite; in places along contact with quartz monzonite porphyry.	Halloysite, kaolin, jarosite, sericite.	Deposited in pronounced fracture zone. Fluorite vein near. Granite contains apatite. Region of copper veins.
Hachita District, N. Mex	Altered trachyte		
Same. Robinson & Porterfield mine.	Altered trachyte and monzonite porphyry, along contact.	Kaolin, limonite, gypsum	Part of trachyte contains much pyrite.
Jarilla Hills, N. Mex	Altered trachyte	At surface, limonite and kaolin; 70 feet from surface, pyrite chalcopyrite, jarosite, kaolin.	
Campbell County, Va	Quartz		Geology not described.

[1] The term "altered" is used to include weathering and deep-seated alteration. The identity of kaolin and of sericite has been verified in many instances by the writer. Their similarity in hand specimens and in some cases under the microscope renders some of the identifications in the literature unreliable. The term kaolin is used to include the crystallized mineral kaolinite, as well as the ordinary, less well-defined product of feldspathic weathering, since the two are not usually distinguished in the literature.

HISTORICAL.

Numerous explanations have been advanced to account for the formation of turquois. The most important of these will be briefly reviewed, under the heading of the respective districts to which they refer.

Sinai Peninsula.—Berthelot[1] believed the Sinai turquois to have been deposited by percolating waters from above. De Launey[2] suggested that the deposits represent the oxidized portions of copper veins, the phosphoric acid having been supplied by a phosphate of some kind in the sandstone. Petrie[3] attributed the phosphoric acid to organisms incorporated in the sandstone at the time of its deposition. Barron[4] assigned the turquois a superficial origin and stated that the pressure, which produced folds and faults in the region, may have been instrumental in its formation.

Nishapur, Persia.—De Launey[5] in 1911 suggested two stages in the formation of the turquois; first, the production of a phosphate of aluminum; and second, its blue coloration by copper. In the case of the Nishapur deposits the small apatite crystals in the trachyte were considered the most probable source of the phosphoric acid, while the copper was thought to be contributed by the copper veins.

France.—Lacroix,[6] writing of the occurrence of turquois in the tin veins of Montebras, Creuse, France, considered the copper derived from a sulphide associated with the cassiterite.

Australia.—In regard to the Edi turquois field of Victoria, Australia, Dunn[7] stated that the constituents of the turquois were probably all present originally in the slate in which the mineral is now found. From the constant association of turquois with weathered pyrite he concluded that the copper was furnished by the latter.

Mineral Park, Ariz.—In a description of the Mineral Park occurrence Sterrett[8] stated that it "appears that some of the turquois may have formed directly from kaolin by the addition of phosphate and copper stains, for specimens are found that show a gradation from good turquois to soft semiturquois and to copper-stained kaolin, and, furthermore, balls or patches of material, which may have once been feldspar phenocrysts, are found that range from kaolin to semiturquois to turquois."

Esmeralda County, Nev.—The Smith Black Matrix mine contains a green variety of turquois which, according to Sterrett,[9] carries a low percentage of copper, and exhibits under the microscope a texture resembling that of variscite (a hydrous aluminum phosphate, without copper). Sterrett therefore suggested that there may be a gradation from variscite to turquois "through a more or less amorphous series of hydrous aluminum phosphates in which copper occurs in amounts varying from nothing to the several per cent necessary to produce normal turquoïs."[9] He further proposed that the constituents of the turquois now occurring in jasperoid may have been leached from above during the decomposition of a rhyolite flow that extended over the turquois-bearing bed before removal by erosion.

Cerrillos Hills, N. Mex.—Silliman[10] in 1881 was the first to advance an opinion on the origin of the Cerrillos turquois. He considered the alteration of the country rock due to hydrothermal action and the formation of the turquois an important accompaniment thereof. Alumina, resulting from the decomposition of feldspar; phosphoric acid, furnished by apatite; and copper, supplied by disseminated copper ores, were deemed competent to produce turquois upon combination.

---

[1] Compt. rend., vol. 123, 1896, pp. 365–374.
[2] Les richesses minerales de l'Afrique. Paris, 1903, p. 285.
[3] Researches in Sinai. London, 1906, p. 36.
[4] The topography and geology of the Peninsula of Sinai (western portion). Surv. Dept. Egypt, Cairo, 1907, pp. 209–212.
[5] La géologie et les richesses minerales de l'Asie, Paris, 1911, pp. 661–663.
[6] Minéralogie de la France et de ses colonies. Paris, 1910, vol. 4, p. 530.
[7] Rec. Geol. Surv. Victoria, vol. 2, 1908, pp. 170–174.
[8] Min. Resources for 1908, pt. 2, p. 48.
[9] Min. Resources for 1909, pt. 2, p. 53.
[10] Amer. Journ. Sci., vol. 22, 1881, pp. 68, 70.

Clarke and Diller,[1] studying the problem in 1886, regarded the turquois as of local origin, resulting from the alteration of some other mineral. They found the turquois under the microscope to be composed of fibers, which in one specimen were arranged at right angles to the vein walls; and this fact is cited as an indication of the replacement of a preexisting substance, probably a phosphate such as apatite.

In 1900 Herrick[2] advanced the opinion that "the turquois owes its origin to action of molten syenite on the copper-bearing sandstone of the Jurassic it had caught up in its escape." This theory, however, as Johnson[3] pointed out, is untenable, since no copper-bearing Jurassic sediments are known in the neighborhood.

Rösler[4] in 1902, in an elaborate paper maintaining that kaolinite is a deep-seated product, attributed the kaolinization and turquois veins at Cerrillos to pneumatolytic processes.

A detailed study of the Cerrillos deposits was completed by Johnson[5] in 1903, and his views regarding their formation may be briefly stated as follows: The turquois originated during the alteration of the country rock; its alumina and phosphoric acid were derived from the feldspar and apatite of the original rock, while its copper was supplied by copper-bearing solutions, which also produced the copper-bearing ores of the region; and the whole process was probably facilitated by hot solutions and vapors rising along crushed and fractured zones. The association of fluorite with the turquois is cited as a significant feature, inasmuch as calcium and fluorine, its components, are the elements remaining if phosphoric acid (P_2O_5) be subtracted from apatite.

Lindgren,[6] after a study of the Cerrillos deposits, "believes it safe to assert that turquois is not a primary vein mineral, but is formed by surface waters of ordinary temperature descending through altered and mineralized rocks." He goes on to say that the Cerrillos turquois-bearing area was evidently greatly altered by mineralizing solutions, with the formation of considerable sericite; and that when the altered rock was brought by erosion within reach of surface waters kaolin was developed by the action on the sericite of sulphuric acid from the pyrite, and the turquois found congenial conditions to form.

Burro Mountains.—Zalinski[7] in 1907 published a detailed account of the Burro Mountains turquois, in which he offered the following explanation of its origin: The turquois was formed by the commingling of two sets of solutions; one, rising along fractures parallel to the vein walls, contributed the phosphoric acid and caused the kaolinization; the other, coming from the footwall of the vein along cross fractures, supplied the copper. Phosphoric acid was derived from apatite, alumina from feldspar; and these combined either at depth or where the turquois was deposited. Intrusion of porphyry not only furnished the solutions, but also produced the fracture zone along which these solutions could easily circulate.

Of this deposit, Graton[8] writes:

The formation of the turquois is undoubtedly related to the intrusion of the quartz monzonite porphyry, as also the accompanying kaolinization and pyritization. It is probable that the phosphoric acid and copper of the turquois were supplied by gases or solutions coming from the intrusive mass, but the alumina may have been derived from the rock in which the turquois was deposited.

Paige[9] has recently made a study of the turquois of the Burro Mountains, and takes exception to the generalizations reached by Zalinski. Paige reviews the mineral associations and geologic relations of this mineral and concludes that the evidence weighs heavily in favor of an origin in the zone of weathering; alumina, phosphoric acid, and copper having been derived from feldspar, apatite, and disseminated copper ores of the country rock. He lays special emphasis upon the association with minerals characteristic of the oxidized zone and upon the physiographic position of the deposits adjacent to a planated surface.

[1] Amer. Journ. Sci., vol. 32, 1886, pp. 211–217.
[2] Rept. Governor of N. Mex. for 1900, p. 258.
[3] School of Min. Quart., vol. 24, 1903, p. 497.
[4] Neues Jahrb., Beilage Bd. 15, 1902, p. 286.
[5] Op. cit., pp. 497–499.
[6] Prof. Paper 68, U. S. Geol. Surv., 1910, p. 166.
[7] Econ. Geol., vol. 2, 1907, pp. 489–491.
[8] Prof. Paper 68, U. S. Geol. Surv., 1910, p. 324.
[9] Econ. Geol., vol. 7, 1912, pp. 382–392.

Jarilla Hills, N. Mex.—According to Hidden,[1] the turquois of the Jarilla Hills was formed directly from kaolin, by the addition of the necessary constituents.

General.—Jones,[2] after considering the turquois deposits of New Mexico, advanced the following explanation for the origin of the mineral: Turquois is deposited by descending surface waters containing aluminum hydrate furnished by kaolinized country rock; phosphoric acid supplied by apatite and perhaps to some extent by organic matter on the surface; and copper derived from disseminated copper ores.

DISCUSSION OF ORIGIN.

TYPES OF DEPOSITS.

Study of the geologic features of turquois deposits throughout the world (see summary, page 60) reveals the fact that this mineral has three modes of occurrence:

Type 1.—The turquois occurs in acid igneous rocks rich in alkalic feldspars and considerably altered by weathering or deep-seated alteration, or both. The majority of commercially important deposits come under this head; as, for example, the Nishapur deposits and the principal deposits of the West, particularly those of the Burro Mountains and the Cerrillos Hills.

Type 2.—The turquois occurs in sedimentary or metamorphic rocks near the contact with igneous masses, and is apparently connected in genesis therewith. The mines in the Mohave Desert, Cal., and several in the Esmeralda-Nye County region of Nevada, most notably the Smith Black Matrix mine, offer examples of this type of deposit.

Type 3.—The turquois is present in a non-igneous matrix (usually sandstone or shale) and has no apparent genetic connection with any igneous body. The Sinai and Australian occurrences are the principal representatives of this type.[3]

HYPOTHESES OF ORIGIN.

Turquois is the result of deposition from solution. The nature of the various occurrences of this mineral limits its possible modes of formation to the following:

Hypothesis 1.—Precipitation from ascending solutions of magmatic origin; the components being supplied wholly by these solutions. Analogy: Chalcopyrite and other primary minerals.

Hypothesis 2.—Formation dependent upon alteration of country rock by magmatic emanations whereby part at least of the components of turquois are supplied through breaking down of minerals in the country rock. Analogy: Hydrothermal sericite.

Hypothesis 3.—Precipitation from cold solutions, formed by atmospheric waters leaching through rocks near the surface. All the components of turquois are supplied by minerals in the country rock. Analogy: Limonite.

(*a*) The process may be independent of prior deep-seated alteration of the country rock.

(*b*) The process may be favored by prior deep-seated alteration of country rock.

(*c*) The process may be dependent upon prior deep-seated alteration of country rock.

Each type of deposit will be examined separately in the light of the three hypotheses just outlined.

ORIGIN OF DEPOSITS OF TYPE 1.

Turquois deposits of type 1 present the following salient features, diagnostic of their origin:

1. The turquois is confined to the altered portions of igneous rocks rich in alkalic feldspars. In many instances these rocks have suffered deep-seated changes; in all instances they have undergone more or less weathering.

2. The turquois is invariably associated with limonite and copper carbonates—minerals not formed below the zone of oxidation.

3. The turquois is generally associated with more or less kaolin, a substance usually resulting from the weathering of alkalic feldspars.

---

[1] Amer. Journ. Sci., vol. 46, 1893, p. 402.

[2] New Mexico mines and minerals. Santa Fe, 1904, pp. 272-273. Also in Min. World, vol. 31, 1909, p. 1252.

[3] The occurrences in Alabama and in Virginia appear to form further examples, but their geology is not sufficiently known to accept this with confidence.

4. The turquois in many instances is associated with sericite, partly, at least, of hydrothermal origin.

5. The turquois in some instances is associated with chrysocolla, alum, jarosite, and copper sulphate.

6. In the country rock apatite has usually been identified.

7. Pyrite and copper sulphides are usually present below the turquois deposits.

8. The turquois deposits are invariably near the surface. The mineral does not extend to depth (is seldom below 100 feet).

Applying these eight criteria to the three hypotheses of origin it is seen that an origin from magmatic solutions is opposed by points 1, 2, 3, 5, 7, 8; an origin through alteration of the country rock by magmatic emanations alone is opposed by points 2, 3, 5, 8; while an origin through alteration of the country rock by atmospheric waters is favored by all points but No. 4. The weight of evidence therefore favors a superficial origin for turquois of type 1, although some occurrences present features, notably a close association with abundant sericite, not readily compatible with a formation from descending meteoric waters. In the ensuing discussion this question receives further attention.

Turquois is a hydrous phosphate of copper and aluminum ($CuO.3Al_2O_3.2P_2O_5.9H_2O$), and an explanation of its formation must account for phosphoric acid, alumina, and copper.

Source of phosphoric acid.—Apatite disseminated in the country rock is the most probable source of the phosphoric acid. This mineral is "one of the most widespread, if not the most widespread, of all the subordinate constituents of rocks." Its presence has been noted in the country rock at Nishapur, Cerrillos, several Nevada localities, and the Burro Mountains. At the last-named locality, as pointed out by Paige,[1] fresh crystals are only found below the zone of oxidation. The presence of fluorite near the deposits of the Burro Mountains and the Cerrillos Hills is suggestive, inasmuch as the components necessary for its formation are left if phosphoric acid be subtracted from apatite. Fresno County, California, has yielded a pseudomorph of turquois after apatite.

It is well known that apatite is readily dissolved in the zone of weathering by carbonated waters.[2] As shown by a series of analyses by Endell,[3] this mineral is leached away during kaolinization. Some of the phosphoric acid removed in solution will react upon the other products of rock decomposition to form new secondary phosphates.[4] From carbonated solutions ferric hydroxide and aluminum hydroxide have the ability to extract phosphoric acid and to form with it phosphates of iron and aluminum.[5]

Source of alumina.—The fact that turquois of type 1 is confined to altered feldspathic rocks implies that the latter are essential to its formation, and points to the feldspars as the source of the alumina. The feldspars have universally undergone kaolinization and in places sericitization; the former due to weathering, the latter (in large part, at least) due to deep-seated alteration. These processes, one or both, must have liberated from the feldspars sufficient alumina to produce the turquois. Each possibility will be examined.

Liberation of alumina during kaolinization.—The decomposition of aluminous silicates presents a complex chemical problem that has been as yet by no means fully solved. Kaolin is mostly a product of superficial weathering, formed by the action of percolating acid waters on aluminous rocks.[6] It may result from the decomposition of many aluminous minerals, but the alkalic feldspars are its principal source. In the change of the latter into kaolin the lime and alkalis are practically removed, a part of the silica is liberated, water is absorbed, and alumina is concentrated. The condition of aluminum during the transformation is not

[1] Op. cit., p. 388.

[2] Bischof, Elements of chemical and physical geology. London, 1855, vol. 2, p. 32. Müller, Tsch. Min. Mitth., 1877, p. 25. Cameron and Hurst, Journ. Amer. Chem. Soc., vol. 25, 1904, pp. 903–911. See also Clarke, The Data of Geochemistry, 1911, pp. 337, 495.

[3] Sprechsaal, vol. 42, 1909, pp. 495–496.

[4] Clarke, op. cit., p. 495.

[5] Warington, Journ. Chem. Soc., vol. 19, 1866, p. 316.

[6] Lindgren (Trans. Amer. Inst. Min. Eng., vol. 30, 1900, p. 614) states that "kaolinite is formed most abundantly in the upper oxidized zones of many ore deposits."

The statements of Rösler (Neues Jahrb., Beil. Band 15, 1902, p. 231) and of a few others, to the effect that kaolin is only produced by pneumatolitic action, can not be accepted (see Merrill, Rocks, Rock-weathering, and Soils, 1906, p. 17), although kaolin of deep-seated origin is not uncommon.

known; is it entirely retained in the kaolinite, or is part removed in solution? Some light may be shed upon this question by considering the formation of bauxite and laterite—related substances, in origin directly connected with the derivation of aluminum from aluminous silicates.

Bauxite, the principal ore of aluminum, is an aluminum hydroxide mixed with small quantities of ferric hydroxide, silica, and other impurities. No one origin will explain its varied occurrence, but in general it has been derived from preexisting aluminous rocks; in some instances remaining as a residual deposit after the removal of more soluble constituents; in other instances transported and deposited by solutions. To consider the Georgia bauxite deposits as a single example: Hayes [1] believed that ordinary surface waters, percolating through shales, oxidized the sulphides contained therein, and by virtue of the sulphuric acid thus formed dissolved aluminum as a sulphate; and that the solutions, later rising through dolomites, were reacted upon by calcium carbonate with the precipitation of aluminum hydroxide.

Laterite is a product of rock decay confined principally to tropical and semitropical regions. It is found either in place or transported, and is essentially a mixture of ferric hydroxide, aluminum hydroxide, and free silica in varying proportions. It has resulted from extreme decomposition, whereby the silicates are completely broken down. During the process aluminum hydroxide is liberated and may be transported in solution. Lateritization is a type of weathering predominating under special conditions, yet it can not be separated by hard and fast lines from kaolinization; laterites, indeed, usually contain some kaolinite. Mohr [2] and Harrison [3] hold that laterites are formed from rocks rich in plagioclase feldspars, whereas alkalic feldspars, under the same conditions, yield mainly kaolin.

In view of the preceding consideration it appears extremely probable that during kaolinization some aluminum is separated from the silicate radical and taken into solution. It is believed that the association of kaolin with turquois is indicative that the alumina was so derived. It is further believed that the presence of pyrite, yielding sulphuric acid upon oxidation, is helpful in the extraction of the aluminum, which would then enter solution as a sulphate.[4] This view is rendered very probable by the occurrence of alum, copper sulphate, etc., in some deposits of turquois; by the constant presence of limonite (although much of it may have resulted from iron-bearing silicates); and by the appearance of pyrite at depth, as noted at some localities.

Sericitization as productive of alumina.—The repeated presence of sericite in the country rock adjacent to turquois has been noted. Rarely, however, is it in excess of kaolin. The possibility that sericitization has in some instances conditioned the production of turquois must be examined.

Sericite is derived from feldspars, usually as a result of hydrothermal or dynamic metamorphism. It may also be produced by weathering agencies. The sericite of the turquois deposits is probably mostly of deep-seated origin. Little is known of the details of the reaction whereby feldspar is converted into sericite, but there is no reason why some aluminum may not escape during the process. It is entirely possible, chemically, that heated solutions may have extracted sufficient aluminum during sericitization to produce turquois, and in some instances this may have happened. This hypothesis, however, fails of broad application because of the confinement of the turquois to the zone of oxidation and its constant association with minerals ordinarily formed only under conditions of oxidation.

The sericite, however, has probably some bearing upon the formation of turquois. It is believed to be this: That sericitization is favorable to subsequent kaolinization by which the aluminum is supplied. In the case of the Cerrillos deposits, Lindgren [5] distinguished between original sericitization due to mineralizing solutions and subsequent kaolinization as a result

---

[1] Trans. Amer. Inst. Min. Eng., vol. 24, 1894, p. 352.
[2] Bull. Dept. Agr., Indes Néerlandaise, No. 28, 1909, through Clarke, op. cit., p. 470.
[3] Geol. Mag., vol. 7, 1900, pp. 440, 560.
[4] It is known that aluminum is abundantly transported as a sulphate.
[5] Prof. Paper 68, U. S. Geol. Surv., 1910, p. 166.

of the action of surface waters on the sericite. The formation of kaolinite from sericite has been noted in other connections.[1]

Source of copper.—Disseminated copper ores are the source of the copper combined in the turquois. Copper stains are always, and copper deposits frequently, recognized at turquois localities. Copper, easily oxidized and easily reduced, enters readily into reactions. Dissolved as a carbonate or sulphate, it would easily unite with the aluminum and phosphoric acid radicals to form turquois. Possibly copper in solution is capable of converting precipitated hydrous aluminum phosphate into turquois. An experiment by Sullivan[2] is instructive in this connection. He has shown, by passing a solution of copper sulphate through kaolin, pulverized feldspar, etc., that a certain quantity of copper is extracted and an equivalent quantity of bases goes into solution.

Summary.—The conditions necessary to the formation of turquois (deposits of type 1) are believed to be: Igneous rocks, rich in alkalic feldspars and containing disseminated apatite and copper minerals (in small quantity), undergoing weathering, with kaolinization of the feldspars. Favorable to its formation, in addition, are: Disseminated pyrite (or other sulphides); a prior hydrothermal metamorphism with production of sericite; and fracture and shear zones especially pervious to descending waters.

ORIGIN OF DEPOSITS OF TYPE 2.

The origin of deposits of type 2 will now be considered. The examples are not many and are confined to the Mohave Desert region of California and some of the deposits of Nevada.

At the Smith Black Matrix mine (Nevada) the turquois occurs in a jasperoid beneath a rhyolite flow now eroded away. This occurrence appears to be a contact deposit, the components of the turquois having been supplied by the rhyolite; it is equally probable, however, that the turquois was produced during, and as a result of, the weathering of the overlying rhyolite. In the Mohave Desert and at several other localities in Nevada the turquois lies along the contact between igneous and sedimentary (or metamorphic) rocks, occurring in each. The portion in the igneous rock is identical in all its associates and relations with turquois of type 1. This fact is strongly indicative that the deposits in question, instead of being directly due to contact action, resulted during the subsequent weathering of the igneous rock, the more altered and fractured condition of the rocks along the contact increasing chemical activity and facilitating circulation, so that the deposition was mainly in that zone.

ORIGIN OF DEPOSITS OF TYPE 3.

The origin of turquois occurring in sedimentary rocks, not directly associated with igneous masses, remains to be considered. The Sinai occurrence is the principal representative; here the turquois occurs in sandstone along with limonite. Not sufficient is known of the geology and mineralogy of this occurrence to afford safe detailed deductions as to origin. The turquois, however, was unquestionably deposited from solutions, but whether these came from below or above can not be determined with the information in hand, although the latter source is more probable.

In Australia the turquois occurs in shale and slate. Here, too, the geologic information is too meager to afford accurate deductions as to origin.

The presence of turquois in sandstone and shale is analogous to the occurrence in many parts of the world of certain ores of copper, lead, vanadium, and uranium in similar rocks. The geology of such deposits has recently been well summarized by Lindgren,[3] who states that these ores have clearly been concentrated by atmospheric waters from small quantities of metals disseminated in the rocks, and that the metals were probably carried down as sediments and solutions from older ore deposits in the adjacent continental areas. Similarly, turquois of type 3 is believed to have been deposited by circulating surface waters that derived their alumina,

---

[1] Selle, Journ. Chem. Soc., vol. 96, pt. 2, p. 63. Through Clarke, loc. cit., p. 409.
[2] Econ. Geol., vol. 1, 1905, p. 69. See also Bull. 362, U. S. Geol. Surv., 1907.
[3] Econ. Geol., vol. 6, 1911, pp. 568–581.

phosphoric acid, and copper from the sediments. The source of these components, with present information, is a matter of conjecture, but it may be surmised that the alumina was derived from feldspathic or clayey material, the copper from disseminated copper ores, and the phosphoric acid either from some phosphate of organic origin distributed through the sediments or from sparse apatites which survived decomposition during erosion, transportation, and deposition.[1]

Under this third type of occurrence may also be included those instances in which turquois has been deposited in ordinary veins. The reported occurrence in a copper mine in New Jersey, the presence of turquois in the Mizpah vein at Tonopah, and the Virginia occurrence are such examples. Its formation is analogous to the development of other copper minerals in veins, the constituents of the turquois instead being present. The source of these constituents may have been deep-seated or superficial.

SUMMARY.

Turquois, like many minerals, has more than one mode of origin. It is dominantly formed, however, by the percolation of surface waters through aluminous rocks containing apatite and disseminated copper minerals.

---

[1] This last assumption implies a dependence upon arid climatic conditions. Wherry (Amer. Journ. Sci., vol. 33, 1912, pp. 574–580) has attributed the formation of carnotite in Pennsylvania to the accumulation of sediments rich in black silicates, supposedly carrying traces of vanadium and uranium, which upon later attack and decomposition by surface waters yielded components that were deposited as carnotite.

CHAPTER V.

THE USE OF TURQUOIS.

Turkomans, countless as their flocks, led forth
From th' aromatic pastures of the north;
Wild warriors of the turquoise hills.

Thomas Moore: Lalla Rookh.

The maid threw the breast-plate thick with jade,
Upon the turquoise anklets.

Kipling: The Sacrifice of Er Heb.

In a turquoise twilight, crisp and chill
A Kafila camped at the foot of the hill.

Kipling: The Ballad of the King's Jest.

Of crystal carven was the cup,
With turquoise set along the brim,
A lid of amber closed it up;
'Twas a great king that gave it him.

Edwin Arnold: The Caliph's Daughter.

INTRODUCTION.

Turquois has been used extensively from a very early period and today finds employment amongst peoples widely separated geographically and greatly differing in social and cultural development. Its application, both historically and ethnographically, covers a wide range and is largely dependent upon the appeal that its color [1] has made to the minds of those who have valued it.

Precious stones have played an interesting part in the history of mankind. We may suppose that upon the first development of a desire for ornamentation, the savage was attracted by bright colored minerals found in the beds of streams, and, with advancing discrimination, was pleased by pebbles presenting shades of yellow and red. It is a matter admitting of little doubt that the rolled alluvial gems were sought long before the first attempts were made to obtain the less evident and more inaccessible minerals hidden in the rocks. It is likely that some primitive digging was engaged in before means were devised for boring the stream pebbles, yet strings of bright stream stones probably formed the earliest jewelry that pleased the

---

[1] To appreciate fully the bearing of the color of turquois upon its use, especially among primitive peoples, it is necessary to examine certain recently advanced ideas regarding the significance of fundamental colors, of which the turquois is represented by two, green and blue. It has been found by Prof. Victor Goldschmidt of Heidelberg that the spectrum colors, yellow, red, green, and blue, when arranged in a descending series according to their wave-lengths, and reduced to their simplest numerical expression, yield a series of harmonic numbers

$$N_3 = 0 \quad . \quad \tfrac{1}{2} \quad . \quad 1 \quad . \quad 2 \quad 3 \quad \infty$$

red   yellow   green   blue

in which the figures indicate the relative complexity of each color. The relations brought out in this series are in accord with a fundamental law, known as the *law of complication*, which was formulated by Goldschmidt from extended observations on crystal forms and later applied to the theory of music and of colors.

It is impossible within brief space to give to the general reader a satisfactory comprehension of the *law of complication*. It is based on a fundamental concept in crystallography, namely, that upon every crystal the faces lying in the same zone are related to one another in a simple mathematical manner; and that these relations may be expressed by simple harmonic ratios, thus:

$$N_0 = 0 \quad . \quad . \quad . \quad . \quad . \quad . \quad \infty$$
$$N_1 = 0 \quad . \quad . \quad . \quad 1 \quad . \quad . \quad . \quad \infty$$
$$N_2 = 0 \quad . \quad . \quad \tfrac{1}{2} \quad . \quad 1 \quad . \quad 2 \quad . \quad \infty$$
$$N_3 = 0 \quad \tfrac{1}{3} \quad \tfrac{1}{2} \quad \tfrac{2}{3} \quad 1 \quad \tfrac{3}{2} \quad 2 \quad 3 \quad \infty$$

etc.

The most complicated relations, if in accord with the law, may be reduced by the proper means to one of these "normal series;" the color series above, for example, corresponding to N_3. (For a fuller exposition of the law of complication and its application to music and colors, consult Ueber Harmonie und Complication, by Victor Goldschmidt, published at Berlin in 1901. English reviews of this law may be found in Journ. Frank. Inst., vol. 156, 1903, p. 230, and School of Mines Quart., vol. 25, 1904, p. 415.)

Philological research has shown that in the historical development of color-sense yellow is the first color recognized, then red and green, and lastly blue. (See Geiger, Zur Entwicklungsgeschichte der Menschheit. Stuttgart, 1871, p. 45.) This order corresponds to that derived from the development of the number series, N_3, noted above, according to the principles of the *law of complication*, and indicates that the development follows from the simple to the complex in a definite mathematical manner. According to Goldschmidt (op. cit., pp. 98–99) the development of color-sense proceeds in four stages, as follows:

vanity of primitive man. A long period intervened before metals became known and were utilized for enhancing the beauty of precious stones, and it was during this interval that the turquois found its earliest use, following the development of a taste for its colors. It is safe to say that its greener shades were prized long before its blue tones were appreciated; indeed, today, there are some peoples who have not yet formed a liking for the latter. Of only moderate hardness and lending itself to shaping with comparative ease, the turquois, once known, must soon have been fashioned into rough beads and crude pendants.

AFRICA.

Turquois seems to have been little used in Africa outside of Egypt. Garcia ab Horto,[2] writing in the sixteenth century, however, stated that the mineral was employed medicinally by the inhabitants of Mauretania, an ancient country of northern Africa.

EGYPT.

At what remote time the turquois became known to the Egyptians can not be precisely stated. It is certain, however, that this mineral was used by them as an ornament long before the dynastic period was entered upon, as amply demonstrated by the presence of turquois beads in prehistoric graves.[3] By the beginning of the first dynasty (about 5500 B. C.[4]) an Egyptian mining colony had been established at turquois deposits in the Sinai Peninsula and records left by the ancient workers show that operations were continued there at intervals until the close of the twentieth dynasty (about 1100 B. C.).

In addition to evidence furnished by remains of early turquois mining, the use of turquois by the Egyptians is exemplified by ornaments of this material found from time to time in graves and ruins of the Nile country. By far the most important discovery of this kind was made in 1900 by Petrie[5] during the course of excavations in the cemetery of the royal tombs at Abydos in Upper Egypt. While clearing out the tomb of King Zer, who was the second ruler of the first dynasty, a workman noticed a portion of a mummy lying in a broken hole in the wall. This relic proved to be the desiccated arm of Queen Zer, and when freed from its bandages revealed four encircling bracelets of gold and precious stones (see Pl. 5, Fig. 3), representing the oldest group of jewelry known in the world.[6] The bracelets are illustrated in plate 5 and are of skilful workmanship. The finest example (Fig. 1, Pl. 5) is fashioned of alternate plaques of cast gold and carved turquois, each surmounted with the royal hawk and paneled to imitate the front

---

First stage.—Characterized by the harmonic series, $N_0=0$ . . . . . . ∞ , shows only light and darkness. A definite color-sense is lacking.

Second stage.—Characterized by the harmonic series, $N_1=0$ . . 1 . . . ∞ , witnesses the perception of yellow.
yellow

Third stage.—Characterized by the harmonic series, $N_2=0$. $\frac{1}{2}$ 1 . 2 . ∞ , reveals the introduction of red and later of green.
red yellow green

Fourth stage.—Characterized by the harmonic series, $N_3=0$. $\frac{1}{2}$ 1 . 2 3 ∞ , shows the final perception of blue, thus completing our
red yellow green blue
present appreciation of basal (spectrum) colors.

Goldschmidt gives an interesting and significant discussion of colors, based upon the observations of many investigators and the application of the *law of complication* to this subject. Such of his conclusions as bear upon blue and green, the colors of turquois, follow: The course of development of color-sense is the same amongst all peoples; following the order, yellow, red, green, blue. With some the development is completed at an early period; with others, much later; and among others still this sense is not yet fully developed. Experiments with children have shown that the development of their color-sense follows the same order, namely, yellow, red, green, blue. The development of the color-organ precedes the development of the corresponding color-concept. It is therefore not correct to believe, for example, that when the concept of blue is lacking the organ for blue has not been developed. Color-concepts develop before words are invented expressing them, and in many inferior languages words are lacking for some of the elemental colors. When a word is wanting for only one, each time it is blue, and this color is termed either gray or green. When two words are lacking the second is always green and either red or yellow serves to designate this color. Light-blue is more primitive than dark-blue; and since there is a greater contrast between blue and red than between green and red, the taste for blue, once developed, will probably be stronger than that for green.

It is interesting to note in this connection that the Welsh, Chinese, and Hebrew languages at present lack words for blue (Rivers, Pop. Sci. Monthly, vol. 59, 1900, p. 58) and that Homer used no word for this color in his writings (ibid., p. 50). Characteristics of primitive language, therefore, are an indefinite nomenclature for green, and either an absence of a word for blue or a confusion of the terms for blue and green (ibid., p. 50).

[2] Aromatum et simplicium aliquot. Antwerpiæ, 1567, p. 199.

[3] As the result of excavations in the cemeteries of Abadiyeh and Hu, Petrie found that turquois was here employed from S. D. 55–63. [S. D. refers to a system of "sequence dating," whereby S. D. 30 is placed approximately at 8000 B. C. and S. D. 80 at 5000 B. C.] See Diospolis Parva, Publ. Egypt Expl. Fund, London, 1901.

[4] According to Petrie. See p. 30 for statement as to Egyptian chronology.

[5] The royal tombs of the earliest dynasties. Publ. Egypt Expl. Fund, London, 1901, pt. 2, pp. 16–18.

[6] In the New Museum in Berlin are also two necklaces from Abydos; one is composed of beads of gold, turquois, carnelian, amethyst, and faience, and the other of roughly polished balls of amethyst, rock-crystal, carnelian, and turquois.

of a tomb or palace. The turquois had been cut with a saw and worked over with a drill and a graving point. This piece of jewelry represents a turning point in Egyptian art, containing archaic work along with that more highly developed. The next bracelet (Fig. 2) is entirely different in design. The center piece of gold, apparently copied from the seed vessel of a desert plant, is accompanied on each side by beads of turquois and gold, and lastly by large amethyst balls of deep color. The back half is of similar material, and the two groups of beads are united by a plaited braid of gold wire and thick hair probably from tails of oxen. The fastening of this, as of the other bracelets, is by ball and loop. The gold beads are hollow balls made by hammering out and soldering two half spheres, in much the same manner as the silver beads of the Navaho Indians are fashioned, but the joining is so nicely done that no trace of soldering can be discerned. The third bracelet (Fig. 4) consists of beads of turquois and dark lapis-lazuli, with hollow beads of gold. The fourth bracelet (Fig. 5) is made of hour-glass beads of amethyst, gold, and dark brown limestone, with lozenge-shaped turquoises capped on the ends with gold to prevent wear.

These interesting examples of early art are now in the Cairo Museum. It is remarkable that they should have escaped destruction. As Petrie points out: [1]

The chances against this jewelry having been preserved seem almost numberless. The king's tomb was first plundered in early times, and holes broken in the walls in search of hidden treasure. After that the queen's body was found, and broken up, and one plunderer thrust this fragment of the mummy into the hole in the wall, while probably returning to secure more in the scramble. Then the tomb was cleaned out, and a shrine of Osiris built into it about 1400 B. C., which was frequented constantly for a thousand years, every visitor passing within a few feet of the treasure. About 500 A. D. the Copts utterly destroyed the shrine, and the other royal tombs; yet the arm lay untouched. Again, three years ago, a French explorer turned out the whole place in search of valuable objects, but his workmen neglected the arm, which they must have seen. Time after time it would have seemed impossible that such valuables could escape, lying openly in the wall, yet our thorough search was thus most unexpectedly rewarded.

Turquois ornaments have been found at many other places in Egypt, but none equal in interest the examples brought to light by the excavations at Abydos. A few examples will suffice. In the early nineties a series of excavations at Dahshur yielded jewelry of the twelfth dynasty (about 3400–3200 B. C.), including quantities of amethyst, carnelian, turquois, and lapis-lazuli, carved in the form of scarabs, beads, and pendants, many set in gold with exquisite workmanship; and a breastplate of gold inlaid with lapis-lazuli, turquois, carnelian, and other stones.[2] In 1905 a necklace of carnelian, shell, turquois, garnet, and amethyst with turquois pendant rudely fashioned into the form of an ibex, was found at Abusir el-Meleq in remains of about 3500 B. C.[3] Maspero[4] describes a bracelet[5] of massive gold, consisting of three parallel bands set with turquoises, found on the wrist of Queen Aahotep of the seventeenth dynasty. In the coffin of the same queen was discovered a battle-axe placed there for the defense of the soul, its handle fashioned of cedar wood covered with sheet gold, with the legend of Aahmes inlaid thereon in characters of lapis-lazuli, carnelian, turquois, and green feldspar. Green turquoises are known among the jewels of Ptolemy. Petrie[6] states that from prehistoric times the minerals most used by the Egyptians were quartz, amethyst, agate, carnelian, turquois, lapis-lazuli, hematite, and serpentine.

Students of Egyptian art can not fail to be impressed by the importance of blues and greens amongst its objects. As so strikingly illustrated in the Egyptian Room of the British Museum, beads, scarabs, figures, and other ornaments, showing these colors, are in such profusion as to give to the entire collection a blue-green aspect. Many objects of faience indeed

---

[1] Harper's Monthly Magazine, vol. 53, p. 685.

[2] Morgan, Ann. Rept. Smithsonian Inst., 1896, p. 599. This breastplate is exhibited among the magnificent collections of the Cairo Museum. Budge (The Egyptian Sûdân, London, 1907, vol. 1, p. 538) refers to these objects in the following citation: "In * * * the reign of Amenemhat II * * * the Egyptians were bringing the products of the Sudan to their country both by sea and by land. From the Peninsula of Sinai also they were obtaining turquoises during this reign, and these, with the gold and carnelians which came from the Sudan, were made into jewelry, of which such splendid specimens were discovered by M. J. de Morgan at Dahshur."

[3] Aegyptischer Goldschmiedearbeit, ed. by H. Schäffer Berlin, 1910, pp. 25–37; plate 5. Through Kunz, The curious lore of precious stones, 1913, p. 37.

[4] Manual of Egyptian archaeology. London, 1902, pp. 323, 328.

[5] Now exhibited in the British Museum.

[6] The arts and crafts of ancient Egypt. Chicago, 1910, p. 80.

so closely simulate the color and texture of turquois as to suggest that they were made in imitation of it. Still others by mere inspection can not be distinguished from this mineral, and the writer ventures the belief that turquois is actually present in collections in more instances than has been recognized.

On the basis of the examples of Egyptian art here mentioned and the almost constant interest maintained for several thousand years in the Sinai deposits, it is safe to assert that the turquois was a prized possession among the ancient dwellers along the Nile, forming with gold, amethyst, and the other quartz gems, objects highly prized for purposes of decoration and personal adornment.[1]

ASIA.

Asia, the home of precious stones, has from time immemorial produced the turquois and assigned to it a varied and extended use. In Persia and Tibet it is used profusely, and the nomad tribes roaming the barren stretches of Arabia and Turkestan value no other adornment so highly. India also employs this gem, and in China very elaborate carvings are prepared of this material. The famous mines near Nishapur in Persia have long supplied to western Asia quantities of the finest turquois, while scarcely known deposits in central Asia have yielded larger though inferior stones to the hordes of people inhabiting the interior portion of that continent.

PERSIA (INCLUDING ARABIA).

At what period the turquois became known to the inhabitants of Persia must remain a matter of doubt, for history does not record its earliest use and archaeology has not elucidated this question.[2] The presence of turquois ornaments in graves of great antiquity in Russian Turkestan[3] and of turquois objects in burial places of the first to third centuries in the Caucasus,[4] suggest an early exploitation of the Nishapur locality; but such evidence is indirect and not at all conclusive, and the fact, as pointed out by Laufer,[5] that there is no ancient Iranian word for turquois and Avestan literature makes no allusion to it, casts some doubt on the widely accepted idea that turquois has been known to the Persians since remote antiquity.

The earliest references to the turquois mines of Nishapur were made by Ibn Haukal (978 A. D.), al-Beruni (973–1048), and al-Ta'alibi (961–1038).[6] A Persian manuscript of the eleventh century, quoted by Ouseley,[7] states that the turquois, being a stone without brilliancy, was not reckoned fit for the decoration of kings, although it was regarded as lucky; and Ibn-el-Beithar,[8] the famous Arabic botanist, mentioned a similar limitation in its use about the year 1200. In an Arabic work of 1175,[9] it is stated: "Many kings hardly have the desire to wear a turquois, because the vulgar frequently utilize it as sigillum and wear finger rings which are imitations of its best kind."

Teifascite,[10] a well-known Arabian author on precious stones, writing toward the middle of the thirteenth century, distinguished two species of turquois, the finer called in Persian "buschechica" and the other "lahahica."

Muhammed Ibn Mansur, in an Arabian work on mineralogy, written about 1300, devotes considerable space to the turquois. He writes:[11]

The turquois is divided according to its different sources into different qualities, and experts, as soon as they see a turquois, can tell from what mine it came. There are five kinds: Nishapuri, Ghaznewi (Afghanistan), Ilagi (Transoxania), Kermani, and Charezmi (Chiwa). The Nishapur stones are valuable; the other kinds are soft, impure, and soon lose their color. The former are hard, beautiful and pure, and do not change in color; there are seven kinds

1 See the legend of Zazamankh, p. 111.

2 See discussion on p. 35.

3 See p. 74. The locality is within 200 miles of Nishapur.

4 See p. 75.

5 Op. cit., p. 38.

6 See Laufer, op. cit., pp. 40–41.

7 Nozhat Namah Ellaïy in Travels in various countries of the East, London, 1819, vol. 1, pp. 210–212.

8 See p. 13.

9 Wiedermann, Beiträge zur Geschichteder Naturwissenschaften XXX. Zur Mineralogie im Islam, Erlangen, 1912, p. 234. Through Laufer, op. cit., p. 30, note 3.

10 Translated into Italian by Ant. Raineri under the title, Fior di Pensieri sulle Pietre Preziose, etc. Bologna, 1906, pp. 70–73.

11 Translated by the writer from a German translation by Schindler, Jahrb. k. k. geol. Reichs., vol. 36, 1886, pp. 303–314.

of them: Abu Ishagi, which have a beautiful dark color and are brilliant and pure; Azheri, like the first, but not so good; Soleimani, which are somewhat milky; Zarbumi, with golden spots (pyrite), not so brilliant as the first kinds; Chaki, sky-blue; Abdul Medjidi, dark-blue, but not pure; Andelibi, milky. The turquois in clear weather is bright and brilliant; with cloudy sky, dull and insipid. Some turquoises are pale, and if they are smeared with butter their color becomes darker; but the color obtained in such a manner is only temporary. Jewelers call this quality Sedja (also Mescha and Messiha). A turquois with two colors is termed *abresch* (mottled). The hard turquois is bored with diamond; the softer with steel. There are three kinds of false turquoises: (1) glass paste, (2) hard green stones composed of copper and other minerals, (3) Madjun i Tschini, also called Boreizeh (Chinese paste). It is very easy to distinguish real from false stones. The turquoises, according to their age, are separated into the old and the new. The luster and color of the old do not change; the new soon lose their color. It is said that a beautiful, faultless turquois of more than twenty-three grams has never been found, although large stones are not rare. Jewelers, however, speak of an Ilagi turquois, weighing more than 920 grams, and whose price was $170,000.[1] In the story of Seldjugen it is recorded that to King Alparstan, when he captured Fars, was brought from the castle of Istachr a turquois dish which held 6 kilos of musk and amber, and that the name Djamschids was engraven upon it. Sultan Sadnjar is said to have had a turquois the size of an apple. In the treasury of the (Samaniden) king, Noh Ibn Mansur, was a turquois vessel which held 6 flasks of rosewater, each containing 4½ liters. In the vicinity of Nishapur occurs a turquois-like stone which is fashioned into chess men, but the color soon fades. Turquois mines are located at Ilag, Ghazni, Chaarezm, in the mountains between Yezd and Kerman, and in the mountains between Tus and Nishapur at the village Paschan (the old name for the village Maden). The best mines are at Nishapur; there are seven mines, from which come the seven grades of turquois mentioned. The best mine is that which was discovered by Isaac, the father of Israel, and consequently known as Isaac's mine. The worst mine is the Andelibi. Stones are cut on a wheel, then polished with a white stone and willow wood. The best kind of turquois is the Nishapuri and its best quality is the Abu Ishagi; next in value is the Azheru turquois, then the Soleimani, then the Zarbumi, then Chaki and Abdul Medjidi, and finally the Andelibi, which is the least desirable of all. The best color is dark-green; the next best, whitish-milky; then sky-blue. The most popular form in Khorassan and Transoxania is the piekani (pointed), while the Arabs and Syrians prefer the mussateh (flat) stones. The Chinese[2] fancy the Tarmaleh (?), which are turquoises furrowed by other stones; these they use for decorating their idols and their wives.

A good turquois feels soft (weich), and is pure and brilliant. An *Abu Ishagi* or *Azheri* of beautiful dark color, flawless, 2.3 grams in weight, is worth $24 to $34;[1] 4.6 grams, $68 to $102; 9.2 grams, $170 to $238. The milk-colored turquois of 4.6 grams costs $2.80; the middle quality costs 75 cents for 4.6 grams; the poorest quality has little value. The turquois is a copper ore changed by heat.

The eye is strengthened by looking at a turquois. If one sees a turquois early in the morning, he will pass a fortunate day. One should view a turquois at the time of the new moon. The turquois helps its owner to victory over his enemies, protects him against injury, and makes him liked by all men. Moisture, oil, and strong odors impair the luster of the stone; mutton fat strengthens its color, therefore on the hands of butchers are turquoises always beautifully colored.

A further manuscript, quoted by Ouseley,[3] entitled "Nozhat al Colub" and written between 1300 and 1400, states in a chapter on minerals that the Firuzedje (turquois) was worn by women and considered inferior in value to the emerald. A later and better known compilation on precious stones, entitled "Juaher Nameh," probably written in India in the seventeenth century, described the mines at Nishapur as most celebrated from early ages for a particular kind of turquois entitled "Abu Ishaki" which "is worthy of a place among the treasures of emperors."[4] In an article[5] derived principally from information contained in the Juaher Nameh, it is stated regarding the turquois:

The name Firozeh is said in the *Jawahir-nameh* to have been given to this stone by Firoz Shah, but this must be a matter of doubt; as also whether the Sanskrit synonyme in Hunter's Dictionary, *peroj*, is not a corruption of *beruj*, beryl, quite a different stone. From the localities and from the characteristics of the two varieties in the books before us, it might be conjectured that the two species of this mineral known to European mineralogists as the calaite, or mineral turquois, and the *odontolite*, or bone turquois, are equally familiar to the Persian jewellers, under the epithets of *Abu-Is'haqi* and *Badakshani*.

The *Abu-Is'haqi* (father of Isaac), or genuine turquois, is the product of the mines of *Ansar*, near *Nishapur*, in Khorasan (the same place mentioned as *Michebourg* in Tavernier's Travels in India). All authorities concur that these are the only turquois mines in the world; the stones are said to vary from pale blue to green and white, but all except the azure are worthless. A curious fact is mentioned also, which from the nature of the mineral may readily be believed, though it has not been observed in Europe: "The real blue turquois of *Nishapur* changes its color when kept near musk or camphor, also from the dampness of the ground, as well as from exposure to the fire; the inferior stones

[1] Values only approximate. Schindler quotes the values in francs, which the present writer has turned into dollars (5 francs equal $1).
[2] This is probably an error and should read "Tibetans." See Laufer, op. cit., p. 42, note 2.
[3] Loc. cit.
[4] From Ouseley, loc. cit.
[5] Prinsep, Journ. Asiat. Soc. Bengal, vol. 1, 1832, pp. 361–362.

become discolored even without this test," by gradual decomposition or efflorescence.   The *Khawis-ul-hejar* makes the clearness or dulness of the turquois vary according to the atmospheric changes.   "It brightens the eyes; is a remedy for opthalmia and bites of venomous animals; it is used in enameling sword handles, etc."

"The *Badakshani* turquois essentially differs from the *Nishapuri* in being able to withstand the heat of a fire for ten days without alteration; for this quality it is much esteemed, although in other respects not so good as the produce of *Ansar*."

Now the calaite, which contains 18 per cent of water, would be entirely destroyed by such an operation, while the *bone turquois* is actually made in many places by exposure to the fire of fossil bones impregnated with iron and the fossil bones brought from the north of the Himalayan range, when exposed to a red heat, are found to assume the very appearance of *odontolite;* it is possible, therefore, that a supply of this artificial gem may find its way into Persia through Balkh, and take its name from that country as its known market.

Arguments are not wanting, on the other hand, to show that the *Badakshani* turquois is nothing more than *lapis lazuli*, or *lajaward*, and the descriptions of the two are mixed up together in the books before us, like those of the emerald and topaz.

Jean Baptiste Tavernier, the celebrated merchant traveler, who visited Persia during the seventeenth century, writes as follows on the use of the turquois at that period: [1]   .

> There are there two mines, one they call the *old rock*, the other the *new;* those of the *new* are but of a bad blew, inclining to white, and little esteemed, and it is free for any man to take as many of them as he pleaseth.   But the King of Persia some years since forbad the digging in the *old* for any besides himself, because, having no goldsmiths but such who work in the thread, and are wholly ignorant how to enamel upon gold, as people who know neither the design nor manner of it, they make use for the garnishing of their swords and ponyards and other works of these toikoses, instead of enamel, and cause them to be cut and set in the bearit of rings, according to the flowers and other figures, that do best please him.

A later writer [2] narrates that "the women of Lars and Ormuz pierce the upper portion of their nose, the bone itself, and pass through the hole a hook that fastens a sheet of gold shaped to cover the nose, and enriched with rubies, emeralds, and turkoises."

Turquois the Persian word for which is *ferozah* or *firozah*, meaning "victorious," is the national stone of Persia, and is to be seen in all quarters.   At every important town small turquoises set in silver rings may be purchased; and even the lowest classes, such as muleteers, grooms, and tent-pitchers, wear such rings set with stones the size of wheat grains. [3]   The high officials lay great store on seals and most of these are made of gold adorned with diamonds, or of turquois decorated with pearls and rubies. [4]   Great numbers of stones are purchased by pilgrims, "everyone of whom, according to his means, thinks it incumbent upon him to furnish himself with a ring of turquois." [5]   Persian goldsmiths and jewelers, particularly at Meshed, buy quantities of the Nishapur turquois, which they use for incrusting articles of jewelry, amulets, dagger and sword hilts, sheaths, horse-trappings, pipe heads (see Pl. 14, Fig. 1), etc. They are very skilful in embellishing the larger stones with scroll-work of gold so as to hide the flaws and imperfections.   A favorite treatment also is to ornament the surface with passages from the Koran, inlaid in letters of gold.   A large heart-shaped, polished turquois, decorated in this manner, was worn of old by the Nadir Shah, and in 1860 was in the possession of a jeweler in Moscow.   In the Townshend collection of the Victoria and Albert Museum, London, is a rather pale, greenish-blue stone, heart-shaped and inlaid with gold wire.   Many stones bearing Persian proverbs and other quotations in incised gilt characters are mounted on small sticks covered with red paper to form seals, and are carried as amulets. [6]

An interesting example of fifteenth century Persian art is displayed in the American Museum of Natural History in the form of a greenish slab of turquois, presenting scarcely two square inches of upper surface but incised in this restricted area with 2,000 words of the Koran. King [7] describes a magnificent turquois of Persian workmanship engraved with the heads of a modern Shah and his queen, with the field inlaid in ornaments of gold.

---

[1] Voyages en Turquie, en Perse, et aux Indes.   Amsterdam, 1678, pt. 2, p. 374.   The translation is taken from Kemp (The history of jewels. London, 1671, pp. 62–64).

[2] Tagore, Mani-mala.   Calcutta, 1879, p. 793.

[3] Ouseley, loc. cit.

[4] Khan and Sparrow, With the pilgrims to Mecca.   London, 1895, pp. 43, 260.

[5] Fraser, Journey into Khorassan.   London, 1825, pp. 468–469.

[6] Dr. Geo. F. Kunz has kindly shown the writer a large and interesting collection in possession of Tiffany & Co. of New York.

[7] Antique gems and rings.   London, 1872, vol. 1, p. 85.

The Shah of Persia has for a long period reserved for himself the choicest stones found at Nishapur, and his collection of turquoises is said to be the finest in existence. He has a turquois costume,[1] and in his palace at Teheran is the celebrated peacock throne, captured from the Grand Mogul in former days by the victorious Nadir Shah. This is described as a "dazzling marvel; it is covered with sheets of gold on which precious enamels, fantastic birds, and chimeras set with rubies, emeralds, sapphires, and turquoises shine, culminating in the supreme radiation of a diamond sun. It is said to be worth six million pounds."[2] In the drawing room of the palace is the famous terrestrial globe, resting in a frame of solid gold incrusted with diamonds.[3] The geographical divisions of the sphere are represented by precious stones of various shades: Persia, by turquois; and the town of Teheran by a large diamond; the seas are made of emeralds; India, of amethysts; Africa, of rubies; England and France of diamonds, etc. The work is stated to have cost about $10,000,000. Precious stones excite the greatest covetousness in the Shah's harem, and he is said to distribute them prodigally at New Year's, giving away turquoises, sapphires, pearls, rubies, emeralds, and even diamonds by the handful.[4]

The Persians, in their art, show a strong taste for turquois-blue, lapis-lazuli-blue and turquois-green. Many of their porcelains and carpets exhibit these colors. In their ancient enamels, in addition to metallic oxides, finely pulverized minerals, principally amethyst and turquois, were utilized.[5]

The Arabs prize the turquois, but care more for its size than its color.[6] Many inferior stones therefore are current among them, and large, off-color slabs find a ready sale. They regard the turquois as possessing talismanic virtues and wear seals and amulets of this mineral.[7] They use it also for inlaying arms, trappings, etc., and wear it in rings of plated tin. Sir Richard Burton[8] on his first expedition to western Arabia noted a fine turquois adorning the handle of a Bedawyn's matchlock.

TURKESTAN.

Throughout Turkestan, and especially among the nomad tribes of Bokhara, the turquois finds wide application. Earrings, belt ornaments, brooches, pendants, rings, dagger handles, bridles, horse trappings, and other objects are decorated, sometimes in elaborate fashion, with inlays of this precious stone. Magnificent examples are to be found in the Museum for Ethnology, Berlin, and the India Museum, London. Deserving particular notice in the latter is a saddle from Yarkand, E. Turkestan, with its bridle, stirrups, martingale, and crupper profusely adorned with turquois inlay. In the United States National Museum is a necklace from Yarkand (Cat. No. 175131) consisting of 10 repoussé silver-gilt charm boxes set with turquoises.

Turquoises are utilized by the Sart in and around Tashkend for the decoration of silver necklaces, bridles, girdle-clasps, etc.[9] Dr. Karutz, of the Museum of Lübeck, who has traveled extensively in Russian Turkestan, writes to Dr. Laufer, of the Field Museum, that he "encountered two areas in which turquois is diffused among the Tatars of Russia and among the Sart of Turkestan, but that he did not find it among the Turkmen and the Kirghiz; he therefore concludes that it occurs only in the town population, but not among the nomads of the steppe; he learned nothing about indigenous sources of the stone, but is convinced that it is imported from Afghanistan. There is, he says, a rumor to the effect that turquois is found in the Kirghiz steppe,[10] but he doubts the fact, as it is not employed by the Kirghiz in their ornaments."[11]

Turquois beads have recently been found during explorations of the ancient ruins of Anau,[12] near the Transcaspian Railway, in Russian Turkestan. The culture of this oasis region is very

[1] Lorey and Sladen, Queer things about Persia. Philadelphia, 1907, p. 181.
[2] Ibid., pp. 173–174.
[3] Ibid., p. 175.
[4] Ibid., p. 159.
[5] Gayet, L'Art Persan. Paris, 1895, p. 249.
[6] On the authority of Ibn-el-Beithar and al-Beruni, stones of fine blue color took foremost rank among the Arabs.
[7] Fraser, loc. cit.
[8] The gold mines of Midian, etc. London, 1878, p. 302.
[9] H. Moser, A travers l'Asie centrale. Paris, 1885, pp. 104–107. Through Laufer, op. cit.
[10] See p. 41.
[11] Laufer, op. cit., p. 36.
[12] Pumpelly, Explorations in Turkestan. Washington, 1908, vol. 1.

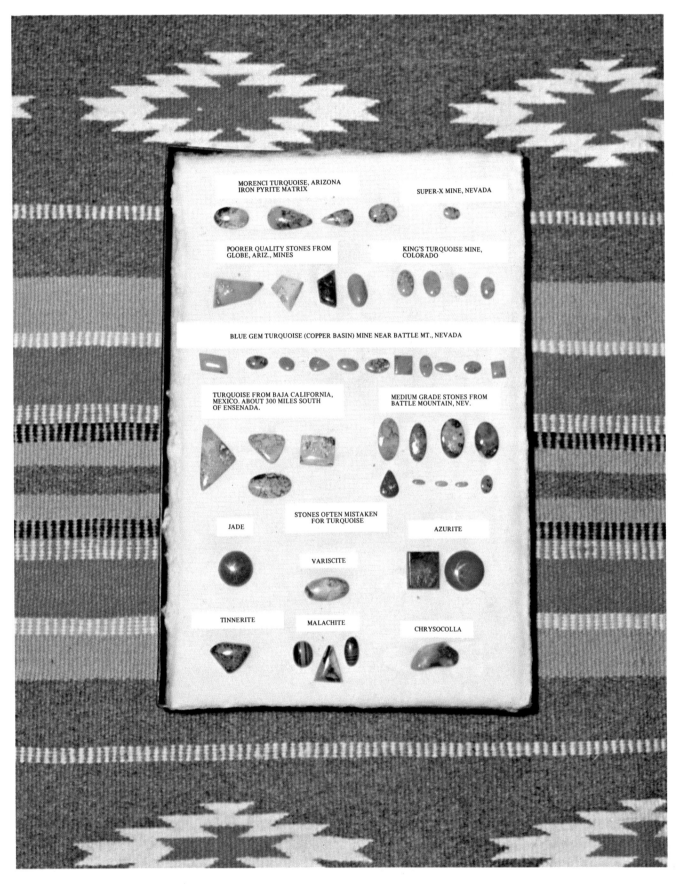

Various specimens from the collection of Joan Patania Wheeler.

Plate No. 10

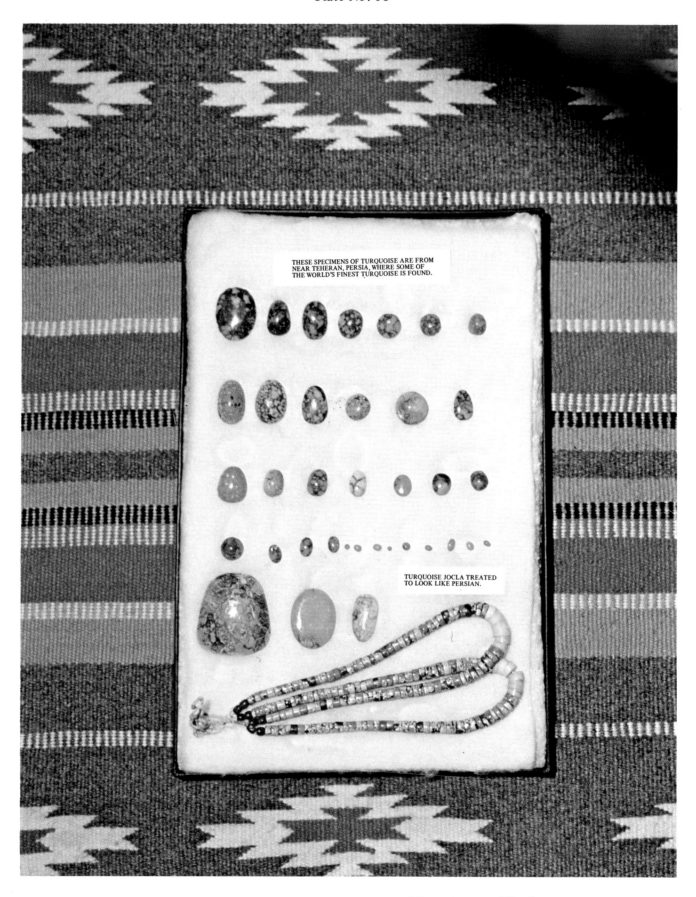

THESE SPECIMENS OF TURQUOISE ARE FROM
NEAR TEHERAN, PERSIA, WHERE SOME OF
THE WORLD'S FINEST TURQUOISE IS FOUND.

TURQUOISE JOCLA TREATED
TO LOOK LIKE PERSIAN.

Various specimens from the collection of Joan Patania Wheeler.

ancient, antedating, according to Pumpelly, even that of Babylon and Egypt.[1] There are three epochs of culture, and in all three the turquois was used.[2] A peculiar custom, characteristic of the earliest epoch, was the practise of burying children under the earthen floor of dwellings, and in many burials turquois beads, used as burial gifts, were exhumed with the skeletons.[3] In the lower and middle strata of North Kurgan (one of the ruins) were found six peculiar and primitive bean-shaped turquois beads, transversely pierced.[4] The easternmost of the old Merv ruins, which are known today as Ghiaur Kala (City of the Infidel), yielded many cylindrical, barrel-shaped, annular, and disk-shaped beads of turquois.[5] The source of the turquois utilized in this region is not certainly known.[6]

AFGHANISTAN.

In Afghanistan the turquois is employed in much the same manner as in Turkestan. The India Museum contains an Afghan girdle of damasked velvet, with eight bossed ornaments of turquois in cloissoné mounts, surrounded by colored stones and terminating in a silver gilt clasp set with turquoises.

TRANSCAUCASIA.

The region including and adjacent to the Caucasus Range is one of peculiar significance because of its position of contact between Europe and Asia. The cemeteries of Kertch, of ancient Olbia, of Taman, and of the southern Caucasus, have yielded ornaments of gold and bronze, inlaid with precious stones, that not only reflect the taste that prevailed during the Roman Era, but also present an oriental imprint.[7] These objects of the first to third centuries in particular, comprising bracelets, necklaces, ear-pendants, etc., are characterized by embellishments in garnet, turquois, rose-coral, and blue enamel in imitation of lapis-lazuli. A collar found in a cave at Kertch is adorned with pendants set with emeralds, turquoises, and corals.[8]

SIBERIA.

The Hermitage collection of St. Petersburg possesses a number of turquois-adorned objects of ancient Siberian workmanship,[9] which indicate an employment of this precious stone by the prehistoric inhabitants of that region. The ornaments, many of which are elaborate and show both taste in design and technical skill in execution, present a perplexing problem not only in time of origin, but also in cultural relations and source of materials. Some appear to bear a Persian impress and the turquois entering into them is probably from the famous mines near Nishapur; others, included amongst the antiquities of the bronze age and representing, next to Egyptian jewelry and Turkestan beads, perhaps the oldest application of turquois of which we have record, show a resemblance to modern Tibetan technique that suggests a related origin. It is, therefore, probable that the Tibetan turquois, which has been produced since remote times and at an early period was introduced into Mongolia,[10] was also drawn upon by the Siberian tribes to the northwest. Deserving of special notice in the Hermitage collection are two small ram heads in gold, with necks incrusted with turquoises, following a system of ornamentation in use in central Asia;[11] several plaques, fashioned of electrum and inlaid with turquoises, emeralds, and other stones in very striking designs of animal figures;[12] a cylindrical diadem of gold,

---

[1] Pumpelly's chronology must be accepted with caution. Many authorities hold that these ruins are not of great antiquity (less than 3,000 years old).)

[2] Pumpelly, op. cit., p. 176.

[3] Ibid., p. 64.

[4] Ibid., p. 157.

[5] Ibid., p. 199.

[6] Pumpelly (ibid., pp. 39, 64) believes that it came from Persia; Laufer (op. cit., p. 39) questions this assumption and suggests that it may as well have been derived from Siberia, Tibet, or some forgotten mine in Turkestan.

[7] Kondakof, Tolstoï, et Reinach, Antiquités de la Russie méridionale. Paris, 1891, pp. 316–317.

[8] Ibid., p. 318 (fig. 282, p. 316).

[9] The Siberian antiquities, which form one of the chief treasures of the Hermitage collection, are part of more extensive collections brought to Russia during the first half of the 18th century, and owe their preservation to the care of Peter the Great. Unfortunately, no information has survived as to the localities from which the specimens were obtained nor of the conditions under which they were found; it is only known that graves and ruins in the general region of western Siberia have supplied them.

[10] See p. 82.

[11] Kondakof, Tolstoï, et Reinach, Antiquités de la Russie méridionale. Paris, 1891, p. 855.

[12] Ibid., pp. 378 et. seq.

decorated with turquois and garnet, and surmounted by four tigers rampant; and [1] a small eagle holding in its grasp a swan inlaid with turquoises.[2] In the museum of the University of Siberia a bronze plaque with turquois inlay [3] is worthy of note.

INDIA.

The turquois was apparently unknown to the peoples of ancient India; they possess no indigenous word [4] for this substance nor is it mentioned in the older Sanskrit treatises on precious stones. Archæological work also has failed to produce a single turquois from ancient graves, although numerous finds of other precious stones have been made. The earliest reference of importance to the turquois is found in a mineralogical treatise, *Rajanighantu*, written by Narahari, a physician from Kashmir, not earlier than the beginning of the fifteenth century, wherein its supposed medicinal efficacy is noted. It is therefore highly probable that the turquois did not appear on Indian soil until very late during the Middle Ages, in the Mohammedan period (probably between the tenth and fifteenth centuries), and that it was imported from Persia.[5] The earliest testimony of its presence in India is that of the Arabic traveler, al-Beruni, who, writing between 973 and 1048, remarked that the people of Irag prefer the smooth stones, while the inhabitants of India like the round ones with convex surfaces.[6]

The northernmost Provinces of India, which lie in close proximity to Tibet, where turquois has been found and used for centuries, may have earlier come to know this mineral; at any rate the inhabitants of these frontier regions [7] today import supplies of it from Tibet and use it in much the same way as do their Tibetan neighbors.[8]

In modern Indian art, turquois holds a fairly prominent position, although it is subordinate in importance to the diamond, ruby, sapphire, emerald, spinel, and perhaps one or two other precious stones. It finds application not only in jewelry, but also in the decoration of arms, trappings, and other objects and for inlaying in jade. The Indian section of the Victoria and Albert Museum in London is rich in objects adorned with precious stones and the following descriptions, based upon examination of this admirable collection, will indicate the ornamental purposes to which turquois has been applied:

Delhi (Punjab), the bazaars of which are famous for precious stones and jewelry, is the source of many objects in the India Museum. Among these may be mentioned a bracelet of gold adorned with turquoises and rubies; gold rings set with turquoises; a whip-handle elaborately decorated with an inset of turquoises; a head-ornament of pearls, turquoises, and rubies; a small carved bottle (seventeenth century) of rock crystal set with rubies, sapphires, diamonds, and turquoises; a walking-stick handle (eighteenth century) of gray-white jade inlaid with gold set with garnets and turquoises.

Bengal has furnished a beautiful necklace with pendent ball entirely inlaid with fine blue turquoises. From Hulwa, Bengal, comes a saddle with cloths, pistol holder, etc., embroidered with gold and set with turquoises. Cuttack, Bengal, is the source of two turquois-set silver rings. Some of the embroidery from Madras is inset with turquois. Among objects from Bombay is a horse-collar of silver-gilt, consisting of 16 leaf-shaped plaques ornamented with relief representation of a flowering plant, the flowers and leaves of which are formed of turquoises and rubies. A gold nose-ring, labeled Sind (Bombay), is decorated with turquoises and rubies, and a similar ornament set with turquois, from Sultanpur (Oudh), is displayed. Among other ornaments of Indian workmanship may be mentioned an amulet for wearing on the arm,

---

[1] Kondakof, Tolstoï, et Reinach, Antiquités de la Russie meridionale. Paris, 1891, p. 408.

[2] Ibid., p. 405.

[3] Ibid., p. 402.

[4] According to Laufer, the Sanskrit term for turquois, *peroja*, is a recent loan word from the Persian, and the Sanskrit designation *haritāçma* is a compound meaning "greenish stone."

[5] Turquoises are brought from Persia through Bokhara to India. (Cunningham, Ladák, physical, statistical, and historical. London, 1854, p. 253.)

[6] Turquois in India is fully treated by Berthold Laufer (Field Museum of Natural History, Anthr. Ser., Publ. 169, vol. 13, No. 1, 1913, pp. 1–5), and the facts in the foregoing paragraph are derived from this authority.

[7] The use of turquois in these States will be considered under Tibet, with which they are closely connected ethnologically.

[8] Considerable jewelry of Tibetan workmanship reaches India by way of Sikkim, Bhutan, Nepal, and Kashmir.

consisting of three pieces of turquois engraved with Persian characters and mounted in silver;[1] another and somewhat similar piece in silver gilt frame inset with rubies; and a jardiniere, 7½ inches high, of green jade jeweled with garnets and turquoises and mounted on a silver base set with large turquoises.

In an exhibition of Indian art metal work at South Kensington, London, in 1892 was a set of leather horse trappings from Jeypoor, enriched with turquoises, rubies, and emeralds.[2] In the Museum for Ethnology in Berlin are pieces of turquois jewelry from Lucknow and Calcutta. The Higinbotham collection of jewelry in the Field Museum of Chicago contains several fine specimens of Indian jewelry in which turquois is employed.

TIBET.

Turquois not only finds wide application in Tibet today, but it has been known to the inhabitants of that country since remote times. It can not be ascertained at what early period this mineral first entered into the adornment of the people, but its Tibetan name *gyu* is indigenous [3] and indicates that the knowledge of the stone came from within and not through outside influences. As early as the eighth century tradition points to the knowledge of turquois,[4] and from this time on the mineral finds mention in the voluminous literature of that country. Much of the material employed in Tibet is of local origin,[5] although a considerable quantity of perforated beads, roughly polished stones, and carved pieces are imported from China. It is probable that little if any of the Persian product reaches Tibet proper, although the States along its western border (Bultistan, Ladakh, Kashmir, etc.) are in likelihood affected by other than Tibetan or Chinese sources.[6] The turquois used in Tibet is usually of mediocre quality, most of it being greenish in color [7] with the larger masses seamed and mottled with black matrix; and it is neither of great value according to our standards, nor has it ever among the Tibetans themselves assumed a value at all comparable with gold.[8] It is universally esteemed, however, and, with coral, enters into the decoration of nearly all ornaments and many objects of worship and utility. As Gill [9] says:

> The Tibetans, both men and women, are possessed of a taste almost amounting to a frenzy for coral and turquoises, and the immense quantities of these that are used is surprising.

Berthold Laufer [10] has made a detailed study of turquois in Tibet, and the following extract is a condensed review of his statements on the use of turquois in that country:

> As jade is the recognized jewel of the Chinese, so turquois is the standard gem of the Tibetans. * * * To call a turquois a stone means an offense to the Tibetan, and he will exclaim indignantly, * * * "this is a turquois, and not a stone." * * * Two special sorts of turquois are called *drug-dkar* and *drug-dmar*, that is white *drug* and red *drug;* the word *drug* designates the number 6, and the two terms are explained to designate very fine kinds of turquoises supposed to be one-sixth part white or red in tint, respectively. * * * The appreciation of turquoises by the ancient Tibetans was graduated as follows: Deep-blue, lustrous stones without flaw took foremost rank; white and red strips or layers were not considered a blemish, but rather a special beauty; the lighter the blue, and the more approaching a gray and green, the more it sank in estimation; stones with black veins and streaks and with cloudy strata were looked upon as common, also those of greenish hues. It is interesting to note that this scale of valuation doubtless going back to ancient times holds good also for the present age. * * * The small turquoises not larger than a lentil and used for the setting in rings are designated *pra.*

> As famous swords, daggers, saddles, and coats of mail receive in Tibet individual names, so also celebrated turquoises were given special designations. * * * Turquoises, usually in connection with gold, belong to the most

---

[1] According to Hendley (Journ. Indian Art and Ind., vol. 12, 1907 p. 51) flat turquois slabs inlaid with Persian or Arabic sentences from the Koran are sometimes worn in the Punjab Province by Mohammedans.

[2] Taylor, Precious stones and gems. London, 1895, p. 34.

[3] See Berthold Laufer, op. cit., 1913, p. 5.

[4] See Laufer, op. cit., 1913, pp. 6–9.

[5] See p. 42 for localities.

[6] Cunningham (Ladák, physical, statistical, and historical. London, 1854, p. 253) states that stones are brought into Ladakh from Yarkand. Lawrence (The valley of Kashmir. London, 1895, p. 64) writes that the lapidaries of Kashmir import valuable stones (including turquois) from Badakhshan, Bokhara, and Yarkand.

[7] The Tibetans, however, have long held the blue stones in greater esteem than the more common green ones.

[8] Turquois ranks above coral and amber. "It has never been, even in times of old, a stone of any exaggerated value." Laufer, op. cit, p. 12.

[9] The river of the golden sand. London, 1880, vol. 2, p. 107.

[10] Notes on turquois in the East. Field Museum of Natural History, Publ. 169, Anthr. Series, vol. 13, No. 1, 1913, pp. 5–20. The reader is referred to this paper for many details that space forbids inserting here.

ancient propitiatory offering to the gods and demons; in the enumeration gold always precedes turquois as the more valuable gift. They also figure among the presents bestowed on saints and lamas by kings and wealthy laymen. The thrones on which kings and lamas take their place are usually described as adorned with gold and turquoises, and they wear cloaks ornamented with these stones. * * *

In the popular medicine of the present time turquois is, as far as I know, not employed, but it is officially registered as a medicament in several medical standard works derived from or modeled after Sanskrit books. * * * A curious utilization of turquois is mentioned in the Biography of Padmasambhava (ch. 53), who is said to have availed himself of gold, silver, copper, iron, lapis lazuli, turquois, and minium inks for writing on light-blue paper of the palmyra palm and on smoothed birch bark. * * *

In the religious service turquoises are employed, strung in the shape of beads, for rosaries, 108 beads being the usual number. * * * Turquoises are, further, offered on the altars of the gods, and their brass or copper images are adorned with them. * * * This is not intended as a mere ornamental addition, but the turquoises are to signify the actual jewelry with which the deities are adorned, and which forms part of their essential attributes. * * * In the pictorial art of Lamaism jewels (including turquois) take a prominent place.

The men in most parts of Tibet wear an earring in the left ear. In northern Tibet it is a large gold or silver hoop about 2 inches in diameter, set with a coral or turquois bead.[1] (See Pl. 6, Fig. 1.) Among the pastoral tribes of central Tibet the men frequently suspend from their left ear, in addition, a pendant of gold or silver adorned with coral and ending in a hoop, on which is fastened a circular or heart-shaped plaque set with turquoises.[2] (See Pl. 6, Fig. 6.) A single piece of turquois is often tied to the right ear, and this ornament is abundant throughout Tibet, even among the wealthy people in the most civilized parts of the country.[2] The officials in Lhasa and other parts of central Tibet usually wear in their ears a plain gold hoop, to which is fixed a long pendant adorned with pearls, corals, and turquoises.[2] Among other ornaments of Tibetan men are finger rings of chased silver, many set with turquois or coral beads. The United States National Museum contains several examples, of which three are shown in plate 6, figure 8. Similar rings are seen among the Mongols of Ts'aidam, who procure them either from Tibetan travelers or when visiting Lhasa or Tashilunpo on a pilgrimage.[3] The only Tibetan men who wear ornaments on their hair are members of the pastoral tribes. Upon their queues, which are usually of false hair wound around the head, they string turquois-set finger rings and rings of ivory, or attach a strip of red cloth bearing large perforated turquois beads and small charm boxes set with the same material.[4]

The Tibetan women wear earrings of gold and silver which are commonly set with turquois. A favorite style in central Tibet, Chamdo, and other districts,[5] consists of a silver hoop over 2 inches in diameter, on the front of which is a heart-shaped plaque thickly studded with bits of turquois. Laufer[6] figures a pair of Tibetan earrings of gold inlaid with mosaic of turquois. He says: "The requirement of these mosaics is that the stones shall be well matched in color, resulting in a harmonious color arrangement. With this end in view, Tibetan women gather turquoises during many years, till they have the desired colors in the required number of stones. Such earrings belong to the most cherished property of a Tibetan woman and range from 100 to 600 rupees and more in price." The example shown in plate 6, figure 4, was worn by the native wife of a Chinese soldier stationed near Chamdo, and a jade ring, such as is worn on earrings in China, has been added by the Chinese husband.[7] Small gold finger-rings set with a cluster of small turquoises are often seen. The shirts worn by the women of eastern Tibet are buckled at the throat with a gold or silver clasp set with beads of coral and turquois.[8] A fine example is shown in figure 3 of plate 10. This object is of Nepalese workmanship, made in Lhasa, and shows a wheel and butterfly design in gold set with coral and turquois. Other examples are of silver, in butterfly and flower patterns, adorned with beads of turquois

---

[1] Rockhill, Ann. Rept. U. S. National Museum, 1893, p. 691.

[2] Ibid., p. 691.

[3] Ibid., p. 692.

[4] Ibid., p. 690. Also Rockhill, Diary of a journey through Mongolia and Tibet in 1891 and 1892. Washington, 1894, p. 253.

[5] Rockhill, op. cit., 1893, p. 693.

[6] Op. cit., Pl. V.

[7] Rockhill, op. cit., p. 693.

[8] Ibid., p. 694.

and coral. (See Pl. 6, Fig. 3.) Some of the chatelaines, from which small objects are suspended, are adorned in similar manner. The Bhotiya women, according to Waddell,[1] wear "massive amulets and charms like breastplates of gold and silver filigree set with turquoises; and their prayer wheels and rosaries are also bejeweled."

The Tibetan women wear quantities of ornaments in their hair. Among the Panaka of northern Tibet (Kokonor) the women's hair is dressed with three broad bands of red cloth, to which are attached large beads of carnelian, shell, turquois, coral, and glass.[2] Plate 7 shows an ornament worn by the women of Markams and adjacent country fastened along the length of their queues. The portion illustrated represents only one-third of a string and consists of seven oblong silver beads, each set with a large turquois and separated on the string by small coral beads. In parts of eastern Tibet the married women wear on their heads large gold plaques, and many of these are enriched with turquois and coral. In figure 10, plate 6, is shown an example in silver from Hor Chango; figure 9 illustrates a silver head ornament from the Ta-chien-lu richly ornamented in raised work and bordered with a row of coral beads including a single turquois. When the Lh'ari women (Province of Ts'ang) marry they make a kind of "mirror-shaped plaque" set with turquoises, which they wear on their foreheads and call yü-lao.[3] The women from K'amba djong in southern Tibet are described[4] as wearing a band about the forehead from which coins, corals, and turquoises hang down to the eyebrows, while lappets of these ornaments fall over the ears. Sarat Chandra Das[5] thus describes the head-dress of the wealthy women at a festival at Tashilhunpo:

Their headdresses struck me much. The prevailing form consisted of two, or sometimes three, circular bands of plaited hair placed across the head and richly studded with pearls. * * * Coral and turquois beads as large as hens' eggs, pearl drops and various sorts of amber and jade encircled their heads like the halo of light round the heads of goddesses. These circles were attached to a circular headband, from which six or eight strings of pearls and regularly shaped pieces of turquois and other precious stones hung down over the forehead.

The women in Ladakh[6] and the neighboring regions wear, suspended from the back of the head, bands of red cloth decorated with large perforated beads of turquois, turquois-incrusted charm boxes, and other ornaments. Figure 1, plate 8, shows an example from Leh (Ladakh) in the United States National Museum, and figure 4, plate 10, illustrates another of slightly different design in the British Museum. The owners are very loath to part with these ornaments,[7] many of which are heirlooms. Bishop,[8] writing of the dress of the women about Leh, says:

Their hair is dressed once a month in many much-greased plaits, fastened together at the back by a long tassel. The headdress is a strip of cloth or leather sewn over with large turquoises, carbuncles, and silver ornaments. This hangs in a point over the brow, broadens over the top of the head, and tapers as it reaches the waist behind. The ambition of every Tibetan girl is centered in this singular headgear. Hoops in the ears, necklaces, amulets, clasps, bangles of brass and silver, and various implements stuck in the girdle and depending from it complete a costume preeminent in ugliness.

An oil portrait of the late Queen of Sikkim in the Field Museum shows her in state attire. Laufer[9] in describing her adornment says:

Her crown, the peculiar headdress adopted by the queens of Sikkim, is composed of broad bandeaux made up of pearls, interspersed with turquoises and corals alternating. Her gold earrings are inlaid with a mosaic of turquoises in concentric rings. The necklace consists of coral beads and large yellow amber balls and has a charm box (gau) attached to it, set with rubies, lapis lazuli, and turquois. She wears a bracelet of corals and two gold rings set with turquois and coral.

[1] Among the Himalayas. Westminster, 1900, p. 46.

[2] Ibid., p. 692.

[3] Rockhill, Journ. Roy. Asiat. Soc., vol. 23, 1891, p. 76.

[4] Hooker, Himalayan journals, vol. 2, 1855, p. 86.

[5] Journey to Lhasa and central Tibet. Ed. by W. W. Rockhill, London, 1902, p. 119.

[6] According to Cunningham (Ladák, physical, statistical, and historical. London, 1854, p. 253) turquoises are brought into Ladakh from Yarkand (Turkestan), but most of the turquois used comes from Tibet.

[7] Knight (Diary of a pedestrian in Cashmere and Tibet. London, 1863, p. 184) says that the women regard these ornaments as sacred and as their own property only during their lifetime, and that they revert to the church upon decease of the owner.

[8] Among the Tibetans. New York, 1894, p. 44.

[9] Op. cit., frontispiece. The portrait is reproduced in colors.

The headdress of the Bhot women, who live in Ladakh, is thus described by Bellew:[1]

The hair, parted in the centre of the forehead, is plaited over the crown into two broad fillets * * * united along the middle line by a mixed row of cowries, bits of red coral, agate, turquois, malachite, and gold coins * * * hanging from the ears below their edges are strings of large beads of glass, or coral, or turquois * * * a chatelaine hangs from the girdle and is loaded with white bosses of conch, or strung with cowries, and beads of agate and turquois * * *.

The men and women of Bultistan, northwest of Ladakh, according to Paske,[2] wear earrings and necklaces, enriched with turquois and coral mixed with glass, rock crystal, and amber. Of the fashion of dressing the hair in vogue among the women, this author writes:

The women in Spitti and in neighboring provinces wear a very peculiar headdress, consisting of a broad band of red cloth studded with large turquoises and other stones, and arranged to hang from the brow down the back of the head and neck to the waist, which is called a Pirak. Usually a Pirak forms part of the dowry given to the bride by her parents, and the value of the ornaments varies according to the means and position of the family. The Nono, or chief man in the Spitti, when once asked why his daughter was still unmarried replied that he had not been able to secure all the ornaments for her Pirak. On one occasion, when resting near a Tartar encampment, I tried to purchase a Pirak from an old Tartar woman, but we could not come to terms about the price. I offered her $50, while she would take nothing less than $75, and as the band of the Pirak was very old, greasy, and dirty I declined the bargain.

Writing of the women of the same region, Knight[3] says:

The women * * * wore a curious headdress. * * * It consisted of a broad band extending from the forehead to the waist behind, and studded thickly with large, coarse turquoises. These generally decrease in size from the forehead, where there is a larger turquois than the others, down to the waist, and where the hair ends it is joined into a long worsted tail terminating at the heels. Some of these bands must be of considerable value, but the proprietors, although otherwise in complete rags, will not part with them for any consideration.

This writer describes a dance in the Waka Valley:[4]

They (the women dancers) were attired most picturesquely. * * * They all wore caps; * * * these were hung round with little silver ornaments, something in the shape of wine labels for decanters, but studded with turquoises; some of them also wore brooches, generally formed of three carnelians or turquoises in a row. The broad bands of turquois, worn usually on the forehead, were for the time derated (disrated) from their post of honor, and were suspended instead from the nape of the neck, over a square piece of stiff cloth, embroidered with strings of red beads.

In figure 5, plate 10, is shown a belt clasp made at Srinagar, in Kashmir. This object is of silver, richly adorned with mosaic of turquois, and is of special interest in comparison with the mosaics from North America, described below.

Most Tibetans carry charm boxes of wood, copper, silver, or leather, suspended from their necks or attached to some other part of their person. Some of these objects are very elaborately decorated with turquoises. Figure 6, plate 10, illustrates an example of gilt made in Lhasa by a Nepalese workman.[5] Other examples, shown in figure 4, plate 10, and figure 1, plate 8, are worn by women in Ladakh attached to the headbands. In the India Museum, London (see Pl. 8, Fig. 2), is a Lamaist charm box from Gau made of copper incrusted with silver and set with turquoises, in its center carrying a mystic monogram. This piece was worn attached to the girdle. In figure 1, plate 10, is a very elaborate example, forming part of a silver waistband, also set with turquoises.

Many objects of utility are enriched with turquoises and corals. Knife handles, scabbards, pouches, needlecases, bells, and other trappings are commonly studded with silver ornaments that almost invariably carry a turquois or coral bead. Plate 9 shows interesting examples of leather work in the United States National Museum. Its collections also contain a snuff horn set with ivory, coral, and turquois, and a silver stopper for snuff bottle, with snuff spoon attached, carrying a top set with coral and turquois. (See Pl. 6, Fig. 7.) In the Metropolitan Museum of Art, in New York, are displayed two Tibetan trumpets (nineteenth century) of gilt bronze, set with turquois and coral. The Bishop collection in the same museum contains a snuff bottle fashioned of a single piece of turquois, but this may be of Chinese origin.

[1] Kashmir and Kashgar. London, 1875, pp. 129–130.
[2] Journ. Anthr. Inst. Great Britain and Ireland, London, vol. 8, 1878–9, p. 199.
[3] Diary of a pedestrian in Cashmere and Tibet. London, 1863, pp. 168–169.
[4] Ibid., p. 217.
[5] Rockhill, Ann. Rept. U. S. Nat. Museum, 1893, p. 692. The best silversmiths in Tibet are Nepalese and Chinese.

By men and women rosaries are worn around the neck or wrist, and the strings usually seen contain 108 beads. The materials are ivory, seed, wood, coral, turquois, rock crystal, or glass. Many of the strings have small pendent beads of coral or turquois. The rosaries of the priests are more elaborate than those of the laity and are an essential part of every Lama's dress. A turquois rosary is occasionally used in the worship of the popular goddesses Dö-ma[1] and Tara,[2] who are conceived to be of bluish-green complexion. Prayer wheels are not uncommonly adorned with turquois. A fine example in silver and bronze is in the United States National Museum (Cat. No. 130392), and another set with turquoises and incrusted in chased silver, in the India Museum, London. Turquois is further used in the adornments of censers,[3] holy water vases,[4] ceremonial musical instruments, bells, etc. In the India Museum is a natural size idol-head of gold inlaid in turquois, coral, and other stones, with ears adorned with elaborate turquois earrings. The same collection contains a Buddhist wheel of the law (see Fig. 3, Pl. 8) of copper gilt set with turquoises and rubies. The United States National Museum possesses a Tibetan bowl from Kumbum, made of a human skull, with elaborately chased cover and base of copper gilt, set with small turquoises. One of the finest monuments in Tibet is the sarcophagus of the first Tashi Lama, in the monastery at Tashilhunpo. It is "of gold, covered with beautiful designs of ornamental work and studded with turquoises and precious stones. The turquoises appear all to be picked stones, arranged in patterns and in such profusion as to cover every available spot, including the polished concrete of the floor."[5] In the Ranwchhe Temple in Lhasa are small figures carved from turquois.

A recent writer,[6] in a description of the great Temple of Lhasa, says:

> The most notable feature of this temple is an image of Buddha. It is 30 feet high. The entire body is gold plated and inlaid with pearls, coral, turquois, and other kinds of precious stones. The design of this extraordinary work is so curious and elaborate that the like of it can scarcely be imagined. So difficult was the transportation of this idol that the natives claim that it was moved to Tibet from China by the gods in a night.

Supplies of turquois from Tibet, and stones coming even from China via Tibet, find their way into the Himalayan Provinces of Nepal, Sikkim, and Bhutan, along the north-central frontier of India, where they are worked into jewelry and ornaments that differ little from those fashioned in Lhasa and other parts of Tibet. The Nepalese, indeed, are noted as clever silversmiths, and much of the jewelry made in Tibet is made by Nepalese artisans. In the Museum for Ethnology in Berlin and the India Museum, London, are fine examples from those States of turquois- and coral-encrusted jewelry in gold and silver. Hooker,[7] writing of the Lepchas of Sikkim, says that these people are "fond of ornaments, wearing silver hoops in their ears, necklaces of carnelian, amber, and turquois brought from Tibet, and pearls and corals from the south, with curious silver and golden charm boxes or amulets attached to their necks or arms." Of the inhabitants of eastern Nepal the same author writes:[8]

> Both sexes wore silver rings and earrings, set with turquoises, and square amulets upon their necks and arms, which were boxes of gold or silver, containing small idols, or the nail parings, teeth, or other relics of some sainted Lama, accompanied with musk, written prayers, and charms.

Turquois will pass for currency in many parts of Tibet.[9] According to Rockhill,[10] no traveler going from China into Tibet should omit laying in a supply of turquois beads, "for with them he can buy better than with money all the necessaries of life."

---

[1] Waddell, Journ. Asiat. Soc. Bengal, vol. 61, pt. 1, 1892, p. 29.

[2] Laufer, op. cit., 1913, p. 13.

[3] Examples in Musée Guimet, Paris, and India Museum, London.

[4] Example in U. S. National Museum.

[5] Rawling, The great plateau. London, 1905, p. 184. See also Laufer, op. cit., p. 13.

[6] Chuan, Nat. Geogr. Mag., vol. 23, 1912. p. 966.

[7] Himalayan journals. London, vol. 1, 1855, p. 122.

[8] Ibid., p. 192.

[9] "* * * like coined money it continues to circulate in the country as a medium of exchange." (Campbell, The Phoenix. London, vol. 1, 1871, p. 143). "Tibetans use tea and beads of turquois largely for payment, instead of metal." (Gill, The river of the golden sand. London, 1880, vol. 2, p. 77.) Beads and stones, purchased at Si-ngan, are employed by Chinese commercial travelers trading with Tibetans as a means of barter. Laufer (op. cit., p. 63) obtained many ethnological specimens in Tibet in exchange for turquoises.

[10] The land of the Lamas. New York, 1891, p. 24.

MONGOLIA.

The turquois has long been known to the Mongols, who early became acquainted with this material through Tibetan or Turkish tribes or through both,[1] and later (during the thirteenth or fourteenth centuries) introduced a knowledge of it into China. The stone is employed in much the same manner in Mongolia as in Tibet, and a number of the turquois-adorned objects previously described under Tibet are found also in use in Mongolia. Indeed, considerable Tibetan jewelry finds its way into the latter country, either brought by traders or obtained by Mongolians when on pilgrimages to Tibet. Figures 1, 2, and 7 of plate 6 show turquois-encrusted objects in use among the Mongols. China also supplies quantities of turquois beads[2] and carvings, and from Peking a regular trade in these articles is carried on.[3] The twelve animals of the zodiac, shown in plate 13, were carved from turquois in Peking for export trade; such sets are made for wealthy Mongols to facilitate the counting of years.[4] Dr. A. Hrdlička, who visited Mongolia in 1912, informs the writer that flat, irregularly rounded pendants of turquois are common ear ornaments among the women of that country.

Dr. Berthold Laufer has shown the writer an elaborate regalia worn by noble Mongol women. This beautiful ornament, now in the Field Museum in Chicago, consists of head-piece, ear-pendants, necklace, and breastpiece, of silver-gilt filagree richly studded with coral and turquois.

Mme. A. Kornacoff, a student of Mongolian customs, has kindly communicated the following information on the turquois in Mongolia:

I have seen the turquois adorning the golden rings and gold-silver head ornaments worn by princesses and wives of Khans. This stone I have not seen in the ornaments of single women. The Mongolian obtains turquois from China.

The Mongolian designation for turquois is *ughiu*, a comparatively recent loan word from the Tibetan. An older word for this mineral is *kiris*, which probably represents the ancient Mongol term before the introduction of *ughiu*.[5]

CHINA.

The turquois,[6] though found at present in Central China in situ and commercially exploited by Chinese traders for export trade into Tibet and Mongolia, is not generally known to the Chinese people, for the apparent reason that it is but little employed by them, and plays no significant part in their life. Outside of Peking and Si-ngan fu, where the trade is monopolized by a few of the initiated, the stone is hardly familiar to the people at large, nor to the educated classes; in Shanghai, Hankow, and Canton it is entirely unknown. * * * Traders who have come in contact with Tibetans or Mongols or even settled among these peoples are certainly acquainted with it, and may even be induced to wear a turquois button, but a "barbarous" odor is always attached to it, and it seldom enters the ornaments of a self-respecting Chinese woman.[7] * * * The present Chinese name for turquois is *lü sung shi*, that is "green fir-tree stone," or *sung êrh shi* (also *sung-tse shi*) that is, "fir-cone stone."[8]

According to the historical inquiries of Laufer,[9] the Chinese became acquainted with the turquois not earlier than the Yüan or Mongol period, that is to say, the thirteenth or fourteenth centuries.[10] There are early records of turquois mining in Yün-nan Province in 1290 and in Hu-pei Province in 1366, but the operations were probably restricted and knowledge of the mineral came principally through intercourse with the Turks, Persians, Tibetans, and Mongols. Laufer is "under the impression that the Mongol rulers were the first to introduce

---

[1] Laufer, op. cit., 1913, p. 58.

[2] According to Rockhill (The land of the Lamas. New York, 1891, p. 24) the Mongols prefer greenish or off-color beads.

[3] See p. 83.

[4] Laufer, op. cit., p. 63.

[5] Ibid., p. 5.

[6] This quotation is a condensed excerpt from Laufer's careful study of the turquois in China (op. cit., 1913, pp. 20–60), to whose work the reader is referred for further details.

[7] The use of turquois in China has been scarcely mentioned by western writers. Besides Rockhill (The land of the Lamas. London, 1891, p. 24), who refers to its occurrence in Honan, Williams (The Middle Kingdom. New York, 1883, vol. 1, p. 310), merely states that it is employed in China, and Pumpelly (Geological researches in China, Mongolia, and Japan. Smiths. Contr., vol. 15, 1868, p. 118) observes that a mineral "similar to the turquois" is carved by the Chinese into very intricate forms.

[8] Laufer (pp. 21–24) reviews what Chinese authors have to say concerning petrified fir wood, and concludes that turquois was named "green fir-tree stone" because it was regarded as a transformation from the fir tree. In this connection it may be mentioned that the present writer has recently seen opalized fir cones from Nevada, with their outer form beautifully preserved, though converted completely into opaline silica. Laufer (pp. 25–55) then goes with great care into the significance of the Chinese word *sê-sê*, assumed by some authors to have the meaning of turquois. The question is of considerable importance, for such an interpretation would considerably extend the rôle of turquois in the East. The conclusion is reached, however, after a most critical investigation of the problem, that *sê-sê* can not be accepted as referring to turquois.

[9] Op. cit., pp. 56–62.

[10] Probably the earliest authentic use of a word for turquois in the Chinese language occurs in a Chinese work, "Cho keng lu," first published in 1366, in which turquois is called *tien-tse*. See p. 15.

it into China, and that their utilization of the stone gave impetus to the discovery of turquois mines on Chinese soil, and led to the turquois monopoly related by Marco Polo.[1] * * *"

Quoting further from Laufer: [2]

It is thus evident that in the Mongol period at least three turquois mines were in operation, in Hu-pei, Yün-nan, and Sze-ch'uan (Marco Polo's Caindu). Also from Tibet turquoises were imported into China during that period. * * * The modern word *lü sung shi* (turquois), as far as I can see, does not occur earlier than the eighteenth century, and it may be presumed also that the exploitation of turquois mines in China was taken up again only at that time, while it was interrupted during the Ming period. In the K'ien-lung period (1736–1795) turquois was occasionally used in the imperial manufacture at Peking. * * * It appears that the Manchu Emperors with their predilection for Lamaism and their interest in the Mongols and Tibetans derived the application of turquois from these peoples, and followed in this respect the trail of the Mongol Emperors. * * * It was the first time also in the K'ien-lung period that the stone was officially adopted and its use sanctioned for the imperial cult. Turquoises enter the imperial robe on some occasions, as recorded in the "Institutes of the Manchu Dynasty."

The native product ranges from green to blue in color, much of it is marked with black veins, and it is obtainable in comparatively large masses. It is regarded more as an ornamental material than a precious stone. Consequently it has been chiefly used for carvings of various kinds, resembling in design the more familiar examples in jade and agalmatolite, and for shaping into slabs and large perforated beads. To some extent also it has been employed for inlaying and along with other stones in the manufacture of composite pieces, such as floral designs.

In the Bishop collection of jade in New York, the beautiful objects of which have been admirably catalogued [3] in chronological order, the turquois makes its first appearance in two products of the K'ien-lung period (1736–1795), made in the imperial manufactory in Peking. These are a scabbard of chiselled gold adorned with Buddhist emblems of carved turquois, and a jade-handled knife studded with lapis-lazuli, carnelian and turquois. In the Chinese section of the British Museum is a magnificent turquois carving which is probably to be correlated with work of the K'ien-lung dynasty.[4] The object is fashioned from a single mass of turquois, measuring about 8 by 6 by 6 inches, of greenish color, and veined with black oxide hair lines. The design is very elaborate and represents a hillside, with trees, houses, figures, etc.[5] The subject is splendidly worked out and the piece represents not only one of the largest single blocks of turquois in existence, but one of the finest examples of carving in this material extant.[6] In the Victoria and Albert Museum, London, is another product of the same period; namely a peach-shaped box with a cover of red lac, richly decorated in fruit and flower designs inlaid with green and yellow jade, lapis-lazuli, turquois, and amethyst.[7] The Bishop collection,[8] also, contains two vases of jadeite carrying flowers of jade and quartz with leaves of moss-green jade and turquois, made during the reign of Chai-Ch'ing (1796–1820). Other stone plants of the same period, with leaves of carved turquois, may be found in this and other collections. In a recent elaborate study of jade, Berthold Laufer [9] has figured and described a beautiful pomegranate tree of the K'ien-lung period (1736–1795), now in the Field Museum of Natural History of Chicago, which is fashioned of carved jade, agate, and carnelian, with leaves of jade and turquois.

At present the turquois trade in China is practically confined to Peking and Si-ngan fu, where the rough stones are fashioned into beads, slabs, and carved ornaments of various sorts.[10] (See Pls. 11, 12, and 13.) From Peking considerable material is exported into Mongolia, while Si-ngan fu supplies a portion of the turquois used in Tibet.

---

[1] Marco Polo passed through the Province of Caindu (corresponding to the western part of the present Chinese Province of Sze-ch'uan) during the latter part of the thirteenth century, and mentioned a mountain in that country "wherein they find a kind of stone called turquois in great abundance and it is a very beautiful stone. These the Emperor does not allow to be extracted without his special order." See Laufer, p. 16.

Muhammed Ibn Mansur, in the thirteenth century, referred to the use of turquois by the Chinese. (See p. 72 and footnote 2.)

[2] Pages 59–62.

[3] Bishop, Investigations and studies in jade. New York, 1906.

[4] The Bishop collection contains a carving of that period of similar design in green nephrite.

[5] This carving is doubtless the one described by King (Antique gems and rings. London, 1872, vol. 2, p. 5) from the collection of Octavius Morgan. "The general outline" (of the original mamillary mass), writes King, "suggested the idea of a rounded mountain; the protuberances lent themselves for minor hills, forests, and villages rising in tiers one above another, with due gradation of distance, and every portion enlivened with numerous figures engaged in various occupations."

[6] A somewhat similar carving is to be seen in the Museum of Industrial Art in Berlin.

[7] Bushell, Chinese art. London, 1910, p. 125.

[8] Op. cit., vol. 2, p. 247.

[9] Field Mus. Nat. Hist., Anthr. Ser., vol. 10, 1912, p. 335, plate 66.

[10] Described by Laufer, op. cit., 1913, p. 63.

JAPAN.

Turquois does not occur in Japan, and until recently has remained unknown to the Japanese. Their mineralogists upon coming acquainted with this mineral from Western literature coined the word *turkodama* to designate it.[1]

EUROPE.

The turquois appears to have played only a minor rôle among the Europeans of ancient times.

The extent of its employment by the Greeks is difficult to ascertain, but judging from jewelry now extant its application was limited. The extensive collection of Grecian objects in the British Museum contains only a single example, a turquois pendant in the shape of a seated cat, obtained from excavations at Curium in Cyprus.[2] King[3] suggests that the turquois probably became known to the Greeks in the days of Theophrastus by its presence in the spoils brought home from Persia by the Macedonian soldiers; but this is merely conjectural.

Among the Romans the turquois found limited application as an ornamental stone. Pliny is thought by some to have described this mineral;[4] and in modern collections a few Roman cameos in turquois are known.[5] In the Marlborough collection are two examples, one showing the heads of Livia and the young Tiberius carved in relief on a large green turquois,[6] and the other comprising a small cameo portrait of a Grecian prince.[7] King[7] mentions a further example in Florence, consisting of a head of Tiberius, large as a walnut, in full relief. Antique turquois intaglios are rarer than cameos, and according to Middleton[8] the only ones known are probably of Sassanian (Persian) workmanship.[9] King[10] also doubted the existence of intaglios of classical time, although Buffon[11] in 1802 mentioned a fine specimen then in the cabinet of the Grand Duke of Tuscany, bearing the incised portrait of Julius Caesar. Kluge[12] has noted supposedly antique turquois carvings in the Orleans cabinet[13] and in collections in Vienna,[14] Florence, and Turin,[15] but according to Fischer[16] he later found them to be spurious. Of the Roman jewelry in the British Museum no examples show turquois save a single pair of gold earrings (see Fig. 2, Pl. 14) of the third century, which are set with garnet, turquois, and green porcelain.[17]

Perforated, discoidal, and cylindrical beads of a green turquois-like mineral have been found in prehistoric graves in France and Spain. A number of writers[18] have characterized these as turquois and discussed the possibility of their indicating ancient intercourse with the East, but judging from a single analysis made in 1864 by Damour[19] the material more nearly approximates variscite. This identification, however, can not be accepted as conclusive for

---

[1] Laufer, op. cit., p. 66.

[2] Marshall, Catalogue of the jewelry, Greek, Etruscan, and Roman, in the British Museum. London, 1910, p. 229. Middleton (The engraved gems of classical times. 1891, p. 149) goes so far as to say that turquois was apparently not used for Greek gems.

[3] The natural history, ancient and modern, of the precious stones and gems, etc. 1865, p. 138.

[4] See pp. 10–11.

[5] Maxwell Somerville (Engraved gems. Phila., 1889, pp. 688–689) lists among the Greek and Roman cameos 27 specimens engraved on turquois.

[6] Middleton, op. cit., p. 150.

[7] King, op. cit., p. 139.

[8] Op. cit., p. 150.

[9] According to Osborne (Engraved gems. New York, 1912, p. 284) the turquois was rarely employed for engraving by the Græco-Roman artists.

[10] Op. cit., p. 139.

[11] Histoire naturelle, 1802, vol. 13, p. 323. Mentioned also in the seventeenth century by de Boot.

[12] Handbuch der Edelsteinkunde, 1860, p. 361.

[13] Said to have contained two engraved turquoises; one representing Diana, with her quiver upon her shoulder, and the other, the elder Faustina. Dieulafait, Diamonds and precious stones. London, 1874, p. 143.

[14] The Katalogue der Sammlung des Herrn Tobias Biehler in Wien, 1871, lists the following turquois objects: (1) Scarab with lower side engraved in hieroglyphics, (2) scarab in ring, (3) Greek cameo, (4) Roman antique cameo, (5) Cupid, entire figure.

[15] According to Dieulafait (ibid.) the Genevosio collection of Turin contained an "amulet, convex on one side and flat on the other, showing on one side an engraving of a veiled Diana holding two branches in her hands, upon the other a sort of sistrum, a star, and a bee. Greek letters are inscribed on both faces."

[16] Archiv. Anthrop., vol. 10, 1878, p. 191.

[17] Marshall, op. cit., p. 307. Figured in plate 55.

[18] Aveneau de la Grancière, Les parures prehistoriques et antiques en grains d'enfilage et les colliers talismans Celto-Armoricains. Paris, 1897. Compte de Limur, Bull. Soc. Polymathique du Morbihan, 1st sem., 1893, p. 85; also 2d sem., 1893, pp. 206–207. Siret, L'Anthropologie, vol. 20, 1909, p. 138.

[19] Compt. rend., vol. 59, 1864, pp. 936–940. Damour suggested the name *callais*, thinking the mineral identical with the one described by Pliny under this name. Dana (System of mineralogy, 1892) changed the name to *callainite*, listing the mineral, however, as an independent species. Bauer (Edelsteinkunde, Leipzig, 1896, p. 457) suggested its probable identity with variscite.

all the occurrences. At any rate, beads of this material were in extensive use during the Neolithic period, and numerous specimens have been exhumed from graves in Morbihan,[1] Loire-Inférieure, Marne, Aveyron, Lozère, Provence, the Pyrenees, the eastern coast of Spain, and Portugal.

Excavations in Russia have revealed that the turquois found an early application in that country. The resemblance of the objects to those found in Siberia and in the environs of the Caucasus Range,[2] all of which bear a distinct Oriental imprint, indicate an early intercourse with the East. In 1890 a tumulus near Gouloubinskaïa, Province of Don, southern Russia, yielded ornaments, including two bracelets incrusted with turquoises;[3] and in 1873 two somewhat similar bracelets, decorated with vestiges of turquois or enamel, were found near the village of Petrik, on the Dnieper River, Government of Kiev, southwest Russia.[4] Among the treasures of Novotcherkask, Don Province, are enumerated small figures in gold, incrusted with plates of blue enamel, rose coral, and turquois; vases with handles in the shape of animals, adorned with turquois;[5] and a very elaborate diadem of massive gold, surmounted by a frieze of animal figures in turquois mosaic.[6] Even the magnificent treasure of Petrossa, found between Bucharest and Galitz in Roumania, included a fine golden vase adorned with silver tigers inlaid with turquois and rubies.[7]

Throughout the Middle Ages the beauty or rarity of a stone counted for less than its reputed virtue in the Pharmacopœia.[8] During that period the turquois came into high esteem, and a wonderful array of properties was ascribed to it. Because of its fickleness of color it was thought to possess remarkable powers of divination, and regarded as productive of good luck and efficacious in securing health and prosperity to the wearer, it was consequently in much demand.

It was very generally used for the adornment of every kind of sacred vessel, such as the chalice, ciborium, altar-cross, mitre, and pastoral staff;[9] and also found application in the decoration of medieval manuscripts. In the British Museum is a psalter, with wooden covers faced with two fine Byzantine ivory carvings of the twelfth century inlaid with small rubies and turquoises of unusually fine color. The Victoria and Albert Museum, London, contains an eleventh century manuscript copy of the Book of Gospels, with its upper cover, stated to be of twelfth century workmanship, overlaid with plaques of gold enriched with cloisonné enamel work and cabochon precious stones, including chalcedony, sapphire, rock crystal, jade, garnet, emerald, and greenish turquois. In the Morgan collection, in the same Museum, is a French (Limoges) reliquary shrine of the thirteenth century, covered with gilt copper plaques variously decorated and set with rows of glass beads and cabochon turquoises.

A notable example of an antique gem used in ornaments of the Middle Ages is the Schaffhausen Onyx, preserved among the archives in Schaffhausen, Switzerland. It is a Roman cameo of sardonyx, representing a female figure, in a beautiful setting of gold-work embellished with garnets, sapphires, pearls, and turquoises.[10]

The turquois was much used by the Renaissance artists for small beads and cameos, and, according to King,[11] such is the origin of nearly all the small carved turquoises usually regarded as antique. In the time of the Medici the people of Italy wore turquois cameos as charms.[12] De Boot, writing in 1609, remarked that the turquois possesses such authority that no one feels satisfied with his dress if he can not wear a fine one. Yet, de Boot naïvely added, the ladies prize it not greatly because, being brought rather abundantly from the Orient, it does not command an exorbitant price. The turquois, however, was valuable enough for princely gifts, for the young and beautiful Anne of Brittany, Queen of Louis the Twelfth of France, sent

---

[1] A number of specimens are preserved in the collection of the Société Polymathique of Morbihan.

[2] See p. 75.

[3] Kondakof et al., Antiquités de la Russie méridionale. Paris, 1891, p. 488.

[4] Ibid., p. 290.

[5] Ibid., pp. 494–495.

[6] Ibid., p. 490.

[7] Ibid., p. 504.

[8] King, The natural history of precious stones. London, 1865, p. 6 of preface.

[9] Lee, A glossary of liturgical and ecclesiastical terms. 1877, p. 425.

[10] Smith, H. C., Jewellery. London, 1908, p. 104.

[11] The natural history of precious stones. 1865, pp. 136–140.

[12] Encyclopædia of superstitions, folklore, and the occult sciences of the world. Chicago, 1903, vol. 2, p. 762.

a turquois ring to James the Fourth of Scotland.[1]   Sir Walter Scott [2] refers to it in the following stanza:

> For the fair Queen of France
> Sent him a turquois ring and glove;
> And charged him as her knight and love,
> For her to break a lance.

The use of the turquois at that period is further exemplified by Shakespeare, who has Shylock to say that he would not have lost his turquois ring "for a whole wilderness of monkeys." In Pepys's Diary (1667–68) appears the following line:

> She shows me her ring of a Turkey-stone, set with little sparks of dyamonds.

Evelyn in his Mundus Muliebris (1690) refers to a lady's ornaments as including:

> A saphire bodkin for the hair.
> Or sparkling facet diamonds there;
> The turquois, ruby, emerald rings
> For fingers.   *   *   *

The art collections of London and Berlin contain a number of European objects of the sixteenth, seventeenth, and eighteenth centuries that show the application of turquois during that period. The most important [3] may be noted. In the British Museum may be seen an onyx cameo of the time of George II set in gold, with its four corners adorned with turquoises; two jeweled alabaster cups of seventeenth century Russian workmanship, inset with turquoises; and two Hungarian brooches (eighteenth century) of elaborate design in metal work, inlaid with large, roughly rounded turquoises and other stones (see Fig. 3, Pl. 14). The Victoria and Albert Museum is rich in turquois jewelry; of particular interest are the following: Pendant (English, sixteenth century), set with diamonds, rubies, and a turquois cameo portrait of Queen Elizabeth; silver-gilt cross (Greek, sixteenth or early seventeenth century) carved and set with turquoises and garnets; cross of cypress wood (Greek, from Mount Athos, no date given), carved in openwork with the Ascension and other subjects and mounted in silver-gilt frame-work, enameled and decorated with filigree, pearls, turquoises, and imitation stones; boxwood cross (Russo-Greek, seventeenth century), decorated with enamel, filigree, turquois, and other jewels; fine octagonal turquois cameo (Italian, eighteenth century), representing the rape of Proserpine; elaborate morse of gold openwork (Hungarian, seventeenth century), inset with sapphires, pearls, turquoises, aquamarines, garnets, and enamels;[4] two girdle clasps (one Georgian, eighteenth century, one Anatolian, nineteenth century), of silver filigree set with turquois;[5] modern Hungarian pectoral cross and locket, fashioned of silver-gilt, enameled with garnet and turquois; elaborate Turkish belt-clasp of silver, ornamented with jade, turquois, garnet, and coral. The Wallace Collection in London contains a magnificent cup and cover (German, eighteenth century) of silver-gilt, adorned with precious stones including turquois. In the Museum of Industrial Art in Berlin are displayed a magnificent Hungarian mantle-clasp of the sixteenth century, and a girdle (seventeenth-eighteenth centuries) from Siebenburgen, made of gold and set with turquoises. Among the imperial treasures at Moscow is a throne covered with gold and studded with 2,000 turquoises.[6]

In 1912 the writer saw a fine cameo portrait of Queen Elizabeth in turquois, probably of European origin, which had been purchased from a dealer in New York. (See Fig. 2.)

Fig. 2.—Turquois cameo, probably of European origin. Purchased in New York in 1912. Height 5 cm. Photo. by courtesy of S. Varni.

---

[1] Edwards, The history and poetry of finger rings. New York, n. d., p. 158.
[2] In a note he says that a turquois ring, "probably this fatal gift" is preserved in the College of Heralds, London.
[3] These were seen by the writer in 1912.
[4] Morgan collection.
[5] Loan court.
[6] Hipponax Roset, Jewelry and precious stones. Philadelphia, 1856, p. 34.

During recent times in Europe the turquois has found a continual use, varying, of course, according to the dictates of fashion.[1] It has taken the lead among the opaque stones, but never recently has it approached to the value possessed by a number of the transparent gems. At present (1914) it is in demand and many fine specimens are to be seen on the London and Paris markets.

In a mystical theologic work,[2] published in Paris in 1909, the virtues of Mary are symbolized by the various precious stones, and the turquois is deemed particularly appropriate for this purpose. "It is a fine symbol," says the author, "of Mary considered as Mother and Queen of the elect."

SOUTH AMERICA.

The turquois was used rather extensively by certain prehistoric tribes in South America, especially those that inhabited the present countries of Peru and Argentina.

The mineral was known to the Incas. Garcilaso de la Vega[3] says that the "Torquoise is a stone of a blew color, some of them of a more deep Azure, and finer than the others, but not so much esteemed by the Indians as the emerald." Among the presents sent by the Inca Atahualpa to the Spanish Conqueror Pizarro, after the latter had mastered Tumpiz, were gold, many emeralds, and turquoises. Raimondi[4] states that the turquois was worked into small objects by the ancient inhabitants of Peru; and many examples have been found in the neighborhood of a turquois deposit near Ayacucho. Bandelier[5] discovered a single turquois bead interred in a cyst with two skeletons, on the island of Titicaca, in the lake of that name—a region comprising the very center of the culture of the ancient Incas. Amongst the extensive South American collections in the Museum for Ethnology in Berlin are displayed many turquois beads of Inca time, and four small objects of greenish turquois, crudely carved to represent the human figure, which were collected near Cuzco. Graves in the Pacasmayo Valley of northern Peru have yielded necklaces of turquois beads of which two good examples may be seen in the British Museum.

In Peru inlaying upon wood, shell, and bone was widely practised and turquois was one of the materials used. This type of art, however, never reached the perfection attained in North America. In a recent work on the archæology of South America,[6] a necklace decorated with white shell frogs inlaid with beads of turquois is figured. Amongst the Peruvian antiquities in the British Museum are two examples, described in 1908 by T. A. Joyce.[7] The first is an implement, probably a dagger or scraper, carved from a long mammalian bone to represent a forearm and clenched fist surmounting a flat blade. The surface of the handle is decorated with engravings of various objects and figures and is inlaid with pyrite and scattered blue-green turquoises.[8] The fragments of the inlay are cemented in cavities by means of some resinous material. The specimen came from a grave in the Santa Valley on the border line between the Provinces of La Libertad and Ancachs. The second object, from near the same locality, consists of a flat wooden knob, about $1\frac{3}{4}$ inches in diameter, covered by a mosaic of shell in the design of a bird, the eyes of which are of blue-green turquois.

The catalogue of the Bishop collection[9] states that a tooth incrusted with turquois and labeled "Peru" is exhibited in the Berlin Museum for Ethnology. Boman[10] is inclined to doubt the authenticity of this specimen, since, as he says, W. Lehmann was unable to locate it in that museum. Dental mutilation was practised by the ancient tribes of both North and South America; but especially by those formerly inhabiting Central America and Mexico, where the turquois was one of the materials used for this purpose.[11] The example just referred

1 For instance, John Mawe (A treatise on diamonds and precious stones), writing in 1815, says that the turquois was then in vogue, the demand at that time exceeding the supply, and paste imitations were frequently seen.

2 Valere, Marie et le symbolisme des pierres precieuses.

3 The Royal Commentaries of Peru, Rycaut's trans. London, 1688, p. 341.

4 Minerales del Perú. Lima, 1878, p. 218.

5 The Islands of Titicaca and Koati. New York, 1910, p. 181.

6 Joyce, South American Archæology. London, 1912, p. 206.

7 Amer. Anthrop., vol. 10, 1908, pp. 16–23.

8 Identified by G. T. Prior.

9 Investigations and studies in jade. New York, 1906, vol. 2, p. 101.

10 Antiquitiés de la région Andine de la République Argentine et du désert d'Atacama, Paris, 1902, p. 583.

11 See p. 97.

to, which is called into question by Boman, is the only one known to the writer of such use of the turquois among South American tribes.

Another interesting application of turquois is cited by Dall,[1] who quotes from Maginus:[2] "In Peru they make holes in their cheeks in which they put turquois and emeralds." This practise of wearing labrets,[3] peculiar to certain aborigines of Central Africa and America, is now partly extinct, and usually entirely so in the case of tribes that have come in contact with civilization. The extent to which the custom prevailed is very vividly attested by an old writer,[4] who says:

> The Brasilians have their lips bored wherein they wear stones so big and long that they reach to the breast * * * great Jasper stones being a kind of bastard emerald inwardly flat with a thick end because they shall not fall out; when they take out the stones they play with the tongue in the holes, which is most ugly to behold, for that they seem to have two mouths one above the other.

In Argentina a wealth of turquois ornaments has been found. According to Ambrosetti,[5] many collars consisting of graduated discoidal beads similar in shape to those of the Pueblo Indians, were obtained from the valley of Calchaquies east of the Andes. A. Hrdlička, on an expedition to Argentina in 1910, found a pale-green bead not far from the seashore near Niramir. This is slightly oval, measuring $7\frac{1}{2}$ by 9 mm., perforated near one end, the other end being slightly thicker, and was identified by the present writer as turquois.

In 1902 Eric Boman published an elaborate treatise entitled "Antiquités de la région Andine de la République Argentine et du desert d'Atacama," and in this a great many turquois ornaments are described in detail. The descriptions carry exceptional weight, as the turquoises were identified by Alfred Lacroix, the eminent French mineralogist. The information contained therein bearing on the turquois may be briefly reviewed as follows:

The so-called Diaguite Region (also called Calchaquie) occupies a series of secondary parallel chains on the western slopes of the Andes in Argentina. It was formerly the seat of considerable pre-Spanish culture and is now rich in ruins. Small beads of turquois and other green minerals are very abundant in graves of that region. The material most widely employed, however, is turquois of various shades, ranging from green to green bordering upon sky-blue.[6] In the region of Quebrada del Toro, in the southern part of the high plateau of Puna de Jujuy, beads and pendants of turquois were found interred with many of the skeletons,[7] and their position about the necks of the bodies indicated that they served as necklaces. The beads are discoidal, slightly irregular, polished, and centrally perforated; they range from 2 to 10 mm. in diameter and from 4 to 5 mm. in length. Their shapes are very similar to those seen in many Pueblo necklaces. (See Pl. 22, Fig. 3.) The pendants are triangular or oval and most are larger. A single turquois bead was discovered upon the summit of Nevada del Chani,[8] the highest peak of the Quebrada del Toro region, and another in the ruins of the pre-Spanish village of Tastil.[9] At Morohuasi, and especially at Golgota, villages of the same general region probably inhabited at the time of the Spanish Conquest, turquois beads were found in considerable abundance, and Queta yielded both disks and cylinders of turquois.

The pre-Spanish ruins of Bolivia contain many similar beads and ornaments, but turquois appears to have been more rarely used there than farther south in Argentina. An interesting necklace composed of pendants of sodalite, chrysocolla, and turquois, was taken from a body dug up near Pucara de Rinconada;[10] many small, perforated, discoidal beads of tur-

---

[1] Bur. Amer. Ethnol., 3rd Ann. Rept., 1881-82, p. 84.

[2] Geogr. Ptolem. Descr. dell' America, pt. 2, 34, p. 207.

[3] A labret is a plug or button, of various materials, which is inserted through a hole pierced in the thinner portions of the face about the mouth and thus worn as an ornament. By gradual enlargement the hole may become a permanent opening, in many instances occasioning frightful disfigurement; that is, to our own eyes. Doubtless the results of this practise were pleasing to the participants.

[4] Bulwer, Anthropometamorphosis, etc. London, 1655, p. 180. Through Dall, loc. cit.

[5] Antigüedades Calchaquies. Buenos Aires, 1902, pp. 42–43.

[6] Fig. 129 in Boman's work illustrates the shape and appearance of a number of the beads and pendants from various sources.

[7] Boman, op. cit., p. 329.

[8] Ibid., p. 353.

[9] Ibid., p. 373.

[10] Ibid., p. 655.

quois were also obtained from just beneath the surface in the plateau of Pucara de Rinconada.[1] At Calama, situated on the high Bolivian Plateau, on the railway between Antofagasta and Ururo, were found some rare beads of turquois, both disk and pendant shaped. The Museum for Ethnology in Berlin possesses turquois beads from Caracoto near Tupiza, and from San Blas near Tarija, both localities in southern Bolivia. In the United States National Museum are turquois beads from Tiohuanaco (Cat. No. 27068).

Chile, also, has supplied examples of the early use of the turquois. At Chimba,[2] on the Bay of Antofagasta, many discoidal beads, some of which were chrysocolla but the majority turquois, were exhumed in 1902. A few small cylindrical beads of turquois were also collected at Sansana, Region of Omaguacas.[3]

The source of the turquois employed by the ancient tribes is an important question, but one that can not be satisfactorily settled with the present meager knowledge concerning the mineralogy of South America. As has been noted (p. 44) the turquois occurs in limited quantity near Huari, Department of Ancachs, in the Andes of northern Peru; probably also in Chile at San Lorenzo and possibly near Copiapo.[4] By the present writer these sources are considered inadequate to have supplied all the turquois that recent archeological investigations have brought to light. No prehistoric turquois workings analogous to the Cerrillos excavations in New Mexico are known upon the South American continent. Furthermore, it is unwarranted to attribute the turquois to intercourse with tribes living north of the Isthmus of Panama. One is therefore led to the conclusion that deposits of turquois, worked in pre-Spanish times, await rediscovery in west-central South America, probably near where the present countries of Bolivia, Chile, and Argentina adjoin one another.

NORTH AMERICA.[5]

INTRODUCTORY STATEMENT.

The use of turquois in North America, apart from modern application in jewelry, has been confined to Central America, Mexico, and the southwestern portion of the United States, and within this territory it has been known and prized for centuries. At the time of the Spanish Conquest there were, broadly speaking, three somewhat distinct groups of aborigines within this region: The Zuñi, Hopi, and allied tribes dwelling in pueblos in the elevated plateau of New Mexico, Arizona, and northern Mexico; the Nahuan tribes, commonly designated as Aztecs, with a higher degree of culture than the Indians to the north, occupying the mountainous region of Mexico; and the Maya, Quiché, and kindred peoples of Central America. In all three provinces the turquois found both religious and ornamental use, and there are striking analogies between its application among widely separated tribes. With the passing of the ancient Nahuan and Mayan cultures, however, the use of turquois dwindled to unimportance south of the northernmost provinces of Mexico; but not so in the Pueblo region, where the mineral holds the same high place today that it did centuries ago.

The information concerning the use of turquois by modern Indians is drawn from writings of ethnologists and other observers, and study of the objects themselves, a number of which are in the ethnologic collections of the United States National Museum.[6] The evidence for deducing the application of turquois among the ancient tribes is derived from two different and wholly independent sources: First, the objects now existing in various collections and available through accurate descriptions; second, the writings of the old Spanish chroniclers,

---

[1] Boman, op. cit., p. 640.

[2] Ibid., p. 766.

[3] It is only within the past 20 years that the turquois has been found to any extent in South America. It is notable that in a very elaborate folio work, with large and magnificent colored plates, illustrating the arts and crafts of South American tribes (Kultur und Industrie südamerikanische Völker, Berlin, 1889, by Stübel, Reiss, Koppel, and Uhle) the turquois is in no place figured. One plate shows several beads and cylindrical ornaments labeled chrysocolla; some of these may be turquois.

[4] G. Bodenbender (Los minerales de la Republica Argentina. Cordoba, Argentina, 1899) does not mention turquois.

[5] Pages 89–104 were printed by the author as a separate article, under the title "The aboriginal use of turquois in North America," in the American Anthropologist, vol. 14, 1912, pp. 437–466.

[6] The writer had occasion to spend three months among the Navaho and Hopi of northern Arizona in 1910 and was afforded good opportunity to observe the use of turquois among those tribes. He has also inspected with profit the ethnologic collections in the British Museum and the Berlin Museum for Ethnology.

who were first-hand observers of the actual conditions. A few words concerning the relative weight of the two classes of evidence: The first, in most instances, can hardly be questioned; the turquois in the objects described has in many instances been identified as such by competent mineralogists. The historical evidence is more open to doubt; we can not always be sure that the precious stone described as turquois is really such. Many of the descriptions of it are confusing and conflicting, and were the historical accounts the only basis the entire ancient use of turquois might be open to reasonable doubt. So many turquois objects are known, however, and some of these so closely fit the descriptions of the old writers, that the historical evidence, by corroboration, assumes a weight it would not have alone and in the main can safely be accepted.

In the old Spanish writings there is repeated mention of a green precious stone prized by the Aztecs and called by them *chalchihuitl* (pronounced chal-che-we'-tl). This has been the subject of much discussion, some maintaining that it represented jade, others that it was turquois, others that it was in part jade and in part turquois, still others that the term included many varieties of green gems, and so on. This subject receives special treatment in Chapter VI; it is desirable here only to state the conclusions reached by the author, namely, that the early writers confused several green stones under this term; the natives, however, used it more strictly to designate one of their most valued precious stones, in the Southwest this being turquois, in Mexico and Central America probably jade. The uses of *chalchihuitl* and turquois were very similar, and in discussing the latter an occasional allusion to the former can not be avoided.

It may be useful to bear in mind the relative, rather than the absolute, antiquity of the races that have used turquois.[1] For example, the culture of Mexico at the time of the Conquest was more archaic than that of Egypt under the Pharaohs, and certain of the tribes of our Southwest, the Hopi, for example, are almost as primitive today as the dwellers in the lake villages of Switzerland during Neolithic time.

THE USE OF TURQUOIS IN MEXICO AND CENTRAL AMERICA.

USE AS ATTESTED BY HISTORICAL EVIDENCE.

The first European to come in contact with turquois in the New World was probably Juan de Grijalva, the discoverer of Yucatan. In 1518, according to Gomara,[2] he procured by barter from the natives of that country three gilded masks of wood covered with mosaics of turquois. It is not unlikely that one, if not all, of these is in existence today.[3] Proceeding on the same expedition to San Juan de Ulloa, Grijalva obtained further ornaments from the natives, including four turquois-incrusted ear pendants and five gilded mosaic masks (nature of mosaics not known).

It was in the following year that Fernando Cortés made the first of a series of daring moves that quickly resulted in the overthrow of the "Aztec Empire." It is related that upon landing at San Juan de Ulloa he was met by numbers of natives, of whom it was reported[4] that "Among the rest or rather aloofe off from the rest were certaine Indians of differing habit, higher than the other and had the gristles of their noses slit, hanging over their mouthes, and rings of jet and amber hanging thereat; their nether lips also bored and in the holes rings of gold and Turkesse-stones[5] which weighed so much that their lips hung over their chinnes leaving their teeth bare. These Indians of this New Cut Cortez caused to come to him and learned that they were of Zempoallan a citie distant thence a dayes journey whom their Lord had sent; * * * being not subject to Montezuma but onely as they were holden in by force."

Cortés immediately dispatched envoys to enter into negotiations with Montezuma, ruler of the Aztecs, who returned ambassadors to the Spanish camp bearing princely gifts. Sahagun[6]

[1] For a good discussion of the degrees of culture embraced by the terms savagery, barbarism, and civilization, consult Fiske, The discovery of America, Boston, 1892, vol. 1, pp. 24–38.

[2] Histoire générale des Indes Occidentales, et Terres Neuues. French trans. by M. Fumée, Paris, 1606, pp. 64, 65.

[3] See pages 93–96.

[4] Purchas, Pilgrimes. London, 1626. Vol. 5, book 8, chap. 9, p. 859, quoted by Dall, 3d Ann. Rept. Bur. Ethnol., 1881–82, p. 85.

[5] The custom of wearing labrets of turquois was also practised in South America. See p. 88.

[6] Histoire générale des choses de la Nouvelle-Espagne, French trans. by Jourdanet and Siméon. Paris, 1880, pp. 799–800.

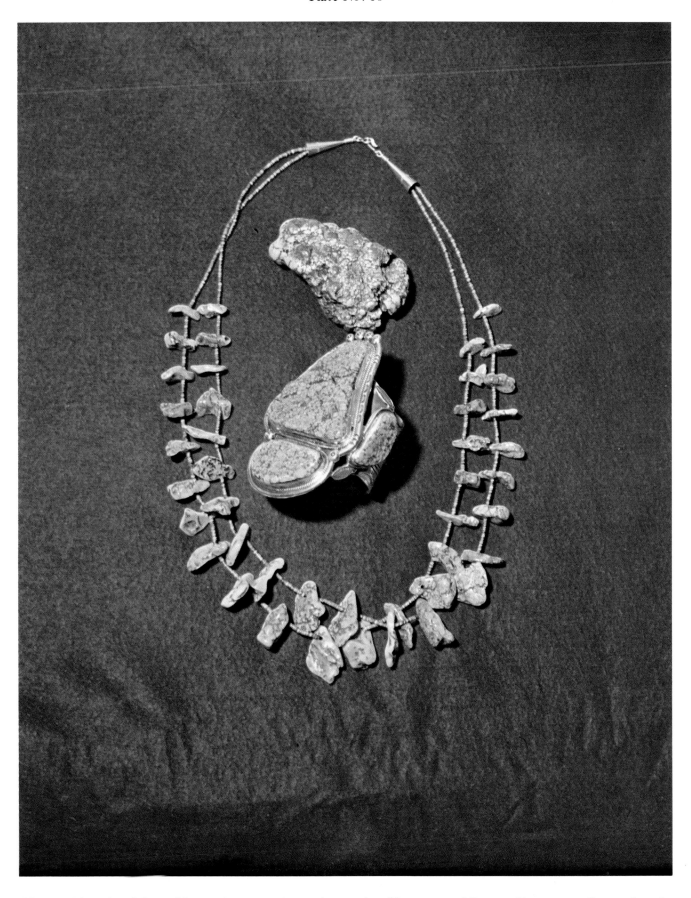

The necklace is of Lone Mountain turquoise and contains 43 nuggets of fine quality stones. Separating the nuggets are shell beads. The necklace is of two strands and is 30 inches long. The turquoise nugget at the top of the picture is from the Steinich Mine, and is 3¾ inches long. The bracelet at the bottom of the picture has four fine spider web stones from the Lone Mountain mine in it; it is 4½ inches long.

Squash-Blossom necklace of Blue Gem turquoise, 5½ inches long. Larger bracelet has Blue Gem turquoise. Smaller bracelet of Cerrillos turquoise. Collection of Oscar Branson.

enumerates in detail these presents and his inventory includes: (1) A mask, incrusted with mosaic of turquois, carrying upon it a snake, coiled and twisted, worked of the same stone; (2) a bishop's crozier [1] all made of turquois in mosaic work and terminating in a coiled snake's head; (3) large earrings of chalchihuitl in serpent design; (4) a miter [1] of ocelot's skin, surmounted by a large chalchihuitl and decorated with turquois mosaic; and (5) a staff [1] adorned with mosaic of turquois.

According to other accounts,[2] Montezuma later sent further gifts, intended for the Spanish King, including four chalchihuitls, each, according to the estimates placed upon them by the Mexicans, "worth a load of gold." The identity of the four stones can not be definitely settled. Kunz,[3] however, remarks that "it is a well-authenticated fact that the gems referred to were turquoises, and it is believed that they are among the crown jewels of Spain."

The Spaniards soon penetrated to the high plateau of Mexico and seized the person of Montezuma. They found the turquois esteemed throughout the country, and the many uses to which it was put are recorded in the writings of their chroniclers.

The turquois was employed not only as an ornament, but found an important religious and ceremonial application as well. A Nahuan king was interred with great pomp, a mask either painted or of gold or of turquois mosaic being placed over his face.[4] A pendant of turquois hung from the underlip of Topiltzin, the chief of six priests customarily engaged in human sacrifice;[5] "under the lip upon the midst of the beard hee had a peece like unto a small canon of azured stone."[6] In the month of Izcalli a feast was celebrated in honor of Xiuhtecutli,[7] the God of Fire, and an image of this Aztec Vulcan was clothed in fine raiment; from its ears hung pendants wrought in mosaics of turquois,[8] and its left hand grasped a shield surmounted by five green chalchihuitl stones placed in the form of a cross upon a gold plate.[9]

Quetzalcoatl, Lord of the Winds and mysterious hero-god of the Mexicans, is supposed to have introduced the art of working precious stones.[10] In the sacrifices and fetes held in his honor he is represented as wearing blue turquois earrings in mosaic.[11] He was worshiped as the god of commerce by merchants who bought, sold, and worked in precious stones.[12] According to tradition the palace of this personage was composed of four apartments, lavishly decorated; the easternmost one "called the hall of emeralds and turquoises, because its walls were embellished with stones of all kinds arranged in mosaics of wonderful perfection."[13] Catmaxtli, the father of Quetzalcoatl, was adorned with a mask of turquois mosaic during the feast of Catmaxtli.[14]

Each Aztec god was represented as carrying some form of atlatl as a symbol,[15] and these objects, fashioned in snake design and inlaid with turquoises, were in ceremonial use at the time of the Conquest. In the great festival in honor of Quetzalcoatl, his high priest was preceded by a "mace bearer with a scepter shaped like a monstrous serpent, all covered with mosaic composed of turquoises."[16] Similar insignia were presented to Cortés by Montezuma,

[1] These were among the insignia of Quetzalcoatl and their presentation to Cortés suggests that the latter was thought to be this fair-skinned god, returning from the east as had been prophesied. Mrs. Nuttall (The Atlatl or Spear-thrower, Peabody Museum Papers, Cambridge, 1891, vol. 1, No. 3, pp. 21–23) deems these examples to be a form of atlatl, or spear thrower, and states, "It appears that all three were sent to Europe."

[2] Clavigero, History of Mexico, Cullen's trans. Phila., 1817, p. 282. The Memoirs of Bernal Diaz, Lockhart's trans. London, 1844, vol. 1, p. 93.

[3] Gems and precious stones. New York, 1890, p. 63.

[4] Bancroft, Native Races of the Pacific States of North America. New York, 1874, vol. 2, p. 606. "Speaking of the obsequies of Tezozomac of Azcapuzalco, Ixtlilxochitl says that a turquois mask was put over his face * * *" Relaciones, in Kingsborough, Mex. Antiq., vol. 9, p. 370. Veytia states that it was a gold mask "garnecida de turquezas."—Hist. Ant. Mej., Tom. IV, p. 5.

[5] Clavigero, op. cit., 1817, vol. 2, p. 52.

[6] Purchas, Pilgrimes. London, 1626, vol. 5, book 8, chap. 9, p. 871, quoted by Dall, 3d Ann. Rept. Bur. Ethnol., 1881–82, p. 85.

[7] xiuitl = turquois, herb, year, or comet; and tecutli = lord.

[8] Sahagun, op. cit., p. 27.

[9] Ibid., p. 50.

[10] Torquemada, Monarchia Indiana. Madrid, 1723, vol. 2, p. 48.

[11] Sahagun, op. cit., p. 16.

[12] Peñafiel, Monuments of Ancient Mexican Art. Berlin, 1890, p. 12.

[13] Sahagun, op. cit., vol. 2, p. 656. See also Bancroft, op. cit., vol. 2, p. 173. Emerson, Indian myths or legends, Boston, 1884, p. 9. Nuttall in Peabody Mus. Papers, Cambridge, 1901, vol. 2, p. 294.

[14] Bancroft, op. cit., vol. 2, p. 314.

[15] Nuttall in Peabody Mus. Papers, Cambridge, 1891, vol. 1, No. 3, p. 29.

[16] Sahagun, op. cit., p. 169. See also Nuttall, 1891, op. cit., p. 23.

as has been noted.   The serpent-shaped atlatl of the hero-god Huitzilopochtli was called *xiu-atlatl*, meaning blue or turquois atlatl.[1]

The ornamental use of turquois was no less interesting.   Montezuma, as high priest and representative of a god, wore necklaces of precious stones, fine and large, consisting of chalchihuitls and turquoises of finest quality.[2]   The latter, indeed, were of such value that they could be worn only by the first of the land.   The dress of the nobles is thus described by Sagahun:[3]

> The Mexican lords wear wrist bands of black leather made pliable with balsam and decorated with strings of chalchihuitl or other precious stones.   They used to wear chin ornaments of chalchihuitl set in gold and implanted in the flesh.   Some of the ornaments are large crystals with blue feathers in them, which give to them the aspect of sapphires.   They wear many other precious stones protruding through openings made in the lower lip.   The noses of the great lords are also pierced and they wear in the openings fine turquoises and other precious stones, one on each side.

Annually the tribes under the dominion of Montezuma were required to pay tribute, including jewelry and ornaments of great value.   As recorded in the "Book of Tribute" and translated by Penafiel,[4] these consisted of a "gold circle, gold diadem, gold necklace, pearls of chalchihuitl, masks of turquois stone, turquois stone not cut, stones of rock crystal with shades of blue and with gold mounting, pendants of beryl enameled in blue and with gold mounting, and plates mounted with turquois stones."   Included also therein, according to Clavigero,[5] were "ten small measures of fine turquoises and one cargo of ordinary turquoises."   It is known from the Chronicle of Tezozomoc[6] that in the fifteenth century the Mexicans imported shields and ear plugs bedecked with turquois mosaics from the people of the Zapotecan tribes and accepted these objects as tribute.

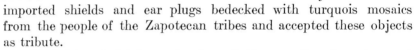

Little historical information is available regarding the nature and occurrence of the turquois employed by the old Mexicans.   Sahagun[7] writes:

> The turquois occurs in mines.   There are some mines whence more or less fine ones are obtained.   Some are bright, clear, fine, and transparent; while others are not.

Again:

> Teoxiuitl is called turquois of the gods.   No one has a right to possess or use it, but always it must be offered or devoted to a divinity.   It is a fine stone without any blemish and quite brilliant.   It is rare and comes from a distance.   There are some that are round and resemble a hazelnut cut in two.   These are called xiuhtomolli.[8]

FIG. 3.—Aztec lapidary from ancient Codex. (After Seler, 1904.)

In another place [9] he says:

> There is another medicinal stone called xiuhtomoltetl (from *xiuhtomolli*, turquois, and *tetl*, stone), which is green and white at the same time like chalchihuitl.   It is very beautiful.   Its moistened scrapings are good for feebleness and nausea.   It is brought from Guatemala and Xochonuchco.   They make it into strings for hanging around the neck.[10]

Finally, in relating the traditions of the first settlement of Mexico by the natives, Sahagun [11] states:

> The Toltecs also discovered the mine of precious stones, called in Mexico Xivitl (Xihuitl), which means turquois.   This mine, according to the ancients, was in a large hill situated near the village of Tepotzatlan.   * * *   At present the same name is borne by an inhabited village near Tulla.[12]

---

[1] Nuttall, 1891, op. cit., p. 188.

[2] Sahagun, op. cit., p. 514.   Nuttall in Peabody Mus. Papers, Cambridge, 1888, vol. 1, No. 1, pp. 1–52.

[3] Op. cit., p. 511.

[4] Monuments of ancient Mexican art.   Berlin, 1890, p. 79.

[5] Storia antica del Messico.   Ceseno, 1780.

[6] See Lehmann in Globus, vol. 90, 1906, p. 322.

[7] Op. cit., p. 771.   From this description one would suppose that Sahagun's "turquois" included more than one mineral, for turquoises are not transparent.

[8] Sahagun, op. cit., p. 772.

[9] Op. cit., p. 763.

[10] In a manuscript copy of Sahagun in Madrid (quoted by Seler, Gesammelte Abhandlungen zur amerikanischen Sprache- und Alterthumskunde, Berlin, 1904, vol. 2, p. 637) it is stated that the turquois was not very hard and that it was first polished with fine sand and then with another polisher.   Emery was not utilized as with many other precious stones.

[11] Quoted by Peñafiel, Monuments of ancient Mexican art.   Berlin, 1890, pp. 26–28.

[12] Not far from Mexico City.

USE AS ATTESTED BY OBJECTS.

Turquois has been identified in numbers of objects originating within the region of ancient Aztec dominion and coming from farther south in Central America. Its presence substantiates, to an important extent, the historical descriptions of its use as developed in the preceding section, and attests the position it held at the time of the Spanish Conquest.

Mosaics.—One of the most interesting and highly developed arts in prehistoric America was that of incrusting objects for ceremonial and ornamental purposes with precious and semiprecious stones.[1] Ancient mosaics, showing skill in workmanship and taste in design, are to be seen in many of the leading museums. This form of art reached its highest development in ancient Mexico (including Central America), although excellent examples are known from ruins in the southwestern portion of the United States, and objects from Peru inlaid with turquois[2] indicate a similar though less perfected application in South America. The materials usually employed were turquois, jadeite, malachite, quartz, beryl, garnet, obsidian, pyrite, gold, and varicolored shell, cemented to a base of wood, bone, or stone by means of a tenacious vegetal pitch of local origin. Only 24 examples from Mexico and Central America are now known. As a result of a peculiar coincidence of circumstances, 23 of these are to be found in European museums, most of this number having reached the continent during Spanish occupancy of the region in question. The best preserved of these objects are very beautiful and are among the highest types of art attained in aboriginal America.

The mosaics are distributed as follows: Nine[3] in the Christy collection of the British Museum in London; five[4] in the Prehistoric and Ethnographical Museum in Rome; three[5] in the Royal Museum for Ethnology in Berlin; three[6] in the Imperial Museum in Vienna; two[7] in the Ethnographical Museum in Copenhagen; one[8] in the Ducal Museum in Gotha; and one[9] in the United States National Museum at Washington. These will be described briefly in the order given, followed by a discussion of their origin and significance.

Of the nine specimens in the British Museum the most interesting and best known is the mask shown in plate 15, figure 1. It consists of a human skull, the front of which is covered with a mosaic of five transverse bands alternately of turquois[10] and highly polished obsidian. The rear portion has been cut away and leather thongs attached, to admit of its being hung over the face of an idol, as was the custom in Mexico to mask the gods on state occasions.[11] The eyes are disks of shiny pyrite surrounded by circles of white shell; and the nasal cavity has been slightly enlarged, with the insertion of pink shell.[12] This interesting object was acquired from the Hertz collection, having previously been obtained about the year 1845 at a sale of a collection in Bruges, suggesting that it was brought from Mexico soon after 1521 and before the expulsion of the Spaniards from Flanders during the revolt of the Low Countries in 1579.[11] No. 2 (Pl. 16, Fig. 1)[10] is a mask of cedar wood, formed of two rattlesnake carvings entwined to represent a human face. The front is covered with a mosaic of turquois, of bright-

---

[1] Gomara (Histoire généralle des Indes Occidentales, et Terres Neuues, trans. into French by Fumée, Paris, 1606, p. 46) refers to the Aztec custom of inlaying figures and masks of wood with various colored stones.

[2] See p. 87 of this paper.

[3] Tylor, Anahuac: or Mexico and the Mexicans, ancient and modern, London, 1861, app. 5, pp. 337–339. Bourbourg, Recherches sur les ruines de Palenqué et sur les origines de la civilisation du Méxique, Paris 1866. Franks, Guide to the Christy Collection, British Museum, 1868. Stevens, Flint chips, London, 1870, pp. 324–328. Brocklehurst, Mexico today, London, 1883, p. 194. Read in Archæologia, Soc. Antiquaries, London, vol. 54, 1895, pt. 2, pp. 383–398. Oppel in Globus, vol. 70, 1896, pp. 4–13. Lehmann in Globus, vol. 90, 1906, pp. 318–322.

[4] Pigorini, Gli antichi oggetti messicani incrostati di mosaico, Reale Accad. dei Lincei, Rome, 1885. Andree, Ethnographische Parallelen und Vergleiche, Leipzig, 1889, pp. 127–130. Read, loc. cit. Oppel, loc. cit. Peñafiel, Indumentaria Antigua; Vestidos Guerreros y Civiles de los Mexicanos, Mexico, 1903, pp. 101–103. Bushnell in American Anthropologist, vol. 8, 1906, pp. 243–255. Lehmann, loc. cit.

[5] Bastian in Verh. Berliner Gesellsch. Anthrop., 1885, p. 201. Uhle in Congrès intern. Américanistes, 7me. sess., 1888, Berlin, 1890, p. 738. Uhle in Veröff. Kgl. Museum für Völkerkunde, Berlin, 1889, pp. 2, 20. Andree, loc. cit. Peñafiel, 1903, loc. cit. Lehmann, 1906, loc. cit. Lehmann in Congrès intern. Américanistes, 15th sess., Quebec, 1906, vol. 2, 1907, pp. 339–349.

[6] Steinhaur, Handkatalog für die Besuchenden, Copenhagen, 1880, p. 19; 1886, p. 22. Heger in Annalen des k. k. Naturhistor. Hofmuseum, Wien, vol. 7, 1892, pp. 379–400. Lehmann, 1906, loc. cit.

[7] Duc in Archives de la commission scientifique du Méxique, Paris, 1867, vol. 3, pt. 1, pp. 157–158. Anon., Congrès International d'anthropologie préhistorique, C.-R. 4me. sess., Copenhagen, 1869, p. 462. Stevens, loc. cit. Andree, loc. cit. Lehmann, 1906, loc. cit.

[8] Andree, loc. cit. Ibid., Internat. Arch. Ethnogr., vol. 1, 1888, pp. 214–215. Ibid., Congrès intern. Américanistes, 7th sess., 1888, Berlin, 1890, pp. 146–149.

[9] Blackiston in American Anthropologist, vol. 12, 1910, pp. 536–541.

[10] Read, loc. cit.

[11] Tylor, loc. cit.

[12] The mask is figured in colors in the publications by Bourbourg and by Brocklehurst, previously cited.

blue and dull-green color, so distributed as to give to the two snakes a different shade. The specimen is 6.9 inches high, and was purchased in Paris in 1870 from the Demidoff collection. No. 3 (Pl. 16, Fig. 2)[1] is a mask of cedar cut to fit the face; its surface is covered with a beautiful mosaic of accurately fitted, polished slabs of turquois, mostly of a brilliant-blue. The face is studded with numerous knobs of polished turquois, and the eyes are mother-of-pearl.[2] The specimen, which is in an excellent state of preservation, came from a collection in Florence or Venice. No. 4[3] is a sacrificial knife with blade of yellowish, opalescent chalcedony. The handle is of light-colored wood carved in the form of a crouching human figure wearing an eagle mask, its face appearing through the widely opened mouth of the bird. The figure is incrusted with a mosaic of turquois blended with malachite and white and red shell; much of the mosaic has now disappeared from its setting. This piece was previously in the Hertz collection, having been acquired in Florence or Venice. No. 5[4] is a headpiece, or helmet, cut from a single block of wood with the interior hollowed and painted green. It is carved in ornamental shape, pointed at the back and front, probably to represent the upper mandible of an eagle, and was covered with a mosaic of turquois, malachite, pearl shell, and pink shell. Much of the mosaic is gone, but sufficient remains to show an involved design, including two conventional rattlesnakes. Its history may be traced back to 1854, when it was purchased in Paris. No. 6[4] consists of a circular disk or shield of cedar, about 12 inches in diameter, with a mosaic of turquois and shell in elaborate design, including the snake, human figure, and geometric patterns. This example was purchased in 1866 from a dealer, who stated that it came from Turin. It resembles in design the famous "Reloj de Montezuma," or calendar stone, in Mexico City. No. 7[4] is a pendant of white wood, 4 inches high, carved to represent an apelike head, with open mouth, as shown in plate 15, figure 2. The front is covered with mosaic of turquois, malachite, and other stones. The turquois is mostly pale-green in color, but two patches above the sides of the mouth are bright-blue. This specimen was obtained in 1866 from a dealer who had procured it in northern Italy. No. 8[4] is a breast ornament of light-colored wood, fashioned in the form of a two-headed snake with body disposed in meander loops. (See Pl. 15, Fig. 3). It is 17.5 inches in length, and is covered on the front with a mosaic of fairly uniform turquois slabs, with a line of larger pieces following the middle of the body. It was obtained from an old collection in Rome. No. 9,[4] the final example, consists of the figure of a feline animal, with open mouth and protruding tongue, crouching upon its haunches. It is 6.8 inches in height, and was carved from a block of brown wood; its surface shows the remains of a mosaic of turquois, malachite, pink shell, and pyrite. Its history is not known.

The five incrusted objects in Rome have been described and illustrated in colors by Pigorini, and a photographic reproduction of them is shown in plate 17 of this paper. They include two masks, two knife handles, and a musical instrument or rattle. Mask No. 1 (Pl. 17, Fig. 3) is made of wood, the back hollowed out to fit the human face, and the outside incrusted with a partly preserved mosaic consisting of malachite, turquois, red, white, and blackish shell, and pearl shell, besides a little garnet and several squares of pyrite. The eye cavities and half-open mouth are colored red, and out of the latter issue two white tusks and a tongue that projects to the chin, where it joins an appendage below, resembling the head of an animal. The piece was acquired in 1878 from the University of Bologna; during the seventeenth century it was in the collection of Aldrovandus.[5] Mask No. 2 (Fig. 4) is somewhat similar to that just described, although its back is not hollowed out. It was obtained in Florence in 1880, and its history can be traced by inventories back to the middle of the sixteenth century, the first mention of it being in the Inventario della Guardarobo Medicea (1553–1559). The two knife handles (Figs. 1 and 2) are in the form of crouching figures, the one human, and the other with a human body and an animal's head with widely opened mouth. Both are entirely covered with mosaic of turquois and other minerals, and are somewhat similar to the knife handle in the Christy col-

[1] Read, loc. cit. Tylor, loc. cit.
[2] Figured in colors in Bourbourg.
[3] Tylor, loc. cit. Read, loc. cit.
[4] Read, loc. cit.
[5] Aldrovandus, Musæum Metallicum. Bologna, 1647, p. 550.

lection in the British Museum.   These two pieces are figured in an old catalogue of 1677. [1]   The musical instrument or rattle (Fig. 5) is made of a human femur, with the ball covered with mosaic, a few pieces of which still remain.   Its history is not known.

The three ancient mosaics deposited in Berlin include a skull mask and two animal figures. The most interesting of these is the first, [2] which is fashioned from a human skull inlaid over the surface with small slabs of sky-blue to pale turquois.   This specimen was previously in the Ducal Museum of Braunschweig.   The second piece [3] is a two-headed jaguar, 12.5 inches long, carved from a piece of wood and covered with plates of turquois and malachite, with some obsidian, shell, and mother-of-pearl.   The eyes are malachite.   It came to the museum through the estate of Alexander von Humboldt, who must have procured it during his journey in Mexico, though he left no note concerning its acquisition.   The third example is a jaguar head of wood, inlaid with shell, turquois, and malachite.   This specimen was formerly in the Ducal Museum of Braunschweig.

Of the three turquois incrusted objects in Vienna, the most notable [4] is a circular, slightly convex, wooden shield, about 16.5 inches in diameter.   Except for a narrow border it was formerly covered with an elaborate design in turquois mosaic, which has almost entirely fallen away, leaving impressions in the gum indicating its original extent.   The object probably formed the center of a shield somewhat similar to those presented to Cortés by Montezuma.

The second object represents the head of an animal, carved of light-colored wood and covered with an inlay of pieces of shell, jadeite, turquois, and glass or obsidian. This is of somewhat different make from the other mosaics and is executed in a much bolder and rougher style.   The earliest mention of these two objects was in an inventory for the year 1596.   In 1891 they were found by Mrs. Zelia Nuttall in the Ambras collection, and were subsequently transferred to the Imperial Hofmuseum in Vienna.   The third [5] mosaic is a Xolotl figure.   Its history is not known.

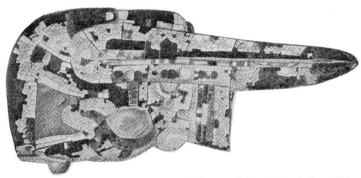

FIG. 4.—Ancient Mexican turquois mosaic. Bird mask. Gotha. (After Andree, 1889.)

The two specimens in Copenhagen are masks of wood, ornamented with mosaics of turquois, mother-of-pearl, and small shells. [6]

The single specimen in Gotha is a well-made mask in the shape of a bird's head. [7]   (See Fig. 4.) It is decorated with an inlay of malachite, turquois, mother-of-pearl, red coral, and white shell, but most of the mosaic has fallen out.   This object was obtained from a Jesuit collection in Rome about 1800.

The final example forms part of the Blackiston collection in the United States National Museum, and has an added interest in being the only specimen of ancient Mexican or Central American mosaic art now known on this continent.   The object [8] is a life-sized mask which was formerly covered by a mosaic of turquois [9] and other stones set in a thick layer of gum or pitch.   Three greatly elongated projections serve for the nose and two lips.   There are two cir-

[1] Legati, Museo Cospiano, Bologna, 1677, p. 477. Licetus (Pyronarcha sive de fulminum natura deque febrium origine libri duo, Padua, 1634, pp. 123–126) figures and describes two knife handles similar to those in Rome and the one in London. Lehmann (1906, loc. cit.) thinks that these two represent the ones described by Aldrovandus (1647, loc. cit.) and are now apparently lost.

[2] Bastian, loc. cit.

[3] Lehmann, 1907, loc. cit.

[4] Heger, loc. cit. The turquois was identified by F. Berwerth.

[5] Lehmann, loc. cit.

[6] Congrès International 1869, loc. cit. Steinhaur, loc. cit.

[7] Andree, loc. cit.

[8] Blackiston, loc. cit. U. S. National Museum, Cat. No. 258271.

[9] Identification verified by the present writer.

cular openings for the eyes, and smaller ones on the side to carry thongs which bound it to the head. In the forehead is an oval hollow which possibly formed a setting for a large ornamental stone, since fallen out. Along the sides of the face are impressions in the gum of regularly shaped stones, larger than those of the rest of the mosaic. The remainder of the mask was covered by thin, polished slabs of turquois, a number of which are still in place. The turquois is fine blue and green to dirty-grayish or yellowish. The mask was recently collected by A. H. Blackiston from a cave in Honduras, near the ruins of the ancient city of Naco.

The 24 known mosaics, by way of summary, are as follows:

10 masks
- Human skulls, 2 (London, Berlin).
- Wood, 7 (2 London, 2 Rome, 2 Copenhagen, Washington).
- Bird mask, 1 (Gotha).

5 beasts
- Beast heads, 3 (London, Berlin, Vienna).
- Beast figures, 2 (London, Berlin).

3 knife handles (1 London, 2 Rome).
2 shields (London, Vienna).
1 helmet (London).
1 double snake (London).
1 bone musical instrument (Rome).
1 Xolotl figure (Vienna).

Except one mask (Washington) recently collected in Honduras, the other mosaics have been in Europe for a long period. Nearly all of them were acquired by European museums from old continental collections. More than half were at one period in Italy [1] (distributed in Florence, Venice, Turin, Bologna, and Rome), the principal owners being the Medici in Florence, Ferdinando Cospi, a relative of the Medici, and Ulysses Aldrovandus, in Bologna. As has been noted, some of these (or analogous examples, now lost) were mentioned in old catalogues of the years 1553, 1596, 1643, 1647, and 1677. It is probable that the majority reached Europe during and immediately after the Spanish Conquest of Mexico. Most of these are of Aztec origin, though some were probably fashioned by tribes living farther to the south.

According to Lehmann [2] the mosaic art seems to have centered within the country east of the Mexican highland where, be believes, it existed in a specially flourishing condition. The turquois utilized was possibly derived from nearby deposits now unknown. There is some authority [3] for believing that this mineral was imported from Guatemala and Xochonuchco, and ancient tradition points to the village of Tulla as a source. [4] It is almost certain, however, that part of it at least was obtained through trade from the Cerrillos locality in New Mexico, which was extensively exploited in pre-Spanish time.

The mosaics were not ordinary ornaments. They had a symbolical meaning and were apparently confined to ceremonial application. They were the insignia of the Aztec gods, and, as such, were employed to adorn their representatives, both idols and priests. They had, moreover, a legendary significance, and tradition frequently attributed their use to the deities. The presents sent by Montezuma to Cortés included objects elaborately adorned in turquois mosaic; these gifts carried a special meaning in that they were the regalia dedicated to the memory of Quetzalcoatl, of whom Cortés was believed to be the reincarnation. [5]

Beads and other ornaments.—Turquois beads and objects adorned with turquois are comparatively rare in Mexican graves and ruins. This circumstance suggests that here the mineral was less commonly employed as an ornament and more exclusively confined to objects of ceremonial application than in the Southwest where ornaments of this material are frequent and beads usual in burial places. According to Dr. Nicolas Leon [6] the regions most productive of turquois objects are Oaxaca, Chiapas, Guerrero, and Michoacan—a group of States along the

---

[1] Lehmann, 1906, loc. cit.

[2] Globus, vol. 90, 1906, p. 322.

[3] Sahagun, book 2, edition of H. Siméon, p. 763. Hernandez, Hist. Animalium et Mineralium Novæ Hispaniæ, book 1, tr. 6, p. 90, cited by Lehmann, 1906, p. 319.

[4] See p. 122.

[5] Sahagun, op. cit., book 12, chap. 4. See also Nuttall, The Atlatl or Spear-thrower, Peabody Museum Papers, Cambridge, 1891, vol. 1, No. 3, pp. 21–23.

[6] Private communication.

southern coast of Mexico. Examples have been found also in Chihuahua.[1] In the American Museum of Natural History in New York is a suite of perforated discoidal beads made of turquois, from San Pablo Huitzo, State of Oaxaca.

Dr. Nicolas Leon has kindly furnished the writer with the following note concerning such objects in the National Museum in the City of Mexico:

The Museo Nacional has only a few objects made of or adorned with turquois. They are:

A beautiful gold pendant representing an escutcheon (chimali) ornamented with turquois lamellae, found in Yanquitlan (Mixteca), State of Oaxaca.

A necklace of gold beads alternating with turquois beads, from Nochixtlan (Mixteca), State of Oaxaca.

A stone figure with turquois eyes, found in Cozcatlan (Mixteca), State of Puebla.

Some necklaces made of turquois lamellae, from Michoacan (Tarascos).

Formerly there were many objects of turquois encountered at Teotihuacan, but none are to be seen at the Museum at present.

Dental mutilation.—A peculiar custom of aboriginal America, and one more frequently practised in Central America and Mexico than elsewhere, was that of altering the shape of the teeth or modifying their appearance by the insertion of different materials. Several of the early Spanish historians refer to this fashion, and in the catalogue of the Bishop collection of jade [2] is a reproduction of three teeth incrusted with green jadeite. A mythological personage known as Vukub-Cakix is described as possessing teeth incrusted with blue stones that shone like the face of the sky,[3] and this appears to refer directly to the use of turquois for adorning the teeth. That such was actually done is attested by an upper jawbone exhumed in 1882 from a sepulcher near Campeche in Yucatan, which bore six teeth inset with convex and polished turquoises of blue-green color.[4]

ANCIENT USE OF TURQUOIS IN THE SOUTHWEST.[5]

USE AS ATTESTED BY HISTORICAL EVIDENCE.

Vague rumors reached the Spaniards of enormous riches to the north of Mexico, and toward the middle of the sixteenth century we find them turning their attention to this unknown and alluring region. In 1535 Cabeza de Vaca, with three companions, made an extraordinary journey from eastern Texas to Sonora on the Pacific coast,[6] which subsequently led to the discovery of New Mexico. Cabeza de Vaca was the first to note the use of turquois among the sedentary tribes. When near the Pacific coast he was given presents of turquois by the Indians. Among the Sierra Madre, about 90 miles east of the Yaqui River in Sonora, he found the Indians owning turquoises, and, inquiring their source, was informed that they were obtained in the distant north in exchange for parrot plumes.[7]

In 1539 Fray Marcos de Niza, with a negro companion named Estevan, penetrated northward into the present New Mexico in search of the "Seven Cities of Cibola." [8] While his account of the adventuresome journey is exaggerated as to detail, in the main it is reliable. He found the natives of the region valuing turquois as ornaments and using it for exchange. He was impressed by the great number of turquoises worn by the Sobaipuris of the Rio San Pedro in southern Arizona, the last region inhabited by village Indians before Zuñi was reached.[9] The natives along his course gave Fray Marcos presents of turquois and oxhides.[10] Nearing Cibola he reached a village on the edge of the desert, where the inhabitants wore turquoises suspended from the ears and nostrils; these ornaments were called *cacona* and the wearing of them *cas-*

[1] See also p. 99.

[2] Investigations and studies in jade. New York, 1906, vol. 2, p. 101.

[3] Bourbourg, Popol-Vuh, Paris, 1861, quoted by Boman, Antiquités de la région Andine, etc., Paris, 1902, vol. 1, p. 583.

[4] Hamy in Bull. Soc. d'Anthr. de Paris, vol. 5, 1882, p. 884, figured. This object is also described by the same writer in Décades américanæ, Mem. d'arch. et d'ethn. américaines, déc. III, No. 28, p. 92.

[5] This term is used to include the plateau region now comprising Arizona, New Mexico, and adjacent parts of Mexico, California, Nevada, and Colorado.

[6] Bandelier, Contributions to the history of the southwestern portion of the United States. Cambridge, Mass., 1890.

[7] Ibid., pp. 42, 61.

[8] A group of pueblos, now in ruins, centering about the present pueblo of Zuñi.

[9] Bandelier, ibid., p. 442.

[10] Extracts from journal of Fray Marcos de Niza, published in the Indian Report by Lieut. Whipple, Pacific R. R. Expl. and Surv., vol. 3, pt. 3, 1856, pp. 105–108.

conados.[1] Many turquoises were offered the friar, who was told that these gems abounded in Cibola as well as in the kingdoms of Marata, Acus, and Tontonteac.[2] Estevan, who had shown undue zeal in collecting turquoises,[3] had been sent ahead to Cibola, where he became involved in difficulties with the Indians and was killed. Niza followed and found that the people of Cibola "have emeralds and other jewels, although they esteem none so much as turquoises, wherewith they adorn the walls of the porches of their houses, and their apparel and vessels; and they use them instead of money through all the country."[4] Niza took formal possession of Cibola and returned to Mexico, where he gave a glowing account of the riches of the new country. A force was then raised under Coronado and dispatched to conquer Cibola.

In 1540 Coronado visited the newly discovered country of Cibola, and reported that Niza had enlarged upon the richness of the place, and denied that the houses were decorated with turquoises.[5] However, he noted that the natives possessed turquoises of good quality, as well as "turquois earrings, combs and tablets set with turquoises;"[5] and he further observed that they sometimes offer turquoises in their worship, which is principally of water.[6] When Coronado had occupied Cibola he heard of Tusayan (the present Hopi pueblos) and dispatched Don Pedro de Tobar to capture its villages. After a brief fight, in which the natives were defeated, the latter sued for peace, offering gifts including turquoises.[7] Somewhat later Alvarado was dispatched by Coranado on a short journey past Acoma to Cicuye (the present Pecos), where he was presented with cloth and turquoises, "of which," he reported, "there are quantities in that region."[8]

In a letter[9] from Mendoza to the King of Spain, written in 1540, it is observed that the people of Cibola have turquoises in quantity, though not so many as Marcos de Niza at first affirmed. Castañeda,[10] who accompanied Coronado to Cibola, referred to the custom in Culiacan (Sinaloa) of making presents of turquoises to the devil and of decorating certain classes of women with bracelets of fine turquoises. According to Bandelier[11] the Seri of Sonora, in early Spanish time, exchanged iridescent shells from the Gulf of California for the turquois of Zuñi; and the Opata gave parrot skins and plumes to the people of Zuñi in return for turquois and turquois ornaments. The Apache between the years 1630 and 1680 were accustomed to come to the pueblo of Pecos to trade in turquois.[12] The Yaqui in former times held the turquois in place of money.[13] The Tano during the sixteenth century owned the Cerrillos turquois deposits in New Mexico and guarded them jealously,[14] and the turquois obtained therefrom proved quite an important resource for purposes of commerce.

There is little evidence that turquois was used in Spanish times by tribes living to the north and east of the Pueblo region. It is stated in one place,[15] however, that in the region of the lower Mississippi the Spaniards saw shawls of cotton, brought, it was said, from the west, and probably from the Pueblo country, as they were accompanied by objects which from their description may have been of turquois. More than 100 minute discoidal beads and a small pendant of turquois, believed to have been derived through trade with the Pueblos, were found with the skeleton of a child in a mound in Coahoma County, Miss.[16]

[1] Davis, Spanish conquest of New Mexico. 1869, p. 125.

[2] Ibid., p. 125. Marata has been identified as the ruined Makyata near Zuñi; Acus as the pueblo of Acoma; and Tontonteac as the Tusayan, or Hopi province, northwestward from Zuñi. See Winship, The Coronado Expedition, 14th Ann. Rept. Bur. Amer. Ethnol., 1892–93, pt. 1, p. 357.

[3] Winship, op. cit., p. 357.

[4] Marcos de Niza in Whipple's Report, 1856, loc. cit.

[5] Coronado, Extracts from journal, published by Lieut. Whipple in Pacific R. R. Expl. and Surv., vol. 3, pt. 3, 1856, pp. 108–111. According to F. H. Cushing the custom of adorning the porches of the houses with turquoises is supported by tradition.

[6] Winship in 14th Ann. Rept. Bur. Amer. Ethnol., 1892–93, p. 573. In Smith's Relación de la Jornada de Coronado á Cibola (Colección de Documentos para la Historia de Florida, London, 1857, vol. 1, p. 148) it is stated that the people of Cibola offered turquoises of poor quality in sacrifice to their springs. This custom of devoting offerings to the sources of water was widespread among the Pueblo Indians. See Hough, Sacred Springs of the Southwest, Rec. of the Past, vol. 5, 1905, pp. 163–169.

[7] Castañeda's narrative in Winship, loc. cit., p. 489.

[8] Ibid., p. 491.

[9] Translated in Winship, loc. cit.; see p. 549.

[10] Narrative, in Winship, loc. cit.; see p. 513.

[11] Bandelier, Final report of investigations among the Indians of the southwestern United States. Cambridge, 1891, pt. 1, p. 39, also p. 63.

[12] Vetancurt, Teatro Mexicano, Mexico, repr. 1870–71, vol. 3, p. 323.

[13] Bancroft, Native races of the Pacific States of North America. New York, 1874, vol. 1, p. 583.

[14] Bandelier, Final report, etc., op. cit., 1890, pt. 1, p. 163.

[15] Holmes, Prehistoric textile art of Eastern United States, 13th Ann. Rept. Bur. Amer. Ethnol., 1891–92, p. 25.

[16] Peabody, Exploration of mounds, Coahoma County, Miss. Peabody Museum Papers, Cambridge, 1904, vol. 3, No. 2, pp. 50–51.

USE AS ATTESTED BY OBJECTS.

Throughout the Southwest turquois ornaments of various kinds have been found in comparative abundance in graves and ruins. Bandelier[1] noted turquoises that came from the ruins of Casas Grandes, in Chihuahua, Mexico. Kunz[2] described and figured two objects found by Frank Hamilton Cushing near Tempe, Maricopa County, Ariz. The first of these is a prairie dog carved from white marble, with turquois eyes; the second, a sea shell incrusted with mosaic of turquoises and garnets (?), fashioned to represent a frog.[3] Blake has referred to a mosaic of turquois dug from the ruins near Casa Grande on the Gila River,[4] and an ancient cross of clam shell bordered with turquois mosaic from a cliff dwelling on Oak Creek,[5] near Jerome, Ariz. In the latter locality Fewkes[6] found some beads in the Honanki Cliff ruin, near Oak Creek. According to Blake[7] the ruins of the Salt River Valley in Arizona have yielded many turquois beads and pendants, formerly used for necklaces, and a marine shell incrusted with turquois.

In 1896 some interesting finds of turquois objects were made by Fewkes[8] in the ancient pueblo ruins near Winslow, Ariz. The most important of these is a beautiful ornament of shell incrusted with turquois,[9] found at Chaves Pass on the breast of a skeleton (Pl. 18, Fig. 1). It consists of one valve of *Pectunculus giganteus*, coated with gum, in which are inlaid rows of green turquois slabs carefully fitted together, the object representing a frog or toad. The nearby ruins along Chevlon Creek, a tributary to the Little Colorado, likewise furnished turquois ornaments, including a square fragment of lignite inlaid with five small turquoises (Pl. 19, Fig. 1), a pear-shaped pendant of bone covered on one surface with turquois mosaic (Pl. 19, Fig. 2), an armlet of shell inlaid with turquois (Pl. 18, Fig. 2), and an object of shell and turquois combined in an incrustation on wood. Of the dress of the ancient Patki people who formerly inhabited these ruins, Fewkes[10] says:

> For ornaments they wore shell, bone, and turquois variously worked. The most elaborate forms of these ornaments were shell and turquois incrustations on wood, shell, lignite, or bone. * * * The women had ear pendants made of rectangular fragments of lignite set with turquois, bone incrusted with the same, or simple turquois. Both sexes had armlets, wristlets, and finger rings made of the marine shell *Pectunculus giganteus*, sometimes inlaid with stone.

From the Black Falls ruins, on the Little Colorado about 35 miles northeast of Flagstaff, Fewkes obtained an interesting pair of ear-pendants, made of lignite slabs, upon which are cemented small squares of turquois and lignite arranged in simple though attractive geometrical design, with a slab of yellow indurated clay in the center (Pl. 19, Fig. 3).

Farther north, in the Sikyatki ruin in the Tusayan Province, many turquois objects have been unearthed[11] during the course of archæological excavations. The ancient Sikyatki people buried their dead with the ornaments worn while living, and many of their skeletons were found with rows of turquois beads about the neck and single pendants near the mastoid process, indicating that the bodies had been adorned with necklaces and pendants. A food vessel collected from the Sikyatki ruin is decorated with the painted head of a woman wearing square ear-pendants of turquois mosaic like those worn by the Hopi women of today. A pair of similar earrings, consisting of flat slabs of wood with one side covered with tiny squares of turquois set in hardened pitch, has been found by Cummings[12] in the Betatakin ruin, a well-known cliff dwelling near Marsh Pass in northeastern Arizona.

---

[1] Final report of investigations among the Indians of the southwestern United States. Cambridge, 1890, pt. 1, pp. 39, 352.

[2] Gems and precious stones. New York, 1890, p. 61.

[3] According to F. W. Hodge, the incrusted frog referred to by Kunz was not found, but was a model of one in possession of Mr. Lincoln Fowler, of Phoenix, Ariz., the source of which was one of the ruins in the Salt River Valley.

[4] Amer. Journ. Sci., vol. 25, 1883, pp. 197–200.

[5] Amer. Antiquarian, vol. 22, 1900, pp. 108–110.

[6] 17th Ann. Rept. Bur. Amer. Ethnol., 1895–96, p. 573.

[7] Amer. Antiquarian, vol. 21, 1899, pp. 278–284.

[8] Ann. Rept. Smiths. Inst., 1896, pp. 517–539.

[9] Figured in colors in the publication cited, p. 529. Also described in American Anthropologist, vol. 9, 1896, pp. 359–367.

[10] Op. cit., p. 534.

[11] Fewkes in 17th Ann. Rept. Bur. Amer. Ethnol., 1895–6, pp. 641, 662, 733.

[12] Bull. Univ. Utah, 1911, vol. 3, No. 3, pt. 2, p. 35.

Turquois beads and ear-pendants are abundant in the ruins of northwestern New Mexico and the adjacent region.[1] In 1899 George H. Pepper found many turquois carvings and some imperfect mosaics in ruins in the Mancos Canyon,[2] near the southwestern corner of Colorado. Of special interest were tadpoles from one-fourth to 1 inch in length, fashioned of turquois and perforated for suspension as pendants, and frogs nearly 3 inches long made of black jet, with raised eyes of turquois and a band of similar material back of the eyes. The turquois was mostly rich green, though some pieces were partly bluish. Dr. J. Walter Fewkes[3] has seen a beautiful bird mosaic inlaid with turquois from one of the ruins near Cortez, in the Montezuma Valley not far from Mancos. This object is made of hematite, with turquois eyes and neckband. The feathers are represented by stripes of inlaid turquois, and upon the back is an hourglass figure in turquois inlay recalling designs on ancient pottery. A single specimen of turquois, probably an ear-pendant, was found in the Cliff Palace ruin in the same region.

The most important series of turquois objects yet found in this country, however, is the result of explorations made in 1896 by George H. Pepper[4] in the ancient Pueblo Bonito of Chaco Canyon, northwestern New Mexico. Mosaics, carvings, beads, and pendants in great quantity and variety were found in the burial rooms and accompanying the skeletons of the former inhabitants. A few are shown on plate 20. One of the objects is a "bone scraper" formed of the humerus of a deer or an elk and decorated about its center with an inlay of jet and turquois, showing considerable taste and skill in execution and design. Another is a head or breast ornament made of polished jet, its four corners set with circular turquoises. Another jet object is designed to represent a frog or toad; its body is carefully rounded and polished; the eyes are two large rounded pieces of turquois standing boldly out, and across the neck is a broad inlaid band of the same material.[5] A suite of eight duck-like birds, carved from decomposed turquois of pale bluish-green color, were prominent among the finds. The figures were probably roughed out with a stone implement and then ground to the desired shape with sandstone grinders. In addition, the ruins yielded a quantity of turquois pendants and discoidal beads, mostly green in color; one pendant, however, showed a delicate blue.

One burial room in particular has served as the subject of a special paper by Mr. Pepper,[6] and the number and variety of turquois ornaments found there is remarkable. From the neck, breast, waist, wrist, and ankles of several of the skeletons, turquois beads to the number of several thousand were collected, together with pendants and carved pieces. Near one of the bodies was a "turquois jewel basket" of cylindrical shape, 3 inches in diameter and 6 inches long, consisting of slender splints, over which a mosaic of turquois slabs had been cemented by means of piñon gum. The basketwork had decayed, but the mosaic was held in place by the sand in which the object was buried. One thousand two hundred and fourteen pieces of turquois had formed the mosaic, and within and near the mouth of the cylinder were found 2,150 disk-shaped turquois beads and 152 small and 22 large turquois pendants, some carved to represent birds. Among thousands of other objects of turquois there may be noted: A stone ornament with inlay of turquois; another object made of turquois and shell mosaic inserted on basketwork, the beads being strung and placed on edge in parallel rows; a pendant with turquois front and trachyte back, showing splendid workmanship; several beads with holes smaller than an ordinary pin; a number of tadpoles, frogs, and buttons of carved turquois, drilled on the underside for suspension; a pear-shaped ornament made of three turquois pieces joined with great exactness; a cylinder of hematite ornamented with turquois inlay, representing a bird; a mouthpiece for a shell trumpet incrusted with turquois; pendants of various shapes and sizes; beads, ornaments, and inlays in great variety.

---

[1] Bandelier, Final report, op. cit., p. 352.

[2] Kunz in 21st Ann. Rept. U. S. Geol. Surv., 1899–1900, p. 456.

[3] Bur. Amer. Ethnol., Bull. 41, 1909, p. 27.

[4] American Anthropologist, vol. 7, 1905, pp. 183–187.

[5] Among the Pueblo Indians of today, as well as among the ancient inhabitants of the Southwest, the frog is a symbol of water, and its conventionalized design is common in both the ancient and the modern art.

[6] The Exploration of a burial-room in Pueblo Bonito, New Mexico, Putnam Ann. Vol., New York, 1909, pp. 196–252.

Pepper [1] states that this burial chamber probably contained the remains of priests, caciques, or other important personages, and that the objects show a high degree of skill and taste, and "afford conclusive evidence that the people of Pueblo Bonito reached as high a degree of proficiency in the arts as those of any other pueblo in the Southwest."

RECENT AND PRESENT USE OF TURQUOIS IN THE SOUTHWEST.

The turquois is today in wide use among the Indians of the Southwest, and it forms one of their most cherished possessions. As in the past, it still finds a ceremonial as well as an ornamental application.

Pueblo-dwelling tribes.—The Pueblo Indians find great pleasure in turquois and seldom is a well-to-do representative seen without ornaments of this material. Especially upon gala occasions and during ceremonies is this stone in evidence, and both sexes bedizen themselves with quantities of it. The turquois is most commonly fashioned into discoidal and cylindrical beads and into various-sized pendants of oblong, triangular, and keystone outline. The work is performed by rubbing the material on sandstone and polishing on finer material, and the objects are perforated with a bow-drill, usually tipped with a fragment of quartz or flint. (See Pl. 21.) The workmanship is rather crude, and the finished piece is seldom symmetrical or highly polished. The beads are usually strung on cord, but sometimes on wire, and one or more strands are used for necklaces, bracelets, and more rarely as ear-ornaments. Discoidal beads are most common (see Pl. 22, Fig. 3); in some strands these alternate with cylindrical shapes, and pendants may be inserted, especially toward the center, to give variety. Beads of coral and white shell are often combined with the turquois, although their introduction lessens the value of the string. Pendants are frequently worn alone, suspended from the ears; indeed this is perhaps the most common ornament seen in the Southwest. A number of pendants of Sia workmanship shown in plate 22, figure 6, illustrate the customary shape and appearance of these objects. Many finger rings are set with turquois, and the mineral is frequently used for purposes of currency. Furthermore, the turquois is employed, though not so universally, for inlaying ornaments and objects of utility, and in some instances small slabs of this material are fashioned into mosaics of beauty, though not equal to the superb examples made of old by the Aztecs.

In addition the turquois finds application by virtue of its supposed efficacy and consequently is prominent in many charms, amulets, and fetiches. Few religious rites take place without its use and the paraphernalia of the priesthood abound in objects adorned with it. Turquois, indeed, may be said to hold a fundamental place in the religious ideas of the Pueblo Indians and in their outward ceremonial expression of them.

The turquois utilized varies from very inferior material to really beautiful stones. The majority, however, are of little value as gem material, according to our standards. Turquois matrix is used along with pure material, although the latter is preferred. The Indian is usually a rather keen judge of quality, although he does not so strongly favor the blue color, to the exclusion of the green, as does the white man.

The Zuñi value the turquois more highly than does any other Pueblo tribe, with the possible exception of the Hopi. A single string of beads of good quality is said to be worth several horses. In former times the Zuñi necklaces were more carefully made than they are today, and numbers of them, worn only on ceremonial occasions, have been handed down from father to elder son for several generations.[2] Two red shells inlaid with turquois and worn pendent to the necklaces during certain religious rites were in possession of the Zuñi from early time; recently Mrs. M. C. Stevenson succeeded in obtaining one of them for the United States National Museum. (See Pl. 22, Fig. 4.) According to Mrs. Stevenson, double loops of turquois beads are worn by the Zuñi in the ears only on ceremonial occasions; at other times they are worn pendent to necklaces. Beautiful mosaics consisting of thin pieces of turquois cemented to wooden slabs are

---

[1] The exploration of a burial-room in Pueblo Bonito, New Mexico, Putnam Ann. Vol. New York, 1909, pp. 251-252.
[2] Stevenson, M. C., Dress and adornment of the Pueblo Indians. Consulted in manuscript.

sometimes suspended from the ears.   A good example, with a piece of abalone shell in the center, is shown in plate 22, figure 1.   In the United States National Museum is a Zuñi cradle with a small turquois inset in a position that would come beneath the heart of the occupant.   Many Zuñi fetiches, particularly such as were supposed to be efficacious in the chase, have pieces of turquois attached to them.[1]   Some are fashioned of stone in crude animal shapes, with inlaid eyes of turquois.   An example of particular interest in the United States National Museum is made of sandstone, dipped in blood, and not only are its eyes of turquois, but several irregular slabs of this material are inset at intervals over the body.

The most characteristic adornments of the Hopi are the mosaic ear pendants worn by the women.   These are very beautiful, and are made of thin slabs of turquois, nicely polished and cemented with piñon gum to a flat wooden base.   An example is shown in plate 22, figure 2. According to Fewkes,[2] the older mosaics of this description are much finer than the modern ones, some of which are made of reworked turquois, containing pieces previously perforated and used for beads.   They have generally dropped out of use on the East Mesa of the Hopi domain, where they are preserved as heirlooms.[3]   Necklaces, ear pendants, bracelets, etc., are used in abundance by the Hopi.   The men wear loop earrings similar to those worn by the Zuñi on ceremonial occasions.   According to Mrs. Stevenson [4] the Hopi in 1882 possessed several shell mosaics similar to one illustrated in plate 22, figure 4.   The Hopi have perhaps the most elaborate ceremonies of any Indian tribe and in many of them the turquois figures.   During the famous Snake Dance each antelope priest is customarily adorned with shell and turquois necklaces.[5]   The Walpi Warrior Society, in certain of its rituals, uses a jet snake with turquois eyes and other emblems adorned with turquois.[6]   In several of the Hopi Katcinas, as described by Fewkes,[7] the figures are represented with ornaments of turquois, and many Hopi fetiches are decorated with this material.

The Keres of Santo Domingo pueblo, New Mexico, wear beads of turquois strung on silver wire and earrings of the same material.[8]   Their medicine men, in their ceremonies to induce rain, use a fetich of gypsum in the form of a prairie dog with eyes of turquois.[9]   Kunz [10] mentions a large, flat, drilled turquois amulet that was employed as a charm by these Indians.   Roughly ground, heart-shaped ornaments, drilled with a bow drill with point of quartz or agate, have been sold to some extent by them.[11]

Each tribe of the Tewa of New Mexico consists of a Sun people and an Ice people.   At San Ildefonso the kiva or ceremonial chamber of the Ice people is known as the "turquois kiva," and in it the Galaxy and Turquois fraternities meet.   For centuries the Tewa cradle has been made with headrest set with turquois.[12]

Pima.—Among these Indians turquois is now rarely seen, though in the earlier days ornaments of this material were common.[13]   Both sexes, but especially the men, wore strands of beads and pendants, usually of turquois and shell, suspended from the ear lobes and the neck, while upon the arms of women and the right arms of men were often seen bracelets of similar material.   A very brave man was accustomed to pierce the septum of his nose and wear suspended from it a bit of polished bone or else a piece of turquois or shell.

---

[1] Examples are displayed in the United States National Museum.

[2] 22d Ann. Rept. Bur. Amer. Ethnol., 1900–1901, p. 86.

[3] Fewkes, American Anthropologist, vol. 9, 1896, pp. 359–367.

[4] Dress and adornment of the Pueblo Indians, op. cit.

[5] Fewkes, 16th Ann. Rept. Bur. Amer Ethnol., 1894–95, p. 282.

[6] Personal communication from Dr. Fewkes.

[7] 21st Ann. Rept. Bur. Amer. Ethnol., 1899–1900, pp. 67, 86, 113, 119.

[8] Kunz, Mem. Intern. Congr. Anthr. Chicago, 1894, pp. 267–281.

[9] In the United States National Museum there is a somewhat similar fetich from Sia, New Mexico, with body of gypsum and eyes of turquois, made probably to represent a bear.

[10] Kunz, Mem. Intern. Congr. Anthr., loc. cit.

[11] Kunz, Min. Resources of the United States for 1883–84, U. S. Geol. Survey, pp. 767–768.

[12] Report of the Secretary of the Smithsonian Institution for 1912. Washington, pp. 44, 46.

[13] Russell, 26th Ann. Rept. Bur. Amer. Ethnol., 1904–05, p. 112.   An old military report of 1848 (Emory, Notes of a military reconnoissance from Fort Leavenworth, in Missouri, to San Diego, in California, Senate Ex. doc. 7, 30th Congress, 1st sess., 1848, p. 88) mentions that at that time the Pima and Maricopa Indians were accustomed to resort to near-by ruins after rains to search for trinkets of shell and a "peculiar green stone" (the turquois).

Navaho.—The wandering Navaho hold the turquois in no less esteem than do the neighboring pueblo-dwelling tribes, from whom they doubtless derived their fondness for this gem. Indeed they value their turquois ornaments above all other possessions, and their regard for this precious stone causes them to go to almost any extreme to obtain it. They are inordinately fond of personal adornment, and not uncommonly a single Indian will bedeck himself on special occasions with regalia to the value of several hundred dollars. In general, a man's position and wealth may be judged from the number of ornaments he wears.

A Navaho is seldom seen without ear pendants and necklaces of turquois. The former are usually large pieces, roughly fashioned into keystone shape and polished, which are attached to the ears with cord; the necklaces consist of small, perforated, discoidal beads, from one-eighth inch in diameter upward, strung frequently for sake of variety with a few cylindrical beads and pendants or combined with beads of red coral and white shell. Occasionally a saddle horn or gun handle will be studded with small knobs of turquois. The Navaho also are clever silversmiths, and turquois is their favorite stone for setting in various objects of jewelry. Bracelets, buttons, buckles, belts, rings (see Pl. 22, Fig. 5), plaques, and other ornaments are fashioned from Mexican pesos and American silver coins, and many are inlaid with roughly polished pieces of turquois. According to Mrs. Stevenson,[1] the first setting of turquois in silver was done in 1880, after which the Navaho became much interested in this type of work. The Zuñi soon followed their example, and both tribes have produced interesting specimens, although the Navaho excel the Zuñi in originality of design.

The turquois passes as currency with the Navaho. He will pay a high price for a desirable stone, and although he has no definite idea of its exact value, he can not be imposed on with a poor, inferior specimen. A Navaho herder was seen on one occation to buy $125 worth of turquoises at a trading store after disposing of $300 worth of wool to the trader.[2] Much of the turquois in use is of various shades of green, but occasionally a fine blue stone is seen, and this is particularly valued by the Indian. In rare instances a small turquois of good color is obtained from one of the cliff ruins in which the region abounds, and upon such a specimen the Navaho places a particularly high value, refusing to sell it under any circumstances, for he realizes that its color has been tested by centuries and will not fade.

In addition to its ornamental use, the turquois figures in many Navaho rituals and possesses a religious significance. It is used in the Mountain Chant [3] and the Night Chant,[4] two of the most important Navaho ceremonies. Certain sacred objects of ceremonial application are customarily painted blue with powdered turquois.[5] The mineral is commonly called *chalchihuitl* and pronounced chal'-chi-we-te by the Navaho.[6]

Other tribes.—The Apache value the turquois and call it *duklij* ("blue or green stone," these two colors not being differentiated in their language). The Apache medicine man is almost invariably provided with some of this mineral, which is supposed to have unusual virtues. It has long been used in this manner, for according to Bourke,[7] "it was the Apache medicine-man's badge of office, his medical diploma, so to speak, and without it he could not in olden times exercise his medical functions."

The Ute are stated to prize the turquois as highly as do the Navaho.[8] Their congeners, the Paiute, use the turquois in much the same manner as do the Navaho, but care less for it.

---

[1] Dress and adornment of the Pueblo Indians, manuscript in the Bureau of American Ethnology.

[2] Sterrett, Min. Resources for 1911.

[3] Matthews, 5th Ann. Rept. Bur. Amer. Ethnol., 1883–84.

[4] Matthews, Mem. Amer. Mus. Nat. Hist., Hyde Expedition, 1902.

[5] Matthews, The Mountain Chant, 5th Ann. Rept. Bur. Amer. Ethnol., 1883–84, p. 421.

[6] Blake, Amer. Journ. Sci., vol. 25, 1858, p. 227. Also according to personal communications of Mr. F. W. Hodge and Dr. Walter Hough, who informed the writer that this Mexican term is commonly employed by the Southwestern Indians to designate the stone. It was the writer's experience that the turquois was also termed "doklisi" by the Navaho. The Zuñi name is *'hli'akwa.*

[7] The medicine-men of the Apache, 9th Ann. Rept. Bur. Amer. Ethnol., 1887–88, pp. 588–591. It should be mentioned that Bourke called the *duklij* malachite, but his description and allusions leave no doubt that turquois was meant.

[8] Pepper, 1909, loc. cit.

DISCUSSION OF THE USE OF TURQUOIS IN NORTH AMERICA.

The portion of North America wherein the turquois has found application among the aborigines is sharply limited on the one hand by the Isthmus of Panama, and on the other by a line drawn eastward from the Pacific coast through southern Nevada and Colorado, thence southward through Texas to the Gulf of Mexico. This is, of course, due to the fact that the American deposits of turquois, except two of little importance,[1] are confined to this area. Rarely, however, has dependence of use upon occurrence been so well exemplified. It indicates, too, the lack of communication between the pueblo-dwelling tribes of the Southwest and the other Indians of the United States.

The aboriginal use of turquois can be further analyzed as due to three principal reasons. First, the mineral occurs upon and near the surface, so that deposits are easily located and readily worked with crude appliances. Second, turquois is comparatively soft and lends itself to primitive methods of shaping that would make no impress upon harder stones. And third, the color of turquois, ranging from the blue of sky to the green of water and plants, seems to make a strong psychological appeal to uncivilized peoples, peculiarly fitting their religious ideas and constantly suggesting symbolical application.[2]

The individual sources of both the ancient and the modern turquois are numerous. Most of them are now known to the whites, although it is believed that certain tribes still obtain stones from localities known only to themselves. The present-day Indians, however, carry on little systematic mining for turquois, obtaining their material through barter with other Indians or by purchase from white traders. They utilize also quantities of turquoises handed down from their fathers. It is a striking circumstance that in America there are no turquois deposits of importance that do not exhibit signs of prehistoric exploitation. At Los Cerrillos, N. Mex., in particular, are immense excavations dating from pre-Spanish times. The source of the turquois used by the ancient Indians of the Southwest is therefore apparent. To trace the source of the turquois used in Mexico and Central America is more difficult. No occurrence at all adequate as an important source has been discovered south of the present Mexican boundary. It therefore seems probable that the Aztecs and allied peoples, through trade with tribes to the north, obtained supplies of turquois from the Cerrillos hills and perhaps other localities of the Southwest.

---

[1] In Alabama and Virginia.

[2] In the development of the color-sense, blue is the last of the pure spectrum colors to be distinguished. (See Goldschmidt, Ueber Harmonie und Complication, Berlin, 1901, pp. 97–104.) The fondness for blue, once formed in primitive people, seems to be a strong one.

CHAPTER VI.

THE CHALCHIHUITL QUESTION.

The Mexicans were accustomed to say that at one time all men have been stones; and, acting literally upon this conviction, they interred with the bones of the dead a small green stone, which was called the principal of life.

Brinton: Myths of the New World (p. 253).

The use amongst the ancient Mexicans of a highly valued green stone called *chalchihuitl* has already been noted. It found employment for decorative and ceremonial purposes in much the same manner as did the turquois. The old descriptions of it are obscure and somewhat conflicting, and its modern equivalent is not certainly known. Many writers, however, have attempted to settle its identity, with results not entirely in accord; and since the turquois is probably embraced among the minerals included under this term, the question requires reconsideration here.

HISTORICAL EVIDENCE.

The early Spanish writers make repeated allusion to *chalchihuitl*.[1] Bernal Diaz[2] calls it "a species of green stone of uncommon value, which is held in higher estimation with them (the Aztecs) than the smaragdus (emerald) with us." Clavigero[3] refers to certain green stones like emeralds and not inferior to them. Torquemada[4] places the *chalchihuitl* with "stones of the class of emeralds." Molina[5] defines *chalchihuitl* as an inferior kind of emerald. Sahagun[6] explains that it is "a kind of rough emerald, unpolished." He says further of it:[7]

The place where the chalchihuitl occurs is always covered by green grass, because these stones exhale a very great freshness and dampness. Dig in the earth here and one finds the chalchihuitl. * * * There is another kind of stone called quetzal chalchihuitl, because it is very green and resembles chalchihuitl. The best have no flaws and are a beautiful transparent green. The inferior ones show a mixture of spots and blemishes. The chalchihuitl is a green stone, mixed with white, without transparence.[8] The fine personages ornament their wrist bands with them, which is a sign of nobility. The common people are not permitted to wear them. * * * There is another stone related to chalchihuitl, which is called *tlilayotic*, and shows a mixture of black and green. * * * Besides the stones just mentioned there are jasper stones of various colors. * * * Some are both white and green and are therefore called *iztacchalchiuitl* or white chalchihuitl. Others have green veins with light blue or other colors mingled with the white. All these stones are good for sickness.

The *chalchihuitl* undoubtedly took high rank among the choicest possessions of the aborigines of Central America and Mexico.[9] Torquemada,[10] however, says that it was not prized by the Spaniards. Among the gifts sent by Montezuma to Cortés, soon after the latter's landing at San Juan de Ulloa, were "four chalchihuitls," each of which was claimed to be worth more than a load of gold.[11] In his enumeration of other gifts from Montezuma, Sahagun mentions *chalchihuitl* and turquois alongside (see p. 91). Later Montezuma is reported to have prepared for Charles V a rich consignment of presents, of which he is quoted as saying:

To this I will also add a few chalchihuis of such enormous value that I would not consent to give them to anyone save to such a powerful emperor as yours; each of these stones is worth two loads of gold.[12]

---

[1] Written also *chalchihuite, chalchiuitl, chalchuite, chalchihuis, calchirites, chalcibetes,* etc.

[2] The memoirs of. Lockhart's trans., 1844, vol. 1, p. 93.

[3] Storia antica del Messico. Ceseno, 1780.

[4] Monarchia Indiana. Madrid, 1723, vol. 2, p. 288.

[5] Vocabulario de la Lengua Mexicano, 1571.

[6] Histoire générale des choses de la Nouvelle-Espagne. French trans. by Jourdanet and Siméon, Paris, 1880, p. 30.

[7] Op. cit., pp. 771–773.

[8] Sahagun in another place (p 763) refers to a variety of "turquois stone" that is green and white like chalchihuitl.

[9] "In the language of the ancient Mexicans blood was called *chalchiuhatl*, or 'water of precious stones', as the quintessence of what was regarded as the most costly things." Kunz, The curious lore of precious stones, 1913, p. 40, who cites Seler, Codex Borgia, Berlin, 1904, vol. 1, p. 16.

[10] Op. cit., vol. 1, p. 462.

[11] Diaz, op. cit., vol. 1, p. 93.

[12] Ibid., p. 278.

The Mexican kings were accustomed to wear collars of precious stones, consisting of *chalchihuitls* and turquoises of finest quality.[1] The nobles were adorned with strings of *chalchihuitl* beads attached to their wristbands and wore chin ornaments of the same material set in gold and implanted in the flesh.[2] Fine *chalchihuitls* were placed in the mouths of distinguished chiefs who died, to supply the heart;[3] and a similar custom is said by Ximenez[4] to have been practised among the tribes of Central America. The *chalchihuitl* served for the adornment of Xiuhteculti, the Nahuan god of fire.[5] It was used in the decoration of the Nahuan nuptial couch.[6] The altar for the dedication of the largest ear of corn was decked with flowers and precious *chalchihuitls*.[7]

The Mexican goddess of water was called chalchihuitlicue, the woman of the *chalchithuils*, and the name of Chalchiuihapan was frequently applied to the city of Tlaxcalla, because of a beautiful fountain of water found near it, "the color of which," according to Torquemada, "was between blue and green."[8] Tezcatlipoca, the god of providence, was assigned during certain ceremonies as companion to the goddess of water, whose likeness was adorned with a green and blue skirt representing the colors of the sea; and his idol was decorated with a rosary of *chalchihuitls*.[9]

According to Torquemada,[10] the Indians claimed that the art of polishing the *chalchihuitl* was taught them by Quetzalcoatl. One account[11] notes that Quetzalcoatl was born of the virgin called Chalchihuitztli, which means the precious stone of penance or sacrifice. An old tradition[12] tells that Queen Chimalman swallowed a *chalchihuitl*, found when sweeping, and gave birth to Quetzalcoatl.

The Aztecs called Cortés *chalchihuitl*, as a captain of great valor.[13] When Alvarado gambled with Montezuma the latter paid in gold, but the former in *chalchihuitls*,[14] which arrangement suited the cupidity of each. Las Casas[15] says:

> He that stole precious stones, and more especially the stone called *chalchihuitl*, no matter from whence he took it, was stoned to death in the market place, because no man of the lower orders was allowed to possess this stone.

Chalchihuitls among the Maya were suspended from the wrists and necks of war captives about to be sacrificed.[16] The chronicler Fuentes speaks of the Indians of Quiché, of the old Kingdom of Guatemala, as wearing "head dresses of rich feathers and brilliant stones, chalchiguites," very large and of great weight.[17] The Pipil Indians of San Salvador wore *chalchihuitls* on their wrists and ankles, supposing it a specific against certain diseases.[18]

Little information can be gathered concerning the source of the *chalchihuitl*. Sahagun throws no light on this question. Torquemada[19] mentions the village and mines of Chalchihuites, not far from San Andres in Zacatecas.[20] Palacio[21] states that in the Cenconatl Province occur some so-called *calchivites*, stones ordinarily used for pleurisy and other ills.

When Ahuitzotl, the ruler of Mexico, conquered the coast tribes near Tehuantepec in 1497, the latter are reported[22] to have promised tribute as follows: "We will pay you tribute of all

[1] Sahagun, op. cit., p. 514.
[2] Ibid., p. 511.
[3] Torquemada, op. cit., vol. 2, p. 521.
[4] Las historias del origen de los Indios de esta provincia de Guatemala, Scherzer's trans. Vienna, 1857, p. 211.
[5] Sahagun, op. cit., p. 30.
[6] Clavigero, History of Mexico, Cullen's trans. Phila., 1817, vol. 2, p. 101.
[7] Bancroft, The Native Races of the Pacific States of North America. New York, 1874, vol. 2, p. 350.
[8] Squier, Carta dirigida al Rey de España por el Lic. Dr. Don Diego Garcia de Palacio año 1576. London, 1859, p. 110.
[9] Peñafiel, Monuments of Ancient Mexican Art. Berlin, 1890, p. 14.
[10] Op. cit., vol. 1, p. 462.
[11] Kingsborough, Antiquities of Mexico. London, 1831, vol. 5, p. 135.
[12] Bancroft, op. cit., vol. 5, p. 257.
[13] Torquemada, op. cit., vol. 1, p. 435.
[14] Ibid., p. 462.
[15] Bancroft, op. cit., vol. 2, p. 458.
[16] Ibid., p. 707.
[17] Squier, Observations on the Chalchihuitl of Mexico and Central America. New York, 1869.
[18] Ibid., p. 7.
[19] Op. cit., vol. 3, p. 341.
[20] Probably between Zacatecas and Guadalaxara.
[21] San Salvador und Honduras im Jarhe 1576. Trans. into German by Frantzius, Berlin, 1873, p. 29.
[22] Chronicle of Tezozomoc. Through Nuttall, Amer. Anthrop., vol. 3, 1901, p. 227.

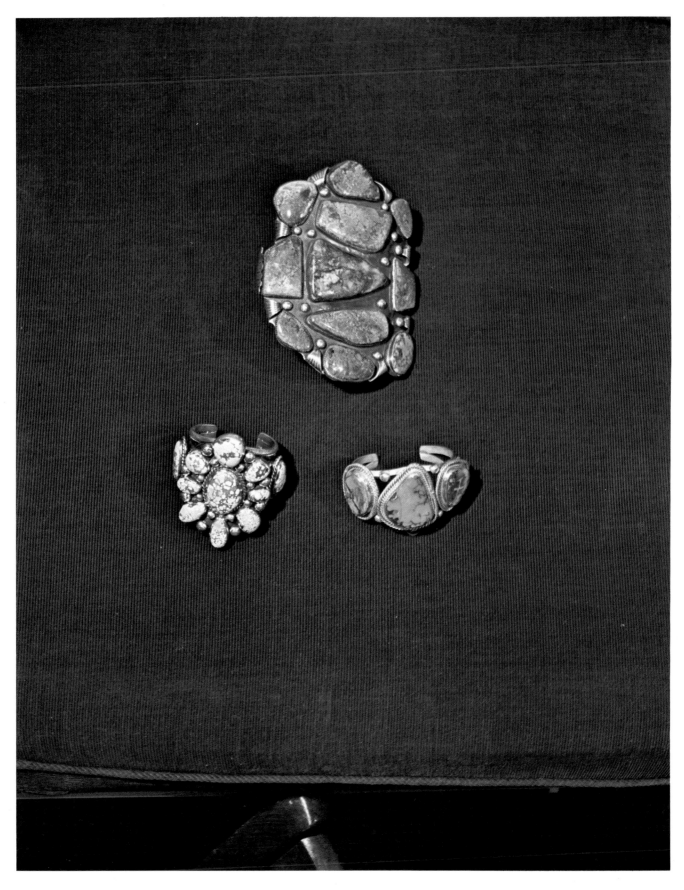

Large bracelet of 11 stones of White Horse turquoise, 5½ inches long. Smaller bracelet has three stones of Bisbee turquoise, two inches across. Cluster bracelet is of light blue spider web turquoise from the Number 8 Mine, 11 stones, 3 1/8 inches long.

Silver box and bracelet both have Morenci turquoise. The box is 6 inches in diameter and 4¼ inches tall. The bracelet is 6½ inches long.

that is produced and yielded on these coasts, which will be *chalchihuitl* of all kinds and shades, other small precious stones named *teoxihuitl* [divine turquois] for inlaying in precious objects, etc." From this time to that of Montezuma, a period of 22 years, the coast tribes of southern Mexico paid tribute of *chalchihuitl* beads,[1] and the tribute roll of Montezuma, a copy of which was sent by Cortés to Charles V, records the names of towns from which the *chalchihuitl* came. Mrs. Zelia Nuttall[2] has located as many as possible of the towns associated with the *chalchihuitl* tribute, and found that these are in the main confined to two comparatively restricted districts— one situated in the northern part of the State of Guerrero and the other occupying a part of Chiapas, near the frontier of Guatemala. In the latter is a place called Chalchihuitan, literally "The Land of Chalchihuitl," and the name is regarded by Mrs. Nuttall as so suggestive that she calls the locality a "promising field of investigation, not only for jadeite, but also for gold and turquois mines." Mrs. Nuttall subjoins a list of Mexican localities, the names of which incorporate the word *chalchihuitl*. Amongst these it is significant that a small range of mountains running north and south in the district of Sombrerete, State of Zacatecas, is termed *Sierra de Chalchihuites;* and that a mining town at the northern end of the range is called *Chalchihuites*.[3]

MODERN VIEWS.

Blake[4] in 1858, on the basis that the Navaho of western and northern New Mexico highly prized green turquois, which they called *chalchihuitl*, held that this name had the same significance in ancient Mexico, and suggested that the New Mexican green turquois be accordingly called *chalchihuitl*. This conclusion was maintained, with elaborations, in several subsequent papers.[5]

Squier[6] in 1859 stated that *chalchihuitl* consisted "generally of green quartz, jade, or the stone known as *madre de Esmeralda* (mother of emerald)"; and in 1869[7] expressed the belief that it was either emerald or nephrite. Fischer,[8] in his elaborate treatise on nephrite and jadeite, identified *chalchihuitl* with the former. Valentini[9] in 1881 called it nephrite. Dall[10] writing in 1881 says: "The 'fair green stones,' 'emeralds,' and 'bastard emeralds' [of the early writers who mentioned their use as labrets] were, without doubt, in most instances, the green turquois-like mineral called 'chalchihuitl' by ethnologists, and which was extensively used for jewels and ornaments from Mexico to Peru by natives at the time of their discovery." Wilson,[11] in an important paper entitled "Jade in America" published in 1902, reviewed the question, with the conclusion that *chalchihuitl* meant jade and jade alone. He placed great stress on the fact that in the Tribute Roll of Montezuma, as published in colors by Peñafiel,[12] the turquois is represented in the hieroglyphics as blue (vol. 2, Pl. 18, p. 245); whereas the *chalchihuitl* is reproduced in green (Pls. 21, 23, and 25). Kunz[13] likewise in 1902 discussed at length the identity of *chalchihuitl*, and while admitting that several green stones were probably included under this term, concluded that "the *chalchihuitl* so highly prized was jadeite in southern Mexico and Central America and turquois in northern Mexico."[14] Seler,[15] one of the greatest authorities on

---

[1] Nuttall, loc. cit., pp. 227–238. See also Kingsborough, loc. cit.; and the inventory given by Peñafiel, loc. cit., p. 79.

[2] Op. cit.

[3] Mentioned by Torquemada. It should be noted (see p. 48) that turquois occurs at two points in Zacatecas, about 100 miles distant from the village of Chalchihuites.

[4] Amer. Journ. Sci., vol. 25, 1858, pp. 227–232.

[5] Blake, Amer. Journ. Sci., vol. 25, 1883, pp. 197–200. Blake here proposed that the green turquois of New Mexico be given the shorter name of *chalchuite*.

Blake, Amer. Antiquarian, vol. 21, 1899, pp. 278–284.

Blake, Intern. Congr. Americanists, 13th sess. New York, 1902, pp. 203–204.

Blake, Minerals of Arizona. Tucson, 1909, pp. 12–13.

[6] Carta dirigida, etc. London, 1859.

[7] Observations on the Chalchihuitl of Mexico and Central America. New York, 1869.

Also Ann. Lyc. Nat. Hist., vol. 9, 1870, pp. 246–265.

[8] Nephrit und Jadeit. Stuttgart, 1880.

[9] Proc. Amer. Ant. Soc. Worcester, vol. 1, 1881, p. 283.

[10] 3d Ann. Rept. Bur. Amer. Ethnol., 1881–82, p. 84.

[11] Congrès intern. Americanistes, XII sess., Paris, 1902, pp. 141–187.

[12] Monuments of ancient Mexican art.

[13] Trans. Amer. Inst. Min. Eng., vol. 32, 1902, pp. 68–83.

[14] Ibid., p. 81.

[15] Gesammelte Abhandlungen zur amerikanischen Sprach- und Alterthumskunde. Berlin, 1904, vol. 2, p. 628.

Mexican antiquities, writes in 1904 that the term *chalchihuitl* included chloritic quartzites, serpentines, and other stones of like aspect; possibly also jadeite. In the monumental work on the Bishop collection of jade,[1] it is stated that the Spanish accounts seem to point to the identity of *chalchihuitl* with the emerald-green varieties of jade. Kunz[2] in 1906 again expressed his opinion that in the Pueblo region north of Mexico Blake's view that the turquois was *chalchihuitl* held; but in Mexico, and particularly its southern portion, jade was so designated. Writing in 1913 Kunz[3] says: "The term *chalchihuitl* was indifferently applied by the ancient Mexicans to a number of green or greenish-white stones; *quetzal chalchihuitl*, which was regarded as the most precious variety, may perhaps have more exclusively denoted jadeite. An inferior kind of *chalchihuitl*, said by Sahagun to have come from quarries in the vicinity of Tecalco, appears to have been identical with the so-called 'Mexican onyx.'"

DISCUSSION.

The available evidence bearing on *chalchihuitl* is of two kinds, historical and ethnologic; the first derived from the old Spanish accounts of the mineral, and the second based upon a few facts regarding the present use of the name, the mineralogic nature of such specimens of Mexican ornaments as are known, etc.

The historical evidence is not wholly dependable. It is derived from accounts of men untrained in the distinctions of mineralogy, who based their statements in most cases either upon casual observation or upon information obtained by interrogating the Indians. There is a double chance of error. In the first place, did the natives apply the name *chalchihuitl* to a definite mineral, so characteristic as to be always recognized by them, or was this term used loosely to embrace a number of green minerals in a general way resembling one another? In the second place, were the Spanish chroniclers keen enough observers to discriminate between the various green minerals in use so as to describe invariably the *actual* chalchihuitl under this name? As to the first question, it is probable that the natives themselves rather closely distinguished between the valuable *chalchihuitl* and other similar but inferior stones. This statement is based upon their analogy to the present Indians of the Southwest, who possess a remarkably keen sense of discrimination between natural objects with which they are familiar. A Navaho or Zuñi Indian can recognize turquois as readily as a New York jeweler. As to the second question, it appears almost certain that the Spanish writers confused a number of green precious stones under the one term; for their statements are too varied and conflicting to refer to a single species. This confusion is but natural; no great degree of scientific accuracy had been attained by the sixteenth century. From the historical evidence alone, therefore, it would be possible, by selection of evidence, to make out a good case for any one of several precious stones. But whether the one chosen would correspond to the actual *chalchihuitl* of the natives is another question.

It is necessary then to supplement the historical by ethnologic evidence. Unfortunately the latter is very meager. The Navaho[4] and Pueblo[5] Indians of the Southwest today call turquois *chalchihuitl*;[6] the term is perfectly definite and no other mineral is included under it. The name therefore is common to the present Southwest and ancient Mexico and Central America; it does not absolutely follow, however, that its mineral equivalent was the same in the two regions. In the State of Zacatecas, Mexico, about 100 miles from a locality where turquois has recently been discovered (see p. 48) is a small Mexican village named Chalchihuites, in a range of mountains of similar name; this place held the same name at the time of the Spanish Conquest.[7] The finding of turquois near the village of Chalchihuites may be due to a coincidence, yet it is suggestive. Mrs. Nuttall has shown that *chalchihuitl* was a recognized product of the hot lands along the Pacific coast in southern Mexico, and it is significant that

[1] Investigations and studies in jade. New York, 1906, vol. 1, pp. 3–4.
[2] Congrés intern. Americanistes, XV sess., Quebec, 1906, vol. 2, pp. 289–303.
[3] The curious lore of precious stones, 1913, p. 251.
[4] Blake, Amer. Journ. Sci., vol. 25, 1858, p. 227.
[5] Blake, Intern. Congr. Amer., 13 sess., New York, 1902, p. 203.
Also according to Hodge as quoted by Wilson, Congrès. Intern. Americanistes, XII sess., Paris, 1902, p. 144.
[6] Or at least by a term that so closely approximates *chalchihuitl* in sound as to warrant the correlation.
[7] It was mentioned by Torquemada.

graves of that region have yielded turquois in greater abundance than other portions of the country. (See p. 97). Our most exact knowledge regarding the precious stones used by the aborigines of Mexico and Central America is derived from the minerals used in mosaics, of which 24 examples are extant. Of the green minerals used therein the turquois occurs in all, and jade, malachite, and beryl in a few. It is probable that the *chalchihuitl* is included among these four minerals.

The principal feature regarding *chalchihuitl*, and the one upon which all accounts agree, is its green color. In the following list are placed all the green minerals which by the most liberal construction might be regarded as the equivalent of *chalchihuitl;* these are emerald, green turquois, jade, chrysocolla, malachite, serpentine, and green quartz.[1] All but the first three are very probably eliminated as unfit to have commanded the high rank among the natives that all Spanish writers unite in assigning the *chalchihuitl.*[2] This leaves the emerald, green turquois, and jade (including jadeite and nephrite). Each will be examined separately.

1. *Emerald.*—The old accounts agree singularly in calling the *chalchihuitl* an emerald-like stone. The Spaniards, however, were familiar with the emerald, and would not have mistaken that precious stone. The descriptions, so far as they can be relied upon, do not fit the emerald, which was assigned a name wholly different from the *chalchihuitl* (namely, *quetzaliztli*).

2. *Green turquois.*—Ordinary blue turquois the *chalchihuitl* certainly was not. Most turquois, however, and particularly that used by uncivilized peoples, is green, and it is entirely possible that the aborigines would assign green turquois a name different from that given to ordinary blue turquois (which was *xiuhtl*, also *teoxiuitl*); particularly as they possessed no adjective in their language to distinguish between blue and green.[3] In the preceding pages some evidence has been advanced in favor of this correlation. On the other hand the various comparisons of the *chalchihuitl* to the emerald, and the historical descriptions in general, correspond more closely to emerald-green jade than to green turquois, and probably outweigh such contrary ethnologic evidence as has been gathered.

3. *Jade.*—This material was extensively used in ancient Mexico, where it found religious as well as ornamental application, and many examples are to be seen in collections of Mexican antiquities. The impression gathered from a careful survey of the whole problem points to green jade as the *most probable* equivalent of *chalchihuitl* among the Aztecs. The possibility can not be entirely eliminated, however, that in certain sections green turquois may have been so designated, just as it is today in parts of the Southwest.

CONCLUSION.

In conclusion, therefore, it appears that the following points are fairly well established.

1. A term either identical with or corresponding closely to *chalchihuitl* has long been used by the Indians of the Southwest to designate the turquois and the turquois alone.

2. The early Spanish writers confused several green stones under *chalchihuitl.*

3. The aborigines of Mexico and Central America used the word *chalchihuitl* to cover one of their most highly prized precious stones; the mineral so designated was probably either jade or green turquois. The historical evidence favors its identification as jade; the ethnologic evidence presents some points in favor of green turquois. The total evidence weighs for jade.

---

[1] Possibly also variscite, a green copper phosphate resembling green turquois. It is probable, however, that this mineral was not known to the ancient Mexicans. It has been suggested to the writer by Mr. C. H. Beers that a beautiful variety of blue-green calamine recently found in Mexico represents the ancient *chalchihuitl*, but this correlation is questionable.

[2] Necklaces of serpentine, green quartz, and green rock beads were extensively used by the Aztecs and are to be seen in all collections representing their culture, but materials so commonplace and so readily found would not have possessed unusual value, nor been restricted in use to the nobility and priesthood.

[3] Torquemada, Monarchia Indiana. Madrid, 1723, vol. 2, p. 47. It is significant that several Indian tribes of the Southwest have identical words for green and blue. Indeed, this is characteristic of many primitive people the world over. The circumstance does not necessarily indicate that these colors are not distinguished, for the color-sense is developed in advance of the color-vocabulary. (See pp. 68–69.) Recognizing green and blue turquois as different in appearance, but having no adjectives to designate this difference, it is possible that the Aztecs distinguished them with different names.

CHAPTER VII.

THE MYTHOLOGY AND FOLKLORE OF TURQUOIS.

> They would pelt me with starry spangles and shells,
> Laughing and clapping their hands between,
>   All night, merrily, merrily.
> But I would throw them back in mine
> Turkis and agates and almondine.
>
> Tennyson: The Merman.
>
> And turcois, which who haps to bear
>   Is often kept from peril.
>
> Michael Drayton: The Muses Elysium.
>
> And true as turquoise, in my dear Lord's ring
>   Look well or ill with him.
>
> Ben Jonnson: Sejanus.

In all ages precious stones have been endowed by the fancy of men with supernatural properties and associations. Even today, in the most enlightened communities, there are individuals—so persistent is superstition—who have not entirely parted with the belief that certain gems are lucky, while others bring bad fortune.

The turquois is peculiarly rich in its list of reputed achievements and in this respect is exceeded by few gems. Its early use, its ready fashioning by primitive people unskilled in the art of working the harder stones, and its occurrence within reach of diverse and widely separated races; its range of color, suggesting both the blue of sky and the green of water and of verdure, and its tendency to alter in shade, bespeaking a power within itself—all these have connected the turquois with many superstitions not only of the Ancients but of the ignorant of today.[1] A singular analogy appears to exist between the beliefs both past and present of the old world and the new; and the turquois serves as an added example of a relation that often has been noted.

From remote ages blue has been a significant color and its emblematic use widespread. The Hindu god Vishnu is represented by this color, "which is supposed to have allusion to the tint of that primordial fluid on which he, as Narayana, moved in the beginning of time."[2] In ancient Chinese ceremonials blue (or green) is symbolical of heaven, while green is usually associated with the East.[3] The Egyptian god Amun was painted blue and the goddess Isis sometimes shrouded in a blue veil.[4] The Nile was named in reference to its blue waters from the Sanskrit word *nila*, meaning blue. The Jews used blue for the high priest's pontifical robes. Blue was the Druid's sacred color.[5] In German folklore the lightning is represented blue.[5] In ancient Mexico blue appears to have been the color of supreme authority,[6] and this color figured prominently in many Aztec ceremonials. Among the Indians of the Southwest, blue is likewise a significant color; it is ordinarily associated with one of the cardinal points and with Heaven, while green is more commonly the emblematic color of the earth.[7] These examples might be multiplied several times. They are sufficient, however, to show that the color of turquois is very significant; and wherever this mineral happens to be used by primitive people it becomes associated with the beliefs of those who value it.

---

[1] Mythology may be defined as the superstitions of the ancients; folklore as the superstitions of the ignorant of today.

[2] Emerson, Indian myths or legends, traditions, and symbols of the aborigines of America. Boston, 1884, p. 456. Mythologies are almost unanimous in assigning the priority to water—"Cosmogenies reach no further than the primeval ocean." (Brinton, Myths of the New World. New York, 1868, pp. 122–123.)

[3] See Laufer, Field Mus. Nat. Hist., Anthrop. Ser., vol. 10, 1912, pp. 120, 149. Green is also symbolic of spring and of growing vegetation. In the imperial worship of the Manchu dynasty, the Temple of Heaven was covered with blue tiles, and everything during the ceremonies was characterized by a blue color. See Laufer, op. cit., 1913, p. 62, note 1.

[4] Emerson, op. cit., p. 456.

[5] Black, Folk-medicine; a chapter in the history of culture. London, 1883, p. 112.

[6] Nuttall, Standard or head-dress? Arch. Ethnol. Papers, Peabody Museum, Cambridge, vol. 1, No. 1, 1888, p. 36.

[7] Nuttall, The fundamental principles of old and new world civilizations. Arch. Ethnol. Papers, Peabody Museum, Cambridge, vol. 2, 1901, p. 129.

AFRICA.

The Egyptians from the earliest times were acquainted with turquois, and this precious stone figures in the legends of that ancient people. One story in particular, as translated by Petrie[1] from a papyrus, carries special interest. It is called *Baufra's Tale*, and recounts a wonder encompassed by the Magician Zazamankh in the days of King Sneferu (about 4700 B. C.). The story runs somewhat as follows:[2] The King, on one occasion, being disconsolate, sought diversion at the suggestion of Zazamankh on the lake of the palace. He was rowed in a magnificent boat by 20 fair maidens, and was made glad by the sight of their rowing. But one of them dropped a jewel of new turquois from her hair and refused to be comforted for its loss. Then Zazamankh, seeing the King chagrined by this untoward event, spoke a magic speech, whereby the waters were divided and the jewel recovered. Then was the King much pleased over the skill of his chief reciter Zazamankh.

In other ancient Egyptian texts the turquois finds a place. For example, in a hymn to the god Ra the color of water is characterized by this term, as follows: "Praises shall be offered unto thee in thy boat; * * *; thou shalt see the ant fish when it springeth into being in the waters of turquois * * *."[3]

ASIA.

INTRODUCTORY.

Asia has long produced the turquois, and this material not only became associated at a very early period with the superstitious beliefs of those who employed it, but even today is invested with very remarkable properties in many parts of the Orient. Just as its application in Persia, Arabia, Afghanistan, and adjacent regions, where the mineral is looked upon as a gem of great value, differs widely from its use in northern India, Tibet, Mongolia, and western China, where though greatly esteemed, this material ranks as an ornamental stone rather than a precious stone;[4] so the ideas concerning it in the two regions differ as completely as if they pertained to separate substances.

PERSIA, ARABIA, AFGHANISTAN, INDIA, AND ADJACENT REGIONS.

The turquois in the Near East has long been the gem paramount of health and success. An early Persian manuscript[5] on precious stones, written in the eleventh century, states that the *piruzeh* (turquois) was regarded as auspicious and lucky on account of its name, which signifies victorious or fortunate. Ibn-el-Beithar, the famous Arabic botanist, writing toward the middle of the twelfth century,[6] remarks:

The turquois shines when the air is pure, and becomes pale when it is dim. * * * It enters into the remedies of the eye. Triturated and administered as a potion, it is useful against the stings of scorpions.[7] * * * It is given also for intestinal ulcerations.[7]

Teifascite,[8] an Arabian mineralogist of the thirteenth century, writes:

The turquois changes its color with the condition of the weather * * * it brightens and refreshes the vision when looked at fixedly, and is beneficial to the eyes when used with eye salve. According to Aristotle, it is a stone with which the Kings of Damascus never omitted to adorn their necks and hands and to employ for many other purposes, because, among the great, the stone possesses the property of removing from its wearer the danger of being killed, and is therefore never to be seen on the hands of a person killed. Furthermore, when reduced to powder, it is of assistance in case of stings of scorpions and dangerous and venomous reptiles.

---

[1] Egyptian tales. First series, fourth to twelfth dynasty. London, 1895, pp. 16–22. In this edition, the jewel is called malachite, but Petrie (in written communication to writer) now considers it to be turquois, the preferable translation of *mafkat*. (See p. 32.)

[2] For the sake of brevity the writer has taken the liberty of considerably condensing the story.

[3] Budge, The book of the dead. London, 1901, vol. 1, p. 78.

[4] One reason for this is that the Persian turquois is much finer in quality than the Tibetan and Chinese product.

[5] Nozhat Namah Ellaÿ by Sehem Ad'din. Quoted by Ouseley, Travels in various countries of the East. London, 1819, vol. 1, pp. 210–212.

[6] In his Treatise on Remedies. See p. 13 of the present treatise.

[7] The early Greek writers attributed these properties to the lapis-lazuli. See p. 10.

[8] See p. 14 of this treatise.

Muhammed Ibn Mansur, in an Arabian treatise on Mineralogy, written about 1300, refers to the supposed virtues of turquois in these terms: [1]

The eye is strengthened by looking at a turquois. If one sees a turquois early in the morning, then he will pass a fortunate day. One should view a turquois at the time of the new moon. The turquois helps its owner to victory over his enemies, protects him against injury, and makes him liked by all men.

In a small mineralogical treatise,[2] written in India not earlier than the fifteenth century, it is stated:

The turquois quickly destroys every poison, whether vegetable or arising within a living body, or a mixture of both; and drives away those pains which result through demoniacal or other evil influences.

The Juaher Nameh, a modern compilation on precious stones, written in the seventeenth century, probably at one of the native courts of India, observes that the mine at Nishapur was celebrated from early ages for a particular kind of turquois entitled *Abu Ishaki*, which is worthy of a place among the treasures of emperors. "And not without reason, if" it is added, "this stone averted evil from those who wore it, conciliated the favor of princes, augmented wealth, preserved the sight, insured victory over an adversary, and banished all unpleasant dreams. The ancient sages, when first they beheld a new moon, fixed their eyes on the Firuzeh (turquois) immediately after." [3]

The Mani-Mala [4] (Chain of Gems) includes the following paragraph on the turquois, derived from the views of Arabian and Persian writers on gems:

The turquoise possesses the virtues of the *Bish* stone. It cures all diseases of the head and the heart. By application over the eyes in the shape of Surmá, it increases their lustre, prevents the fall of fluid therefrom, brings back the color of the pupils if they get white, and restores natural vision to those who are almost blind at night. It is a sovereign remedy for hernia, swellings, flatulence, dyspepsia, insanity, and ulcers inside the stomach or abdomen. In combination with other ingredients, it would relieve and cure the pains and swelling of the body caused by assault. Whether taken with other drugs or simply with honey, it has the power of curing epilepsy, spleen, stricture, etc. In cases of poisoning or snake bite, a durm or a quarter tola weight of turquoise should be given with wine; for scorpion bites, a third of this quantity would suffice. But as the above prescription may cause harm to the stomach, it should always have added to it a quantity of katilá. Hakim Aristatalis (Aristotle?) has limited the dose to one-eighth of a tola. Worn on the fingers as a ring, the turquoise brings about happiness of mind, dispels fear, ensures victory over enemies, and removes all chances of getting drowned or being struck with lightning or of being bitten by snakes or scorpions. He who after looking at the moon on the Pratipada (the first day after new moon) casts his eyes over this stone becomes the master of fabulous wealth.

In Afghanistan it is believed that cataract in the eyes may be cured if a turquois, set in a silver ring and dipped in water, be applied to the part affected during the chanting of the name of the Almighty.[5] In Arabia and Persia the manufacture of the turquois can be attained, supposedly, by mixing five parts of fresh sulphur with one part of mercury, putting the mixture in a cold ground for a period of seven years, and exposing it for the whole time to the rays of the sun and of the star called Zohul.[6]

A strong belief in the evil eye prevails in Persia and blue is the favorite color with which to turn aside its effects.[7] Turquois consequently is very naturally deemed efficacious for this purpose. Even camels, horses, and mules sometimes have beads attached to their tails, and a highly valued animal may wear a blue necklace. A child frequently carries sewn to his cap an amulet case in which is placed a piece of turquois embedded in a sheep's eye brought by a pilgrim from the great holocaust of sheep in Mecca.[7] The Persians believe that to look on a turquois when one first awakes in the morning insures prosperity and highly strengthens and preserves the sight during the entire day.[3] That the stone will avert poverty if worn is a

---

[1] See Schindler, Jahrb. k. k. geol. Reichs., Wien, vol. 36, 1886, pp. 303–314.

[2] By Narahari, a physician from Kashmir. Quoted by Garbe, Die indischen Mineralien. Leipzig, 1882, p. 91. See also Laufer, op. cit., 1913, p. 2.

[3] From Ouseley, op. cit.

[4] Tagore, Mani-Mala, or A treatise on gems. Calcutta, 1879, vol. 2, p. 883.

[5] Tagore, op. cit., vol. 2, p. 946.

[6] Ibid., p. 882.

[7] Sykes, Folk-lore, London, vol. 12, 1901, p. 268.

general belief[1] and the Persian soldiers are said to prize this mineral as a protection against contagion.[2]

The Arabs value the turquois for its supposedly talismanic virtues. They wear seals and amulets, many set in small rings of plated tin, which are firmly expected to bring good fortune and prosperity.[3] Buffon[4] quaintly remarks that this custom, "while not harmful, is only a sign of stupidity."

Near Darjeeling, in upper Bengal, the following love song was heard:

> My love is like the image in a pure silver mirror,
> Beyond the reach of grasping hands, and only won by loving heart.
> Like a tree of costly coral, like a leaf gemmed with turquois,
> Like a fruit of precious pearls, you, my love, are rare.
> You are loveliest of lovely flowers, and where'er you go,
> I, as a turquois butterfly, will follow my flower.

TIBET.[5]

> Mapan, the famed lake of Turquois
> Whose water over water runs,
> So all matter in vacuity is lost.
>
> *Tibetan legend from eleventh century block print.*[6]

The turquois is so extensively used in Tibet and neighboring provinces and has so long figured in the culture of the inhabitants of that region that it has entered very fundamentally into the traditions and ideas of the people. The early history of Tibet, which, like all early history, is a mixture of fact and fancy, includes many references to the turquois; and the religion of that country assigns the substance an ornamental and symbolical application in its paraphernalia and ceremonials. The present-day natives look upon it as a thing distinct in itself and not as a stone.[7]

There is a tradition that King Du-srong mang-po at the beginning of the eighth century found the largest turquois then known in the world on the top of Mount Tag-tse, a few miles north of Lhasa.[8] An ancient family thrived in Tibet during the eighth century, whose name means Turquois-Roof; a celebrated member of this family relates in his biography that the name originated from the fact that he was visited on one occasion by gods and demons, who heaped an immense quantity of turquoises and other precious stones upon the roof of his house.[9] The mansion of this family may be seen today in Lhasa, standing near a bridge called "Turquois-Roof Bridge." In the seventh century the powerful Tibetan King Srong-btsan sgam-po married a Chinese princess. According to the Tibetan story of his wooing, he was required in order to win the hand of his bride to pass a silk thread through a coil of perforated turquois beads arranged in concentric circles; the problem was solved by tying the thread to a queen ant which he placed "in the perforation of the first turquois, gently blowing into the hole, till to the amazement of the lookers-on the ant came out at the other end of the coil dragging the thread along."[10] There is a popular tradition in regard to the blue-glazed tiles with which some temples are roofed that this early king produced the glaze by melting an immense quantity of turquois for that purpose.[11]

Ancient traditions and epic stories lead to the inference that arrowheads were fashioned not only of common flint, but also occasionally of turquois, and to these a high value was

---

[1] Khan and Sparrow, With the pilgrims to Mecca. London, 1895, p. 41.

[2] Fenderson, Min. and Sci. Press., vol. 74, 1897, p. 192.

[3] Fraser, Journal into Khorassan. London, 1825. Edwards, The history and poetry of finger rings. New York, p. 107.

[4] Histoire naturelle. Paris, 1802, vol. 13, pp. 322–323.

[5] The place of turquois in Tibetan tradition is admirably developed by Laufer (op. cit., 1913, pp. 5–20), and his contribution has been freely drawn upon in the present section. He remarks: "During the summer, large patches of blue, red, and yellow flowers abound on the fine pasture lands, and at this sight I could never suppress the thought that the enthusiasm of the Tibetans for turquois, coral, and amber must have been suggested and strengthened by these beautiful shades of their flowers which their women as readily use for ornament as stones; indeed, it seems to me, as if owing to its permanency the stone were only a substitute for the perishable material of the vegetable kingdom."

[6] From Das, Journ. Asiat. Soc. Bengal, vol. 50, 1881, p. 208.

[7] See Laufer, op. cit., 1913, p. 5.

[8] Ibid., p. 8.

[9] Ibid., pp. 8–9.

[10] Ibid., p. 9.

[11] Das, Narrative of a journey round Lake Yamdo. Calcutta, 1887, p. 49.

attached. A powerful saint, it is related, by touching the bow and arrow of a blacksmith, 'transformed the bow into gold and the arrowhead into turquois.[1] The hero Gesar was said to own thirty arrows with notches of turquois.[1]

The Annals of the Tibetan Kings describes a shrine in a temple founded during the eighth century as decorated with beams of turquois and of gold with dragons of turquois attached.[2]

With the Tibetans the word for turquois is a favorite in designating natural objects of sky-blue color. The color of beautiful lakes is often so characterized, and wells are almost constantly distinguished by this epithet. Other objects also, such as flowers, the manes of horses, and even bees and tadpoles, are described in this way; the hair of goddesses and the eyebrows of children born in a supernatural manner are spoken of as turquois-blue; likewise the beauty of the body of such beings may be compared to this mineral.[3] In Spiti the forget-me-not is known as the flower whose essence is turquois. The Tibetans speak poetically of the sky as "the turquois of Heaven" and "thirteen turquois heavens" are mentioned in their ancient mythology. A Tibetan legend as quoted by Laufer [3] gives the following description of the country:

At the foot of the giant mountains (the Himalaya) supporting the sky, lakes and flowing streams gather, forming plains of the appearance of turquois, and glittering pyramids of snow-clad crystal rise. This mountain range spreading like a thousand lotus flowers, is white and like crystal during the three winter months; during the three months of the summer it is azure blue; during the three months of the autumn it is yellow like gold; and in the moons of the spring striped like the skin of the tiger.

An account of the marriage customs of Tibet includes the following poetical description of the recitation that the officiating priest is supposed to make as the bridal party approaches the bridegroom's house: "May there be happiness to all living beings. The lintel of this door is yellow, being made of gold. The doorposts are cut out of blocks of turquois. The sill is made of silver. The doorframe is made of lapis-lazuli. Opening this auspicious door, you find in it the repository of five kinds of precious things. Blessed are they who live in such a house."[4] As described in the Tibetan dramatic play Nang-sa, during a more ancient marital ceremony "the turquois sparkling in rainbow tints" was tied to the end of an arrow fastened to the back of the bride to fix the marriage ties.[5]

The turquois figures in many Tibetan folk-tales. For example, in one entitled "The mouse's three children"[6] it is narrated that the third son of the mouse was a boy, strong and powerful, whose hair, when it was cut and fell to the ground, turned into diamonds, pearls, and other jewels, and whose nail parings became beautiful turquoises. In a Tibetan love song the following couplet [7] is found:

> I'd guard her fragrant body,
> Like white turquois so rare.

Another tale embracing the turquois runs as follows: [8]

THE STORY OF THE HOME-BRED BOY—HOW HE FOUND THE LOST TURQUOIS.

An only boy, reared in great seclusion by his mother, was finally sent forth into the world to seek his fortune. At length, after meeting with several adventures with more or less unfortunate outcome, he took refuge over night in a pile of refuse in the back yard of a large house. The next day the lady of the house came out into the back yard, and the boy, from his hiding place, saw her drop a large and valuable turquois. Over this, upon her departure, he threw an old rag; and shortly after, a maidservant happening by thrust the unsightly bundle into a crevice in the wall. Soon a great uproar was heard in the house when the loss was discovered, and divers magicians and lamas were quickly summoned to try their skill in locating the lost jewel. They met with no luck, however, and toward evening departed. The boy then ventured forward and offered to find the turquois. His proposal was rather scornfully accepted, and next day a great crowd appeared to witness the feat. The boy naturally found it an easy matter, by the aid of a pig's head for effect, to ferret out the jewel's resting place; and he thereby won much praise and a large reward.

[1] Laufer, op. cit., p. 11.
[2] Ibid., p. 13.
[3] Ibid., p. 10.
[4] Das, Marriage customs of Tibet, p. 12. Through Laufer, ibid., p. 15.
[5] Waddell, Buddhism of Tibet. London, 1895, p. 557.
[6] O'Connor, Folk tales from Tibet. London, 1906, p. 70.
[7] Ibid., p. 176.
[8] Ibid., pp. 158–165. The present writer, for the sake of brevity, has taken the liberty of considerably condensing the story as given by O'Connor.

CHINA.

In China the turquois plays so unimportant a part in the lives of the Chinese, and has been known to them for so brief a period, that it has assumed little place in their mythology, and few superstitious ideas have developed concerning it. They look upon it as a transformation from the fir tree, as indicated in their name for turquois, meaning "green fir-tree stone." A modern Chinese author gives the following peculiar view as to its origin: "When the moss growing on rock after many years consolidates and assumes color, turquoises arise, those of a deep hue being called *lü sung*, those light in color *sung êrh* ('fir-tree ears')."[1]

EUROPE.

> If cold December gave you birth,
> The month of snow and ice and mirth,
> Place on your hand a *turquois* blue,
> Success will bless you if you do.

Little is known of the earliest beliefs that prevailed in Europe regarding the turquois. Aristotle is accredited [2] with saying that it protected its wearer against death by accident and was an antidote for scorpion stings; but the Greek philosopher in reality wrote these words in description of lapis-lazuli ($\Sigma\acute{\alpha}\pi\phi\epsilon\iota\rho\sigma\varsigma$), though possibly turquois was regarded as a variety of that mineral. The few other writers of antiquity who touched upon turquois are silent as to its virtues.

Throughout the Middle Ages superstitions ran rampant, and with many of them precious stones were connected. The credulity of mediæval naturalists attributed the most remarkable properties and performances to all the gems, but few were invested with more wonderful powers than the turquois. Its tendency to alter in color and even to fade completely to an unseemly white, coupled with notions brought with it from the Orient, were sufficient to suggest to the credulous minds of the time a more than natural power of independent action. Even to the present day the turquois has not been in all quarters entirely divested of its virtues. As one writer expresses it:

> Other precious stones have lost all the marvelous powers that belonged to them for centuries; the emerald no longer relieves the fatigued eyesight; the diamond can not now dispel fear; the sapphire, though still cold to the touch, has ceased to be able to extinguish fire. In these perverse days the hailstorm comes down even upon the wearer of an amethyst, and bright red coral attracts rather than repels robbers. But the turquois still retains one of its mysterious properties and flaunts it in the face of modern science. Sometimes slowly, sometimes suddenly, it unaccountably turns pale, becomes spotted, or changes from blue to white; and specimens that behave in this capricious manner are found more commonly than those whose color is distinctly permanent.

Another recent writer [3] enthusiastically exclaims:

> Oh, it is truly of celestial aspect, and it should be in the adornment of young girls so as to inspire them with good and sincere thoughts, because it possesses extraordinary virtues and miraculous gifts!

Certain gems have been universally regarded as auspicious, while others have obtained bad reputations for inducing misfortune. Turquois is among the former,[4] and throughout its long career has been made to bear the burden of no undesirable attribute. It was believed that the turquois insured success, happiness, and friends, and through its use lovers and quarreling married couples were reconciled. There is an old saying, "He who possesses a turquois will always be sure of friends." To dream of turquoises was thought to signify prosperity.[5] The mineral was also a potent love charm; hence we find Leah giving a turquois ring to Shylock "when he was a bachelor" in order to win his love and induce a proposal. In some parts of Europe even today "forget-me-not" turquois rings are used as presents, and there is a saying in Germany that worn by loving hands this stone brings good luck and whitens when the good wishes of the donor lessens.[6] In Russia the turquois not uncommonly adorns the wedding ring.[7]

---

[1] From Laufer, op. cit., p. 24.
[2] See Teifascite, p. 14.
[3] Staffe, Les pierres précieuses et les bijoux. Paris, 1896, p. 119.
[4] The diamond, turquois, and emerald are said to be lucky to everyone. (See Bratley, The power of gems and charms. London, 1907, p. 128.)
[5] See Kunz, The curious lore of precious stones, 1913, p. 358.
[6] Kluge, Handbuch der Edelsteinkunde.
[7] Staffe, op. cit., p. 117.

The turquois was supposed to change color when danger threatened its owner. "The Turkeys," says Fenton in his Secret Wonders of Nature, "doth move when there is any peril prepared to him that weareth it." It was even believed to avert accidents, and Russian officers are said [1] in some instances today to carry it for its supposed efficacy against the fatal effects of wounds. It was furthermore deemed good for liberty, "for he that hath consecrated it and duly performed all things necessary to be done in it shall obtain liberty. It is fitting to perfect the stone when you have got it, in this manner: Engrave upon it a beetle, then a man standing under it; afterward let it be bored through its length and set upon a gold fibula; then being blest and set in an adorned and prepared place, it will show forth the glory which God hath given it." [2]

The turquois was believed to indicate the state of the wearer's health; turning pale when he sickened, losing its color when he died, and regaining its former beauty in the hands of a new and healthy owner. Hence the saying:

> The sympathizing Turquois true doth tell,
> By looking pale, the wearer is not well.

According to one writer,[3] "because of the fact that the turquois changes color on the illness of its wearer, and upon his death flies completely to pieces, one concludes that the stone so sympathizes with the wearer that it suffers with him and he prizes it therefore all the more." Ivan the Terrible of Russia is said to have believed that both turquois and coral grew pale in the presence of disease.[4] Furthermore, the turquois was supposed to strengthen the eyes and to aid the vision.[5] It also came to be regarded as a specific against scorpion stings and intestinal ulcerations.[5] As a protection against sudden falls, the turquois was believed to be of signal value by taking upon itself the injury that would otherwise accrue to the wearer. "Whoever," says van Helmont, "wears a turquois so that it, or its gold setting, touches the skin, may fall from any height and the stone attracts to itself the whole force of the blow, so that it cracks and the person is safe." [6] The prevalence of this belief is illustrated in the following anecdote:[7] The Marquis of Villena had a fool who, when asked by a knight what were the properties of a turquois, replied, "Why, if you have a turquois about you, and should fall from the top of a tower and be dashed to pieces, the stone would not break."

The turquois came to be highly esteemed by horsemen, since its presence was thought sufficient to enable them to ride the most dangerous steeds without risk of injury. One writer [8] of the sixteenth century, however, expressed himself a bit sceptical of this property, saying, "I have a beautiful turquois which was given me for a keepsake, but it has never occurred to me to test its virtues, as I do not care, for sake of the experiment, to fall from my horse." It was further believed that the horse would not tire so long as the rider had a turquois about him. According to an old German poem:[9]

> Den rehten turkois, der den hât,
> sô er in dem golde stât,
> der vellet niemer abe daz bein
> noch ander gelide kein,
> sweder er rîtet oder gât
> die wîl er den stein bî im hât.

Suspended by a string in a glass, the turquois would strike the hour, presumably of its own volition. It was also supposed by some to vary in hue with the hour of the day.

---

[1] Fenderson, Min. and Sci. Press, vol. 74, 1897, p. 192.

[2] See King, Antique gems. London, 1860, p. 433.

[3] See Fühner, Lithotherapie. Strasburg, 1902, p. 108.

[4] Hendley, Journ. Ind. Art and Ind., vol. 12, 1909, p. 149. See also The travels of Sir Jerome Horsey, Hakluyt Soc., London, 1856, p. 199; quoted by Kunz, The curious lore of precious stones, 1913, p. 374.

[5] Properties originally attributed to lapis-lazuli.

[6] Tagore, Mani-Mala. Calcutta, 1879, p. 88.

[7] Jones, History and mystery of precious stones. London, 1880, p. 37.

[8] Cardan, De subtilitate.

[9] Das Steinbuch. Ein altdeutsches Gedicht von Volmar. Heilbronn, 1877, p. 19. A free translation is: He who possesses a real turquois, set in gold, will never lose a leg or any other limb, whether he rides or walks, so long as he keeps the stone with him.

In common with most of the precious stones, the turquois was significant in astrology. In an old work entitled "Sympathia Septem Metallorum ac Septem Selectorum Lapidum ad Planetes,"[1] it was associated with Saturn,[2] (see Fig. 5), and under the proper sign was regarded as particularly potent. To be of the greatest efficacy, however, it should be worn in a setting of lead.[3]

Fig. 5.—The planets and their significant stones. (After on old print.)

Precious stones were also assigned to the twelve signs of the zodiac, and were supposed to have particular control over the twelve parts of the human body. Capricorn, the Goat, was

[1] See Tassin, Descriptive catalogue of the collection of gems in the United States National Museum. Washington, 1902, p. 562.

[2] The turquois has also been associated with the planet Venus (see Bratley, The power of gems and charms. London, 1907, p. 128) and with Jupiter (Rantzau, Tractatus de genethliacorum thematum judiciis, Francofurti, 1633, pp. 46–55. Through Kunz, The curious lore of precious stones, 1913, pp. 347–348).

[3] Encyclopaedia of superstitions, folklore, and the occult sciences of the world. Chicago, vol. 2, p. 744.

represented in some old works by the garnet; in others, by the turquois,[1] and its sphere of action was especially potent from December 21 to January 21. Thus the turquois is the birth-stone for December[2] and is symbolical of success and faithfulness; those born in that month should wear this stone, which, to be rendered most appropriate, must be set in lead.

> Friends and lovers for December, Fortune, fame
> If an amulet of turquois bear her name.

The turquois is shown in some modern lists as the birthstone for June and July. Tiffany & Co., of New York, have published a small handbook (1911) containing a "Twentieth Century List" of Birth Stones, as follows:

Month.	Stone.
January	Garnet.
February	Amethyst, hyacinth, pearl.
March	Jasper, bloodstone.
April	Diamond, sapphire.
May	Emerald, agate.
June	Cat's-eye, turquois, agate.
July	Turquois, onyx.
August	Sard, carnelian, moonstone, topaz.
September	Chrysolite.
October	Beryl, opal.
November	Topaz, pearl.
December	Ruby, bloodstone.

Kunz[3] gives turquois as the natal stone for July and includes the two following verses:

> The heav'n-blue turquoise should adorn
> All those who in July are born;
> For those they'll be exempt and free
> From love's doubts and anxiety.

> No other gem than turquois on her breast
> Can to the loving, doubting heart bring rest.

There are, moreover, stones especially suitable for each day of the week. On Friday one should wear, it is said, "a turquois, beryl, or lapis-lazuli set in copper; design, a king on a camel, or a naked maiden."[4] Friday, the day of Venus, is naturally dedicated to the "Works of Love," and the celebrant wears a sky-blue robe; his ring shows a turquois, and his tiara is set with lapis-lazuli and beryl.[5]

Albertus Magnus,[6] writing in the first half of the thirteenth century, remarked that the turquois preserved the sight and protected against harmful accidents. Arnoldus Saxo[7] in the same century stated: "The turquois has the quality of preserving the eyesight from external injuries when superimposed on the eyes; and it induces hilarity."

Sir John Mandeville,[8] toward the close of the fourteenth century, referred to the turquois in these terms:

It aids the vision and is a protection against accidents; it gives boldness and graciousness to the wearer, and the horse of one who carries it can not be chilled from drinking cold water. The Indians say that it is of great advantage in battle and that its use on many occasions has shown that only the diamond is a better protection to the body. It possesses such power that the man who owns it can not engender and the woman can not conceive.

In the fifteenth-century story of the visions of Ste. Françoise,[9] the diamond, garnet, carnelian, turquois, and other stones appear in the crown of the Virgin.

---

[1] Bratley, op. cit., p. 128.

[2] Clouet, Aperçus sur les proprietes occultes, etc. MS. Paris.
The Poles and Russians have long held the turquois to be the natal stone for December.

[3] The curious lore of precious stones, 1913, p. 329.

[4] Bratley, op. cit., p. 140.

[5] Kunz, The curious lore of precious stones, 1913, p. 336, who cites Eliphas Lévi. Rituel de la haute magie, Paris, 1861. A seventeenth century authority states that turquois was most efficacious when worn either on the index finger or the little finger: See Kunz, ibid., p. 375.

[6] See p. 13.

[7] De virtutibus lapidum.

[8] Le Grand Lapidaire. Ed. by Is. del Sotto. Vienna, 1862, p. 109.

[9] L. Pannier, Les lapidaires français du moyen âge. Paris, 1882, p. 225. Through Laufer, op. cit., p. 51, note 1.

The "Mirror of Stones," by Camillus Leonardus, written in Italy in 1502, makes this comment [1] concerning the turquois:

There is a vulgar Opinion that it is useful to Horsemen, and that so long as the Rider has it with him his Horse will never tire him and will preserve him unhurt from any Accident. It strengthens the sight with its Aspect. It is said to defend him that carries it from outward and evil Casualties.

Franciscus Ruëus,[2] in the year 1547, relates the following:

Some wonderful things are claimed for the supernatural powers of the turquois. Indeed there was recently a certain islander greatly bound to me by affection, who so long as he lived took pleasure in the turquois and always wore one in a gold ring. When by chance, or rather by sickness, he came down to death, he had still kept his ring. Then something like a miracle of nature happened in that the turquois, which during the life of its owner could vie with countless numbers of its kind in beauty and perfect purity, appeared at first dimmer, as if mourning the death of its master, and at length showed a continuous crack across its surface of such prominence that the greater part of its beauty was impaired. So I lost in some degree my desire of owning this specimen, although not only on account of the unusual beauty of the stone, but also because of the great powers which this same man always used to assert the gem had in time of danger, I had previously determined to possess one by some means or other if it were in any way possible. I was disappointed, because my own ignorance cheated me—for while I despised that same stone covered with blemishes and stains when it was offered for sale at the auction, another later showed me the stone redeemed from every trace of its defilement, and when I saw it in its former perfection and beauty, as if renewed by right of recovery, having a new master, I began to admire to myself this unexpected prodigy most worthy of nature and to damn my bad luck. I learned by this event that the stone is gifted with a certain divine power. Furthermore, in portending omens the turquois is most remarkable. With its incredible endowments it is employed bravely to defend from danger the one wearing it (as if it were a certain natural amulet and antidote against bad luck). Besides it strengthens the heart and eyes and is believed to bring happiness and prosperity.[3]

Boetius de Boot,[4] writing near the beginning of the seventeenth century, gives a very quaint and amusing account of the supposed accomplishments of the turquois, refusing to accept all the wonderful things it was believed to bring about, yet not entirely able to divorce himself from the superstitious spirit of the times. He speaks as follows:

The turquois is believed to strengthen the sight and spirits of the wearer; but its chief commendation is against falls, which everybody believes it takes upon itself, so that the wearer escapes hurt—a property beyond the scope of reason. I can solemnly affirm that I always wear one set in a ring, the property of which I can never sufficiently admire. Thirty years ago it had been worn by a Spaniard living not far from my father's house. On his death, when his goods were sold off (as is the custom with us), amongst the rest the turquois was put up. No one, however, would bid for it, although many had come to buy it on account of its choice color in the lifetime of the former owner; for it looked more like malachite than a turquois. My father and brother were present, thinking to bid for the gem, which they had often admired aforetime, and were astonished at the change. My father, however, purchased it for a mere trifle, because everybody thought it was not the same that the Spaniard used to wear. When my father came home, thinking it scorn to wear so ugly a gem, he made me a present of it, saying, "Since the story is that a turquois, to exhibit its power, must be presented when one is at home, I now make you a gift of it." I took the gem to an engraver to cut my arms upon it, as is done upon jasper, chalcedony, and other cheap stones, not choosing to wear it, having lost all its beauty, merely as an ornament. I received it back from the engraver, and wore it for a signet ring. Hardly was it on my finger a month when its original color returned, though not so bright as before, in consequence of the engraving and the inequality of its surface. Everybody was surprised, more especially as the colour grew finer every day. Perceiving this, I never took it off my finger, just as I do still. Its wonderful virtue in the case of a fall (if really proceeding from it) I have myself experienced. For returning on horseback to Bohemia from Padua, where I had taken my doctor's degree, a guide I had hired to show me the way shows me a footpath by the side of the high road, which I take, and ride on some time in the dark. Suddenly my horse stands still, and will not move a step. I call my guide; he says there is a well in the path, and that I must go back, the path being very narrow. In turning my horse he stumbles, and puts his left foot outside the path, toward the high road. Immediately I feel myself falling, I throw myself out of the saddle upon the road, which was at least 10 ells lower down than the path. I fall on my side, and my horse on his back close to me. The guide, not hearing me cry out or speak, thought me crushed to death by the horse; but I was safe and sound, had suffered no harm at all, get on my steed, and pursue my journey. But next morning, as I was washing my hands, I found my turquois split, and about a quarter of its substance separated from the rest. I therefore got the larger portion of the stone reset, and continued to wear it some years. One day in attempting to lift out of a river, with a long pike, a weight beyond my strength, suddenly the bones of my chest cracked as though a rib were broken, and I felt a dull pain in the side. Thinking something was fractured, I examined and discovered that the lowest rib was displaced, and its end pushed under the last but one. As the pain was

---

1 Page 236.
2 De gemmis. Paris, 1547, Caput XVIII, pp. 139–140.
3 Translated from the Latin for the writer by Mrs. F. B. Laney.
4 Le parfaict ioaillier ou histoire des pierreries. Ed. by Andre Toll, Lyon, 1644, chap. 116, pp. 340–346.

slight, I applied no remedy to the part affected; but the same day, to my surprise, I see my turquois again broken in two, the smaller portion, however, being no bigger than a hempseed; but lest it should drop out, I had the larger portion, retaining nearly all my arms, set in another ring, which I still wear constantly.[1]

Now it is by no means certain that the accident and the fracture of the precious stone happened at the same moment; I am convinced that naturally this precious stone can not prevent the accident from being harmful, nor attract upon itself the evil. It is necessary then to attribute these results to an occult agent, that is to say, to good and evil spirits (God being willing and permitting this), as I have explained in the chapter on the forces of precious stones. At least, I can certainly assert (which does not attribute power to precious stones, as is commonly done) that I have never believed, nor do I now believe, that such a thing ever naturally happens to the turquois.

The change of color also takes place in a natural manner. Because this precious stone is not perfectly hard, it can easily assume a fine, pale, or ugly color by absorbing the vapors and exhalations that perpetually transpire from the pores of the skin. Yet if it loses its color and beauty when its owner dies, and seems to be doing devilish work by pitying his fate, then this is a circumstance surpassing all human reason and is a matter for metaphysics, as I have mentioned in the case of falls and accidents. All turquoises, however, do not behave in this manner. What miracle is there if the turquois of which I have spoken shortly before is altered by the saline vapors and exhalations which transpire perpetually from a living body, and shall regain its original color when exposed to other vapors and exhalations? It is known by experience that the color of the turquois is amended by vinegar and sal ammonia, in which the sweat and exhalations of the body abound. In truth, I think the reason why the color departs, the owner being dead, and is restituted being possessed by a new owner, is all a very natural fact. Not that the death of the owner is the cause; but because the owner being dead, it is not carried by a person, and consequently its fine color can not be preserved by the exhalations of the body. I recall that after I was sick with jaundice and obstruction, and when my body commenced to breathe out sweat and renewed its good constitution, that my turquois became finer; of such perfection, indeed, that it was an indication to me of health.

Some believe that the turquois performs the office of a clock and sounds the time of day, if held suspended by a thin thread from the thumb and middle finger between the walls of a small glass. It is of a truth admirable that this should be the belief of persons vain and little versed in the nature of things. In fact, however, the stone is ruled by the hand, and the hand by the imagination of the individual, and this happens for every blow, until the true number of hours is sounded; the hand is in accord with the imagination and gives the stone an imperceptible movement, until the number of blows and throbs shall be complete. The hours are not instituted by nature, but by man; and are different in different countries. Now, how can a stone know that man has arranged such things if it has no mind? Further, how can it, without being invested with knowledge, accommodate itself to different countries, which count the hours differently? For in some parts of the world the hours are reckoned from daybreak, in others from the beginning of night, and in others from midnight. Assuredly it must have a mind more intelligent than the mind of man; for he can not know all the hours which he has instituted, and for this reason he has devised and made clocks, by which he measures the quantity of time. Some acknowledge that it does not naturally possess the faculty for striking the hour of day, but the operator must use a certain murmur of words, which being pronounced, the stone performs its office. This has been sometimes done in my presence, but I attribute the cause of the movement, not to words, nor spirits, nor to the stone, but to the hand. I have, indeed, made some experiments along this line myself, and every time I wished I made the stone strike; although in such a natural manner that one could not observe any movement in my hand. Say adieu then to impostures of vain men and enchanters! The turquois should be praised, however, because if carried, it allays and prevents pains in the eye, and in the testes; it serves to stop enmity in some, and reconciles the love of man and woman.

In an odd work entitled "Speculum Mundi, or a glass representing the face of the world," published in 1635 by John Swan, several of the superstitions regarding the turquois are repeated, to wit,[2] that "it helpeth weak eyes and spirits; refresheth the heart; and, if the wearer of it be not well, it changeth colour and looketh pale and dim, but increaseth to his perfectnesse as the wearer recovereth to his health."

Bernardus Caesius [3] in 1636, after noting a number of points about the nature and occurrence of the turquois, remarks:

In the sixth place it should be noted that the following properties are ascribed to the turquois:

1. It soothes the eyesight or vision, and preserves it.
2. It preserves and defends the one wearing it from harm or injury.
3. It cheers and comforts the heart.
4. It causes happiness and prosperity to its wearer.
5. Suspended in a glass it sounds the hour.
6. Worn by the immodest or lewd it loses its power and color.
7. A certain man is said to have possessed a turquois of great value and exceeding beauty, and when he had paid his debt to the laws of fate the gem seems to have wept over its owner's death, its glorious luster becoming dimmed,

---

[1] The translation to this point is taken from King, The natural history of precious stones, London, 1865, pp. 422–424; the remainder is translated by the present writer.

[2] Page 296.

[3] Mineralogia, sive naturalis philosophiæ thesauri. Lugduni, 1636, p. 601.

and it began to appear obscured for a long time. Caussinus relates this and says that this stone is the symbol of the most devoted friendship. The same story is told by Ruëus, who adds that he knew the owner of the stone in question, and that it had become noticeably obscured after his death; and he also adds that the same gem was subsequently bought at a low price by another citizen, but as soon as it had been transferred to a new owner it recovered its pristine brilliancy. But, as we have said, after the death of the first owner it appeared as if dimmed for a long time and exhibited a crack in its median line.[1]

Thomas Nicols,[2] writing in 1655, on the "Nature, Vertue, and Value of Pretious Stones," gives the following section under the caption "Of the Turkey Stone":

THE NATURE, FACULTIES, AND PROPERTIES OF THE TURCHOYS STONE.

Many strange things beyond faith are reported concerning the vertues of this stone, which nothing but excesse of faith can believe.

As that if it be worn in a ring of gold it will preserve men from falls, and from the bruises proceeding of them, by receiving that harm into itself which otherwise would fall upon the man: yet these vertues are said not to be in this gemm except the gemm be received of gift.

It is likewise said to take away all enmity and to reconcile man and wife.

Rueus saith that he saw a *Turchoys* which upon the death of its master lost all its beauty and contracted a cleft, which a certain man afterwards buying at an under price returned again to its former glory and beauty, as if, saith he, by a certain sense it had perceived itself to have found a new master. The same Authour saith of it, that it doth change, grow pale, and destitute of its native colour, if he that weareth it do at any time grow infirm or weak; and again upon the recovery of its master, that it doth recover its own lovely beauty which ariseth of the temperament of its own naturall heat, and becometh ceruleous like a serene heaven.

This stone is very delightfull to the eye and is thought much to strengthen the sight, because it doth not by its overbrightnesse too much dissipate the visive faculty, nor by its overmuch obscurenesse too much concentrate the visive faculty.

Baccius in his Annotations saith that it is sweat as a gumm out of a black stone in Persia, which the Indians call *Perose;* the true *Turchoys* is known by the change of its colour; in the day time it is excellently ceruleous or skie coloured; at night time by candle light it is green.

Another way of triall of it is this, The lower part is sometimes black, from whence issue small veins which do insinuate themselves into the *superficies.*

A third way, which is very much commended for this purpose: dissolve *calx* in water, then anoint the *superficies* of the gemm with it, or put a little of this dissolved *calx* upon the *superficies*, and if upon this the calx receive a tincture or colour from the gemm, this will shew that gemm to be a very excellent *turcuoys.*

SOUTH AMERICA.

Among some of the prehistoric tribes of South America the turquois was a familiar ornament, but practically nothing is known of the ideas that obtained regarding its nature and properties. Its application there, however, paralleled in many respects its use in North America, and the discoidal beads, pendants, and inlays of turquois unearthed from graves and ruins in the territory of ancient Inca dominion indicate that it played a not unimportant rôle in the early culture of that region. We may surmise, therefore, from analogy and from the fact that the superstitions of primitive people are remarkably alike, that the turquois in western South America was invested with fanciful properties and participated in the mythology and religion of the inhabitants in much the same fashion as it did among the prehistoric tribes of southern North America and does at present among the Indians of the Southwest.

NORTH AMERICA.

The turquois has long held an important place in the ceremonies and ornamentation of the native tribes of southern North America. Not only does it form today the most cherished possession of the Indians of the Southwest, but it has figured prominently in the culture of their predecessors; and among the Aztecs and allied peoples of ancient Mexico, at the time of the Spanish Conquest, it shared first rank only with the emerald and the *chalchihuitl.*[3] Attendant upon its wide application, this gem has become intimately associated with the ideas of these peoples, and their religion, legends, and superstitions are replete with allusions to its fancied attributes.

---

[1] Translated from the Latin for the writer by S. M. Gronberger.
[2] Arcula Gemmea: or, a cabinet of jewels. London, 1653 pp. 149–150.
[3] Probably jade. See pp. 108–109.

MEXICO AND CENTRAL AMERICA.

In the section dealing with the use of turquois by the aborigines of Mexico and Central America (pp. 90–97) it proved impossible to distinguish completely the actual employment of this material, as based on historical evidence, from its mythological application, as derived from tradition. Consequently considerable there given might more appropriately come under the heading of the present chapter. It should be noted, however, that the turquois appears to have possessed a very special religious significance, entering frequently into the adornment of priests and idols, and often employed, according to tradition, by the gods themselves; and in particular were turquois-encrusted masks and other symbolical ornaments reserved for ceremonial application and divine use. This was well exemplified in the presents given Cortés by Montezuma. which included turquois insignia dedicated to Quetzalcoatl, whom Cortés was supposed to be.[1]

Sahagun has written extensively of Aztec mythology and traditional history, and the following quotation [2] contains repeated allusions to the turquois:

In the first place the Toltecs who, in Spanish, may be styled first-class artificers, as the saying goes, were the first to people that land, and the first to come to that country, called the land of Mexico. * * * Thence (from Tullant-zinco) they went to a spot on the banks of a river, near the village of Xocotitlan, which now bears the name of Tullan, or Tula. * * * There have also been extracted from the ground some jewelry and precious stones, such as emeralds and fine turquoises. * * * The Toltecs were all called Chichimecans; * * * they were careful and thorough artificers, like those of Flanders at the present time; * * * everything was very good, elaborate and graceful, as for instance the houses that they erected, which were very beautiful, and richly ornamented inside, with certain kinds of precious stones of a green color. * * * There was also a temple, which belonged to their priest, called Quetzalcoatl, much more polished and beautiful than their own houses. This temple had four rooms, one * * * apartment looked toward the West, and was called the "apartment of emeralds and turquoises," because inside, instead of the lace work or the plates of gold, it was ornamented with mosaic work of emerald and turquoises, in a most beautiful manner. * * * The Toltecs had also much experience and knowledge. * * * They * * * found and discovered precious stones, and were the first to use them; for instance, emeralds, turquoises, and the fine blue stone and every kind of splendid stones. Their knowledge of stones was so great, that, even though these were hidden deep in the earth, they discovered them through their natural ingenuity and knowledge, and they knew where to find them. Their manner of making such discoveries was the following: They would get up very early in the morning and go up to an eminence, and turn their heads toward the place where the sun had to rise; when it rose, they carefully looked in every direction, to see in what place any precious stones might be hidden; they would especially look for them in places that were damp or wet, and particularly at the moment when it was rising; then a slight smoke would go up quite high, and there they found the precious stones under the earth or inside of another stone, whence the smoke would issue.

The Toltecs also found and discovered the mine of precious stones called in Mexico Xivitl (Xihuitl), which means turquoises. This mine, according to the ancients, was in a large hill, situated near the village of Tepotzatlan, which bears the name of Xiuhtzone. It was from that mine that they dug said stones, and they would take them to be worked to a stream called Toiac (Atoyae), and there they worked and cleaned them very well; it was for that reason that the stream was called Xippacoian. At present the same name is borne by the inhabited village which now exists near Tulla. * * * Their dress consisted of cloth, which had scorpions painted blue on it; they wore sandals also painted in blue, and the straps of these sandals were of the same color.

As has been noted,[3] Sahagun also described under the head of medicinal stones a mineral called *xiuhtomoltetl*, literally "turquois stone," which was supposed, when cut into shavings and moistened, to be efficacious for feebleness and nausea.

THE SOUTHWEST [4] (UNITED STATES).

The turquois has long occupied and still retains a prominent place in the mythology and folklore of the Indians of the Southwest, not alone because of its wide use among them, but also as a result of the peculiar psychological appeal its color seems to make to the untutored mind.

Pima.—The Pima Indians of southern Arizona, who at an early period had perhaps a higher degree of culture than any other tribe living north of Mexico, believe that the loss of a turquois is due to magic, and that the unfortunate loser will be afflicted with some mysterious ailment which will yield only to the skill of a medicine-man.[5] This functionary as a preventive places

---

[1] See p. 91.

[2] Historia General de los Cosas de Nueva España, 1830, vol. 3, pp. 106–114. The translation is taken from Peñafiel, Monuments of ancient Mexican art. Berlin, 1890, pp. 26–28.

[3] See p. 92.

[4] See p. 97, note, for explanation of this term.

[5] Russell, The Pima Indians, 26th Ann. Rept., Bur. Amer. Ethnol. 1904–1905, p. 112.

The thunderbird pendant at the bottom of the necklace was excavated in Arizona. The necklace itself is an old one, but not prehistoric. From the collection of Forrest Fenn of Lubbock, Tex. The old bow guard at the top of the picture has Smith's Black Matrix turquoise in it. The cluster bracelet is of a combination of Lone Mountain and Smith's Black Matrix turquoise. The bow guard and the bracelet are from the Oscar Branson collection.

These turquoise artifacts were found in Arizona Indian ruins and are from the collection of Forrest Fenn.

another turquois, a piece of slate, or a crystal in water, and gives the remedy to the patient to drink.

Dr. J. Walter Fewkes of the Bureau of American Ethnology has kindly furnished a version of a Pima legend regarding turquois,[1] as follows:

HOW TURQUOISES WERE OBTAINED FROM CHIEF MORNING GREEN.

One day, long ago, the women and girls of Casa Grande were playing an ancient game called *toka*,[2] which was much in vogue at Casa Grande but is no longer played by Pimas. During the progress of the game a blue-tailed lizard was noticed to descend into the earth at a place where the stones were green in color.[3] The fact was so strange that the wonder was reported to Morning Green,[4] who immediately ordered excavations of the earth to be made at this place Here they eventually discovered many turquoises, with which they made, among other things, a mosaic covering for a chair that used to stand in one of the rooms of Casa Grande. This chair was carried away years ago and buried, no one knows where.

Morning Green also distributed so many turquoises among his people that the fame of these precious stones reached the ears of the Sun in the East, who sent the bird with bright plumage (parrot?) to obtain them. When Parrot approached to within a short distance of Casa Grande he was met by one of the daughters of the chief, who returned to the town and announced to her father the arrival of a visitor from the Sun. The father said, "Take this small stick which is charmed, and when Parrot puts the stick in his mouth you lead him to me." But Parrot was not charmed by the stick and refused to take it in his mouth, and the girl reported her failure to induce the visitor to be led to her father. The chief answered that perhaps the strange bird would eat pumpkin seed and told his daughter to offer these to him. She made the attempt without result and returning reported that the bird refused pumpkin seed; the father said, "Put the seed in a blanket and spread it before the bird, then perhaps you may capture him." Still Parrot would not eat, and the father suggested watermelon seed. But Parrot was not tempted by these, nor by seed of cat's claw; nor was he charmed by charcoal.[5]

The chief of Casa Grande then told his daughter to tempt Parrot with corn soaked in water, well cooked, in a new food bowl. Parrot was obdurate; he would not taste it, but noticing a turquois bead of blue-green color, he swallowed it, and when the two daughters of the chief saw this they brought to him a number of blue stones which the bird greedily devoured. When the girls observed this they brought valuable turquois beads, which Parrot ate and flew away. The girls tried to capture him, but without success. He made his way through the air to the home of the Sun in the East, where he drank an emetic and vomited the turquoises, which the sun-god distributed among the people that reside near his house of rising beyond the eastern mountains. This is the reason, it is said, why these people have many stone ornaments made of that material.

But when the chief of Casa Grande heard that Parrot had been sent to steal his turquoises he was greatly vexed and caused a violent rain to fall that extinguished all fires in the East. His magic power over rain gods was so great that he was able even to extinguish the light of the sun, making it very cold. Then the old priests gathered together in council and debated what they should do. Man-Fox was first sent by them into the East to get fire, but he failed to obtain it, and then Rapid Runner was commissioned to visit Thunder, the only one that possessed fire, and steal his lighted torch. But when Thunder saw him running off with the torch he shot an arrow at the thief and sparks of fire were scattered around, setting fire on every tree, bush, and other inflammable objects, from which it happens that there is fire in everything.[6]

Zuñi.[7]—The Zuñi say that the perfect blue turquois is male; the off-color, female.[8] Their upper world is symbolized by the sun, eagle, and turquois; the lower world by the rattlesnake, water, and the toad.[9] Blue with them is the color of heaven; green, that of earth. The west, also, is known as the blue world, "not only because of the blue or gray twilight at evening, but also because westward from Zuñiland lies the blue Pacific."[10] The Zuñi reverenced as fetiches objects of various materials crudely fashioned to represent different animals. A fetich of the blue Coyote of the West is composed of compact white limestone, with traces of blue paint and large turquois eyes.[11] Another fetich,[11] of Navaho origin, but used by the Zuñi, is a sheep of

---

[1] A variant of this legend may be found in the monograph by Russell, op. cit., pp. 221–222.

[2] The players in this game were generally 10 in number facing each other about 100 yards apart. Each participant had a pointed stick with which he caught a rope with a knot at each end.

[3] In a Hopi legend, turquoises are said to be the excrement of lizards.

[4] The chief man of Casa Grande.

[5] Charcoal, the product of fire, is regarded by the Hopi Yaya priests as possessing most powerful magic in healing diseases.

[6] Communicated by J. Walter Fewkes.

[7] The Indians of New Mexico, according to Fenderson (Min. and Sci. Press, vol. 74, 1897, p. 192.), believe that the turquois protects the wearer against contagion and is potent in affairs of the heart.

[8] Stephenson, 23d Ann. Rept., Bur. Amer. Ethnol., 1901–2, p. 58.

[9] Nuttall, The fundamental principles of old and new world civilizations. Arch. and Ethnol. Papers, Peabody Museum, Cambridge, 1901. vol. 2, p. 204.

[10] Cushing, Outlines of Zuñi creation myths. 13th. Ann. Rept., Bur. Amer. Ethnol., 1891–92, p. 369. With the Hopi, also, blue or green is the color symbolical of the west. (Voth, Field Col. Mus., publ. 96, Anthrop. ser., vol. 8, 1905, p. 158.)

[11] Cushing, Zuñi Fetiches, 2d Ann. Rept., Bur. Amer. Ethnol., 1880–81, p. 26.

purplish-pink fluorite, with eyes inlaid with small turquoises. Owned by a shepherd, it is supposed not only to secure fecundity of flocks, but also to guard against disease, wild animals, and death by accidents.

In a legend entitled the "Origin of the Zuñi Salt Lake",[1] the turquois is personified in the form of Hli'akwa (Turquois), "who journeyed on to the southwest and made his home in a high mountain protected by many angry white and black bears." Hither the Zuñi make pilgrimages today to collect turquoises,[2] which they are supposed to obtain only after the bears are appeased by sacrifice of plumes and sacred meal, brought for that purpose.[3]

The turquois figures in several Zuñi folk tales. In "The Maiden of Mátsaki or the Red Feather," the priest-chief of Salt City owned many buckskins and his portholes were covered with turquoises and precious shells;[4] the maiden of Mátsaki also wore earrings as long as one's finger of turquois.[5] In the story of "The Youth and his Eagle," the eagle bore the youth upward into the sky world, where "it alighted with its beloved burden on the summit of the Mountain of Turquoises, so blue that the lights shining on it paints the sky blue."[6] Rare necklaces of sacred shell with many turquoises were given to the Foster Child of the Deer in the story of that name.[7] In the tale entitled "How the corn pests were ensnared" turquois earrings are enumerated amongst the things most prized by a Zuñi maiden.[8] In "The Hermit Mítsina," "collars of shell, and turquois earrings, and other precious things which were plentiful in the days of the ancients" were worn by young men.[9] In the house of Mítsina were many turquoises and turquois ornaments gained by him in gambling, and "even the basket drum old Mítsina played with was fringed with the handsome long turquois earrings which he had worn."[10]

Among the Pueblo Indians the turquois is known as the stone that stole its color from the sky.[11] The mythical Moon Maiden of the Pueblos was the first and loveliest woman of the world and highly honored in all their ceremonies. One of the most important symbols of the medicine men is typical of her; "it is called Mah-pah-roó, the Mother, and is the most beautiful article a Pueblo ever fashioned. A flawless ear of pure white corn (a type of fertility or motherhood) is tricked out with a downy mass of snow-white feathers, and hung with ornaments of silver, coral, and the precious turquois."[12]

Keres.—The Keres of the Santo Domingo Pueblo on the Rio Grande in New Mexico have a fetich of gypsum in the form of a prairie dog, with eyes of turquois, which their medicine men use in invocations to the rain god.[13] They also employ the turquois as a charm to bring good luck. In one of their ceremonies in honor of the patron saint of Indians, a carved wooden image, said to date from the reconquest in 1692, is placed upon an altar, strings of turquois beads of choicest color are suspended from its ears and about the neck, and from its breast is hung a turquois-incrusted marine clam shell.[14]

Hopi.—Among the Hopi the turquois is believed to bring good fortune. It enters into the adornment of fetiches used to insure luck in the chase, and finds application in many ceremonials, such as the famed Snake Dance. Dr. J. Walter Fewkes has kindly furnished the following notes on its participation in the annual Warrior Ceremony at Walpi:

The priesthood of the bow have three fetiches which are arranged in the form of an altar on the floor of the kiva during the ceremony in December. These fetiches are rude effigies made of a prescribed wood (the subterranean branch of cottonwood); two represent quadrupeds, and the third is evidently emblematic of the sky. The largest of

[1] Stephenson, The Zuñi Indians: their mythology, esoteric fraternities, and ceremonies. 23d Ann. Rept. Bur. Amer. Ethnol., 1901-2, p. 58.
[2] Concerning the whereabouts of this mountain, Mrs. Stevenson says she was bound to secrecy.
[3] Stephenson, ibid., p. 58.
[4] Cushing, Zuñi folk tales. New York, 1901, p. 1.
[5] Cushing, ibid, p. 14.
[6] Ibid., p. 40.
[7] Ibid., p. 140.
[8] Ibid., p. 288.
[9] Ibid., p. 384.
[10] Ibid., p. 388.
[11] Lummis, Pueblo Indian folk-stories. New York, 1910, p. 10.
[12] Ibid., p. 71.
[13] Kunz, Mem. Intern. Congr. Anthr., Chicago, 1894, pp. 267-281.
[14] Kunz, Min. Res. for 1891, U. S. Geol. Surv., pp. 544-546.

the quadrupeds is about a foot long and 2 inches in diameter, and is adorned with inlaid fragments of shell and turquois. The fetich representing the sky is a club-shaped body about 10 inches long, with its small end rounded and cross-hatched, to which a number of feathers, as prayer emblems, are attached. On the broad end there are three shell disks representing a star group, possibly Orion, and near the tip of the other end are inlaid fragments of shell and turquois, said to represent the Pleiades or some other constellation. These effigies are reputed to be of great antiquity and are said to have been brought up from the underworld when the races of men emerged from the Grand Canyon.[1]

Many Hopi traditions have allusions to the turquois. The Harúing Wuhti (literally, Hard Being Woman) appears repeatedly in Hopi mythology, and she is said to be the owner of such hard objects as shells, corals, turquoises, etc.[2] In one legend it is stated that the turquois is the excrement of lizards.[3] In the account of how the Hopi came from the underworld, as reported by Voth,[4] a being called Skeleton is described as very handsome, with his neck adorned with turquois strands and his ears with turquois pendants.

In the Snake Myth it is narrated that the chief's son wondered what became of all the water in the Grand Canyon. So he went to investigate. After several adventures he encountered the goddess of hard substances, who gave him a sack filled with all sorts of beads, among them turquoises. Upon his departure he was warned not to open the package until home was reached. The journey lasted several days, and each morning he found that the number of beads had increased. Finally the package became filled, and on the fifth night when nearly home he could resist no longer, but opened the package and spread out the contents. He was very happy over the treasure, but on the ensuing morning all the beads except the few original ones had disappeared, and this is why the Hopi have so few beads at the present time.[5]

In the traditional account of the early wanderings of the Hopi it is narrated that the people, after emerging from the underworld, traveled eastward. They met with many difficulties and were finally beset with grave danger from a great outflow of water from the ground. The chiefs met in council and made two balls of powdered turquois and shell which they sent as a propitiatory offering to the evil water serpent, who was the cause of the deluge, and immediately the ground became dry.[6]

Apache.—Amongst the Apache a small turquois bead affixed to a gun or a bow made the weapon shoot accurately.[7] The gem, moreover, had some relation to the bringing of rain, and could always be found at the end of a rainbow after a storm by diligently searching in the damp earth. In addition, it was a most important emblem of the medicine-man's efficacy, without which he could not exercise his medical functions.[7]

Navaho.—The Navaho of northern Arizona, of nomad habits, differ widely from the village-dwelling tribes around them. Coming from the north into the barren region which they now inhabit, they soon learned through contact with the Pueblo Indians the use of the turquois, and now they are exceeded by none in their admiration for this precious stone.[8] Not only are the Navaho seldom seen without ornaments of turquois, but this mineral also figures conspicuously in their religion, their mythology, and their folklore.

The Navaho attribute talismanic virtues to the turquois, believing that it brings good fortune to the wearer and insures the favor of the gods.[9] Thrown into a river, with the accompaniment of a prayer to the rain god, it is supposed to induce rain. Many stones are offered to the wind spirit, whose anger must thus be appeased in order that the wind may stop blowing and rain result—for the Indians say that when the wind is blowing it is searching for turquoises. Stones carved in the shape of horses are frequently carried, in the belief that the owner is thereby enabled to come into possession of many horses.

---

[1] Dr. Fewkes has sketches and further information pertaining to these objects, derived from Mr. A. H. Stephens.

[2] Voth, Field Columbian Museum, publ. 96, Anthrop. ser., vol. 8, 1905, p. 1.

[3] Communicated by J. Walter Fewkes.

[4] Ibid., p. 12.

[5] Condensed by the writer from the legend as given by Voth, op. cit., pp. 30–34.

[6] Condensed from legend given by Voth, op. cit., pp. 48–54.

[7] Bourke, The medicine-men of the Apache. 9th Ann. Rept. Bur. Amer. Ethnol., 1887–88, p. 589.

[8] The writer spent several months of 1910 amongst the Navaho. Through the kindness of Mrs. John Wetherill of Oljato, Utah, an adept in the Navaho language, he was enabled to gather a few hitherto unpublished beliefs concerning the turquois.

[9] It was included among the 18 sacred things that must be offered to the gods to gain their favor. (Matthews, Navaho Legends. New York, 1897, p. 163.)

Amongst the Navaho the four cardinal points are symbolized by colors. Blue is emblematic of the south and the upper world, and the turquois is constantly associated with these points.[1] The Navaho land is bounded by four mountains corresponding to the four directions and these have a legendary significance. Tsotsil [2] is the mountain to the south. According to one version of the Origin Legend,[3] it was made of earth mixed with turquois, and two supernatural beings called "Turquois Boy" and "Turquois Girl" were put to live in this mountain. Another version of the same legend says:[4]

Tsotsil, the mountain of the south, they fastened to the earth with a great stone knife, thrust through from top to bottom. They adorned it with turquois, with dark mist, she-rain, and all different kinds of wild animals. On its summit they placed a dish of turquois; in this they put two eggs of the blue bird, which they covered with sacred buckskin, and over all they spread a covering of blue sky. The Boy who Carries One Turquois and the Girl who Carries One Grain of Corn were put in the mountain to dwell.

To quote further from the Navaho Origin Legend:[5]

The people now returned to White Standing Rock, where they found on the ground a small turquois image of a woman. This they preserved. Of late the alien gods had been actively pursuing and devouring the people, and at the time this image was found there were only four persons remaining alive. These were an old man and woman and their two children. Two days after the finding of the image, early in the morning, they heard the voice of the Talking God calling four times, and soon he stood before them.

He told the four people to come up to the top of Tsolili after 12 nights had passed, bringing with them the turquois image they had found and at once he departed.

On the morning of the appointed day they ascended the mountain by a holy trail and on a level spot near the summit they met a party that awaited them there. They found there the Talking God, the Home God, White Body, the 11 brothers of Maid Who Becomes a Bear, the Mirage Stone People, the Daylight People standing in the east, the Blue Sky People standing in the south, the Yellow Light People standing in the west, and the Darkness People standing in the north. White Body carried in his hand a small image of a woman wrought in white shell, about the same size and shape as the blue image which the Navahos bore.

The Talking God laid down a sacred buckskin with its head toward the west. The Mirage Stone People laid on the buckskin, heads west, the two little images (of turquois and white shell), a white and a yellow ear of corn, the Pollen Boy, and the Grasshopper Girl. On top of all these Talking God laid another sacred buckskin with its head to the east, and under this they now put Wind.

Then the assembled crowd stood so as to form a circle, leaving in the east an opening through which Talking God and Home God might pass in and out, and they sang a sacred song. Four times the gods entered and raised the cover. When they raised it for the fourth time the images and the ears of corn were found changed to living beings in human form; the turquois image had become the Woman Who Changes (or rejuvenates herself), the white shell image had become the White Shell Woman, the white ear of corn had become the White Corn Boy, and the yellow ear of corn the Yellow Corn Girl. * * * The children of the sun, after many dangers, finally arrived at the house of the Sun God,[6] which was built of turquois. When the boys entered they saw, sitting in the west, a woman; in the south, two handsome young men, and in the north, two handsome young women. The women gave a glance at the strangers and then looked down. The young men gazed at them more closely, and then, without speaking, they rose, wrapped the strangers in four coverings of the sky, and laid them on a shelf. Soon the bearer of the sun entered the house. He took the sun off his back and hung it up on a peg on the west wall of the room, where it shook and clanged for some time.

Then the Sun God turned to the woman and said, in an angry tone: "Who are those two who entered here to-day?" The woman made no answer and the young people looked at one another, but each feared to speak. Four times he asked this question, and at length the woman said: "It would be well for you not to say too much. Two young men came hither to-day, seeking their father. When you go abroad you always tell me that you visit nowhere, and that you have met no woman but me. Whose sons, then, are these?" She pointed to the bundle on the shelf and the children smiled significantly at one another.

He took the bundle from the shelf. He first unrolled the robe of dawn with which they were covered, then the robe of blue sky, next the robe of yellow evening light, and lastly the robe of darkness. When he unrolled this the boys fell out on the floor. He seized them and threw them first upon great sharp spikes of white shell that stood in the east, but they bounded back unhurt from these spikes, for they held their life-feathers tightly all the while. He then threw them in turn on spikes of turquois in the south, on spikes of haliotis in the west, and on spikes of black rock in

---

[1] According to Mrs. John Wetherill (personal communication) the Navaho believe that the heart of the earth lies near the center of the Naciemento Mountains and is composed of turquois.

[2] Means "Great Mountain," and is the Navaho name for Mount Taylor (San Mateo), a lava butte in Valencia County, New Mexico.

[3] Matthews, Navaho legends. New York, 1897, pp. 220–221.

[4] Ibid, p. 79.

[5] Ibid, pp. 104–105. The text as given by Matthews is briefed by the present writer.

[6] In one legend, the medicine basket of the Sun God is made of turquois.

the north, but they came back uninjured from all these trials and the Sun God (Tsohanoai) said: "I wish it were indeed true that they were my children."

Next morning Tsohanoai led the boys out to the edge of the world, where the sky and earth came close together, and beyond which there is no world. There 16 wands or poles leaned from the earth to the sky; 4 of these were of white shell, 4 of turquois, 4 of haliotis shell, and 4 of red stone. They climbed up to the sky on the wands of red stone, and their father went with them.

Further in the Origin Legend the wanderings of the Twelve People are recounted. After many adventures the following incident is described:[1]

They had now been four days without finding water, and their children were dying with thirst. On the fifth day's march they halted at noon and held a council. "How shall we procure water?" said one. "Let us try the power of our magic wands," said another. A man of the gens who owned the wand of turquois struck this wand into the ground, and worked it back and forth and round and round to make a good-sized hole. Water sprang from the hole.

Many other references to the turquois may be found in the Origin Legend. A final quotation will suffice: "The First Man and First Woman decided to make the sun and the moon. For the former they prepared out of clear stone a round, flat object, like a dish, and set with turquois around its edge."[2] There was supposed, at one time, to have descended from heaven among the Pueblos a gambling god named He Who Wins Men, and his talisman was a great piece of turquois; he won constantly from the Indians and finally owned everything they had, including quantities of turquoises.[3] The Navaho, it is related,[4] on first coming upon the earth, found it covered with water and to drain its surface they dug trenches·with spades of turquois tipped with coral.

According to a legend reported by James Stephenson[5] the sun was fashioned of a piece of turquois, upon which eyes and a mouth had been drawn by means of a crystal dipped in pollen. This at first gave little light, but with the aid of many turquoises and a lengthy ritual it was made to blaze; and on account of its great heat it had to be lifted into the sky on four poles (two of turquoises and two of white shell beads) held by twelve men stationed at each of the cardinal points.

In the Natisnesthani Legend,[6] it is narrated:

As they (Natisnesthani and his wife) were passing the other hut she bade him wait outside while she went in to procure a wand of turquois. They went but a short distance when they came, on the top of a small hill, to a large, smooth stone, adorned with turquois, sticking in the ground like a stopple in a water jar. She touched this rock stopple with her wand in four different directions—east, south, west, north—and it sprang up out of the ground. She touched it in an upward direction, and it lay over on its side, revealing a hole which led to a flight of four stone steps.

It is related in another legend[4] that the buffalo originally had horns of turquois. How he lost them came to pass in this wise: One day two boys, while playing, admired the buffalo's horns and longed to possess them; so they ensnared the buffalo in a mesh of sunbeams and said, "We will give you, O buffalo, all the jet we possess and promise nevermore to use jet, if you will give us your beautiful horns of turquois." So he swapped his turquois horns for horns of jet; and to this day the Navaho have turquoises in abundance and believe that the horns of the buffalo are jet.[7]

In the following section from the Yaetso Legend[4] the turquois figures:

Two boys, children of the Sun God, descended from the sun on a bolt of lightning and alighted on a high mountain, supposed to be Mount Taylor. The Yaetso (great god), who was at a spring drinking, was angered by seeing their reflection in the water. He had four knives, one of turquois, one of jasper, one of shell, and one of jet. He threw the blue one at the intruders; they dodged it and picked it up. He then threw the jet, then the jasper, and then the shell, each in turn, which the boys also dodged and picked up as he threw them.

---

[1] Matthews, op. cit., p. 151.
[2] Ibid., p. 80.
[3] Ibid., p. 82.
[4] Communicated by Mrs. John Wetherill.
[5] Ceremonial of Hasjelti Dailjis. 8th Ann. Rept. Bur. Amer. Ethnol., 1886–87, pp. 275–277.
[6] Ibid., pp. 184–185.
[7] According to another version of the same legend (communicated by Mrs. John Wetherill), the two boys, who had ventured afar, encountered some buffalos, who said to them: "Tell the Navaho that when they have the headache it is our fault. We have turquois horns, but do not like them. We much prefer black horns, but can not have them because the Navaho own all the jet. If you will persuade the Navaho to give us jet, then we will promise that their heads will not ache any more."

The Sun, who had been watching the proceedings, was offended by this attack upon his children. He therefore sent down a lightning bolt, which struck the Yaetso, splitting open his head. He followed the first by another and another until four bolts had been dispatched, and after the fourth the Yaetso was dead. The boys then took out his heart and the next day carried it home to their mother.

The Yaetso carried a bag at his waist and when he was dead the boys looked into it and found it filled with blue stones. Wondering what these could be, they submitted the packet to the Chief of the Cliff Dwellers, who said that the stones were called turquoises and that they come from the Big Waters in the West, where the man who made them dwelt, and in time the waters would distribute them all over the world.

In the canyon of Laguna Creek (near Marsh Pass, N. Arizona) is a bubbling spring, in which the Navaho believe the Spirit of the Water dwells.[1] Years ago, it is said, the water became more plentiful than it is today and used to spout to a height of several feet. This was taken to be an indication that the Water Spirit was angry and offerings of many turquoises were made to this spring to propitiate the anger of its occupant.

In the Mountain Chant,[2] a Navaho ceremony of both religious and social significance, four great sand paintings are drawn. In these the cardinal points are important, and the figures to the south are symbolized by blue. In one picture the gods are represented as wearing ear-pendants, bracelets, and amulets, "blue and red (of turquois and coral), the prehistoric and emblematic jewels of the Navaho." During the ceremony, sacrifices are made to the gods, and at one point a blue ornamented stick (kethawn) and five turquoises are buried. In the rites attendant upon the Night Chant[3] the turquois finds also recurrent application.

---

[1] Personal communication from Mrs. John Wetherill.

[2] Matthews, 5th Ann. Rept. Bur. Amer. Ethnol., 1883–84, pp. 385–467. See also Tozzer, Putnam Anniv. Vol., N. Y., 1909, pp. 325, 329.

[3] Matthews, Mem. Amer. Mus. Nat. Hist., vol. 6, 1902.

CHAPTER VIII.

THE TECHNOLOGY OF TURQUOIS.[1]

"She knew * * *
That all the turf was rich in plots that look'd
Each like a garnet or a turkis in it."

Tennyson: Geraint and Enid.

NAME.

The *turquois* or *turquoise*, from the French, meaning *Turkish stone*, is generally supposed to have been so designated because the mineral was introduced into Europe by way of Turkey. It is more probable, however, that the important locality near Nishapur in Persia was once regarded as within the limits of vaguely defined "Turkey" and the term had reference to this source of supply. The word (pronounced ter-koiś, also ter-quoiz, rarely ter-keeź and ter-keeś) is most commonly written *turquoise*, but following the usage of Dana and Webster, and the modern tendency to omit unnecessary letters,[2] the simpler spelling, *turquois*, has been adopted in this treatise.

In the various languages turquois is known as follows: In English, *turquois* or *turquoise*, also *turkois, turkoise, turcois, turkis*, older forms *tourquoise, turqueis, turcas, turchois;* in French, *turquoise*, older form *tourques;* in Spanish, *turquesa;* in Portuguese, *turqueza;* in Italian, *turchese*, also *turchina;* in German, *türkis*, also *turkoys, turkiss, turckiss, turggis;* in Dutch, *turkoois*, also *turckois, turcoys;* in Danish, *turkis, tyrkis;* in Swedish, *turkos;* in Russian, *biruza;* in Turkish, *biruzeh;* in Armenian, *piroza;* in Persian, *ferozah*, also *firuzeh, pirureh, fisure, besoar, bisoura*, older form *firūzog;* in Arabic, *firuzedje;* in Sanskrit, *peroja*, also *perojā, pīroja;* in Tibetan, *gyu;* in Mongolian, *ughiu;* in Chinese, *lü sung shi;* or *sung êrh shi;* in Japanese, *turkodama.*

MINING.

Turquois is a mineral of superficial origin and consequently is never found in quantity at depths exceeding about 100 feet. Its mining is therefore comparatively simple and inexpensive, as deep shafts and extended tunnels are unnecessary. Since, however, the deposits are mostly confined to arid or desert regions, many difficulties and hardships, such as lack of water and timber, excessive heat, and distance from supplies, are experienced. The mineral usually shows upon the surface, and within a few feet thereof good material is often found.

Before the advent of gunpowder turquois was mined by crude tools, probably aided in some instances by the effect of suddenly cooling with water the heated rock. Modernly, however, the material is obtained by blasting. Where the workings are planned on a small scale an open-cut trench or shallow pit suffices; but with more extensive operations a shaft is sunk and tunnels extended horizontally therefrom at intervals following the vein. The loosened rock is broken into portable shape by hammers and raised to the surface in buckets hoisted by rope and windlass. It is there hand picked, after further crushing, with the rejection of all unsuitable material. Turquois mines, in most instances, are not fitted with modern appliances of mining, due in part to the isolated and barren regions in which many deposits occur, and in part to the temporary nature of the enterprise.

CUTTING.

Turquois comes from the mine in rough pieces or nodules and must be cut and polished before it is adapted for use as an ornamental stone. This is rarely done at the mine, but the

---

[1] See Pogue, The technology of turquois. Min. and Sci. Press, vol. 108, 1914, pp. 285-287.

[2] Following this principle consistently the preferable spelling would be *turkois*, but this form is perhaps too great a departure from usage to be advocated.

selected material is usually shipped to some trade center where the work is executed by lapidaries. The most characteristic cut is the *cabochon*, consisting of a flat bottom and polished convex top. The shape ranges from elongated oval to circular, and the convexity or arch varies from nearly flat to dome-shaped. Other forms into which the turquois is fashioned are the *sphere*, the *flat* or *tallow-top cabochon*, the *marquis* (pointed at both ends), the *pointed pendant*, the *drop pendant*, the *heart pendant*, the *flat table*, the *keystone table*, the *truncated cone*, and a variety of fancy forms characterized by simple combinations of plane or curved surfaces. The mineral is also carved into imitative shapes, and some of the results obtained, particularly in China, are very elaborate. It is never faceted, as are the transparent stones.

Turquois is comparatively soft, and is readily worked. The customary procedure in the United States is briefly as follows:[1] A suitable piece is either selected or sawn from a larger mass by means of a revolving metal disk dressed with carborundum or emery powder, and is cemented to the end of a slender wooden or ivory holder about the size of a pencil. The latter is held in the right hand of the operator and pressed against a rapidly revolving wheel or *lap* of lead or tin, upon which emery powder or carborundum is spread. The abrading material works its way into the metal surface, which then "bites" the turquois as a file does steel. The wheel is adjustable to a lathe head and is rotated by foot power or small motor. The turquois is constantly moved in position, especially as the work nears completion, so as to give the desired shape to the specimen. This operation completed, the cutting wheel is replaced by one of wood, flannel, leather, or silk, against which the gem receives its final finish and polish. Stones are bored by means of a rapidly rotating diamond-tipped drill or a steel drill, dressed with an abrasive.

At Idar, in Germany, where centers an important lapidary industry, the turquois is cut on large sandstone wheels, rapidly rotated in a vertical plane by water or steam power. These wheels, resembling immense mill stones, are fashioned with peripheral grooves of various sizes and depths, into which the stones are pressed until, after some manipulation, each assumes a cabochon shape, corresponding in breadth and convexity to the dimensions of the groove selected.

At the famous Persian locality near Nishapur the turquoises are originally purchased by merchants of Meshed or by agents who visit the mines, and some are cut by these dealers before exportation. In 1822 a wheel, composed of gum lac mixed with sand and rapidly rotated by bow and cord, was used by the native lapidaries of Meshed.[2] By 1884 emery had been substituted for the sand.[3] A cruder method rather extensively employed before 1850 and not yet entirely abandoned consisted in rubbing the stones, held by a slit in a piece of wood, into the desired shape on slabs of sandstone. The stones, after cutting, are polished by rubbing first on very fine-grained sandstone and then on leather covered with turquois dust. The two principal shapes are *peikani* and *mussatah*, the conical and the flat, but only the best-grade stones look well with the conical cut, since the apex of mediocre specimens is apt to appear pale. The less the stone is truncated the more highly it is prized, and an elliptical base is preferred to a circular one. Pieces not thick enough for the *peikani* shape and too thick for the *mussatah* are cut *en cabochon*, and the greater the convexity the higher the value. The thinner pieces and slabs yield flat or plane stones, and these are preferred by the Arabs. Flaws in larger gems are very skilfully hidden by scrollwork and letters of gold.

The ancient Mexicans fashioned the turquois into slabs for mosaics and into beads, pendants, and other ornaments. The cutting was effected by copper tools with the aid of siliceous sand[4] or flint-dust.[5] In drilling beads a bronze or copper awl was probably employed, introduced by successive twists and blows and assisted perhaps by water and fine cutting sand.[5]

[1] Claremont, Mineral Industry for 1909, vol. 8, p. 233.

[2] Fraser, Journey into Khorassan, etc. London, 1825, p. 468.

[3] Schindler, Rec. Geol. Surv. India, vol. 17, 1884, p. 139.

[4] Bancroft, The native races of the Pacific States. New York, 1874, vol. 2, p. 481. Sahagun, as quoted by Seler (Gasammelte Abhandlungen zur amerikanischen Sprach- und Alterthumskunde, Berlin, 1904, vol. 2, p. 637), reports that the stones were first polished with fine sand, then with another polisher, and that emery was not utilized as with many other precious stones.

[5] Blake, W. W., The antiquities of Mexico. New York, 1891, p. 76.

The Indians of the Southwest fashion the turquois into the desired shape on a sandstone or other surface. Many pieces are perforated by means of a crude bow drill tipped with quartz or agate.

The stones introduced to the trade are either *pure turquois* (Figs. 1, 4 of frontispieces), i. e., unaccompanied by foreign matter, or *turquois matrix* (Figs. 2, 3, 5, 7, and 8 of frontispiece), in which the mineral is cut with attached country rock, quartz, limonite, or other impurities.[1] Very attractive patterns and contrasts are often yielded by matrix, although it never commands the price of the pure turquois. Much material unfitted for pure gems is cut into matrix. *Cobweb matrix* is a term used to designate a blue ground with markings of cobweb pattern (see frontispiece, Fig. 5). *Mottled matrix* is a turquois matrix showing two shades of blue (or green), and may or may not contain foreign matter (see frontispiece, Fig. 2). Some turquois which occurs in thin, even veins in rock of pleasing shade is carved into attractive cameos.

IMITATIONS.

The turquois has been imitated from the earliest times. The ancient Egyptians had a blue enamel which they called false *mafkat* (turquois).[2] Muhammed Ibn Mansur[3] in 1300 described three kinds of imitation turquois—glass paste, hard green stones composed of copper and other minerals, and *boreizeh*, or Chinese paste—adding that it was easy to distinguish the real from the false stones. Thomas Nicols,[4] writing in 1653, remarked that the Venetians imitated turquois with "Venice glasse, prepared with a convenient skie-colored tincture." Today false turquoises abound, some crude, others clever; and much cheap jewelry is adorned with quantities of them.

Imitations of turquois are of three kinds, as follows: Blue glass or enamel; artificial compounds closely approximating turquois in composition; and other minerals, either naturally resembling turquois or made to do so by stains or dyes.

Glass imitations.—Turquois is perhaps most frequently counterfeited by a blue glass or enamel,[5] and the majority of the imitations to be seen in the cheapest jewelry are of this nature. Most of the paste imitations are very crude and show a glassy appearance and lack of beauty that at once reveal their origin. Others, however, are much more imitative and require careful scrutiny to avoid confusion with the real mineral. Invariably, however, they have a vitreous luster, are slightly harder than turquois, and differ from it in specific gravity. The margin is usually minutely splintered from the grinding, and the small broken surfaces are seen with the hand lens to have a conchoidal or shell-like shape, characteristic of glass. These stones, besides, are apt to contain air bubbles or faint wavy flow lines, indicating that the mass was once molten; and a fragment heated before the tip of a blowpipe flame readily and quietly melts to an enamel.

Synthetic turquois.—The most perfect substitutes for turquois, however, are prepared by mixing precipitated hydrated phosphate of aluminum with copper phosphate and subjecting the whole while damp to hydraulic pressure for a considerable period.[6] The manufactured product, which is in reality a synthetic turquois, can not in all cases be surely distinguished from the natural mineral by mere examination or by the ordinary tests, for it closely approximates the latter in color, texture, hardness, specific gravity, and chemical composition; and even limonite inclosures in some instances are added to simulate matrix. The most decisive proof may be obtained by heating a small fragment, either with the tip of a blowpipe flame[7] or in a small covered crucible.[8] The artificial stone in either instance will fuse quietly and

---

[1] A number of American turquois companies have in the past marked their best-grade stones and guaranteed them to retain their color. The designations are "A" (American Turquois Co.), *circle* (Azure Turquois Co.), *cross* (American Turquois & Copper Co.), "T" (Toltec Turquois Co.), and *arrow* (Himalaya Turquois Co.).

[2] De Morgan, Recherches sur les origines de l'Egypte. Paris, 1896, p. 217.

[3] See Schindler, Jarhb. k. k. geol. Reichs., vol. 36, 1886, pp. 303–314.

[4] Arcula Gemmea. London, 1653, p. 147.

[5] Bauer (Precious Stones. Spencer's trans. London, 1904, p. 401) states that the paste so used is made by adding to a mass of glass 3 per cent of copper oxide, 1½ per cent of manganese oxide, and a trace of cobalt oxide.

[6] Bauer, Zeitschr. angew. Chem., vol. 22, 1909, p. 2177. Heaton, Journ. Roy. Soc. Arts, vol. 59, 1911, p. 584.

[7] Jannetaz, Bull. soc. franç. min., vol. 13, 1890, p. 112.

[8] Pohl, Neues Jahrb. etc., 1878, pp. 364–369.

readily to a black or dark-colored slag; whereas the genuine turquois will either fly to pieces or crumble with a crackling sound into a dark-colored earthy mass or powder. Some artificially produced turquois may be detected from the fact that after lying in water it assumes a darker shade of blue and upon the wet surface discloses a network of cracks; moreover, it is said that such stones become somewhat softer after immersion in alcohol.[1] During the last quarter of the nineteenth century turquoises fabricated in the manner described have come upon the market in considerable numbers, particularly in Europe.[2]

Substitutes.—The third manner in which turquois is imitated is by the substitution therefor of cheaper minerals that either naturally or through artificial coloration resemble it in shade. The minerals which lend themselves for this purpose are the following:

(1) *Odontolite, or bone turquois.*—This material, which was often confused in the Middle Ages with true turquois, is fossil bone or ivory impregnated by phosphate of iron, and possesses a blue color scarcely distinguishable in some instances from that of mineral turquois in daylight, but appearing a dull-gray by artificial illumination.[3] This last feature affords a ready means of recognizing bone turquois. In addition, it differs from mineral turquois by being softer and incapable of taking so brilliant a polish, effervescing in contact with a drop of hydrochloric acid, giving an organic odor upon burning, possessing a greater specific gravity, revealing in cross-section upon close examination the characteristic structure of bone, and gradually fading if placed in water or alcohol.[4] Bone turquois may be prepared artificially by soaking calcined ivory for a week in a warm ammoniacal solution of copper[5] or by slowly baking finely powdered ivory that has been stained by a solution of copper. Odontolite is seldom seen nowadays, and is of slight value.[6]

(2) *Lazulite.*—This is a mineral whose color in some specimens resembles that of turquois. It is a hydrous phosphate of aluminum, with small quantities of other elements, and its specific gravity, inferior hardness (5 to 6 in the scale), and vitreous luster serve to distinguish a polished specimen from turquois. Its use as a precious stone, however, is very exceptional[7] and its substitution for turquois is rarely if ever observed.

(3) *Blue chrysocolla.*—This mineral, which is a hydrous silicate of copper, ranges in color from green to turquois-blue. In its pure state it is too soft (about the same as calcite) for cutting; but when silicified or intermixed with quartz, it becomes available as a semiprecious stone. Blue specimens may be confused with turquois, but the criteria given for copper-stained chalcedony hold also for their distinction. Chrysocolla from the Ural Mountains has been cut to some extent; but only recently, and then but slightly, has the mineral been so utilized in this country.

(4) *Copper-stained chalcedony.*—This substance, also known as blue chrysoprase, may resemble turquois and be mistaken for it. Its greater translucence, superior hardness, and vitreous appearance, serve to distinguish it, however, and a fragment, unlike turquois, will withstand a high temperature.

(5) *Artificially stained chalcedony.*—During the last decade or so great advances have been made by German chemists in staining porous minerals to any desired tint. Of late blue dyes have been found for chalcedony or agate, by means of which the delicate shades of turquois are reproduced, and about 1900 the English and French markets were plentifully supplied with stones of this character.[8] There are several processes, but the details thereof are known to few and are generally held as trade secrets. Bauer[9] mentions that a blue tone varying from a deep indigo through azure to sky-blue may be imparted to agate by first impregnating the stone with potassium ferrocyanide and later warming in a solution of ferrous sulphate, a Berlin-

[1] Bauer, Precious stones. Spencer's trans. London, 1904, p. 401.

[2] Bauer, Zeitschr. angew. Chem., vol. 22, 1909, p. 2177.

[3] Much bone turquois is greenish in color and does not greatly resemble mineral turquois.

[4] Bauer, op. cit., p. 402.

[5] Kluge, Handbuch der Edelsteinkunde. Leipzig, 1860, p. 366.

[6] Claremont, The gem-cutter's craft. London, 1906, p. 250.

[7] Bauer, loc. cit. Doelter, Edelsteinkunde. Leipzig, 1893, p. 151.

[8] Streeter, Precious stones and gems. London, 1898, p. 50.

[9] Op. cit., p. 524.

blue compound being thus deposited in the pores. Good imitations of this kind are difficult to distinguish without careful examination; however, they are harder and show greater translucence about the girdle than turquois, and give none of the chemical tests of the latter. Where the coloring is not skilfully done the specimen presents a crudeness that at once divulges its spuriousness.

(6) *Other minerals.*—Lapis-lazuli and azurite might in rare instances be confused with turquois, but in general the blues of the former are so intense and entirely different from those of turquois as to obviate a substitution. If green turquois were prized by civilized peoples, it would be open to substitution by several minerals; for malachite, chrysocolla, variscite, and green chalcedony may resemble it very closely, but its slight value renders such replacements without purpose.

IMPROVEMENT OF COLOR.

From time to time turquoises that have had their color deepened or otherwise improved by artificial means come into the trade. As such stones are apt to revert to their original shade upon continued wear, those treated in this manner are not sold except in attempts to defraud.

That the turquois may be temporarily improved in color has long been known. Muhammed Ibn Mansur in the thirteenth century mentioned that its color was strengthened by mutton fat or by smearing with butter. The Pueblo Indians of the Southwest, according to Blake,[1] heighten the color of their turquoises by soaking them in tallow or grease. The natives near Nishapur, Persia, often carry stones in their mouths before offering them for sale, and the dealers in Meshed are said to keep turquoises in moist earthenware pots,[2] as by these means, also, the color of inferior specimens is temporarily improved. Doelter[3] states that greenish turquois becomes bluer in contact with carbon dioxide.

Off-color stones are sometimes stained with Prussian blue. Stones so treated may be detected by washing in alcohol, wiping, and soaking in ammonia, whereby the dye is dissolved; or by scraping the superficial coloration from the back of the stone with a steel blade.[4] If the turquois is valuable it is preferable to build a small wall of wax upon its back and partly fill the depression with ammonia, as the solvent effect can thus be noted at one point only, without harm to the specimen. By artificial light the color of stained turquois is gray-blue and unlike pure turquois appears duller instead of brighter.[4]

One process has been patented[5] which is stated to give a permanent coloration to turquois. The stones are first immersed in a dilute solution of tartaric acid and copper or iron sulphate, then placed for 24 hours in a bath of alcohol to which an aniline dye, dissolved in a little water, is gradually added.

PRECAUTIONS IN USE.

The turquois, in common with the pearl and the opal, requires constant care on the part of the wearer in order that its beauty may not be impaired. Its comparative softness and its tendency to change in color afford ample opportunity for its delicate tint to be marred or even entirely destroyed by carelessness. The turquois should never be worn in contact with other stones nor be allowed to strike or rub against objects of any kind, else its surface will become roughened and dull. Moreover, it should never be permitted to come in contact with perspiration,[6] soap lather, or with strong gases, and even perfumes are said to have a harmful effect.[7] Its surface should be kept away from acids or grease, and should be carefully wiped with chamois skin after handling. One should be particular to remove turquois rings before washing the hands.

---

[1] Amer. Journ. Sci., vol. 25, 1883, p. 199.
[2] Curzon, Persia and the Persian question. London, 1892, vol. 1, p. 267.
[3] Edelsteinkunde. Leipzig, 1893, p. 149.
[4] Kunz, Proc. Amer. Assoc. Adv. Sci., vol. 54, 1885, pp. 240–241.
[5] Eng. Pat. 14385. Aug. 25, 1891. See Boult, Journ. Soc. Chem. Ind., vol. 10, 1891, p. 925.
[6] It was noted as early as the 13th century that perspiration, as well as grease and musk, altered the color of turquois. See Teifascite, page 14
[7] Kunz, Mineral Res. for 1892, U. S. Geol. Surv., p. 764.
See also, Investigations and studies in jade, New York, 1906, vol. 1, p. 196.
Hydrogen sulphide in small quantity is said to give blue turquois a greenish cast, and the presence of this compound in exhalations from the skin has been suggested as the cause of fading of stones when worn. (Doelter, Edelsteinkunde, Leipzig, 1893, p. 149.)

PRODUCTION.

It is impossible to speak other than in generalities in discussing the production of the turquois deposits of the world. It will be necessary to consider but four regions which have furnished practically the world's supply of this mineral since the beginning of time; namely, the Sinai Peninsula, the deposits near Nishapur in Persia, scarcely known localities in Central Asia (Tibet and China), and the mines within the southwestern portion of the United States.

1. Little that is definite can be said of the production of the *Sinai turquois deposits.* The mines were extensively and systematically worked under Egyptian control from the first to the twentieth dynasty, and during that period a great quantity of gem material was obtained. At intervals, too, for many thousand years the nomad inhabitants of the Peninsula procured turquoises here, part of which reached Egypt and some doubtless penetrated into the interior of Asia. Since 1855 the Sinai stones have from time to time made some impress upon the turquois trade. Indeed, the material from Sinai is known in the market as Egyptian turquois,[1] and, although of pleasing color, is held in less esteem than the Persian product because of its somewhat glassy appearance and greater tendency to fade.

2. *Nishapur.*—It is impossible to approximate even vaguely the total production of the famous mines near Nishapur. It is neither known when they first were operated, nor are there records until the latter portion of the nineteenth century by which their output may be judged. It is certain, however, that for the past thousand years they have supplied nearly all the turquois used in Europe and western Asia, and until two decades ago, the American trade also. Their total production therefore must be enormous, amounting, by our standards, up into the millions. A few figures may be gleaned from other writers on the subject. In 1881 [2] stones to the value of $60,000 were annually exported to Russia and of $20,000 to Teheran. In 1884 the yearly output valued at the mines, was estimated [3] to average $50,000, but the final purchasers paid probably three times this amount. In 1889 stones to the value of $85,000 were dispatched via the Transcaspian Railway to Europe.[4] The production in 1890 was placed at $115,000.[5] The Reish mine, on the authority of one writer,[6] was the only one in operation in 1900, then producing $400 weekly. In 1905 the registered exports amounted to $46,980, but the production was stated [7] to have probably reached $200,000 in value. In 1911 de Launey [8] placed the annual production at $40,000.

3. *Central Asia.*—Information is entirely lacking whereby the extent of the production of turquois in central Asia may be judged. It is known that this mineral has found wide application since remote times in Tibet and that localities in that country have furnished great quantities of material. Recently also, turquois matrix similar to that employed in Tibet has appeared on the London market.

During the past two hundred years localities in central China have produced considerable turquois, most of which has been exported to Mongolia and Tibet. Modernly much turquois has found employment in the northern provinces of India, and both Tibet and Persia have contributed to this supply.

4. *United States.*—The productive deposits of turquois in North America are confined to five States: New Mexico, Arizona, Nevada, Colorado, and California; and practically every locality that has moderately yielded this precious stone was exploited of old by the Indians. In the Cerrillos Hills of New Mexico in particular are extensive excavations executed in pre-Spanish times, and these workings alone supplied immense quantities of turquois to the aborigines of the Southwest and were probably also the chief source of the turquois so abundantly used by the ancient Aztecs and allied peoples.

Up to the era of modern mining, the yield of the various American localities can not be expressed in figures. One can only judge from the extended native use of the gem during the past thousand years or more, that the total quantity of turquois withdrawn from the mines

[1] Claremont, The gem-cutter's craft. London, 1906, pp. 248–252.
[2] Schindler, Jahrb. k. k. geol. Reichs., vol. 31, 1881, pp. 169–190.
[3] Schindler, Rec. Geol. Surv. India, vol. 17, 1884, p. 139.
[4] Curzon, Persia and the Persian question. London, 1892, vol. 1, p. 214.
[5] Curzon, ibid, p. 266.
[6] Geissel, Sci. Amer., vol. 82, 1900, p. 246.
[7] Kunz, Min. Res. for 1905, U. S. Geol. Surv., pp. 1348–1349.
[8] La geologie et les richesses minerales de l'Asie. Paris, 1911, p.107.

by the Indians is in excess of that of late won by the whites, although its quality and its value (according to our standards) would perhaps fall short of the finer material obtained by modern mining methods.

The recent domestic production of turquois has been very irregular. During certain years a large output has come from a few important mines, while in other years many deposits have shared in the production. Of late turquois matrix has been in demand and the large quantities mined have resulted in an overproduction. For this reason, and because the turquois is temporarily out of vogue, many mines are at present (1914) closed. In 1909 over 17 tons of turquois and turquois matrix were produced; in 1910 nearly 8½ tons; and in 1911 a little over 2 tons.[1] According to statistics gathered by the U. S. Geological Survey, the value of the production in the United States from 1883 to 1912 is as follows:

Production of turquois in the United States from 1883 to 1912.

Year	Value	Year	Value
1883	$2,000	1899	$72,000
1884	2,000	1900	82,000
1885	3,500	1901	118,000
1886	3,000	1902	130,000
1887	2,500	1903	110,000
1888	3,000	1904	100,000
1889	23,675	1905	65,000
1890	28,675	1906	22,250
1891	150,000	1907	23,840
1892	175,000	1908	147,950
1893	143,146	1909	179,273
1894	34,000	1910	85,900
1895	50,000	1911	44,751
1896	40,000	1912	10,140
1897	55,000		
1898	50,000	Total	1,956,600

The figures quoted represent the value of the rough turquois as purchased by dealers. The value of the cut gems would be several times as great. From this point of view the output of the Cerrillos deposits alone from 1890 to 1900, the period of greatest productiveness, is estimated[2] at $2,000,000; and the value of the product of the Azure mine, Burro Mountains, N. Mex., is placed by a former superintendent[3] at "several million dollars."

VALUE.

The turquois varies so considerably in value, not only among different peoples, but also from time to time in the same market, that it is impossible to assign any rule whereby one can at all accurately appraise a given specimen. To do this successfully requires both skill in judging quality and knowledge of market conditions.

At the present time (1914) the turquois is out of fashion and not very popular in the United States. Consequently its value is down, and $10 a carat for good quality is an average price. This applies only to stones of a few carats weight; larger ones of the finest grade are worth more per carat. Inferior stones can be assigned no fixed value. Turquois matrix, according to quality, brings up to about $1 per carat. Frequently, however, matrix stones are sold without specific reference to weight, and command from about 50 cents to $5 each.

A few statements may be cited from other writers. In 1893 turquois from the Azure mine, Burro Mountains, N. Mex., averaged $5 per carat.[4] In 1903 it was stated[5] to bring from $5 to $10 per carat. In 1907 its value per carat was quoted[6] from $6 to $25, and even higher for exceptional pieces, with $15 as an average for good quality. Turquois from the Porterfield mine in the same district is said to have commanded the following figures in 1907: Best quality, deep-blue, from $1 to $10 a carat for stones under 10 carats and $10 or more per carat for those weighing

[1] Sterrett, Min. Resources for 1911, U. S. Geol. Survey, pt. 2, p. 1066.   [4] Kunz, Min. Resources for 1893, U. S. Geol. Surv., p. 693.
[2] See Kunz, Min. Resources for 1900, U. S. Geol. Surv., p. 767.   [5] Reid, Eng. Min. Journ., vol. 75, 1903, p. 786.
[3] Zalinski, Eng. Min. Journ., vol. 86, 1908, p. 846.   [6] Zalinski, Econ. Geol., vol. 2, 1907, p. 492.

over 10 carats; matrix from 25 cents to $1 per carat.[1] Matrix from Ithaca Peak, Mineral Park, Ariz., was valued in 1908 at $1 to $5 per pound in the rough. A single stone from the Castilian mine, near Cerrillos, N. Mex., sold in 1891 for $4,000.[2] In 1904 a number of large stones running from 50 to several hundred carats were obtained from San Bernardino County, Cal., and the best of them brought up to $1,500 each.[3] A turquois of 320 carats, worth $2,600 is said to have been found at Searchlight, Lincoln County, Nev., in 1904.[4]

The Indians of the Southwest value the turquois more highly than do the whites. Among the Zuñi a single string of turquois beads is worth several horses.[5] Blake[6] compared a Navaho's esteem for the turquois to that of a diamond with us. Newberry[7] observed that the Indians of New Mexico and Arizona will give a good horse for a fragment of fine quality the size of the little-finger nail and one-eighth inch in thickness. The writer has witnessed the sale of turquoises by traders to Navaho Indians at a greater profit than could be realized on the stones through ordinary channels.

In Europe good quality turquois is worth about $12.50 per carat, and large stones more.[8] King,[9] writing at London in 1872, stated that turquoises the size of millet seeds, such as were used for incrusting jewels, were worth 12 cents per dozen, while perfect stones one-half inch in diameter sold for $50 each. Kluge[10] mentioned a fine stone in the Museum of the Razel Academy of Moscow, measuring 3 inches long and 1 inch wide, and a large heart-shaped turquois with a passage from the Koran inlaid in letters of gold, purchased by a jeweler in Moscow for 5,000 rubles. At the beginning of the seventeenth century a perfect turquois the size of a hazelnut brought 200 thalers; the same quality stone the size of a large pea, 6 thalers.[11]

In Persia, the home of the turquois, this precious stone commands a good price. According to one writer[12] a flawless stone of fine color, of several carats weight, not uncommonly brings $700 to $1,000 in Teheran. Ibn Mansur,[13] about 1300, referred to a remarkable turquois said to weigh 920 grams and to be worth $170,000.

In Tibet and China the turquois does not command so high a price as in other parts of the world. At Si-ngan fu, China, where centers an export trade in turquoises with Tibet, the ordinary stones, according to Laufer,[14] bring from about $2.60 to $4.10 a pound, and only exceptionally fine pieces are sold as individual stones.

"The wasteful sunset faded out in turkis-green and gold."

—*Kipling: Delilah.*

[1] Sterrett, Min. Resources for 1907, U. S. Geol. Surv., p. 832.
[2] Kunz, Min. Resources for 1891, U. S. Geol. Surv., p. 545.
[3] Kunz, Min. Resources for 1905, U. S. Geol. Surv., p. 1348.
[4] See Sterrett, Min. Resources for 1908, U. S. Geol. Surv., pt. 2, p. 846.
[5] Stephenson, 23d Ann. Rept. Bur. Amer. Ethnol., 1901–1902, p. 378.
[6] Amer. Journ. Sci., vol. 25, 1858, p. 227.
[7] Report of the exploring expedition from Santa Fe to the Colorado, etc., 1859, printed 1876, p. 41.
[8] Bauer, Precious stones. Spencer's trans. London, 1904, p. 392.
[9] Antique gems and rings. London, 1872, pp. 413–414.
[10] Handbuch der Edelsteinkunde. Leipzig, 1860, p. 366.
[11] de Boot, Le parfaict ioaillier ou histoire des pierreries. Ed. by Toll. Lyon, 1644, p. 346.
[12] Benjamin, Persia. London, 1877, p. 408.
[13] See Schindler, Jahrb. k. k. geol. Reichs., vol. 36, 1886, pp. 303–314.
[14] Op. cit., p. 63.

BIBLIOGRAPHY.[1]

AD'DIN, Sehem. Nozhat Namah Ellaiy. Persian manuscript, written in 11th century, quoted by Ouseley, 1819 (q. v.).
Brief note on early use of turquois in Persia.

AGAPHI, Demetrius. Etwas von der eigentlichen Beschaffenheit des orientalischen Türkis. Neue Nordische Beyträge, vol. 5, 1793, pp. 261–265.
Brief description of Nishapur mines, with conclusion that product is a mineral substance and not organic.

AGRICOLA, Georgius (1494–1558). De natura fossilium. Basil, 1657, book 6, pp. 623, 626–627.
Description of callais and blue-jaspers (possibly including turquois), based principally upon Pliny.

AHMED, ben Abd al Aziz. Juaher Namah. [A treatise on precious stones.] •Written during the 17th century, probably
in India. Quoted by Ouseley in 1819 (q. v.).
Notes five Asiatic localities for turquois and mentions its supposed virtues.

AL-AKFANI (died 1347–48). [Treatise on precious stones.] Ed. by P. L. Cheikho, Al-Machriq, vol. 11, 1908, pp.
751–765.
Refers to turquois.

ALBERTUS MAGNUS. De Mineralibus. Written about 1262.
Includes a brief description of turquois.

ALDROVANDUS, Ulysses. Musaeum Metallicum. Bologna, 1647, p. 550.
Brief description, with drawings, of two Mexican turquois mosaics.

AMBROSETTI, J. B. Antigüedades Calchaquies. Buenos Aires, 1902, pp. 42–43
Notes and figures turquois beads found in Argentina.

ANDREE, Richard. Ethnographische Parallelen und Vergleiche. Neue Folge. Leipzig, 1889, pp. 127–130. Also,
Internat. Arch. Ethnogr., vol. 1, 1888, pp. 214–215. Congrès intern. Américanistes, 7th sess., 1888, Berlin,
1890, pp. 146–149.
Description of Mexican turquois mosaic in Gotha. Notes on mosaics in London, Berlin, and Rome.

ANDREYEV, A. (Catalogue of useful minerals of Russian Turkestan. In Russian.) Tashkend, 1912, p. 108.
Gives accurate information on turquois mines in Syr Darya, Samarkand, and Ferghana.

ANGLERIA, Petrus Martyr de. De Insulis nuper inventis. Dec. 4, chap. 9.
Report of presents given Cortés by Montezuma.

ANONYMOUS. Lapidarium omni voluptate refertum. Viennae (no date).
Brief description of turquois, following Albertus Magnus.

———— Congrès International d'anthropologie préhistorique. Compte rendue de la 4me session. Copenhagen,
1869, p. 462.
Notes Mexican turquois mosaics in Copenhagen.

———— Opal, turquoise, amber, and jet. Argosy, London, vol. 12, 1871, pp. 113–118.
Popular account of the turquois.

———— [Note.] Eng. Min. Journ., vol. 31, 1881, pp. 8–9.
Description of Cerrillos deposits. Historical details.

———— Turquois mines and pearl fisheries of Persia. Eng. Min. Journ., vol. 38, 1884, p. 362.
Brief account of Nishapur deposits.

———— The turquois. Chamber's Journ., Edinburg, vol. 63, 1886, pp. 181–183.
Good popular account of the mineral.

———— [In General mining news.] Eng. Min. Journ., vol. 51, 1891, p. 751.
Notes occurrence of turquois near Paschal, Sierra County, New Mexico.

———— [Note.] Eng. Min. Journ., vol. 52, 1891, p. 564.
Notes discovery of turquois near Ibrahim-Olga, 15 miles from Samarkand, Turkestan.

———— Turquoise in southwestern New Mexico. Eng. Min. Journ., vol. 51, 1891, p. 719.
Notes discovery of turquois in Burro Mountains, New Mexico.

———— The turquoise mines of Persia. Eng. Min. Journ., vol. 62, 1896, p. 417.
Brief account of mines at Nishapur.

———— The turquoise mines of Persia. Journ. Soc. Arts., London, vol. 45, 1896, pp. 37–38.
Brief account of Nishapur mines and product.

———— Turquoise in Nevada. Eng. Min. Journ., vol. 64, 1897, p. 456.
Notes discovery of turquois at Sugar Loaf Peak, Lincoln County, Nevada.

---

[1] The writer is indebted to Dr. Berthold Laufer (op. cit. and personal communications) for a number of the references on the turquois in Asia.

ANONYMOUS. Mines of Mount Sinai. Sci. Amer., vol. 82, 1900, p. 134.
> Brief account of mines in Wady Maghareh, Sinai, erroneously located on Mount Sinai.

—— Ein neuer Fundort von Türkis im südlichen Thüringen. Zeitschr. naturw., vol. 72, pt. 6, 1900, p. 453. Neues Jahrb. Min., Geol., und Pal., vol. 1, pt. 2, 1902, p. 187.
> Notes finding of turquois in southern Thuringia.

—— [In General mining news.] Eng. Min. Journ., vol. 71, 1901, p. 347.
> Notes discovery of turquois in Sonora, Mexico.

—— The oldest discovered specimens of Egyptian jewelry. Amer. Antiquarian, vol. 24, 1902, pp. 188, 231.
> Brief account of turquois jewelry (Egyptian) of 1st Dynasty, found at Abydos.

—— Turquoise from ruins. Sci. Amer. Suppl., vol. 53, 1902, p. 21990.
> Notes the finding of turquois beads in cliff ruins of the Southwest (U. S.).

—— [Note.] Arch. Journ., London, vol. 26, 1869, p. 283.
> Notes exhibition in London of Chinese carving in turquois.

ARISTOTLE (Pseudo.). De lapidibus (The book of Aristotle on precious stones, according to the wise accounts of the ancients). Quoted by Rose, 1875 (q. v.). An old work composed before the middle of the ninth century and wrongly attributed to Aristotle.
> Gives brief description of turquois.

ATKINSON, J. A. A locality list of all the minerals hitherto recorded from Victoria. Proc. Roy. Soc. Victoria, vol. 9, 1896, pp. 68–119.
> Notes occurrence of turquois at King River, Victoria.

BACCIUS, Andr. Annot de Nat. Gem.
> Brief account of turquois.

BAEDEKER, K. Lower Egypt and the Peninsula of Sinai. London, 1878, pp. 480–483, 511. See also later editions.
> Good description of Sinai mines, with directions for reaching them.

BANCROFT, Hubert H. The native races of the Pacific States of North America. New York, 1874, vol. 1, pp. 545, 583; vol. 2, pp. 173, 259, 314, 350, 372, 376–377, 458, 481–482, 606, 707; vol. 3, pp. 250, 271, 368, 385, 390; vol. 4, pp. 557–559; vol. 5, pp. 254–257.
> Gives numerous references to, and descriptions of, the use of turquois and *chalchihuitl* in ancient Mexico.

BANDELIER, A. F. Contributions to the history of the southwestern portion of the United States. Cambridge, 1890, pp. 41, 42, 61, 173, 442.
> Early use of turquois in the Southwest.

—— Final report of investigations among the Indians of the southwestern United States. Cambridge, pt. 1, 1890, pp. 39, 40, 63, 163, 196; pt. 2, 1892, pp. 93, 352, 553, 584.
> Early use of turquois in the Southwest.

—— The islands of Titicaca and Koati. New York, 1910, p. 181.
> Notes finding turquois bead in Peru.

BARRERA, (Madame) A. De. Gems and jewels; their history, geography, chemistry, and ana. London, 1860, pp. 147, 150, 248–249.
> Gives general account of turquois. Cites erroneous localities in Mexico.

BARRON, T. The topography and geology of the Peninsula of Sinai (western portion). Survey Dept. Egypt. Cairo, 1907, pp. 209–212.
> Good geologic description of Sinai turquois deposits.

BARTLETT, S. C. From Egypt to Palestine through Sinai, the Wilderness, and the South Country. New York, 1879, pp. 74, 218–223.
> Notes ancient turquois jewelry found in Egypt and reports a visit to the Sinai turquois mines.

BASTIAN, A. Zwei altmexikanische Mosaiken. Verh. Berliner Gesellsch. Anthrop., 1885, p. 201.
> Short description of two Mexican turquois mosaics in Berlin.

BAUER, Max. Edelsteinkunde. Leipzig, 1896, pp. 440–456. Revised edition, 1910. English translation, with additions, by L. J. Spencer, London, 1904.
> Excellent description of the properties and occurrences of turquois.

—— Ueber künstliche Edelsteine. Zeitschr. angew. Chem., vol. 22, 1909, p. 2177. *Abstract:* Chem. Abstr., vol. 4, 1910, p. 734.
> Gives method of preparing synthetic turquois.

BAUERMAN, H. Notes on a geological reconnaissance made in Arabia Petraea in the spring of 1868. Quart. Journ. Geol. Soc., London, vol. 25, 1869, pp. 17–38.
> Geologic description of the Sinai turquois deposits. Includes map.

BECKMANN, John. A history of inventions, discoveries, and origins. Translated by William Johnston. London, 1846, p. 471.
> Does not regard *jaspis aerizusa* as turquois.

BELLEW, H. W. Kashmir and Kashghar. London, 1875, pp. 129–130.
> Describes turquois headdress of Bhot women of Ladakh.

BENJAMIN, G. W. Persia. London, 1877, p. 408.
> Notes on turquois mines of Nishapur and Kerman, Persia.

BERGEAT, Alfred. Der Granodiorite von Concepción del Oro im Staate Zacatecas (Mexiko) und seine Kontaktbildungen. Neues Jahrb. Min., Geol., und Pal., Beilago Band, vol. 28, 1909 p. 499.
> Notes occurrence of turquois at Santa Rosa, Mexico.

—— La granodiorita de Concepción Del Oro en el Estado de Zacatecas. Inst. Geol. Mexico, Bull. 27, 1910, p. 58.
> Preceding paper in Spanish.

BERTHELOT, M. Sur les mines de cuivre du Sinaï, exploiteés par les anciens Egyptiens. Compt. rend., vol. 123, 1896, pp. 365–374.
> Includes a brief mineralogic description of turquois from Sinai.

BEVERIDGE, A. S. The memoirs of Baber.
> Refers to occurrence of turquois near Khojend.

BIRDWOOD, G. C. M. The industrial arts of India. Vol. 2, pp. 25, 28.
> Notes use of turquois in jewelry of India.

BISHOP, H. R. Investigations and studies in jade. New York, 1906, vol. 1, pp. 3–4, 196; vol. 2, pp. 244, 247.
> Includes notes on *chalchihuitl*, brief description of the properties of turquois, and figures of turquois-adorned ornaments of Chinese workmanship.

BISHOP, J. L. Among the Tibetans. New York, 1894, p. 44.
> Describes turquois in dress of women of Kashmir.

BLACKISTON, A. H. Recent discoveries in Honduras. Amer. Anthrop., vol. 12, 1910, p. 539.
> Describes and figures turquois-mosaic mask recently discovered in Honduras.

BLAKE, Wm. P. The chalchihuitl of the ancient Mexicans: its locality and association, and its identity with turquois. Amer. Journ. Sci., vol. 25, 1858, pp. 227–232.
> Describes Cerrillos turquois deposits and maintains identity of product with *chalchihuitl* of ancient Mexicans.

—— New locality of the green turquois known as chalchuite, and on the identity of turquois with the callais or callaina of Pliny. Amer. Journ. Sci., vol. 25, 1883, pp. 197–200. *Abstract:* Zeitschr. Kryst. und Min., vol. 9, 1894, p. 89.
> Notes occurrence of turquois in Cochise County, Ariz., discusses use among ancient and modern Indians, and suggests identity with Pliny's *callais.*

—— Aboriginal turquoise mining in Arizona and New Mexico. Amer. Antiquarian, vol. 21, 1899, pp. 278–284.
> Discusses use of turquois by ancient and modern Indians.

—— Mosaics of chalchuite. Amer. Antiquarian, vol. 22, 1900, pp. 108–110.
> Notes turquois mosaic found in Arizona.

—— The racial unity of the historic and prehistoric aboriginal people of Arizona and New Mexico. Intern. Congr. Americanists, 13th session, New York, 1902, pp. 203–204.
> Notes wide use of turquois by ancient Indians of the Southwest.

—— Minerals of Arizona. Rep. to Gov. Arizona, Tucson, 1909, pp. 57–58.
> Brief notes on occurrence of turquois in Arizona.

BLAKE, W. W. The antiquities of Mexico. New York, 1891, p. 76.
> Notes on the cutting of precious stones (including turquois) by the Aztecs.

BOCCONE, Paolo. Intorno le Turchine o Turquoises della nova rocca. Museo di Fisica, etc., 1697, p. 278.
> Turquois of the *New Rock* is considered to be artificial.

BOGDANOWITSCH, K. Ueber das Türkislager bei Nishapur in Persien. Verh. Russ. Kais. Min. Gesellsch., vol. 23, Protoc. Sitz., pp. 364–365. *Abstract:* Neues Jahrb. Min., Geol. und Pal., vol. 2, 1889, Ref. p. 18.
> Geologic description of the Nishapur deposits.

BOMAN, Eric. Antiquités de la région Andine de la République Argentine et du désert d'Atacama. Paris, 1902, 2 vols., pp. 131, 329, 353, 373, 583, 625–627, 629, 631, 640, 655, 656, 749, 766, 783.
> Detailed description of numerous turquois objects (many of them figured), found in Argentina, Bolivia, and Chile.

BOOT, Boetius de. Le parfaict ioaillier ou histoire des pierreries. Edited by Andre Toll (a French translation of an earlier Latin edition). Lyon, 1644, pp. 338–348.
> An entertaining mediæval account of turquois, relating and discussing its supposed properties.

BOULT, A. J. A process of imparting a permanent colouring to turquoises and other precious stones (English patent 14385, Aug. 25, 1891). Journ. Soc. Chem. Ind., vol. 10, 1891, p. 925.
> Describes process of coloring turquois.

BOURBOURG, Brasseur de. Recherches sur les ruines de Palenqué et sur les origines de la civilisation du Méxique. Paris, 1866.
> Includes colored illustrations of three Mexican turquois mosaics.

BOURKE, John G. The medicine-men of the Apache. Ninth Ann. Rept. Bur. Amer. Ethnol., 1887–88, pp. 588–591.
> Describes use of turquois by the Apache and gives citations on *chalchihuitl.*

BOYLE, Robert. Exercitatio de Origine et Viribus Gemmarum. London, 1673, p. 71.
> Brief description of turquois.

BRARD, C. P. Mineralogie appliquée aux arts. Paris, 1821, vol. 3, pp. 391–396.
> Notes distinction between bone turquois and mineral turquois.

BRATLEY, Geo. H.   The power of gems and charms.   London, 1907, pp. 96, 125, 128, 130, 135, 140.
 Gives the supposed virtues of turquois.

BREASTED, J. H.   A history of Egypt.   New York, 1905, p. 48.
 Briefly describes turquois jewelry of First Dynasty found in Egyptian tomb at Abydos.

BRETSCHNEIDER.   Mediaeval researches.   Vol. 1, pp. 140, 176; vol. 5, p. 5.
 Suggests identity of Chinese *sê-sê* with turquois.   Notes use of turquois in China.

BRINTON, D. G.   Myths of the New World.   New York, 1868, p. 253.
 Notes use of *chalchihuitl* by Aztecs.

BRISTOW, H. W.   A glossary of mineralogy.   London, 1861, pp. 390–391.
 General description of turquois, with notes on specimens from Sinai.

BROCKLEHURST, T. U.   Mexico to-day.   London, 1883, p. 194.
 Brief description, with colored plate, of turquois-encrusted skull from Mexico, now in the British Museum.

BROSSE, Gui de la.   Sur la nature et l'utilitate des plantes.   Paris, 1628, p. 421.
 Maintains that turquois is produced from odontolite through the action of heat.

BRUCKMANN, L.   Etwas über den orientalischen Türkis.   Chem. Ann. (Crell), 1797, pp. 300–301.
 Maintains that the turquois from Nishapur is malachite.

BRUGSCH, Heinrich.   Wanderung nach den Türkis-Minen und der Sinai-Halbinsel.   Leipzig, 1866, pp. 66–68, 70, 78, 80.
 Describes the Sinai turquois mines.   Chiefly historical and archaeological.   Includes map of mines.

——— A history of Egypt under the Pharaohs.   Translated by Philip Smith, London, 1881, vol. 1, pp. 80–81, 160, 195–196, 489–490; vol. 2, pp. 148–149.
 Describes the exploitation of the Sinai turquois mines by the ancient Egyptians.

BÜCHING, H.   Mikroskopische Untersuchung des Türkis.   Zeitschr. Kryst. und Min., vol. 2, 1878, pp. 163–168.
 Abstract: Miner. Mag., vol. 2, 1878–9, p. 144.
 Describes microscopic character of specimens from Sinai, Nishapur, Steine (Silesia), and Oelsnitz (Saxony). Notes color change on heating.

——— Mikroskopische Untersuchung des Türkis aus dem Columbus-District, Nevada.   Zeitschr. Kryst. und Min., vol. 3, 1879, pp. 81–82.
 Describes appearance under microscope.

BUDGE, A. E. Wallis.   The book of the dead.   London, 1901, vol. 1, p. 78.
 Gives reference to turquois in Egyptian text.

——— The Egyptian Sûdân: Its history and monuments.   London, 1907, vol. 1, p. 538.
 Notes the exploitation of turquois deposits in Sinai and Nubia by the ancient Egyptians.

BUFFON, Leclerc de.   Histoire naturelle.   Edited by C. S. Sonnini.   Paris, 1802, vol. 13, pp. 311–325.
 Gives lengthy discussion of bone turquois.

BULWER.   Anthropometamorphosis, etc.   London, 1655, p. 180.
 Describes use of labrets in Brazil.

BURTON, Richard F.   The gold mines of Midian and the ruined Midianite cities.   London, 1878, pp. 302–303.
 Notes occurrence of turquois in Arabia.

——— The land of Midian (revisited).   London, 1879, vol. 1, p. 115; vol. 2, p. 47.
 Brief description of turquois deposits in Arabia.

BUSHELL, S. W.   Chinese art.   London, 1910, p. 125.
 Described Chinese box adorned with turquois.

BUSHNELL, David I., jr.   North American ethnographical material in Italian collections.   Amer. Anthr., vol. 8, 1906, pp. 243–255.
 Brief description of five Mexican turquois mosaics in Rome.

CAESIUS, Bernardus.   Mineralogia, sive naturalis philosophiae thesauri (*also under the title*, De Mineralibus).   Lugduni, 1636, p. 601.
 Includes an account of the turquois.

CAMPBELL, A.   Notes on eastern Thibet.   The Phoenix, London, vol. 1, 1871, p. 143.
 Relates a Tibetan tradition regarding turquois.

CARDAN, Jerome.   De Subtilitate.   Basileæ, 1560.
 Gives an account of the supposed virtues of turquois.

CARNOT, A.   Sur la composition chimique des wavellites et des turquoises.   Compt. rend., vol. 118, 1894, pp. 995–998.
 Abstract: Zeitschr. Kryst. und Min., vol. 26, 1896, pp. 108–109.   *Abstract:* Journ. Chem. Soc., vol. 66, 1894, pp. 355–356.
 Gives two analyses of turquois (Persia and Nevada).

——— Sur la composition chimique des turquoises.   Bull. soc. franç. min., vol. 18, 1895, pp. 119–123.   *Abstract:* Zeitschr. Kryst. und Min., vol. 27, 1896–7, pp. 615–616.   *Abstract:* Journ. Chem. Soc., vol. 72, 1897, p. 325.
 Gives analysis of turquois from Grant County, N. Mex.

CARRERI, Gemelli.   Voyage autour du monde.   Paris, 1719, vol. 2, p. 212.
 Includes a brief note on Persian turquois.

CAZVINI, Hamdallah. Nozhat al Colub. Written about 1300–1400; quoted by Ouseley, 1819 (q. v.).

Notes early use of turquois in Persia.

CHARDIN, Jean. Voyages en Perse et autres lieux de l'Orient. Amsterdam, 1735, vol. 2, p. 70; vol. 3, pp. 30–31.

Notes occurrence of turquois at Nishapur and Firuskuh.

CHUAN, Shaoching H. The most extraordinary city in the world; notes on Lhasa, the Mecca of the Buddhist faith. Nat. Geogr. Mag., vol. 23, 1912, pp. 966, 975, 983.

Includes brief notes on use of turquois in Tibet.

CHURCH, A. H. Revision of mineral phosphates, No. 4, Calaite. Chem. News, vol. 10, 1864, p. 290. *Note:* Journ. Soc. Arts, vol. 32, 1884, p. 1084.

Gives analysis of turquois from Nishapur.

—— Precious stones considered in their scientific and artistic relations, with a catalogue of the Townshend Collection. London, 1905, pp. 70–71, 124–125.

Includes a general account of turquois and described 6 turquoises in the Townshend Collection, Victoria and Albert Museum, London.

CLAREMONT, Leopold. The gem-cutter's craft. London, 1906, pp. 30–31, 248–252.

General description of turquois.

—— The cutting and polishing of precious stones. Mineral Industry, 1909, vol. 8, pp. 229–233.

Notes the method of cutting turquois.

CLARKE, F. W., and DILLER, J. S. Turquois from New Mexico. Amer. Journ. Sci., vol. 32, 1886, pp. 211–217. Bull. 42, U. S. Geol. Surv., 1887, pp. 39–44. *Abstract:* Journ. Chem. Soc., vol. 52, 1887, pp. 116–117.

A mineralogic description of turquois from Cerrillos. Gives three analyses and deduces formula. Describes country rock and discusses origin of mineral.

CLAVIGERO, Francisco Saverio. Storia antica del Messico. Ceseno, 1780.

Notes use of turquois by Aztecs.

—— History of Mexico. Translated by Charles Cullen, Philadelphia, 1817, vol. 2, pp. 52, 101, 287.

Notes use of turquois and *chalchihuitl* by Aztecs. Briefly describes presents given to Cortés by Montezuma.

CLEMENT-MULLET. La turquoise [*In* Essai sur la minéralogie Arabe]. Journ. Asiatique, Paris, vol. 11, 1868, pp. 150–157.

A detailed discussion of turquois, chiefly of historic interest, following Teifascite and other authors.

CLOUET. Aperçus sur les propriétés occultes des pierres precieuses d'apres quelques érudits lapidaires. 1897. Manuscript copy in Bibliothèque nacionale, Paris.

Notes supposed occult properties of turquois.

CORONADO, Francisco Vasques de. Extracts from journal, published in the Indian Report by Lieut. Whipple. Pacific R. R. explorations and surveys, vol. 3, 1856, pp. 108–111.

Notes early use of turquois by Indians of the Southwest (U. S.).

COUREL, M. H., *See* MELY, F. de.

COWAN, John L. American gem mines and mining. Mines and Minerals, vol. 32, 1911, pp. 103–105.

General account of turquois mining in the United States.

CUMMINGS, Byron. The ancient inhabitants of the San Juan Valley. Bull. Univ. Utah, vol. 3, No. 3, pt. 2, 1910, p. 35.

Notes finding turquois mosaic earring in cliff ruin of northern Arizona.

CUNNINGHAM, Alexander. Description of some ancient gems and seals from Bactria, the Punjab, and India. Journ. Asiatic Soc. Bengal, vol. 10, 1841, p. 153.

Figures and describes a turquois brooch of Indian workmanship.

—— Ladák, physical, statistical, and historical. London, 1854, pp. 242, 253, 304, 305.

Notes use of turquois in Ladakh.

CURL, M. A. Ancient gems. Amer. Antiquarian, vol. 22, 1900, pp. 284–291.

Notes superstitions regarding turquois.

CURRAN, J. M. On the occurrence of precious stones in New South Wales, and the deposits in which they are found. Journ. and Proc. Roy. Soc. N. S. Wales, vol. 30, 1896, pp. 214–285. *Abstract:* Journ. Chem. Soc., vol. 74, 1898, pp. 79–80.

Briefly describes occurrence of turquois near Bodalla, New South Wales. Gives analysis.

CURZON, G. N. Persia and the Persian question. London, 1892, vol. 1, pp. 203, 214, 264–267.

Good description of Nishapur deposits. Notes other turquois localities in Persia.

CUSHING, F. H. Zuñi fetiches. Second Ann. Rept. Bur. Amer. Ethnol., 1880–81, pp. 9–45.

Notes use of turquois in Zuñi fetiches.

—— Zuñi folk tales. New York, 1901, pp. 1, 14, 40, 140, 288, 384.

Includes tales in which turquois figures.

CUVIER, G. Extrait d'un ouvrage sur les especes de quadrupeds. Journ. de phys., vol. 52, 1801, p. 263.

Correlates "occidental turquois" with copper-stained teeth.

DALL, W. H. On masks, labrets, and certain aboriginal customs, with an inquiry into the bearing of their geographical distribution. Third Ann. Rept. Bur. Amer. Ethnol., 1881–82, pp. 83–84, 96.

Notes use of turquois labrets in South America. Refers to Aztec turquois mosaics.

DAMOUR, A. Sur la Callaïs, nouveau phosphate d'alumine hydraté recueilli dans un tombeau celtique du Morbihan. Compt. rend., vol. 59, 1864, pp. 936–940.

    Gives analysis of turquois-like mineral from Celtic graves in France.

DAS, Sarat Chandra. Marriage customs of Tibet, p. 12.

    Describes use of turquois in Tibetan marriage ceremony.

—— Contributions on the religion, history, etc., of Tibet. Journ. Asiat. Soc. Bengal, vol. 50, 1881, pp. 208, 223.

    Includes Tibetan legends in which turquois figures.

—— Narrative of a journey round Lake Yamdo. Calcutta, 1887, p. 49.

    Gives a Tibetan tradition relating to turquois.

—— Journey to Lhasa and central Tibet. Edited by W. W. Rockhill. London, 1902, p. 119.

    Describes turquois headdress of Tibetan women.

DAVIS, W. W. H. Spanish conquest of New Mexico. Doylestown, Pa., 1869, pp. 124, 125, 137, 168, 171, 271.

    Notes early explorers' observations on turquoises used by Indians of the Southwest (U. S.).

DIAZ, Bernal. The memoirs of Bernal Diaz. Translated by J. I. Lockhart. London, 1844, vol. 1, pp. 26, 29, 36, 93, 278, 389.

    Describes position and use of turquois and *chalchihuitl* amongst Aztecs. Notes Montezuma's gifts to Cortés.

DIEULAFAIT, Louis. Diamonds and precious stones. London, 1874, pp. 141–144.

    Includes a general account of turquois and notes antique engravings on turquois.

DILLER, J. S. *See* Clarke, F. W.

DINSMORE, C. A. Azure turquois mine, New Mexico. Mining World, vol. 33, 1910, p. 660.

    Description of Azure mine, Burro Mountains, New Mexico.

DOELTER, C. Edelsteinkunde. Leipzig, 1893, pp. 148–152.

    Gives good general account of turquois.

DOMEYKO, I. Mineralogia. Third ed., 1879, pp. 259–260.

    Reports occurrence of turquois at San Lorenzo, Chile.

DUC, Léouzon le. Archives de la commission scientifique du Méxique. Paris, 1867, vol. 3, pt. 1, pp. 157–158.

    Refers to two Mexican turquois mosaics now in Copenhagen.

DUNN, E. J. The Edi turquoise field, King River. Rec. Geol. Surv. Victoria, vol. 2, 1908, pp. 170–174. *Abstract:* Chem. Abstr., vol. 2, 1908, p. 3223.

    Brief geologic description.

EAKLE, Arthur S. The minerals of Tonopah, Nev. Bull. Dept. Geol., Univ. Calif., vol. 7, No. 1, 1912, p. 17.

    Identifies turquois at Tonopah.

EDWARDS, Charles. The history and poetry of finger rings. New York, pp. 106–107, 158.

    Notes superstitions connected with use of turquois in finger rings.

EMERSON, Ellen R. Indian myths or legends, traditions, and symbols of the aborigines of America. Boston, 1884, pp. 9, 340, 455, 456.

    Notes mention of turquois in Aztec legend. Discusses significance of blue color.

EMORY, William H. Notes of a military reconnoissance from Fort Leavenworth in Missouri, to San Diego in California. Senate ex. doc. 7; 30th Cong., 1st sess. Washington, 1848, p. 88.

    Notes use of turquois by Pima and Maricopa Indians.

Encyclopædia of superstitions, folklore, and the occult sciences of the world. Chicago, 1903, vol. 2, p. 744–745, 762.

    Notes superstitions connected with turquois.

FENDERSON, W. C. Turquoise mining in New Mexico. Mining and Scientific Press, vol. 74, 1897, p. 192.

    Description of turquois and methods of mining. Gives superstitions connected with turquois.

FERNIE. Precious stones for curative use. Bristol, 1907, p. 269.

    Refers to London woman said to possess power of restoring color to turquois.

FEUCHTWANGER, L. A popular treatise on gems. New York, 1867, pp. 329–332.

    Notes stones from Arabia exhibited in London in 1851.

FEWKES, J. Walter. Tusayan snake ceremonies. Sixteenth Ann. Rept. Bur. Amer. Ethnol., 1894–5, p. 282.

    Notes use of turquois in Hopi Snake Dance.

—— Archæological expedition to Arizona in 1895. Seventeenth Ann. Rept. Bur. Amer. Ethnol., 1895–6, pp. 573, 641, 662, 733.

    Describes turquois ornaments found in Arizona ruins.

—— Pacific coast shells from prehistoric Tusayan pueblos. Amer. Anthr., vol. 9, 1896, pp. 359–367.

    Describes turquois mosaic found in ruin on Little Colorado River, Arizona.

—— Preliminary account of an expedition to the Pueblo ruins near Winslow, Arizona, in 1896. Ann. Rept. Smithsonian Inst., 1896, pp. 517–539.

    Describes turquois ornaments found in ruins near Winslow, Arizona.

—— Hopi Katcinas. Twenty-first Ann. Rept. Bur. Amer. Ethnol., 1899–1900, pp. 67, 85, 113, 119.

    Notes use of turquois.

—— Two summers' work in Pueblo ruins. Twenty-second Ann. Rept. Bur. Amer. Ethnol., 1900–1901, p. 86.

    Description and discussion of turquois mosaics of Indian workmanship.

Fewkes, J. Walter.   Antiquities of the Mesa Verde National Park: Spruce Tree House.   Bull. 41, Bur. Amer. Ethnol., 1909, p. 27.
   Describes bird ornament of hematite inlaid with turquois mosaic, from ruin near Cortez, southwestern Colorado.

Finot, Louis.   Les lapidaires indiens.   Paris, 1896, pp. 138, 197.
   Gives reference to turquois in Hindu literature.

Fischer, G. de Waldheim.   Addition au Mémoire de Mr. le Dr. John sur la Turquoise orientale.   Mem. Soc. Imp. Nat., Moscou, vol. 1, 1806, pp. 140–149.
   Maintains that oriental turquois is a mineral substance, and proposes three varietal names for it.

———— Onomasticon.   Min. Mus. Imp. Moscou, 1811.
   Nearly same as preceding paper.

———— Essai sur la turquoise et sur la calaite.   Moscou, 1810; also 1816.   Abstract: Ann. Philos., vol. 14, 1819, p. 406.
   General account of mineral and bone turquois.   Gives list of references.

Fischer, Heinrich.   Kritische mikroskopisch-mineralogische Studien.   Freiburg, 1869, p. 59.
   Includes earliest microscopic description of turquois.

———— Die Mineralogie als Hilfswissenschaft für Archäologie, Ethnographie, u. s. w., mit specieller Berücksichtigung mexicanischer Sculpturen.   Archiv. Anthropologie, vol. 10, 1878, pp. 177–214.
   Discusses the use of turquois and gives notes on its microscopic character.

———— Nephrit und Jadeit.   Stuttgart, 1880.
   Includes citations on chalchihuitl, concluding that it is nephrite.

Fraas, Oscar.   Aus dem Orient.   Stuttgart, 1867, pp. 9-10.
   Briefly describes the Sinai turquois deposits.

Francesco Orazio della Penna di Billi.   Breve Notizia del Regno del Thibet.   Written in 1730.   Ed. by Klaproth, Nouveau Journ. Asiat., 1835.   Eng. trans., C. R. Markham, Narratives of the Mission of George Bogle to Tibet, . . . , London, 1876, p. 317.
   Notes occurrence of turquois in Tibet.

Franks, A. W.   Guide to the Christy Collection, British Museum.   London, 1868.
   Describes Mexican turquois mosaics in British Museum.

Fraser, James B.   Journey into Khorassan in the years 1821 and 1822.   London, 1825, pp. 405, 407–421, 468–469.
   Good description of the Nishapur deposits, with notes on the use of the product.

———— Travels and adventures in the Persian Province on the southern banks of the Caspian Sea.   London, 1826, Appendix, pp. 343–347.
   Description of the Nishapur mines.

Frenzel, A.   Mineralogisches.   9. Vorkommnisse von Alexandrien.   Tschermak's Min. und Petr. Mitth., vol. 5, 1883, pp. 182–188.
   Abstract: Neues Jahrb. für Min., Geol., und Pal., vol. 2, 1883, Ref. p. 315.
   Abstract: Journ. Chem. Soc., vol. 46, 1884, p. 269.
   Gives analysis of turquois from Sinai.

Frenzel, A. B.   A turquoise deposit in Mohave County, Ariz.   Eng. Min. Journ., vol. 66, 1898, p. 697.
   Brief description of Burro Mountains locality.

Fuchs, Ed, et de Launey, L.   Traite des Gites Mineraux et Metalliferes.   Paris, 1893, vol. 1, pp. 411–414.
   Brief description of Nishapur deposits.   Notes occurrence of turquois in France.

Fühner, Hermann.   Beitrage zur Geschichte der Edelsteinmedizin.   Bericht d. Deutsch. Pharm. Ges., Berlin, 1901.
   Gives the supposed medicinal properties of turquois, as culled from ancient writers.

———— Lithotherapie.   Strasburg, 1902, pp. 11, 98, 106–108.
   Same as preceding article.

Garbe, Richard.   Die indischen Mineralien, ihre Nahmen und die ihnen zugeschriebenen Kräfte.   Leipzig, 1882, p. 91.
   Gives brief account of supposed properties of turquois.

Garcia ab Horto.   Aromatum et simplicium aliquot.   Antwerpiæ, 1567, p. 199.
   Cites Mesue on turquois and notes confusion arising out of translation of Arabic term for this mineral.

Gayet, Al.   L'Art Persan.   Paris, 1895, p. 249.
   Notes use of turquois in the manufacture of ancient Persian enamels.

Geissel, H. L.   The turquoise mines of Persia.   Sci. Amer., vol. 82, 1900, p. 246.
   Compiled account of the Nishapur deposits.

Genth, F. A.   Gold in turquois from Los Cerillos, New Mexico.   [In Contributions to Mineralogy, No. 48.]   Amer. Journ. Sci., vol. 40, 1890, pp. 115–116.
   The so-called "turquois" is a chromiferous clay.

Gill, William.   The river of the golden sand.   London, 1880, vol. 2, pp. 77, 107.
   Notes use of turquois in Tibet.

Glocker, E. F.   Beiträgen zur mineralischen Kenntniss der Sudetenländer.   1827, vol. 1, p. 58.
   Earliest description of turquois occurring in Silesia.

———— Neues Vorkommen von Calait in Schlesien.   Ann. der Phys. und Chem. (Poggendorff), vol. 64, 1845, pp. 633–636.
   Describes turquois locality in Silesia.

GOMARA, Lopez de. Histoire géneralle des Indes Occidentales, et Terres Neuues. Paris, 1606. Translated into French by M. Fumeé, pp. 64–65.

Refers to turquois mosaics in Yucatan.

GRANCIÈRE, Aveneau de la. Les parures prehistoriques et antiques en grains d'enfilage et les colliers talismans Celto-Armoricains. Paris, 1897, pp. 38, 40, 36, 146–149.

Describes and figures turquois-like material from prehistoric graves in France.

GRATON, L. C. *See* LINDGREN, W.

GROTH, P. Tabellarische Uebersicht der Mineralien. 1898, p. 97.

Gives formula for turquois.

HALSE, E. Gems and precious stones of Mexico. Amer. Inst. Min. Eng., Trans., vol. 32, 1902, pp. 568–569.

Includes note on use of turquois by Aztecs.

HAMY, E. T. Les mutilations dentaires au Mexique et dans le Yucatan. Bull. Soc. d'Anthr. de Paris, vol. 5, 1882, p. 884.

Describes and figures turquois-encrusted teeth from grave in Yucatan.

—— Décades américanæ, Mém. d'arch. et d'ethn. américaines, déc. III, No. 28, p. 92.

Describes turquois-encrusted teeth from grave in Yucatan.

HARPE, de la. l'Abrege des voyages. 1780, vol. 6, p. 507.

Brief account of the Nishapur deposits.

HAUGHTON. Notes of a mineralogical excursion from Cairo into Arabia Petraea [copied from anonymous French manuscript]. Nat. Hist. Rev., London, vol. 6, 1859, pp. 28–47.

Notes finding turquois specimen near well of Nasaiph, Sinai.

HAUSMANN, J. F. L. Handbuch der Mineralogie. 1847, vol. 2, p. 1091.

Notes occurrence of turquois in Persia and Tibet.

HEATON, Noel. The production and identification of artificial gems. Journ. Roy. Soc. Arts, London, vol. 59, 1911, p. 584.

Describes method of preparing synthetic turquois.

HEGER, Franz. Altmexikanische Reliquien aus dem Schlosse Ambras in Tyrol. Annalen des k. k. Naturhistor. Hofmuseum, Wien, vol. 7, 1892, pp. 379–400.

Describes and figures two Mexican turquois mosaics now in Vienna.

HENDLEY, T. H. Indian jewellery. Journ. Indian Art and Industry, vol. 12, 1906–1909, pp. 51, 58, 61, 100, 148–151.

Describes the use of turquois in India. Includes excellent figures and many citations to the literature.

d'HERICOURT, Rochet. Observations géologiques recueillies en Égypte, sur la Mer Rouge, le golfe d'Aden, le pays d'Adel et le royaume de Choa. Bull. soc. géol. France, vol. 3, 1846, pp. 544–545.

Notes occurrence of turquois in Abyssinia.

HERMANN, R. Ueber die Zusammensetzung des orientalischen Türkises (*In* Untersuchungen russischer Mineralien). Journ. für prakt. Chem., Leipzig, vol. 33, 1844, pp. 282–285.

Abstract: Neues Jahrb. für Min., Geol. und Pal., 1846, pp. 227–228.

Brief account of turquois from Nishapur.

HERRICK, C. L. Geological associations in New Mexico mining camps. Rept. Gov. New Mexico for 1900, p. 258.

Discusses origin of Cerrillos turquois. Conclusions erroneous.

HEYD, W. Histoire du Commerce du Levant au Moyen-âge. Leipzig, 1886, vol. 2, p. 653.

Notes occurrence of turquois in Persia and Turkestan.

HIDDEN, W. E. Two new localities for turquois. Amer. Journ. Sci., vol. 46, 1893, pp. 400–402.

Notes locality for turquois in Cow Springs District, New Mexico, and describes occurrence in Jarilla Hills, New Mexico.

—— Zwei neue Fundorte Türkis. Zeitschr. Kryst. und Min., vol. 22, 1893–4, pp. 552–553.

German translation of preceding article.

HILL, JOHN. On the colours of the sapphire and turquois. [A letter appended to the author's translation of Theophrastus.] London, 1774.

Attributes color of turquois to presence of particles of copper.

Histoire de l'Academie des Sciences, 1719, pp. 24-25.

Concludes that bones can not be converted into turquois by heating.

HOLMES, WM. H. Prehistoric textile art of eastern United States. Thirteenth Ann. Rept. Bur. Amer. Ethnol., 1891-2, p. 25.

Notes objects, probably of turquois, in possession of Indians of lower Mississippi region during Spanish times.

—— Mines and quarries; Mosaic; Turquois. [*In* Handbook of American Indians.] Bull. 30, Bur. Amer. Ethnol., 1907 and 1911.

Brief description of the mining and use of turquois by American aborigines.

HOOKER, J. D. Himalayan Journals. London, 1855, vol. 1, p. 122, vol. 2, p. 86.

Describes use of turquois by inhabitants of Sikkim, Nepal, and southern Tibet.

HUME, W. F. The topography and geology of the Peninsula of Sinai (southeastern portion). Survey Dept. Egypt. Cairo, 1906, p. 123.

Notes presence of turquois in the Wady Maghareh and at Serabit el Khadem, and its absence elsewhere in Sinai.

IBN-EL-BEITHAR.   Treatise on remedies.   A French translation by L. Leclerc was published in Notices et extraits des manuscrits de la Bibliothèque Nationale, vols. 23, 25, 26, Paris, 1877–1883, under the title Traité des simples par Ibn-El-Beïthâr.   Article 1713, vol. 3, treats of the turquois.
> A general account of turquois, including its supposed virtues.   Quotes from Dioscorides and Galenus.

JACKSON, A. V. W.   From Constantinople to the home of Omar Khayyam.   New York, 1911, pp. 254, 259.
> Cites Ibn Haukal in reference to the Nishapur mines.   Gives account of Nishapur mines.

JANNETAZ, E.   Note sur la turquoise dite de nouvelle roche.   Bull. soc. franç. min., vol. 13, 1890, pp. 106–112.   *Abstract:* Miner. Mag., vol. 10, 1892–4, p. 172.   *Abstract:* Zeitschr. Kryst. und Min., vol. 21, 1892–3, pp. 268–269.
> Gives analysis and concludes that occidental turquois is of organic origin.

JOHN, J. F.   Experience et Analyse Chimique de la Turquoise.   Mem. Soc. Imp. Nat., Moscou, vol. 1, 1806, pp. 131–139.
> Distinguishes between odontolite and true turquois, giving analysis (no value) of the latter.

——— Chemische Untersuchung des orientalischen Türkisses.   Journ. Chem. und Phys., Berlin, vol. 3, 1807, pp. 93–97.
> Same as preceding article.

——— Bull. scient. nat., 1827, p. 440.
> Gives analysis of turquois from Jordanmühl, Silesia.

JOHNSON, D. W.   The geology of the Cerrillos Hills, New Mexico.   School of Mines Quart., vol. 24, 1903, pp. 493–499. (Areal Geology); vol. 25, 1903, pp. 69–98 (Petrography).
> Good account of the geology, mineralogy, and petrography of the Cerrillos turquois deposits.

JONES, F. A.   New Mexico mines and minerals.   Santa Fe, N. Mex., 1904, pp. 269, 272–277.
> General account of turquois deposits of New Mexico.   Discusses origin.

——— History and mining of turquoise in Southwest.   Mining World, vol. 31, 1909, pp. 1251–1252.
> General account.

JONES, William.   History and mystery of precious stones.   London, 1880, p. 37.
> Notes anecdote connected with turquois.

JOYCE, T. A.   The southern limit of inlaid and incrusted work in ancient America.   Amer. Anthr., vol. 10, 1908, pp. 16–23.
> Describes and figures turquois-encrusted objects from Peru now in the British Museum.

——— South American Archæology.   London, 1912, pp. 206–207.
> Notes turquois inlay work from Peru.

KEMP, Hobart.   The history of jewels.   London, 1671, pp. 62-64.
> Early account of the Persian turquois and its application.

KENNION, R. L.   Extract from Consular Report for 1905.   Min. Journ., London, vol. 80, 1906, p. 522.
> Notes exploitation of Nishapur deposits.

KHAN, Haji, and SPARROW, Wilfrid.   With the pilgrims to Mecca.   London, 1895, pp. 41, 43, 260.
> Notes Persian superstitions regarding turquois.

KHANIKOFF, Nicolas de.   Mémoire sur la partie méridionale de l'Asie centrale.   Paris, 1862, pp. 326–329.
> Brief description of Nishapur mines.   Notes deposit at Taft, near Yezd.

KING, C. W.   Antique gems: their origin, uses, and value.   London, 1860, pp. 59–60, 427, 433.
> Discusses use of turquois in antiquity and gives medieval notions concerning it.

——— The natural history, ancient and modern, of precious stones and gems, and of the precious metals.   London, 1865, pp. 136–140, 422–424.
> Describes use of turquois in antiquity and Middle Ages.   Gives medieval notions concerning it.   Quotes from de Boot.

——— Antique gems and rings.   London, 1872, vol. 1, p. 85, vol. 2, pp. 4, 5, 13, 203, 413–414.
> Good general account of turquois.

KINGSBOROUGH, Edward.   Antiquities of Mexico.   London, 1831, 7 vols.
> Notes use of *chalchihuitl* and turquois by Aztecs.

KLUGE, K. E.   Handbuch der Edelsteinkunde.   Leipzig, 1860, pp. 361–366.
> Contains good general account of the turquois.

KNIGHT.   Diary of a pedestrian in Cashmere and Tibet.   London, 1863, pp. 168–169, 184, 217.
> Describes use of turquois by women of Bultistan.

KOKSCHAROW, N. v.   Die Entdeckung des Türkis.   Bull. l'Acad. Imp. Sci. St. Petersburg, vol. 29, 1884, p. 352.
> *Abstract:* Neues Jahrb. für Min., Geol. und Pal., vol. 2, 1886, Ref. p. 10.
> *Abstract:* Journ. Chem. Soc., vol. 50, 1886, p. 516.
> Gives brief description of occurrence of turquois in the Kirghiz Steppes.   Includes analysis.

——— Türkis.   Materialen zur Mineralogie Russlands, vol. 9, 1881, pp. 83–87.   Verh. russ. min. Ges., vol. 20, 1885, p. 10.
> *Abstract:* Zeitschr. Kryst. und Min., vol. 13, 1887–88, p. 187.
> *Abstract:* Journ. Chem. Soc., vol. 52, 1887, p. 1021.
> Further account of occurrence of turquois in the Kirghiz Steppes.   Gives analysis.

KONDAKOF, N., Tolstoï, J., et Reinach, S.   Antiquités de la Russie méridionale.   Paris, 1891, pp. 290, 316–318, 385, 402, 405, 408, 488, 490, 494–495, 504.
> Figures and describes ancient turquois jewelry from Russia, Roumania, the Caucasus, and Siberia.

KUNZ, Geo. F. [Turquois section in articles on Precious Stones.] Min. Res. of the U. S., U. S. Geol. Surv., 1882, pp. 193–195; 1883–84, pp. 767–768; 1885, p. 441; 1887, p. 562; 1888, p. 582; 1889–90, p. 446; 1891, pp. 544–546; 1892, pp. 763–764; 1893, pp. 693–695; 1900, p. 767; 1901, pp. 760–761; 1902, pp. 856–857; 1903, pp. 951–955; 1904, pp. 957–958; 1905, pp. 1348–1349. Ann. Rept. U. S. Geol. Surv.; Sixteenth, 1894–95, pt. 4, p. 602; Seventeenth, 1895–96, pt. 3, p. 910; Eighteenth, 1896–97, pt. 5, pp. 1209–1211, 1217; Nineteenth, 1897–98, pt. 6, p. 504; Twentieth, pt. 6, 1898–99, pp. 579–584; Twenty-first, 1899–1900, pt. 6, pp. 455–456.

> Describes turquois deposits in the United States.

—— Artificially stained turquoise from New Mexico. [In Mineralogical Notes.] Proc. Amer. Assoc. Adv. Sci., vol. 34, 1885, pp. 240–241.

> Notes method for detecting artificially stained stones.

—— Gems and precious stones of North America. New York, 1890, pp. 54–65.

> General description of turquois, with notes on its use by American aborigines.

—— Folklore of precious stones. Mem. Intern. Congr. Anthr., Chicago, 1894, pp. 267–281.

> Notes turquois charms used by Indians.

—— Gems and precious stones of Mexico. Amer. Inst. Min. Eng., Trans., vol. 32, 1902, pp. 59, 68–83.

> Good discussion of *chalchihuitl* and its identity.

—— Precious stones in the United States in 1901. Eng. Min. Journ., vol. 73, 1902, p. 38.

> Includes brief notes on turquois mining in the United States.

—— Gems, jewelers' materials, and ornamental stones of California. California State Min. Bur., Bull. 37, 1905, pp. 12–13, 107–110, 152–153.

> Describes turquois mines of California.

—— New observations on the occurrence of precious stones of archæological interest in America. Congrès internat. Americanistes, XV sess. (1906), Quebec, 1907, vol. 2, pp. 290–293.

> Gives notes on the occurrence and use of turquois in North America.

—— The curious lore of precious stones. Philadelphia, 1913, pp. 6, 24, 26, 37, 108–114, 246–247, 299, 308, 320, 329, 333, 336, 345, 348, 375.

> Devotes several pages to turquois lore and gives interesting account of numerous beliefs connected with this stone.

LABORDE, Leon de. Voyage de l'Arabie Pétree. Paris, 1830, pp. 43–44.

> Notes modern discovery of turquois at Serabit el Khadem, Sinai.

—— Journey through Arabia Petræa to Mount Sinai [in 1828]. London, 1836, p. 84.

> Notes finding turquoises at Serabit el Khadem, Sinai.

LACROIX, A. Minéralogie de la France et de ses colonies. Paris, 1910, vol. 4, pp. 529–530.

> Notes occurrence of turquois in France.

LAGRANGE, Bouillon. Analyse d'une substance connue sous le nom de turquoise. Ann. de chimie, vol. 59, 1806, pp. 180–195.

> Discusses bone and mineral turquois, giving analysis of former.

LAKES, A. The turquoise mines of the Cerillos Mountains in New Mexico. Mines and Minerals, vol. 21, 1901, pp. 395–396.

> General description.

LANSDELL, Henry. Russian Central Asia, including Kuldja, Bokhara, Khiva, and Merv. London, 1885, vol. 1, pp. 497–498. *Notice:* Miner. Mag., vol. 6, 1884–1886, p. 236.

> Brief description of turquois deposit on Mount Karamazar, Turkestan.

LAUFER, Berthold. Jade: a study in Chinese archæology and religion. Field Mus. Nat. Hist., publ. 154, Anthr. Ser., vol. 10, 1912, pp. 334–335.

> Describes and figures Chinese tree of carved minerals, with leaves of jade and turquois.

—— Notes on turquois in the East. Field Mus. Nat. Hist., publ. 169, Anthr. Ser., vol. 13, No. 1, 1913, pp. 1–71. 8 plates.

> Detailed and critical account of turquois in India, Tibet, and China, based upon travel and exploration in the East and careful research in the literature.

LAUNEY, L. DE Note sur les gisement de Kaolin de la forêt des Colettes (Allier). Bull. soc. géol. France, vol. 16, 1888, p. 1067.

> Notes occurrence of turquois in Colettes Forest, Allier, France.

—— Les richesses minerales de l'Afrique. Paris, 1903, pp. 284–285.

> Good descriptions of Sinai turquois deposits, including map of mines.

—— La géologie et les richesses minerales de l'Asie. Paris, 1911, pp. 107, 606–607, 661–663.

> Description of Nishapur deposits. Notes occurrence of turquois on Mount Karamazar, Turkestan. Discusses origin of turquois.

—— See FUCHS, Ed.

LAWRENCE, W. R. The valley of Kashmir. London, 1895, pp. 64–65.

> Notes use of turquois.

LE CLERC, *see* Ibn-el-Beithar.

LE CONTE, John L. Notes on the geology of the survey for the extension of the Union Pacific Railway, E. D., from the Smoky Hill River, Kansas, to the Rio Grande. Philadelphia, 1868, pp. 36–41.

> Notes occurrence of turquois at Cerrillos, New Mexico.

LEE, F. G.   A glossary of liturgical and ecclesiastical terms.   London, 1877, p. 425.
    Notes use of turquois in Middle Ages for adorning objects of worship.

LEGATI, Di Lorenzo.   Museo Cospiano.   Bologna, 1677, p. 477.
    Figures and describes two Mexican turquois mosaics.

LEHMANN, Walter.   Altmexikanische Mosaiken und die Geschenke König Montecuzomas an Cortés.   Globus, Braunschweig, vol. 90, 1906, pp. 318–322.
    Good description and discussion of Mexican turquois mosaics.

—— Altmexikanische Mosaiken im kgl.   Museum für Völkerkunde zu Berlin.   Congrès intern. Américanistes, 15th session, Quebec, 1906, vol. 2, 1907, pp. 339–349.
    Describes Mexican turquois mosaics in Berlin.

LEONARDUS, Camillus.   The mirror of stones.   Printed in Venice, in 1502, and translated into English in London, 1750.   *See* pp. 235–236.
    Old account of turquois.

LEPSIUS, R.   Reise nach der Halbinsel des Sinai, 1846.
    Discusses Sinai turquois mines.

LICETUS, Fortunius.   Pyronarcha sive de fulminum natura deque febrium origine libri duo.   Patavii (Padua), 1643, pp. 123–126.
    Describes two Mexican turquois mosaics.

LIMUR, Compte de.   Bull. Soc. Polymathique du Morbihan.   1st sem., 1893, p. 85; 2nd sem., 1893, pp. 206–207.
    Describes ornaments of turquois-like material from prehistoric graves in France.

LINDGREN, W., GRATON, L. C., and GORDON, C. H.   The ore deposits of New Mexico.   Prof. Paper No. 68, U. S. Geol. Surv., 1910, pp. 17, 163–167, 296, 321, 324.
    Includes good geological description of turquois deposits of New Mexico.   Discusses origin.   Includes analyses of country rock at Cerrillos.

LOEW, O.   Geological and mineralogical report on portions of Colorado and New Mexico.   *In* Report Chief of Engineers, 1875, pt. 2, p. 1027.
    Brief description of Cerrillos deposits.   Includes analysis.

LOMMER.   Beschreibung der versteinerten Thierzähne bei Lessa in Böhmen.   Abhandl. einer Privatgesellsch., Böhmen, vol. 2, 1776, pp. 112–118.
    Maintains that turquois is formed by the action of fire upon fossil teeth of animals.

LORD, J. K.   The Peninsula of Sinai.   Leisure Hour, London, vol. 19, 1870, pp. 358–360, 398–399, 423–427.
    Popular description of Sinai turquois mines.

LOREY, E. de, and SLADEN, Douglas.   Queer things about Persia.   Philadelphia, 1907, pp. 159, 173–175, 180–181, 245.
    Notes use of turquois in Persia.

LUMMIS, Charles F.   Pueblo Indian folk-stories.   New York, 1910, pp. 10, 71.
    Notes turquois in Pueblo folk-tales.

MAGINUS.   Geogr. Ptolem.   Descr. dell' America, pt. 2, 34, p. 207.
    Notes use of turquois for labrets in Peru.

MANDEVILLE, Sir John.   Le Grand Lapidaire, ou sont declarez les noms de Pierres orientalles, avecque les Vertus et Proprietes d'icelles, aussi les isles et pays ou elles croissent et don ou les aporte.   Ed. by Is. del Sotto, Vienne, 1862, p. 109.
    Gives an early account of turquois, noting superstitions connected with it.

MANSUR, Muhammed Ibn.   Mineralogy [an Arabian work written about 1300].   Section on turquois translated into German by Schindler, Jahrb. k. k. geol. Reichs., Wien, vol. 36, 1886, pp. 303–314.
    Good account of turquois in Persia, its occurrence, use, etc.

MARSHALL, F. H.   Catalogue of the jewelry, Greek, Etruscan, and Roman, in the British Museum.   London, 1910, pp. 229, 307; pl. 55.
    Lists antique turquois pendant from Cyprus and Roman turquois-set earrings of third century.

MARTIN, A. H.   Gem mining in California a profitable industry.   Min. World, vol. 33, 1910, pp. 1227–1228.
    Notes occurrence of turquois in California.

MARX, Karl.   Documents relating to the history of Ladakh.   Journ. Asiat. Soc. Bengal, vol. 60, pt. 1, 1891, p. 123.
    Refers to importation of turquoises into western Tibet.

MASPERO, Gaston, Egyptian archæology.   New York, 1889, pp. 241, 316, 320.
    Describes turquois jewelry and objects of Egyptian workmanship.

—— Histoire ancienne de l'Orient classique.   Paris, 1895, vol. 1, pp. 355–358, 473–476.
    Gives account of inscriptions, remains, and ancient mining in Sinai.

—— History of Egypt.   Translated by M. L. McClure.   London, 4 vols. (no date given), vol. 2, pp. 161–166, 262, 281, 333, 336; vol. 4, pp. 370–371.
    Good historical account of ancient turquois mining in Sinai.

—— Manual of Egyptian archæology.   Translated by A. B. Edwards.   London, 1902, pp. 245, 323, 327–328.
    Describes turquois ornaments and objects, of Egyptian workmanship.

MATTHEWS, Washington.   The Mountain Chant: a Navajo ceremony.   Fifth Ann. Rept. Bur. Amer. Ethnol., 1883–84, pp. 421, 449, 455.
    Notes ceremonial application of turquois amongst the Navaho.

MATTHEWS, Washington. Navaho legends. Boston and New York, 1897, pp. 63, 71, 79, 80, 82, 104–105, 111, 151, 163, 221.
Notes position of turquois in Navaho legends.
—— The Night Chant, a Navaho ceremony. Mem. Amer. Mus. Nat. Hist., vol. 6, 1902.
Notes ceremonial application of turquois.
MAWE, John. A treatise on diamonds and precious stones. London, 1815, pp. 151–155.
General description of turquois.
MEDER, P. Ueber den orientalischen Türkis. Chem. Ann. (Crell), 1799, pp. 185–199.
Shows that oriental turquois is a mineral substance and different from odontolite.
MELY, F. de, and COUREL, M. H. Les lapidaires de l'antiquité et du moyen age. Vol. 1, Les lapidaires Chinois, Paris,
1896; vol. 3, Les lapidaires Arabes, Paris.
MELY, F. de. Les lapidaires de l'Antiquité et du moyen age. Vol. 2, Les lapidaires Grecs. Paris, 1898, pp. 32, 207.
Notes mention of turquois (?) in old Greek works.
MESUE. Electuario de Gemmis (cited by Garcia ab Horto).
Confuses emerald and turquois.
MIDDLETON, J. H. The engraved gems of classical times. Cambridge, 1891, pp. 149–150.
Discusses *callais* and *callaina*. Mentions Roman turquois cameos.
MILLIN. Étude des Pierres Gravées. p. 18.
Notes ancient engraved turquois.
MOLINA, Juan Ignacio. Histoire naturelle du Chili. Translated into French from Italian by Gruvel, Paris, 1789, p. 56.
Notes occurrence of turquois in Chile.
MOORE, G. E., and ZEPHAROVICH, V. von. Kallait pseudomorph nach Apatite aus Californien. Zeitschr. Kryst. und
Min., vol. 10, 1885, pp. 240–251. *Abstract:* Journ. Chem. Soc., vol. 48, 1885, pp. 958–959.
Describes pseudomorph of turquois after apatite from California, giving analysis.
MOORE, N. F. Ancient mineralogy; or, an inquiry respecting mineral substances mentioned by the ancients. New
York, 1859, pp. 214–215.
Describes the *callais* of Pliny.
MORGAN, J. De. Account of the work of the Service of Antiquities of Egypt and of the Egyptian Institute during
the years 1892, 1893, and 1894. Ann. Rept. Smithsonian Inst., 1896, p. 599.
Describes turquois jewelry excavated at Dahshur, Egypt.
—— Recherches sur les origines de l'Egypte. Paris, 1896, pp. 217–225.
Describes Sinai turquois mines. Discusses meaning of *mafkat*. Includes article by Berthelot, 1896, q. v.
MORTIMER, Cromwell. Some remarks on the precious stone called the turquoise. Philos. Trans., vol. 44, pt. 2, 1747,
pp. 429–432.
Early account of turquois, distinguishing between the mineral and odontolite.
MOSER, H. A traverse l'Asie centrale. Paris, 1885, pp. 104–107.
Notes use of turquois around Tashkend.
MOUCHKETOFF, J. Les richesses minerales du Turkestan Russe. Paris, 1878, pp. 11–12.
Describes turquois deposit on Mount Karamazar, Turkestan.
MYLIUS, Joannes Daniel. Opus medico-chymicum. Tractatus II, Basilicae chymicae. Francofurti, 1618, lib. 4,
cap. 13, pp. 360–361.
Gives brief account of turquois, noting superstitious ideas connected with it.
NEWBERRY, J. S. Report of the exploring expedition from Santa Fe to the Colorado, etc., 1859. (Macomb's expe-
dition.) Printed 1876, p. 41.
Notes occurrence of turquois at Cerrillos and use by Indians.
NICOLS, Thomas. Arcula Gemmea; or, a cabinet of jewels. London, 1653, pp. 146–151.
Includes an account of turquois, giving superstitions connected with its use.
NIZA, Fray Marcos de. Extracts from journal, published in the Indian Report by Lieut. Whipple, Pacific R. R.
Explorations and Surveys, vol. 3, pt. 3, 1856, pp. 105–108.
Notes early use of turquois by Indians of the Southwest (U. S.).
NUTTALL, Zelia. Standard or head-dress? Arch. and Ethnol. Papers, Peabody Museum, Cambridge, vol. 1, No. 1,
1888, pp. 36–37.
Notes use of turquois by Aztecs.
—— The Atlatl or Spear-thrower. Arch. and Ethnol. papers, Peabody Museum, Cambridge, vol. 1, No. 3, 1891,
pp. 21, 23, 29, 188.
Notes use of turquois in Aztec ceremonials.
—— The fundamental principles of old and new world civilizations. Arch. and Ethnol. Papers, Peabody Museum,
Cambridge, vol. 2, 1901, pp. 67, 70, 72, 128, 129, 192, 204, 293–294.
Notes ceremonial use of turquois by Aztecs.
—— Chalchihuitl in ancient Mexico. Amer. Anthrop., vol. 3, 1901, pp. 227–238.
Discusses use and source of *chalchihuitl.*
O'CONNOR, W. F. Folk tales from Tibet. London, 1906, pp. 70, 158–165, 176.
Gives Tibetan folk tales in which turquois figures.
OLEARIUS, Adam. Voyages and travels of the ambassadors. Translated by John Davies, London, 1669, pp. 148, 189.
Gives brief account of Persian turquois.

OPPEL, A.　Die altmexikanischen Mosaiken.　Globus, vol. 70, 1896, pp. 4–13.
　　　Description of Mexican turquois mosaics.

ORDNANCE SURVEY of the Peninsula of Sinai, 1868.　One vol. text, 3 vols. photos., 1 vol. maps and plans.
　　　Describes Sinai turquois deposits.　Gives maps and photographs.

OSBORNE, Duffield.　Engraved gems: signets, talismans and ornamental intaglios, ancient and modern.　New York, 1912, p. 284.
　　　Notes that the turquois was hardly ever engraved by the Greeks and was rarely employed for this purpose by the Graeco-Roman artists.

OUSELEY, William.　Travels in various countries of the East; more particularly Persia.　London, 1819, vol. 1, pp. 210-212.
　　　Notes use of turquois in Persia.　Quotes from Persian manuscripts on superstitions, etc.

PAIGE, Sidney.　The origin of turquoise in the Burro Mountains, N. Mex.　Econ. Geol., vol. 7, 1912, pp. 382–392.
　　　Discussion of origin, in which weight of evidence favors superficial formation.

PALACIO, Diego Garcia de.　San Salvador und Honduras im Jahre 1576.　Amtlicher Bericht . . . an den König von Spanien.　Translated into German, with notes, by A. von Frantzius.　Berlin, 1873, p. 29.
　　　Notes use of chalchihuitl by Aztecs.

PALMER, E. H.　The desert of the Exodus.　Cambridge, 1871, pp. 196–197, 201, 234.
　　　Gives account of Sinai turquois deposits.

PANNIER, L.　Les lapidaires français du moyen âge.　Paris, 1882, p. 225.
　　　Refers to fifteenth century legend in which turquois figures.

PASKE, Edward.　Buddhism in the British Province of Little Tibet.　Journ. Anthr. Inst. Great Britain and Ireland, London, vol. 8, 1878–9, pp. 195–210.
　　　Notes use of turquois in Little Tibet (Bultistan).

PATKANOV, K. P.　(Russian translation of Armenian lapidarium: Precious stones, their names and properties, according to the notions of the Armenians.)　St. Petersburg, 1873, p. 48.
　　　Refers to Khojend as a source of turquois.

PEABODY, Charles.　Exploration of mounds, Coahoma County, Mississippi.　Peabody Museum Papers, Cambridge, 1904, vol. 3, No. 2, pp. 50, 51.
　　　Notes turquois beads found in Indian grave in Coahoma County, Miss.

PEÑAFIEL, Antonio.　Monumentos del Arte Mexicano Antiquo (Monuments of ancient Mexican art.)　Berlin, 1890; one vol. of text in Spanish, French, and English; 2 vols. of plates; pp. 7–9, 11, 12, 14, 16, 17, 26–28, 79.
　　　Describes use of turquois and chalchihuitl by Aztecs.　Quotes extensively from Sahagun.

——— Indumentaria Antigua; Vestidos Guerreros y Civiles de los Mexicanos.　Mexico, 1903, pp. 101–103.
　　　Gives description (with 6 colored figures) of Mexican turquois mosaics.

PENFIELD, S. L.　On the chemical composition of turquoise.　Amer. Journ. Sci., vol. 10, 1900, pp. 346–350.
　　　Abstract: Journ. Chem. Soc., vol. 79, 1901, p. 27.
　　　Gives analysis of turquois from Lincoln County, Nevada, deducing formula therefrom.

——— Ueber die chemische Zusammensetzung des Türkis.
　　　Zeitschr. Kryst. und Min., vol. 33, 1900, pp. 542–547.
　　　German translation of preceding article.

PEPPER, Geo. H.　Ceremonial objects and ornaments from Pueblo Bonito, New Mexico.　Amer. Anthr., vol. 7, 1905, pp. 183–197.
　　　Describes and figures turquois ornaments and objects found in ruin in New Mexico.

——— The exploration of a burial-room in Pueblo Bonito, New Mexico.　Putnam Anniversary Vol., New York, 1909, pp. 196–252.
　　　Detailed description, with illustrations, of turquois ornaments and objects found in burial-room of ancient Pueblo Bonito in New Mexico.

PETERSON, Theodor.　Zur Kenntniss der natürlichen Phosphate.　Jahresber. phys. Ver., Frankfurt a. M., 1898.
　　　Neues Jahrb. für Min., Geol. und Pal., vol. 2, 1900, Ref. p. 31.
　　　Gives analysis of turquois from Burro Mountains, N. Mex.

PETRIE, W. M. Flinders.　Egyptian tales, translated from the papyri.　First series: IVth to XIIth Dynasty.　London, 1895, pp. 16–22.
　　　Relates Egyptian tale in which turquois figures.

——— Diospolis Parva.　The cemeteries of Abadiyeh and Hu.　Publ. Egypt Expl. Fund, London, 1901.
　　　Notes turquois beads from prehistoric Egyptian graves.

——— The royal tombs of the earliest dynasties.　Publ. Egypt Expl. Fund, pt. 2, London, 1901, pp. 16–18.
　　　Figures (in colors) and describes turquois jewelry of First Dynasty unearthed at Abydos.

——— Researches in Sinai.　London, 1906.
　　　Gives excellent detailed description of inscriptions, ruins, and turquois mines of Sinai.　Includes maps and many photographs.

——— The royal tombs at Abydos.　Harper's Monthly Magazine, vol. 53, pp. 682–687
　　　Includes description of turquois jewelry of First Dynasty found at Abydos.

——— The arts and crafts of ancient Egypt.　Chicago, 1910, pp. 80, 85
　　　Notes use of turquois by ancient Egyptians.

PIGORINI, Luigi. Gli antichi oggetti messicani incrostati di mosaico. Reale Acad. dei Lincei. Rome, 1885.
    Describes and figures in colors five Mexican turquois mosaics in Rome.
PINKERTON, John. A general collection of the best and most interesting voyages and travels in all parts of the world. London, 1811, vol. 9, pp. 186–187.
    Includes an account of the Nishapur turquois deposits.
PITTMAN, E. F. The mineral resources of New South Wales. Sydney, 1901, p. 409.
    Brief description of turquois occurrence near Bodalla, N. S. W.
PLINY (Caius Plinius Secundus). Natural history. Translated into English by Bostock and Riley. London, 1857. Book 37, chapter 33; also parts of chapters 18, 37, 54, and 56.
    Describes callais, callaina, and other turquois-like minerals.
POGUE, Joseph E. The aboriginal use of turquois in North America. American Anthropologist, vol. 14, 1912, pp. 437–466.
    Essentially the same as pages 89–104 of this treatise.
——— The technology of turquois. Min. and Sci. Press, vol. 108, 1914, pp. 285–287.
    A condensed account of chapter VIII of this treatise.
POHL, J. J. Eine einfache und sichere Unterscheidungsweise der echten Türkise von deren Nachahmungen. Neues Jahrb. Min., Geol., und Pal., 1878, pp. 364–369. Abstract: Journ. Chem. Soc., vol. 36, 1879, pp. 209–210. Abstract: Zeitschr. Kryst. und Min., vol. 3, 1879, p. 86.
    Gives method for distinguishing turquois from its imitations.
POLO, Marco. The travels of Marco Polo. Translated by Henry Yule; revised by Henri Cordier. London, 1903, vol. 1, p. 90; vol. 2, p. 53.
    Notes occurrence of turquois in Kerman, Persia, and Caindu, Central Asia.
PRESCOTT, Wm. H. History of the Conquest of Mexico. 1860, vol. 1, pp. 324–325.
    Includes account of presents given Cortés by Montezuma.
PRINSEP, James. Oriental account of the precious minerals. Chiefly from the Jawahir-námeh, translated by Raja Kalikishen. Journ. Asiat. Soc. Bengal, vol. 1, 1832, pp. 361–362.
    Includes an account of turquois.
PUMPELLY, Raphael. Geological researches in China, Mongolia, and Japan, during the years 1862 to 1865. Smithsonian Contr. to Knowl., vol. 15, 1868, p. 118.
    Notes carvings in turquois made by Chinese.
——— Explorations in Turkestan. Washington, 1908, vol. 1, pp. 38, 39, 42, 60, 64, 120, 157, 176, 199.
    Records finding turquois beads in ruins of Anau and Old Merv, in Turkestan.
PURCHAS. Pilgrimes. London, 1626, vol. 5, book 8, chap. 9, p. 859.
    Describes use of turquois for labrets by ancient Mexicans.
RAIMONDI, A. Minerales del Perú. Lima, 1878, pp. 218, 222.
    Briefly describes occurrence of turquois in Peru and notes use amongst ancient inhabitants.
RAINERI, Antonio. See TEIFASCITE, Ahmed.
RAMMELSBERG, C. F. Handbuch der Mineralchemie. 1860, p. 337.
    Gives analyses of turquois and deduces formula.
RAMSAY, H. Western Tibet: A practical dictionary. Lahore, 1890, p. 162.
    Notes on turquois in Tibet.
RANSOME, F. L. The turquoise copper-mining district, Arizona. Bull. 530, U. S. Geol. Survey, 1911, p. 134.
    Brief geologic description of turquois in Dragoon Mountains, Cochise Co., Ariz.
RAUNHEIM, S. E. Santa Fe, N. Mex. Eng. Min. Journ., vol. 51, 1891, pp. 654–655.
    Gives short account of Cerrillos turquois deposits.
RAWLING, C. G. The great plateau. London, 1905, pp. 117, 184, 294–295.
    Notes use and occurrence of turquois in Tibet.
RAWLINSON, George. History of ancient Egypt. Boston, 1882, vol. 2, p. 389.
    Notes ancient exploitation of Sinai turquois mines.
READ, C. H. On an ancient Mexican headpiece coated with mosaic. Archaeologia, Soc. Antiquaries, London, vol. 54, pt. 2, 1895, pp. 383–398.
    Detailed description, with illustrations, of Mexican turquois mosaics in British Museum.
REAUMUR, De. Observations sur les Mines de Turquoises du Royaume; sur le nature de la Matiere qu'on y trouve, et sur la maniere dont on lui donne la couleur. Mem. l'Acad. Royale des Sci., Paris, 1715, pp. 174–202.
    Demonstrates that "occidental turquois" is copper-stained bone or tooth.
REID, G. D. The Burro Mountain Turquoise District. Eng. Min. Journ., vol. 75, 1903, p. 786.
    Brief description of the deposits.
REINACH, S. La representation du galop dans l'art ancien et moderne. Paris, 1901, p. 66.
    Notes turquois in Siberian ornaments of bronze age.
——— See KONDAKOF, N.
RITTER, Carl. Die Erdkunde. Berlin, vol. 7, 1837, pp. 671, 735, 746, 760; vol. 8, 1838, pp. 325–330; vol. 14, 1848, pp. 745–808.
    Describes several occurrences of turquois.

RITTER, Carl. The comparative geography of Palestine and the Sinaitic Peninsula. Translated and condensed from Erdkunde by W. L. Gage. New York, 1866, vol. 1, pp. 335, 352–355, 358.
    Includes an account of the Sinai turquois deposits.
ROCHSCHILD, M. D. Handbook of Precious Stones. New York, 1890.
    Gives general account of turquois. Not entirely reliable.
ROCKHILL, W. W. The land of the Lamas. New York, 1891, p. 24.
    Notes occurrence of turquois in China.
——— Tibet from Chinese sources. Journ. Roy. Asiat. Soc., vol. 23, 1891, p. 76.
    Notes on use of turquois in Tibet. Includes turquois tradition.
——— Notes on the ethnology of Tibet. Ann. Rept. U. S. Nat. Mus., 1893, pp. 669–747.
    Describes and figures many turquois-adorned ornaments and objects used in Tibet.
——— Diary of a journey through Mongolia and Tibet in 1891 and 1892. Washington, 1894, pp. 69, 253.
    Notes on use of turquois in Tibet.
ROERO, Osvaldo. Ricòrdi dei viaggi al Cashemir, Piccolo e Medio Tibet e Turkestan. Torino, 1881, vol. 3, p. 72.
    Notes importation of Persian turquoises into Ladakh.
ROMANOWSKY, G. v. Verh. Russisch-Kais. Min. Gesellsch., St. Petersburg, vol. 10, 1876, p. 221.
    Notes occurrence of turquois in land of Syr-Daria, Turkestan.
ROSE, Valentin. Aristoteles de lapidibus und Arnoldus Saxo. Zeitschr. deutsch. Alterthum, Berlin, vol. 18, 1875, pp. 391, 408, 446.
    Quotes from Pseudo-Aristotle and Arnoldus Saxo on turquois.
ROSET, Hipponax. Jewelry and precious stones. Philadelphia, 1856, p. 34.
    Gives general description of turquois.
RUDLER, F. W. Note on Mexican turquois. Archaeologia, Soc. Antiquaries, London, vol. 54, pt. 2, 1895, p. 398.
    Notes ancient working at Cerrillos (N. Mex.) and Cochise County (Ariz.) turquois localities.
RUËUS, Franciscus. De gemmis. Paris, 1547, Caput XVIII, pp. 139–140.
    Gives mediaeval account of the turquois.
RUSKA, Julius. Das Steinbuch des Aristoteles. Heidelberg, 1912.
    Gives section on turquois. Notes that this old work, wrongly imputed to Aristotle, was written before middle of ninth century.
RUSSELL, Frank. The Pima Indians. Twenty-sixth Ann. Rept. Bur. Amer. Ethnol., 1904–5, pp. 112, 163, 221, 222, 248.
    Notes on use of turquois by the Pima. Gives legend in which turquois figures.
SAHAGUN, Bernardino de. Histoire générale des choses de la Nouvelle-Espagne. Translated into French by Jourdanet and Siméon, Paris, 1880, pp. 30, 511, 514, 547, 763, 771, 772, 799–800.
    Notes on use of turquois and *chalchihuitl* by Aztecs.
SAXO, Arnoldus. De virtutibus lapidum (Properties of stones). Written near the beginning of the thirteenth century. Sec. 76.
    Brief account of turquois, giving superstitions connected with it.
SCHALLER, Waldemar T. Crystallized turquoise from Virginia. Amer. Journ, Sci., vol. 33, 1912, pp. 35–40. Journ. Washington Acad. Sci., vol. 1, 1911, pp. 58–59. Bull. 509, U. S. Geol. Surv., 1912, pp. 42–47. Zeitschr. Kryst. und Min., vol. 50, 1912, pp. 120–125.
    Gives crystallography, optical properties, and chemical composition (deducing formula) of crystallized turquois from Campbell County, Va.
SCHINDLER, A. H. Neue Angaben über die Mineralreichthümer Persiens und Notizen über die Gegend westlich von Zendjan. Jahrb. k. k. geol. Reichs., Wien, vol. 31, 1881, pp. 169–190.
    Describes Persian turquois localities.
——— The turquois mines of Nishâpûr, Khorassan. Rec. Geol. Surv. India, vol. 17, 1884, pp. 132–142.
    Good detailed description of the Nishapur turquois mines.
——— Die Gegend zwischen Sabzwar und Meschhed in Persien. Jahrb. k. k. geol. Reichs., Wien, vol. 36, 1886, pp. 303–314.
    Describes Nishapur turquois deposits. Notes occurrence in Tabbas district. Quotes from Muhammed Ibn Mansur.
SCHLAGINTWEIT. Die Könige von Tibet, pp. 837, 862.
    Notes use of turquois in Tibet and Ladakh.
SELER, Eduard. Gesammelte Abhandlungen zur amerikanischen Sprach- und Alterthumskunde. Berlin, 1904, vol. 2, pp. 620–621, 635–637.
    Discusses identity of *chalchihuitl*. Quotes from Sahagun on cutting of turquois by Aztecs.
SILLIMAN, Benjamin. Turquoise of New Mexico. Science, vol. 1, 1880, p. 289.
    An account of the Cerrillos turquois deposits.
——— Turquoise of New Mexico. Amer. Assoc. Adv. Sci., Proc., vol. 29, 1880, pp. 431–435.
    Describes Cerrillos turquois deposits.
——— Turquoise of New Mexico. Amer. Journ. Sci., vol. 22, 1881, pp. 67–71. *Abstract:* Zeitschr. Kryst. und Min., vol. 6, 1882, p. 519. *Abstract:* Neues Jahrb. Min. Geol. und Pal., vol. 1, 1883, Ref. p. 27. *Abstract:* Journ. Chem. Soc., vol. 44, 1883, p. 431.
    Describes Cerrillos turquois deposits.

SIRET, Louis. Les Cassitérides et l'Empire Colonial des Pheniciens. L'Anthropologie, vol. 20, 1909, p. 138.
> Notes turquois beads from neolithic graves in Spain.

SLADEN, Douglas. See LOREY, E. de.

SMITH, Buckingham. Relación de la Jornado de Coranado á Cibola. Colección de Documentos para la Historia de Florida. London, 1857, vol. 1, pp. 148, 150.
> Notes early use of turquois by Indians of the Southwest (U. S.).

SMITH, H. Clifford. Jewellery. London, 1908, pp. 5, 104.
> Refers to use of turquois in Egypt and in Europe.

SMITH, R. V. Mining in New Mexico during 1907. Eng. Min. Journ., vol. 85, 1908, p. 198.
> Notes operation of turquois mines in New Mexico during 1907.

SNOW, C. H. Turquoise in southwestern New Mexico. Amer. Journ. Sci., vol. 41, 1891, pp. 511–512. *Abstract:* Zeitschr. Kryst. und Min., vol. 22, 1893–94, p. 422.
> Notes an occurrence of turquois near Silver City, N. Mex.

SOMMERVILLE, Maxwell. Engraved gems. Philadelphia, 1889, pp. 688–689.
> Lists 27 turquois specimens among Greek and Roman cameos.

SPENCER, L. J. *See* BAUER, Max.

SPURRELL, F. C. J. Some flints from Egypt of IVth dynasty. Arch. Journ., London, vol. 49, 1892, pp. 48–52.
> Note on ancient mining operations in Sinai.

SQUIER, E. G. Carta dirigida al Rey de España por el Lic. Dr. Don Diego Garcia de Palacio año 1576. London, 1859, p. 110.
> Discusses identity of *chalchihuitl.*

—— Observations on the Chalchihuitl of Mexico and Central America. New York, 1869.
> Discusses identity of *chalchihuitl.*

—— On a collection of Chalchihuitls from Central America. Ann. Lyc. Nat. Hist., New York, vol. 9, 1870, pp. 246–265.
> Same as preceding paper.

STAFFE, Baronne. Les pierres précieuses et les bijoux. Paris, 1896, pp. 116–119.
> Gives general account of the turquois.

STEINHAUER, C. L. Das königliche Ethnographische Museum zu Copenhagen. Handkatalog für die Besuchenden. Copenhagen, 1880, p. 19; 1886, p. 22.
> Brief description of two Mexican turquois mosaics in Copenhagen.

STEPHENSON, James. Ceremonial of Hasjelti Dailjis. Eighth Ann. Rept. Bur. Amer. Ethnol., 1886–87, p. 275.
> Gives Navaho legend in which turquois figures.

STEPHENSON, Matilda Coxe. The Zuñi Indians: their mythology, esoteric fraternities, and ceremonies. Twenty-third Ann. Rept. Bur. Amer. Ethnol., 1901-2, pp. 58, 60, 377-378.
> Notes use of turquois by Zuñi Indians, and superstitions connected with it.

—— Dress and adornment of the Pueblo Indians. (Consulted in manuscript.)
> Gives use of turquois by Pueblo Indians.

STERRETT, D. B. [Turquois section in articles on Precious Stones.] Min. Res. of the U. S., U. S. Geol. Surv., 1906, pp. 1234–1235; 1907, pt. 2, pp. 827–832; 1908, pt. 2, pp. 845–853; 1909, pt. 2, pp. 778–795; 1910, pt. 2, pp. 885–887; 1911, pt. 2, pp. 1065–1073; 1912, pt. 2, pp. 1055–1056.
> Geological and mineralogical descriptions of the turquois deposits of the United States, based upon field examinations.

STEVENS, Edward. Flint chips. London, 1870, pp. 324–328.
> Describes seven Mexican turquois mosaics in the British Museum and two in Copenhagen.

STREETER, E. W. Precious stones and gems. London, 1877, pp. 169–172; 1898, pp. 50, 221–233.
> Gives good general account of the turquois.

SUESS, Eduard. The face of the earth. Translated by Sollas and Sollas. Oxford, 1904, vol. 1, p. 370.
> Notes occurrence of turquois in Nubian sandstone in Abyssinia.

SWAN, John. Speculum Mundi, or a glass representing the face of the world; shewing both that it did begin, and must also end: the manner how, and time when, being largely examined. Cambridge, 1635, p. 296.
> Gives superstitions connected with turquois.

SYKES, Ella C. Persian folklore. Folk-lore, London, vol. 12, 1901, p. 268.
> Notes talismanic use of turquois in Persia.

SYKES, Percy M. Ten thousand miles in Persia or eight years in Irán. London, 1902, p. 74.
> Notes occurrence of turquois in Kerman, Persia.

TAGORE, S. M. Mani-mala or a treatise on gems. Calcutta, 1879, pp. 88, 793, 802–803, 809, 945–946, 882–883.
> Gives oriental superstitions connected with turquois.

TAVERNIER, Jean Baptiste. Voyages en Turquie, en Perse, et aux Indes. Amsterdam, 1678, pt. 1, p. 421; pt. 2, p. 374.
> Notes occurrence and use of turquois in Persia.

—— Travels in India. Translated from French edition of 1676, by V. Ball. London, 1889, vol. 2, pp. 103–104.
> Briefly notes occurrence and use of turquois in Persia.

TAYLOR, Langdon. Precious stones and gems, with their reputed virtues. London, 1895, pp. 33–34.
    Gives general account of the turquois.

TEIFASCITE, Ahmed. Fior di Pensieri sulle Pietre Preziose di Ahmed Teifascite. Translated from the Arabian by
    Antonio Raineri. Bologna, 1906, pp. 70–73.
    Gives an early account of the nature, occurrence, and use of the turquois.

THEOPHRASTUS. History of stones. Translated by John Hill. London, 1774, p. 159.
    Refers briefly to bone turquois.

THE FOUR TANTRA (ancient Tibetan medical work). Peking edition, vol. 2, fol. 145b.
    Describes briefly Tibetan turquois.

THOMAS, E. S. Turquois mining in Egypt, prehistoric and modern. Abstract from Cairo Sci. Journ., March, 1912,
    Min. and Eng. World, vol. 37, 1912, p. 53.
    Brief notes on ancient and modern mining in Sinai.

TIBETAN ANNALS OF THE KINGS OF TIBET. Manuscript in possession of Berthold Laufer, chap. 13, fol. 45a.
    Narrates Tibetan legend in which turquois figures.

TIETZE, E. Das Vorkommen der Türkise bei Nishapur in Persien. Verh. k. k. geol. Reichs., No. 6, 1884, p. 93.
    Abstract: Zeitschr. für Kryst. und Min., vol. 10, 1885, p. 428. Abstract: Journ. Chem. Soc., vol. 50, 1886, p. 25.
    Gives geologic description of Nishapur deposits.

TOLSTOÏ. J. See Kondakof, N.

TOQUE. Mines de turquoises de Nishapour, Province de Khoraçan (Perse). Ann. des mines, Paris, vol. 13, 1888,
    pp. 563–577.
    Gives good account of Nishapur deposits.

TORQUEMADA, F. Juande de. Monarchia Indiana. Madrid, 1723, vol. 2, pp. 47–48, 288, 435, 462, 521; vol. 3, p. 341.
    Notes on use of turquois and chalchihuitl by Aztecs.

TOZZER. A. M. Notes on religious ceremonials of the Navaho. Putnam Ann. Vol., New York, 1909, pp. 325, 329.
    Refers to symbolical application of turquois in Navaho sand paintings.

TRALLIANOS, Alexander. Treatise on epilepsy (Περὶ ἐπιληψίας). See Theodor Puschmann, Alexander von Tralles.
    Wien, 1878, vol. 1, pp. 566, 570.
    Notes early use and virtues of a sky-blue "jasper" (possibly turquois).

TYLOR, E. B. Description of three very rare specimens of an ancient Mexican mosaic work (in the collection of Henry
    Christy, Esq.). Appendix 5 to Anahuac; or Mexico and the Mexicans, ancient and modern. London, 1861, pp.
    337–339.
    Describes three Mexican turquois mosaics in British Museum.

TYRWHIT, R. Sinai. In Vacation Tourists. London, 1862–3, pp. 337, 350.
    Gives brief account of Sinai turquois deposits.

UHLE, M. Congrès intern. Américanistes, 7me sess., 1888, Berlin, 1890, p. 738. Veröff. Kgl. Museum für Völker-
    kunde, Berlin, 1889, pp. 2, 20 (with plate).
    Describes turquois-incrusted skull-mask of Aztec workmanship in Berlin.

VALENTINI, P. J. J. Two Mexican Chalchihuitls. Proc. Amer. Ant. Soc., Worcester, vol. 1, 1881, p. 283.
    Discusses identity of chalchihuitl.

VALERE, Abbe Em. Marie et le symbolisme des pierres precieuses. Paris, 1909, pp. 227–237.
    Gives symbolical application of turquois.

VARTHEMA. The travels of Ludovico di Varthema. Translated by J. W. Jones. Edited by G. P. Badger. Published
    by Hakluyt Soc., 1864.
    Notes use of turquois in Persia.

VEGA, Garcilaso de la. The Royal Commentaries of Peru. Translated by Paul Rycaut, London, 1688, book 8, chap.
    23, p. 341.
    Notes use of turquois by Incas.

VETANCURT, Agustin de. Teatro Mexicano. Mexico, repr. 1870–71, vol. 3, p. 323.
    Notes early use of turquois by the Apache.

VOLMAR. Das Steinbuch. Ein altdeutsches Gedicht. Ed. by Hans Lambel. Heilbronn, 1877, p. 19, lines 551–556.
    Includes verse giving superstitious belief connected with turquois.

VOTH, H. R. Traditions of the Hopi. Field Columb. Museum, publ. 96, Anthrop. ser., vol. 8, 1905, pp. 1, 12, 33, 53.
    Refers to turquois in Hopi legends.

WADDELL, L. A. Lamaic rosaries: their kinds and uses. Journ. Asiatic Soc. Bengal, vol. 61, pt. 1, 1892, pp. 24–33.
    Notes ceremonial use of turquois in Tibet.

——— Buddhism of Tibet. London, 1895, p. 557.
    Describes ancient Tibetan marriage ceremony in which turquois poetically figures.

——— Among the Himalayas. Westminster, 1900, p. 46.
    Notes use of turquois by Bhotiya women.

WALCOTT, R. H. Additions and corrections to the census of Victorian minerals. Proc. Roy. Soc. Victoria, vol. 13,
    1900, pp. 253–272. Abstract: Zeitschr. Kryst. und Min., vol. 37, 1903, pp. 310–311.
    Notes occurrence of turquois at Lurg, Victoria.

Watson, J. W. Pearls and gems. Harper's Magazine, vol. 21, 1860, pp. 764–780.
Gives general account of turquois, noting superstitions connected with it.
Weill, Raymond. Recueil des inscriptions Egyptiennes du Sinai. Vol. 1, 1904, pp. 21–25, 27, 32–33, 42, 72, 81.
Gives good account of Sinai turquois deposits. Includes good topographic map of Wady Maghareh.
——— La Presqu'ile du Sinai. Paris, 1908, pp. 141–183, 345.
Describes Sinai turquois deposits.
Wiedemann, E. Ueber den Wert von Edelsteinen bei den Muslimen. Der Islam, vol. 2, 1911, p. 352.
Notes exportation of turquoises from Persia into India.
——— Beiträge zur Geschichte der Naturwissenschaften, XXX. Zur Mineralogie im Islam. Erlangen, 1912, pp. 234, 242.
Quotes Arabian authors on turquois.
Williams, S. W. Chinese repository. Canton, 1833–51, vol. 1, p. 310.
Reports occurrence of turquois in Belour Mountains, Turkestan.
——— The middle kingdom. New York, 1883, vol. 1, p. 310.
Lists turquois amongst precious stones used in China.
Wilson, Thomas. Jade in America. Congrès intern. Americanistes, 12 sess., Paris, 1902, pp. 144–145.
Discusses identity and use of *chalchihuitl*.
Winship, George Parker. The Coronado expedition. Fourteenth Ann. Rept. Bur. Amer. Ethnol., 1892–3, pp. 357, 518, 540, 549, 561, 573.
Notes early use of turquois in the Southwest (U. S.).
Women of all Nations. Ed. by T. A. Joyce and N. W. Thomas. London, 1909.
Notes use of turquois among women of Tibet, northern India, Turkestan, etc.
Ximenez, Francisco. Las historias del origen de los Indios de esta provincia de Guatemala. Translated by C. Scherzer. Vienna, 1857, p. 211.
Notes use of *chalchihuitl* in Central America.
Zalinski, E. R. Turquoise in the Burro Mountains, New Mexico. Econ. Geol., vol. 2, 1907, pp. 464–492. *Abstract:* Chem. Abstr., vol. 1, 1907, p. 2789. *Abstract:* Zeitschr. für Kryst. und Min., vol. 46, 1909, pp. 388–389.
Detailed geologic and mineralogic description of Burro Mountains turquois deposits, with conclusions as to origin.
——— Turquois mining, Burro Mountains, N. M. Eng. Min. Journ., vol. 86, 1908, pp. 843–846. *Abstract:* Chem. Abstr., vol. 3, 1909, p. 161.
Gives an account of Burro Mountains turquois deposits.
Zellner. Isis. 1834, p. 637.
Gives analysis of turquois from Jordansmühl, Silesia.

INDEX.

PLATES.

PLATE 1.

Fɪɢ. 1. Specimen showing turquois vein in country rock, from Mineral Park, Ariz. Photograph by D. B. Sterrett, U. S. Geol. Survey.

Fɪɢ. 2. Specimen showing turquois vein, from Los Cerrillos, N. Mex. U. S. National Museum.

Fɪɢ. 3. Specimen of crystallized turquois, from Campbell County, Va. U. S. National Museum. Photograph supplied by W. T. Schaller.

164

SPECIMENS OF TURQUOIS.

PLATE 2.

FIG. 1. Turquois workings on Ithaca Peak, Mineral Park, Ariz. Photograph by D. B. Sterrett, U. S. Geol. Survey.

FIG. 2. Turquois Mountain, Hachita District, Grant County, N. Mex., showing desert character of region in which turquois occurs. Dumpheaps from turquois workings may be seen on the hill. Photograph by D. B. Sterrett, U. S. Geol. Survey.

166

1.

2.

TURQUOIS LOCALITIES IN ARIZONA AND NEW MEXICO.

Fig. 1. Mount Chalchihuitl (near Los Cerrillos, N. Mex.) in foreground, showing open cut on side. Main ancient turquois workings on opposite side of hill. Mount McKensie in distance. Photograph by D. B. Sterrett, U. S. Geol. Survey.

Fig. 2. Ancient stone hammers found in turquois workings on Mount Chalchihuitl. Photograph by D. B. Sterrett, U. S. Geol. Survey.

168

I.

2.

TURQUOIS WORKINGS NEAR LOS CERRILLOS, NEW MEXICO; AND ANCIENT STONE TOOLS.

PLATE 4.

Ancient turquois working on northwest side of Mount Chalchihuitl, Los Cerrillos, N. Mex., showing immense pit excavated in pre-Spanish times.   Photograph by D. B. Sterrett, U. S. Geol. Survey.

170

ANCIENT TURQUOIS WORKINGS NEAR LOS CERRILLOS, NEW MEXICO.

PLATE 5.

Figs. 1, 2, 4, 5. Ancient Egyptian turquois jewelry found on arm of mummy of Ist Dynasty, at Abydos.   After Petrie, 1901.

Fig. 3. Arm of mummy showing bracelets in place.   After Petrie, 1901.

172

1

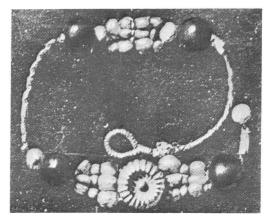

2

3

4

5

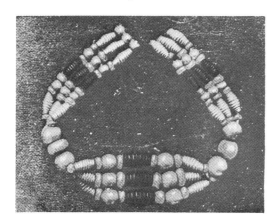

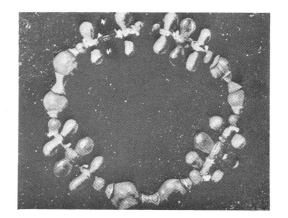

ANCIENT EGYPTIAN TURQUOIS JEWELRY.

PLATE 6.

Turquois jewelry from Tibet and Mongolia. After Rockhill, 1893.

FIG. 1. Man's earring. Carnelian and two turquoises set on hoop. Made in Korluk Ts'aidam. Worn by Mongols. U. S. National Museum, Cat. No. 167212.

FIG. 2. Breast ornament of copper, set with turquois and coral beads. Worn by Mongol women. U. S. National Museum, Cat. No. 167340.

FIG. 3. Silver shirt buckle, set with coral and turquois. From Ta-chien-lu, eastern Tibet. U. S. National Museum, Cat. No. 131179b.

FIG. 4. Woman's earring of silver, with heart-shaped plaque studded with turquoises. Jade ring on hoop. From Chamdo and Lhasa. U. S. National Museum, Cat. No. 167210.

FIG. 5. Chatelaine of gilded brass with large turquois in center. Tibet. U. S. National Museum, Cat. No. 167222.

FIG. 6. Earring of silver set with turquois and coral. Worn by men in central Tibet. From Lhasa. U. S. National Museum, Cat. No. 167282.

FIG. 7. Silver stopper for snuff bottle, with snuff spoon. Top set with turquois and coral. From Ts'aidam. Used by Mongols. U. S. National Museum, Cat. No. 167294.

FIG. 8. Silver rings, set with coral and turquois. Tibet. U. S. National Museum, Cat. Nos. 167277, 167278, 167280.

FIG. 9. Silver plaque, bordered by coral beads and single turquois. Worn in Chala, eastern Tibet. U. S. National Museum, Cat. No. 167242.

FIG. 10. Head plaque of silver, set with coral and turquois. From Hor Chango, eastern Tibet. U. S. National Museum, Cat. No. 167243.

174

TURQUOIS JEWELRY FROM TIBET AND MONGOLIA.

176

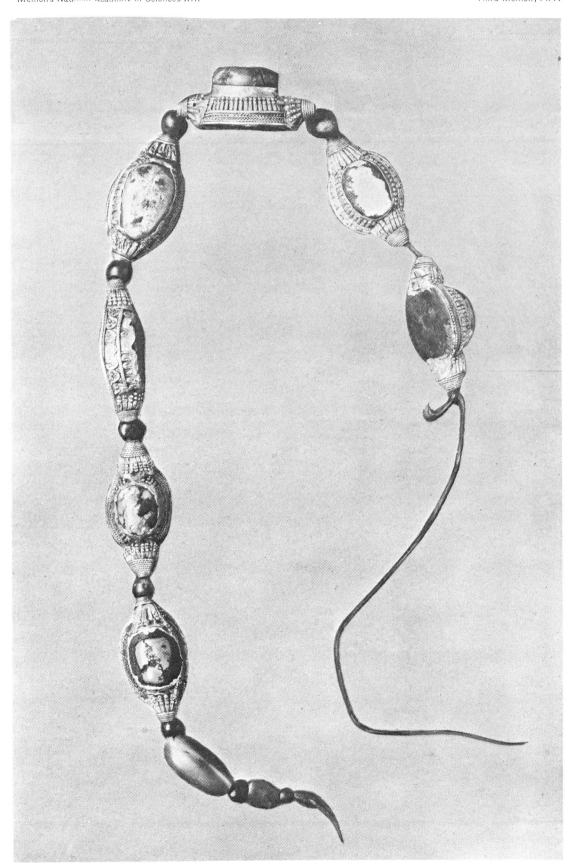

TURQUOIS QUEUE ORNAMENT FROM TIBET.

PLATE 8.

Fig. 1. Head ornament of red cloth, adorned with rough turquoises and turquois charm box. Worn by women of Ladakh. From Leh. U. S. National Museum.

Fig. 2. Lamaist charm box from Gau. Copper encrusted with silver and set with turquois. Eighteenth or nineteenth century. India Museum. After Hendley, 1906.

Fig. 3. Buddist wheel of the law, of brass, set with turquois, from Tibet. India Museum. After Hendley, 1906.

178

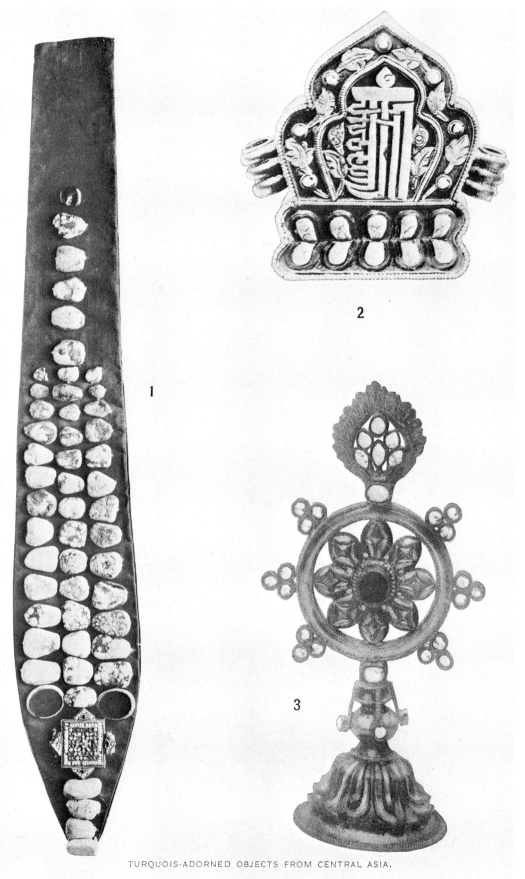

TURQUOIS-ADORNED OBJECTS FROM CENTRAL ASIA.

Tibetan leather work, ornamented in silver, set with turquois and coral.   Knife, scabbard, tinder and flint pouch, and needle case.   U. S. National Museum.   After Rockhill, 1893.

180

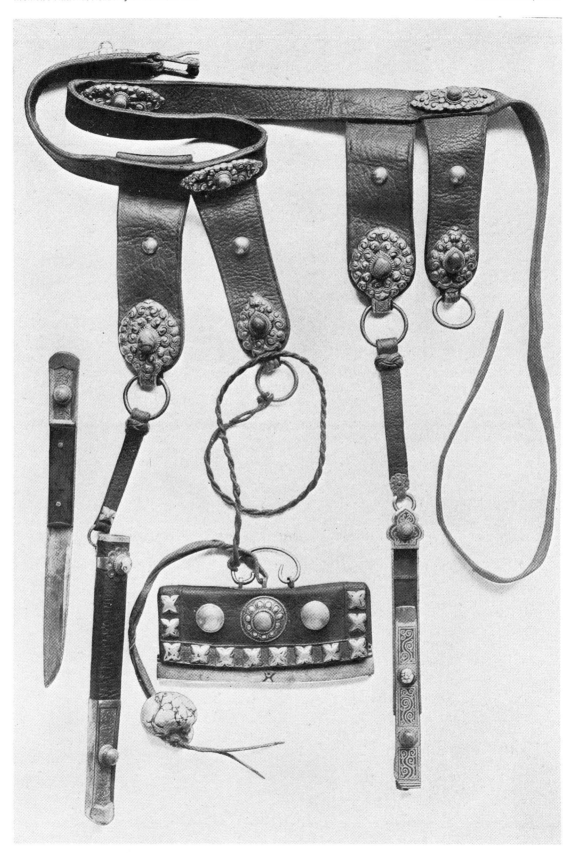

TIBETAN LEATHER WORK, ORNAMENTED IN SILVER, SET WITH TURQUOIS AND CORAL.

PLATE 10.

Turquois ornaments from Tibet and Kashmir.

Fɪɢ. 1. Waistband of silver, set with turquois and coral. India Museum. After Hendley, 1906.

Fɪɢ. 2. Brass earring, adorned with turquois. India Museum. After Hendley, 1906.

Fɪɢ. 3. Gold shirt buckle, set with turquois and coral. Lhasa. U. S. National Museum, Cat. No. 131399. After Rockhill, 1893.

Fɪɢ. 4. Hair ornament of red cloth, adorned with turquoises, glass, and turquois-encrusted amulet. British Museum. After Hendley, 1906.

Fɪɢ. 5. Belt clasp of silver, adorned with turquois mosaic. Made at Sringar in Kashmir. After Hendley, 1906.

Fɪɢ. 6. Gilt charm box, set with turquois. Made in Lhasa. U. S: National Museum, Cat. No. 167244. After Rockhill, 1893.

TURQUOIS ORNAMENTS FROM TIBET AND KASHMIR.

PLATE 11.

Fig. 1. Turquois carving, representing Buddha, made in Peking, China. Height 7 cm. Field Museum, Cat. No. 116673. Photograph supplied by Berthold Laufer.

Fig. 2. Turquois carving, made in China and purchased in London. Height 4 cm. U. S. National Museum, Cat. No. 87026.

184

1.

2.

CHINESE TURQUOIS CARVINGS.

PLATE 12.

Turquois carvings. Chinese. Photographs furnished by Berthold Laufer.

FIG. 1. Square bead of Chinese turquois matrix. Field Museum, Cat. No. 116679.

FIG. 2. Chinese carving in turquois. Height 10 cm. Field Museum, Cat. No. 116663.

FIG. 3. Girdle ornament or pendant in shape of lion. 5.3 by 3 cm.; 2.2 cm. high. Field Museum, Cat. No. 116668.

FIG. 4. Girdle ornament in shape of fish. 5.4 by 3.3 cm. Field Museum, Cat. No. 116667.

FIG. 5. Snuff-bottle. 3.3 by 2.5 cm. Field Museum, Cat. No. 116670.

FIG. 6. Ornamental button. 3.5 by 3 cm. Field Museum, Cat. No. 116669.

186

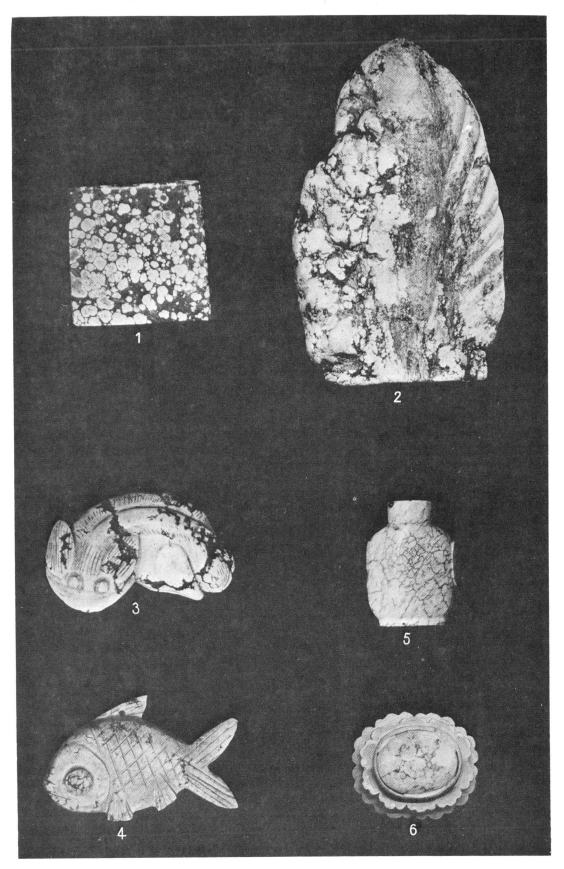

CHINESE CARVINGS IN TURQUOIS.

188

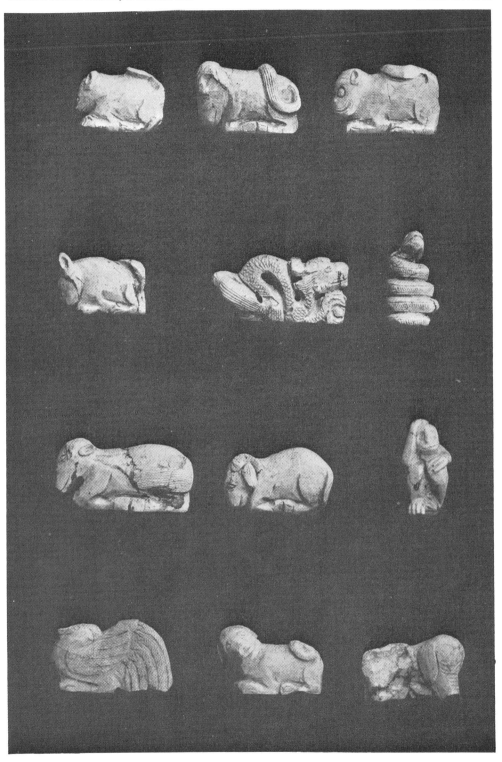

CHINESE TURQUOIS CARVINGS.   TWELVE ANIMALS OF THE ZODIAC.

PLATE 14.

Fig. 1. Persian pipe bowl of brass, studded with turquoises and garnets. U. S. National Museum, Cat. No. 272509.

Fig. 2. Roman earring of third century, A. D., made of gold and set with garnet, green porcelain, and turquois. British Museum. After Marshall, 1911.

Fig. 3. Hungarian brooch of eighteenth century, set with pearls, turquoises, and garnets. British Museum. After Hendley, 1906.

190

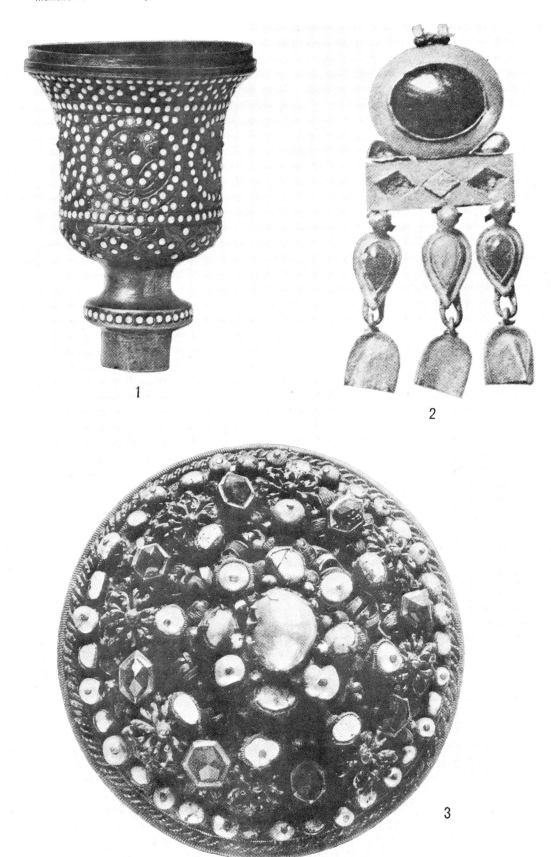

TURQUOIS-ADORNED OBJECTS, PERSIA AND EUROPE.

PLATE 15.

Fig. 1. Ancient Mexican mask. Human skull, inlaid with turquois and obsidian. British Museum. After Read, 1895.

Fig. 2. Ancient Mexican pendant. Ape-like head of wood, inlaid with mosaic of turquois and other stones. British Museum. After Read, 1895.

Fig. 3. Ancient Mexican breast ornament of wood, covered with turquois mosaic. British Museum. Photograph supplied by T. A. Joyce.

192

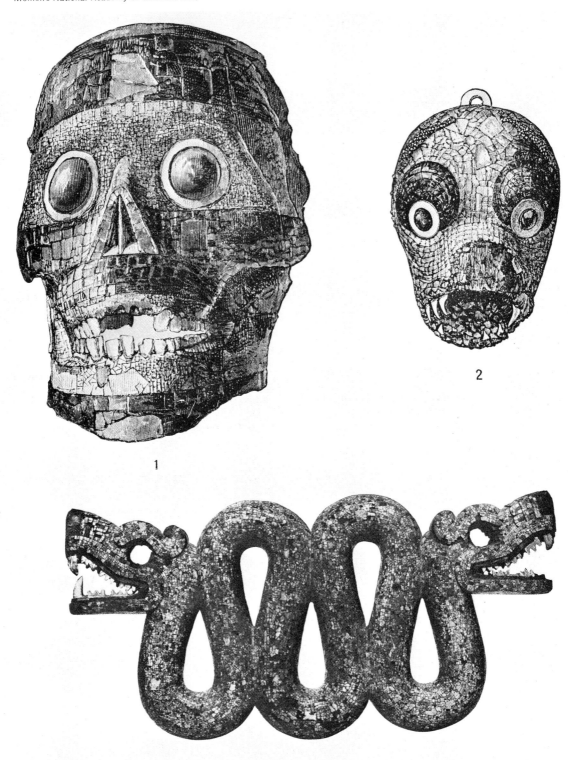

1

2

3

ANCIENT MEXICAN TURQUOIS MOSAICS, BRITISH MUSEUM.

194

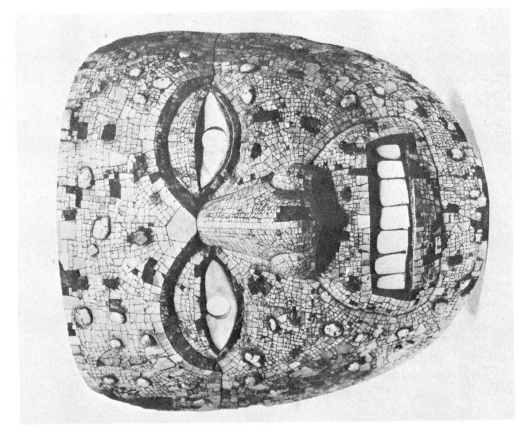

2.

1.

ANCIENT MEXICAN TURQUOIS MOSAIC MASKS, BRITISH MUSEUM.

PLATE 17.

Ancient Mexican objects, adorned with mosaics of turquois and other stones. Prehistoric and Ethnographical Museum in Rome. After Pigorini, 1885.

196

ANCIENT MEXICAN TURQUOIS MOSAICS, ROME.

PLATE 19.

Fɪɢ. 1. Lignite pendant, inset with turquoises, from Chevlon Ruin, Arizona. U. S. National Museum.

Fɪɢ. 2. Bone pendant, partly covered with crude turquois mosaic. From Chevlon Ruin, Arizona. U. S. National Museum, Cat. No. 157251.

Fɪɢ. 3. Ear pendants of lignite, covered with mosaic of turquois and lignite slabs, with piece of yellow indurated clay in center. From Black Falls Ruins, Arizona. U. S. National Museum, Cat. No. 205398.

Fɪɢ. 4. Fetich of sandstone dipped in blood, inset with irregular turquois slabs. Used by Zuñi Indians. U. S. National Museum, Cat. No. 73684.

Fɪɢ. 5. Fetich of gypsum with turquois eyes, used by Indians of Sia pueblo, New Mexico. U. S. National Museum, Cat. No. 152739.

200

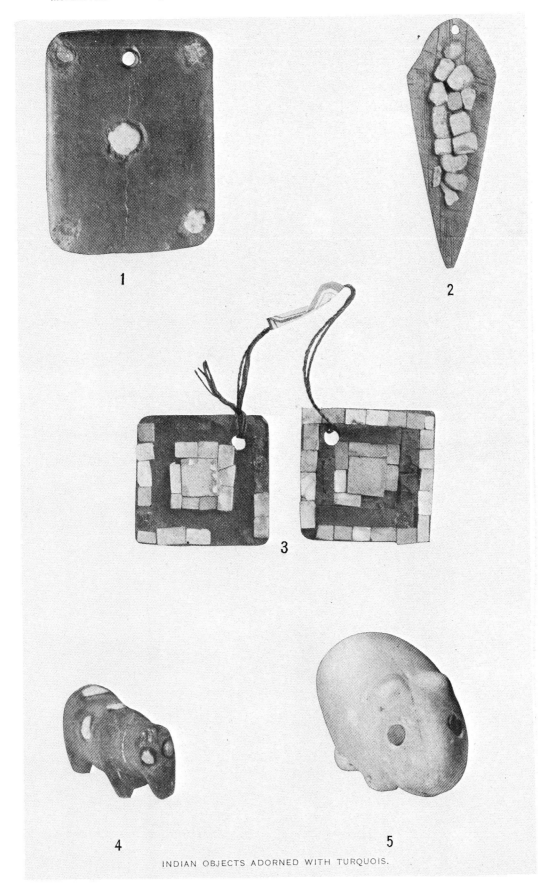

INDIAN OBJECTS ADORNED WITH TURQUOIS.

PLATE 20.

Objects decorated with turquois from ancient Pueblo Bonito, Chaco Canyon, New Mexico. Bone inlaid with jet and turquois; frog of jet and turquois; and breast ornament of jet inset with turquois. After Pepper, 1905.

202

OBJECTS DECORATED WITH TURQUOIS FROM ANCIENT PUEBLO BONITO,
CHACO CANYON, NEW MEXICO.

PLATE 21.

Pueblo Indian drilling turquois beads. Photograph furnished by Walter Hough.
204

PUEBLO INDIAN DRILLING TURQUOIS BEADS.

PLATE 22.

Indian turquois ornaments, United States National Museum.
Fig. 1. Zuñi ear pendants in turquois mosaic.
Fig. 2. Hopi ear pendants in turquois mosaic.
Fig. 3. Pueblo necklace. Turquois, coral, and shell beads.
Fig. 4. Zuñi ornament. Shell inlaid with turquois.
Fig. 5. Navaho ring of silver set with carved turquois.
Fig. 6. Pendants of turquois. Sia workmanship.

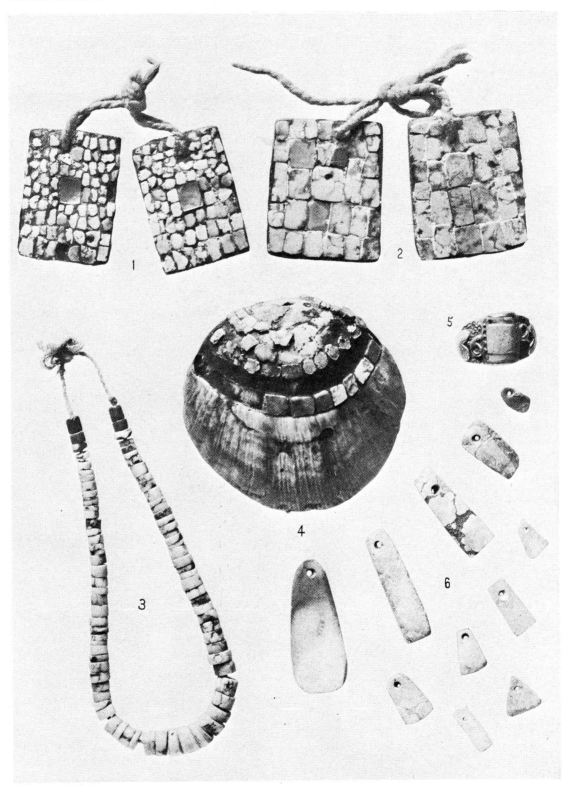

INDIAN TURQUOIS ORNAMENTS.

PLATE 18.

Fɪɢ. 1. Ornament of shell incrusted with turquois, representing a frog or toad. Found in an Indian ruin at Chaves Pass, Ariz. After Fewkes, 1896. U. S. National Museum.

Fɪɢ. 2. Bracelet of shell, inset with turquois. From Indian ruin on Chevelon Creek, Ariz. U. S. National Museum, Cat. No. 157295.

198